COLONIZATION
IN THE ANCIENT WORLD

UNIWERSYTET JAGIELLOŃSKI
INSTYTUT HISTORII

ELECTRUM

Journal of Ancient History

VOL. 20 (2013)

COLONIZATION
IN THE ANCIENT WORLD

JAGIELLONIAN UNIVERSITY PRESS

Electrum, vol. 20 (2013)

COVER DESIGN
Barbara Widłak

Cover photography: © Lagui - Fotolia.com

TECHNICAL EDITOR
Jadwiga Makowiec

PROOFREADER
Gabriela Niemiec

TYPESETTER
Wojciech Wojewoda

The publication of this volume was financed by the Jagiellonian University in Krakow – Faculty of History.

ISBN 978-83-233-3640-2
ISSN 1897-3426
e-ISSN 2084-3909

The digital version of the "Electrum" (ISSN 2084-3909) – which counts as the original – is published in the journals section of the Jagiellonian University Press website (www.ejournals.eu/electrum/).

Number of copies: 250

WYDAWNICTWO UNIWERSYTETU JAGIELLOŃSKIEGO
www.wuj.pl

Jagiellonian University Press
Editorial Offices: Michałowskiego St. 9/2, 31-126 Krakow
Phone: +48 12 663 23 81, +48 12 663 23 82, Fax: +48 12 663 23 83
Distribution: Phone: +48 12 631 01 97, Fax: +48 12 631 01 98
Cell Phone: + 48 506006 674, e-mail: sprzedaz@wuj.pl
Bank: PEKAO SA, IBAN PL80 1240 4722 1111 0000 4856 3325

Contents

Abbreviations

The journals *sigla* utilized are similar to the rules used in *L'Année Philologique*. The other abbreviations used in this volume are as follows:

AE	–	L'Année Épigraphique, Paris
ANRW	–	H. Temporini, W. Haase (eds.), *Aufstieg und Niedergang der römischen Welt*, Reihe II: *Principat*, Berlin–New York 1970–
BMC	–	W. Wroth, *British Museum Catalogue of Greek Coins: Galatia, Cappadocia and Syria*, London 1899
CAH^2	–	*The Cambridge Ancient History*, 2nd edition, Cambridge
CID	–	G. Rougemont *et al.*, *Corpus des inscriptions de Delphes*, 3 vols., Paris 1977–1992
CIL	–	*Corpus Inscriptionum Latinarum*
FD	–	*Fouilles de Delphes*, III : *Épigraphie*, Paris 1909–1985
FGrH	–	F. Jacoby, *Die Fragmente der Griechischer Historikern*, Berlin–Leiden 1928–
FHG	–	K. & Th. Müller, *Fragmenta Historicorum Graecorum*, 5 vols., Paris 1878–1883
GGM	–	K. Müller, *Geographi Graeci Minores*, 2 vols., Paris 1855
GIBM	–	*The Collection of Ancient Greek Inscriptions in the British Museum*, 4 vols. 4, Oxford 1874–1916
I. Délos	–	*Inscriptions de Délos*, 7 vols., Paris 1926–1972
I. Iasos	–	W. Blümel, *Die Inschriften von Iasos*, 2 vols., Bonn 1985
I. Magnesia	–	O. Kern, *Die Inschriften von Magnesia am Maeander*, Berlin 1990
I. Magnesia am Sipylos	–	T. Ihnken, *Die Inschriften von Magnesia am Sipylos*, Bonn 1978
I. Philae	–	A. Bernand, *Les inscriptions de Phialae*, vol. 1: *Époque ptolémaïque*, Paris 1969
IG	–	*Inscriptiones Graecae*
IGLS	–	L. Jalabert, R. Mouterde *et al.*, *Inscriptions grecques et latines de la Syrie*, Paris–Beyrouth 1920–
IGRR	–	R. Cagnat, *Inscriptiones Graecae ad Res Romanas pertinentes*, 3 vols., Paris 1906–1927
ILLRP	–	A. Degrassi, *Inscriptiones Latinae liberae rei publice*, 2 vols., Firenze 1957–1963
ILS	–	H. Dessau, *Inscriptiones Latinae Selectae*, 3 vols., Berlin 1892–1916
I. Milet	–	P. Herrmann *et al.*, *Inschriften von Milet*, 2 vols., Berlin 1997–
ISE	–	L. Moretti, *Iscrizioni storiche ellenistiche*, 2 vols., Firenze 1967–1976

MGH AA – *Monumenta Germaniae Historica Auctores Antiquiores*

OGIS – W. Dittenberger, *Orientis Graeci Inscriptiones Selectae*, 2 vols., Leipzig 1903–1905

PIR^2 – E. Groag, A. Stein *et al.*, *Prospopographia Imperii Romani saec. I.II.III*, editio altera, Berlin 1933–

P. Petrie – W.M. Flinders Petrie, J.P. Mahaffy, J. Gilbart Smyly, *The Flinders Petrie papyri: with Transcriptions, Commentaries and Index*, 3 vols., Dublin 1891–1905

RC – C.B. Welles, *Royal Correspondence in the Hellenistic Period. A Study in Greek Epigraphy*, Rome 1966 (reprint)

RE – *Paulys Realencyclopädie der classischen Altertumwissenschaft*, Stuttgart 1894–1980

RE S. – *Paulys Realencyclopädie der classischen Altertumwissenschaft*, Supplementbände, Stuttgart

RGA – *Reallexicon der Germanischen Altertumskunde*, Berlin–New York 1968/1972–

RPC – A. Burnett, M. Amandry, O.P. Ripollès, *Roman Provincial Coinage*, vol. 1: *From the Death of Caesar tot he Death of Vitellius (44 BC–AD 69)*, London–Paris 1992

SEG – *Supplementum Epigraphicum Graecum*

SGDI – H. Collitz, F. Bechtel *et al.*, *Sammlung der griechischen Dialekt Inschriften*, 5 vols., Göttingen 1884–1915

Syll^3 – W. Dittenberger, *Sylloge Inscriptionum Graecarum*, 3 ed., 4 vols., Leipzig 1915–1924

TAM – *Tituli Asiae Minoris*, Wien 1901–

TIB – *Tabula Imperii Byzantini*, Wien 1976–

ELECTRUM * Vol. 20 (2013): 9–22
doi: 10.4467/20800909EL.13.001.1430

THE TRADITION OF THE IONIAN COLONISATION OF ASIA MINOR: REMARKS ON THE SOURCES[1]

Jakub Kuciak
Uniwersytet Jagielloński, Kraków

Atheniensium res gestae,
sicuti ego aestumo, satis amplae magnificaeque fuere,
verum aliquanto minores tamen quam fama feruntur.
Sed quia provenere ibi scriptorum magna ingenia,
per terrarum orbem Atheniensium facta pro maxumis celebrantur.

Sallustius, *Bellum Catilinae* 8

Abstract: This article discusses the tradition of the Ionian colonisation preserved in ancient literary sources. The author focuses on the time and circumstances in which the view that the Athenians were responsible for the Ionian colonisation emerged. He also examines whether there is any support in the sources for the opinion expressed by some historians that such a belief was already strong in the Archaic period.

Key words: colonisation, Ionia, Athens, Euripides, Thucydides, Herodotus.

Ionian migration is a familiar term in historiography. Certainly, there is an ongoing debate about the extent to which accounts about the Ionians' arrival from Attica in Asia Minor reflect the actual events at the turn of the 1st millennium BC. However, it is generally accepted that as early as the 6th century BC the myth of the Ionian migration played a significant role in forming a bond between Athens and the Greek cities in Asia Minor. This paper is an attempt to critically re-examine the problem. We will start our examination by quoting a fragment of the *Compendium of Roman History* by Velleius Paterculus, who wrote at the turn of the eras:

> Subsequenti tempore magna vis Graecae iuventutis, abundantia virium, sedes quaeritans in Asiam se effudit. Nam et Iones, duce Ione, profecti Athenis nobilissimam partem regionis maritimae occupavere, quae hodieque appellatur Ionia, urbesque constituere Ephesum, Miletum, Colopho-

[1] The author would like to thank Prof. Sławomir Sprawski for all his input concerning the content.

na, Prienen, Lebedum, Clazomenas, Phocaeam, multasquae in Aegaeo atque Icario occupavere Myuntem, Erythram insulas, Samum, Chium, Andrum, Tenum, Parum, Delum alias que ignobiles.[2]

The passage paints a rather consistent picture of the colonisation of Ionia. According to the Roman historian, Ionia was settled by incomers from the territory of Athens. The campaign that populated the territory of Asia Minor and the neighbouring islands was reportedly led by Ion.[3] The reason behind organising a colonisation expedition was overpopulation. This image of the colonisation, carried out from the territory of Athens and making the city into something of a metropolis for the whole of Ionia, had such a powerful influence on historians studying the Greek past that some believed this tradition to be a completely, or at least largely, faithful depiction of actual events. N.G.L. Hammond, a British historian who studied migrations in ancient Greece, wrote in his *A History of Greece* that the Athenians initiated the process of the Ionian colonisation.[4] What is more, he suggests that as a result of the colonisation process initiated by Athens, which brought new settlers to these territories, a bond was formed between the Ionians and the Athenians. Using the example of the festival of Apaturia, mentioned by Herodotus,[5] he writes that even in the 8th century BC its role was to emphasise the ties binding the Ionians and the Athenians, and that the Ionians saw Attica as their homeland.[6] Hammond, then, believed that the sense of unity between the Athenians and the Ionians was formed very early on.

Herodotus, who devoted quite a lot of space to the Ionian colonisation, mentions that having arrived at the territories of Asia Minor, the Ionians founded twelve cities, because their tribe had been divided into twelve parts on the Peloponnese.[7] The Ionians are described as an *ethnos* in *Histories*. However, Herodotus' observation that some of the Ionians avoided using a common name must give us pause.[8]

We should also ask ourselves about the prevalence (in the Archaic and Early Classical Periods) of the sense of belonging to the Ionian *ethnos* and the belief in the tradition that the Ionian cities had been established by Athenian colonists. There is a theory which holds that it was the Ionians who tried to make their bond with the Athenians visible. This supposedly took place at the turn of the 5th century, when Ionian cities in Asia Minor found themselves in the Persian yoke and needed the support of a stronger ally.[9]

From the perspective of the Ionian cities in Asia Minor, the sense of such a union with the Athenians is not apparent in the sources. The local traditions of these Ionian cities include colonisation myths which have little to do with the territory of Attica. According to Mimnermus of Colophon (7th/6th century BC), his city was reportedly founded

[2] Vell. Pat. 1, 4, 3.

[3] We should point out that Ion arriving in Asia Minor and founding colonies there is not known in Greek literature. Only Velleius Paterculus and Vitruvius (4,1) recorded this version.

[4] Hammond 1973, 120.

[5] Hdt 1, 147.

[6] Hammond 1973, 124.

[7] Hdt 1, 145.

[8] Hdt 1, 143.

[9] Lamboley 2007, 58.

by Messenian settlers from Pylos (fr. 9 West). Hellanicus of Lesbos, a writer from the 5th century BC, relates that the founders of Priene came from Boeotian Thebes.[10]

The above fragments of works concerning the foundation of cities in Ionia (κτίσεις) and describing their history do not contain evidence of a unity of the region, and foundation myths treat each *polis* separately, without any references to common Ionian traditions. The graffiti at Abu-Simbel, probably left behind by Greek mercenaries in the early 6th century BC, is an interesting source. The inscriptions follow the same pattern of a person's name and country of origin. Among them, we find some names from Ionian cities, e.g. Pambis of Colophon.[11] The inscriptions found at Naucratis in the Nile Delta, created by people from Chios, Phocaea, and Cladzomenai, follow a similar pattern. It is puzzling that not one of these Greeks called himself an Ionian. Literary sources and inscriptions lead us to posit that perhaps in the archaic period the Ionians did not think of themselves as one community, and it was the *polis* that generated a sense of unity.[12]

On the basis of the surviving sources, it is difficult to prove that the Greeks in Asia Minor found it important to emphasise the existence of ethnic ties binding them to the Athenians. Therefore, it could be assumed that it was not in Ionia but in Athens that the tradition of common ancestry originated.

Historians put forward various theories regarding the time and circumstances in which this conviction emerged. In his article *Myth as Propaganda: Athens and Sparta*, Jan Bremmer stated that around 600 BC the ties between Athens and Ionia were well documented in Athens. This claim is based on one of the fragments attributed to Solon, who calls Attica the oldest part of Ionia.[13] In his comprehensive monograph, Michel Sakkelariou, in turn, dates the origin of the idea that the Ionians were descended from the Athenians to the first half of the 5th century BC.[14] His interpretation is based on the work of one Panyassis, who was supposedly more or less contemporary to Herodotus.

Since this interpretation does not appear very convincing, we must turn to ancient accounts. According to Sakellariou, the work of Panyassis, entitled *Ἰωνικά*, presented Neleus, the son of Kodros (king of Athens) as the leader of the colonisation expedition. However, Sakellariou's conclusions should be taken with caution. Panyassis' work has not survived, and very little is known of its content. *Liber Suda*, which is our source of information on Panyassis, merely states: ἔγραψε (Πανύασις – J.K.) [...] Ἰωνικὰ ἐν πενταμέτρῳ ἔστι δὲ τὰ περὶ Κόδρον, καὶ Νηλέα, καὶ Ἰωνικὰς ἀποικίας.[15] Based on this one mention, it is impossible to determine what role Neleus played in the colonisation of Ionia. Additionally, the mention should be interpreted as "on Kodros and Neleus," not "on Kodros, the son of Neleus," as Sakellariou claims. We should be very cautious indeed when it comes to chronology connected with Panyassis, as very little information

[10] *FGrH* 4 F 101 = Hesych. *s.v. Καδμεῖοι.*

[11] Pernigotti 1998, 63.

[12] Crielaard 2009, 43.

[13] Bremmer 1997, 10. Similarly, Morris 2009, 133.

[14] Sakellariou 1958, 30: «L'idée que les Ioniens seraient issus d'Athènes est donc postérieure à la révolte ionienne, mais antérieure à 460, date à laquelle est mort Panyasis, dont l'oeuvre, nous l'avons dit, présentait Nélée, fils de Codros, comme chef de la migration en Ionie».

[15] *Liber Suda*, s.v. *Πανύασις*.

about the writer has survived, while the work which supposedly described the colonisation of Ionia is mentioned only in *Liber Suda*, a very late source.

According to Sakellariou, the second oldest writer to relate the tradition about the Athenian origin of the Ionians is Pherecydes of Athens.[16] In one of the fragments attributed to the writer, which survived in Strabo's *Geography*, we read that the Ionians drove away the barbarian Carians and Leleges. Androklos – son of Kodros, king of Athens – reportedly led the colonisation campaign; he also founded Ephesus.[17] In the above fragment, the initiative to colonise Ionia does indeed become linked to Athens through Androklos. It must be noted, however, that Pherecydes is a contentious figure among scholars. The first serious problem is the fact that ancient sources relate information about two writers going by the name of Pherecydes, and even ancient writers found it difficult to distinguish between them. In his *Lives and Opinions of Eminent Philosophers*, Diogenes Laertius writes:

> Andron of Ephesus says that there were two natives of Syros who bore the name of Pherecydes: the one was an astronomer, the other was the son of Babys and a theologian, teacher of Pythagoras. Eratosthenes, however, says that there was only one Pherecydes of Syros, the other Pherecydes being an Athenian and a genealogist.[18]

Two figures emerge from the cited fragment: Pherecydes of Syros and Pherecydes of Athens. The former probably lived in the 6th century BC,[19] while Pherecydes of Athens (cited by Strabo) was a mythographer whose life and work is dated to the 5th century BC. It should be noted, however, that sources are not unanimous with regard to the seniority of the two writers named Pherecydes. Strabo writes that Pherecydes of Syros lived before his namesake from Athens.[20] According to *Liber Suda*, however, Pherecydes of Athens was older than Pherecydes of Syros.[21] Modern historians have tried to establish the exact period when the Athenian Pherecydes lived and wrote, but as yet without reaching a consensus. Felix Jacoby, who believes that one of Pherecydes' works, *Historiai*, was written between 508/507 and 476/475, dates his activity to the early 5th century BC.[22] George Huxley, in turn, links the period of Pherecydes' activity to the times of Cimon.[23] We must also mention the opinion of Ulrich Wilamowitz-Moellendorf, who questioned the existence of Pherecydes of Athens. He believed Pherecydes of Syros to have been a historical figure, and thought that Pherecydes of Athens had been invented by Eratosthenes.[24] According to this theory, in ancient times mythographic works were credited to the invented Pherecydes of Athens by the same principle by which laws were ascribed to Solon and medical treaties to Hippocrates.[25] The disputes which Phere-

[16] *FGrH* 3.

[17] *FGrH* 3 F 155 = Strabo 14, 1, 3 (C 632): ἄρξαι δέ φησιν Ἄνδροκλον τῆς τῶν Ἰώνων ἀποικίας, ὕστερον τῆς Αἰολικῆς, υἱὸν γνήσιον Κόδρου τοῦ Ἀθηνῶν βασιλέως, γενέσθαι δὲ τοῦτον Ἐφέσου κτίστην.

[18] Diog. Laer. 1,11. English translation edited by R.D. Hicks (Perseus Digital Library).

[19] Engels 2010, 70.

[20] Strabo 10, 5, 8 (C 487).

[21] *Liber Suda*, s.v. *Φερεκύδης Ἀθεναῖος: πρεσβύτερος τοῦ Σύριου.*

[22] Jacoby 1947, 33.

[23] Huxley 1973, 137.

[24] Fowler 1999, 2.

[25] Jacoby 1947, 33; Fowler 1999, 2.

cydes of Athens has provoked since Antiquity (particularly Wilamowitz's theory) put a question mark over a matter that is key for this article – the time when the fragment cited by Strabo was written. This means that we cannot definitively conclude that a strong tradition concerning the colonisation of Ionia by the Athenians existed in the first half of the 5th century BC.

In our search for the link between the Athenians and the Ionians, we should also turn to older sources. The first literary mention of the Ionians can be found in Homer; they were mentioned only once by the poet. It should be added that they were not placed in Asia Minor; Homer lists them as participants in the battle against the Trojans. Since Homer mentions them right next to the Boeotians, it could be assumed that according to the epic poet they lived somewhere in central Greece, perhaps Attica. This is just one possible interpretation; some historians place the Ionians in the *Iliad* on Euboea.[26] Others, in turn, believe this fragment to be an interpolation made by the Athenians.[27] It seems likely that Homer could have placed the Ionians in Attica.[28] However, the poet does not mention Ion (present in Paterculus' work) – the leader of the colonisation campaign and their eponym. His absence may be due to the fact that at the time the *Iliad* was written, Ion was not yet perceived as the eponym of the Ionians and coloniser.

The name of the famous Athenian statesman and poet Solon also appears in this discourse. One of the fragments attributed to him reads:

Γιγνώσκω καί μοι φρενὸς ἔνδοθεν ἄλγεα κεῖται,
Πρεσβυτάτην ἐσορῶν γαῖαν [Ἰ]αονίας κλινομένην.[29]

The author of this fragment expresses his sorrow at the bad condition of the Athenian *polis*, called "the oldest of the Ionian lands." On the basis of this fragment, historians conclude that the view that the Athenians and the Ionians had common ancestors was prevalent at the beginning of the 6th century BC in Attica (since 594/593 is the traditionally accepted date of Solon becoming *archon*).[30] Such a reference to the territory of Attica was to express a sense of unity of the Athenians and the Ionians. However, Solon's account must also be treated with the utmost caution, since there are more and more doubts as to whether all the fragments of poetry attributed to Solon were indeed his works. It

26 Burkert 1995, 11–12.

27 Hom. *Il.* 13, 685: Ἰάονες ἑλκεχίτωνες; Crielaard 2009, 41 n. 25.

28 Let us add that the Ionians are linked to Attica in late works penned by Strabo and Pausanias. It should also be mentioned, however, that the territory of the Peloponnese played an equally important role in these writers' accounts. They relate that apart from Attica, Achaea (which was called Aigalos in mythical times) was another land inhabited by the Ionians at the beginning of their history. However, information about Aigalos and Attica differs somewhat in Strabo's and Pausanias' accounts. Strabo derives the Ionians from the Athenians (ἐξ Ἀθηναίων τὸ γένος ὄντες). The Ionians from Attica sent colonists to the Peloponnese, where they settled in Aigalos, see Strabo 8, 7, 1 (C 383). Pausanias (7, 1, 1–9) on the other hand, identifies Aigalos as the cradle of the Ionians, who migrated to Attica after many trials and tribulations (Pausanias includes the earliest history of the Ionians and the progress of the colonisation of the Ionian cities in Asia Minor in the book on Achaea).

29 Frg. 4 (Diehl) = *Athenaion Politeia* 5.

30 Hall 1997, 53; 2002, 69; Miller 1997, 26. Zacharia (2003, 47) also posits that this view was known in Solon's times. She also suggests that Phrynichus' tragedy, *The Fall of Miletus,* may have contained similar content (Zacharia 2003, 49).

has been pointed out that since Solon's poetry was preserved only in oral form for a long period of time, it may have been distorted or even manipulated. Therefore, some scholars believe that at least some fragments attributed to Solon are not genuine.[31] If supporters of this theory are right, we cannot be certain that the one cited above reflects a view which was prevalent in Athens in the early 6th century. It could just as well have been composed at any moment preceding the writing of the *Athenaion Politeia*, whose author attributed these verses to Solon.[32] The matter is even more complicated because the manuscripts in which the relevant verses survived are damaged, which means that the cited fragment must be reconstructed, and the version presented above is not the only possible reading.[33]

A source-based depiction of the unity of the Athenians and the Ionians can only be found in works from the 5th century BC, penned by Herodotus, Thucydides, Euripides, and Hellanicos of Lesbos. In one of the chapters of *Histories*, Herodotus states that the Ionians who came from the Athenian Prytaneion considered themselves to be the highest born.[34] Euripides, in turn, shows Ion (the eponym of the Ionians) as a descendant of the Athenian king Erechteus.[35] Thucydides' account is a very important source; in the first part of Book I of the *History of the Peloponnesian War*, which is called the Archaeology, he states twice that the colonisation of the Ionian territories was carried out from Athens and by the citizens of the *polis*. This story is part of a broader description of the history of the Hellenes after the Trojan War. That time saw numerous migrations of peoples, although these were not experienced by Attica, meaning that this territory was always inhabited by the same population (τὴν γοῦν Ἀττικὴν [...] ἄνθροποι ᾤκουν οἱ αὐτοὶ αἰεί).[36] When the turmoil ended, Athens started to grow so quickly that it faced the prob-

[31] Lardinois 2006, 32–33; we should remember that the Athenian was regarded as a legend in the 5th century BC. He was listed among the Seven Sages and credited with deeds which, on the one hand, are very difficult to prove, but on the other hand are so fixed in the collective awareness that they are almost taken for granted even today (e.g. the creation of the Council of Four Hundred). Solon is already presented as a wise man in Herodotus' *The Histories* (Book I), where he gives advice to the Lydian king Croesus and Cyrus the Great. He is also named in the oldest extant list of the Seven Sages, which has survived to our times in Plato's *Protagoras* (342e–343c), where he is listed as a wise man along with Thales of Miletus, Bias of Priene, Pittacus of Mytilene, Cleobulus of Lindos, Myson of Chenae, and Chilon of Sparta, see Snell 1943, 26–56; Engels 2010, 49–52.

[32] Keaney 1992, 14.

[33] Masaracchia 1958, 272–273. Mülke (2002, 165–168) discussed the difficulties with interpreting this fragment. For alternative readings, cf. Rhodes 1993, 122–123. Some sources say that Ionia is the original name of Attica, but these sources are late, as well as few and far between, see Strabo 8, 7, 1 (C 383); Steph. Byz., *s.v. Ἰωνία:* ἡ Ἀττικὴ πρότερον [...].

[34] Hdt 1, 146.

[35] M. Sakellariou (1958, 26) claims that Plato's *Euthydemus* (302c) also relates the information that the Ionians in Asia Minor were descended from Athens. However, this fact cannot be established on the basis of the text. The fragment reads that all the Ionians – those in Athens, and those who left the city (ἐκ τῆσδε πόλεως ἀπῳκισμένοι) – worship Apollo as their protective deity; it does not mention where the Ionians migrated to. Asia Minor is the first place that comes to mind, but we should remember that according to the tradition recorded in Strabo's *Geography*, the Ionians from Attica also colonised the Peloponnese. See Strabo 8, 7, 1 (C 383): οὕτω δὲ πολυανδρῆσαι τὴν χώραν τότε συνέπεσεν ὥστε καὶ ἀποικίαν τῶν Ἰώνων ἔστειλαν εἰς Πελοπόννησον Ἀθεναῖοι [...].

[36] Thuc. 1, 3. The autochthonous origin of the Athenians is already mentioned by Herodotus. In the description of the refusal to give the command of the Athenian fleet to Gelon, the tyrant of Syracuse, the

lem of overpopulation, which was solved by sending colonists to Ionia.[37] Thucydides also points out the kinship between the Athenians and the Ionians when he depicts the Hellenes' customs and style of dressing in the oldest times. As a result of their common ancestry, both the Athenians and the Ionians wore long chitons and tied their hair with pins.[38] We should also note that some of the extant fragments by Hellanicos, a writer more or less contemporary to Thucydides, refer to the colonisation of Ionia. Neleus, son of the Athenian king Kodros, plays an important role in the events. According to one of the fragments, Neleus was the founder of the twelve cities in Ionia.[39] Another fragment calls Neleus the founder of the city of Erythrai.[40]

In our search for evidence of a sense of unity between the Athenians and the Ionians, we should not overlook the figure of Ion. He appears for the first time in the *Catalogue of Women (Eoie)*, a work credited to Hesiod.[41] There is a debate among scholars concerning the dating and authorship of this work. Some scholars claim, that the *Catalogue of Women* is indeed the work of Hesiod, written at the turn of the 7th century BC.[42] However, it is increasingly often posited that the work was probably written in the 6th century BC. Martin West, an editor of the *Catalogue of Women*, also subscribes to this theory. This dating is based on text analysis, which sets the work's *terminus ante quem non* at the second half of the 7th century BC, and the *terminus post quem non* at the early 5th century BC.[43] There is also a hypothesis that the writer had connections with Attica.[44] Although the text of the *Catalogue of Women* is fragmentary and Ion only appears in one of the fragments, it can be a basis for some very important observations. In the account of the author of the *Catalogue of Women*, Ion is the son of Xuthus and Creusa (daughter of the mythical king of Athens, Erechteus), and on his father's side he is descended from Hellen himself.[45] Ion is mentioned next to his uncle Dorus, regarded in Greek mythology as a hero and the eponymous founder of the Dorians. In doing so, the text includes Ion in the Panhellenic genealogy, which systematised accounts about the ancestry of various Hellenic tribes, trying to reconcile various local traditions.[46] Since Ion does not appear

---

envoys say: ἀρχαιότατον μὲν ἔθνος παρεχόμενοι, μοῦνοι δὲ ἐόντες οὐ μετανάσται Ἑλλήνων; Hdt 7, 161. Cf. also Isoc. *Panegyricus* 24.

[37] Thuc. 1, 3, 12.

[38] Thuc. 1, 6.

[39] *FGrH* 4 F 125 = Schol. Platon. *Symp.* 208D.

[40] *FGrH* 4 F 48 = Harp. s.v. *Ἐρυθαῖοι*; traditions about the colonisation of Ionia in which Neleus played an important role are also recorded in later sources, e.g. Aristotle (frg. 76 Rose).

[41] Ps.-Hes. *Cat.Mul.* F 10 (Merkelbach – West):
Ξοῦθος δὲ Κρείουσαν ἐπήρατον εἶδος ἔχουσαν
Κούρην καλλιπάρηον Ἐρεχθῆος θείοιο
ἀθανάτων ἰότητι φίλην ποιήσατ' ἄκοιτιν·
ἥ οἱ Ἀχαιὸν ἐγείατ' Ἰάονά τε κλυτόπωλον
μιχθεῖσ' ἐν φιλότητι καὶ εὐειδεα Διομήδην.

[42] P. Dräger (1997, 1–27) takes this position, disagreeing with West.

[43] West 1985, 130–136; cf. Hall 2002, 238–239.

[44] West 1985, 169–171; West states that if the author himself did not come from Attica, he "learnt the form from another who was." See Hall 2002, 239.

[45] Ps.-Hes. *Cat. Mul.* F 9 = Plut. *Quaest. conv.* 747f: Ἕλληνος δ' ἐγένοντο φιλοπτολέμου βασιλῆος Δῶρός τε Ξοῦτός τε καὶ Αἴολος ἱππιοχάρμης.

[46] Hall 2002, 26–27.

in the Asia Minor tradition, we may consider the possibility that Ion is a creation of the Athenian tradition (if we agree with West's opinion that the *Catalogue*'s author had connections with Attica). However, it is impossible to say with certainty how important Ion was in the eyes of the author of the *Catalogue of Women*, since he appears only once in the work, in the cited fragment.[47]

Perhaps Herodotus continued the tradition represented by the author of the *Catalogue of Women*, since in *Histories* he twice states that Ion was the son of Xuthus (just like the author of the *Catalogue of Women*).[48] The context in which Ion's name appears in Herodotus' *Histories* is significant. He appears clearly in connection with Athens and Attica, but not in the description of the colonisation of Ionia in Asia Minor, which Herodotus also mentions.[49] In Book V, in the passage discussing Cleisthenes and his administrative reform dividing Attica into ten phyla, it is also mentioned that the previous division into four tribes was linked to Ion, as those administrative units were named after his sons.[50] It should be emphasised that *Histories* is the first work in which Ion is presented as an eponymous figure. However, Herodotus claims that it was the Athenians who adopted the name "Ionians," derived from their leader.[51] The inhabitants of Athens were not the only ones to adopt Ion's name; so did those who had lived in Achaea before the arrival of Xuthus and had called themselves Aegialian Pelasgians.[52] Considering the fact that in *Histories* Ion is linked to the territory of Attica and the northern Peloponnese, it could be surmised that the myth used by Herodotus originated in those regions. On the other hand, the figure must have been absent from the stories taken from the Asia Minor, Ionian tradition. Herodotus discusses both the topic of the colonisation of Ionia and the topic of the oldest history of the *poleis* situated there[53] – but not a word is written about Ion in those passages.

It is worth noting that Herodotus did not devote much attention to Ion, despite the fact that the writer himself was connected with both Ionia and Attica. His links to the former are obvious because of his origin (although Halicarnassus was where Ionian and Doric influences met) and his stay on the Ionian island of Samos, where, as tradition has it, he wrote *Histories*.[54] He subsequently went to Athens, where – if ancient accounts are to be believed – the Athenians rewarded him with ten talents for praising their par-

[47] In her commentary on the *Catalogue of Women*, M. Hirschberger (2004, 184–185) writes rather boldly, "Ion ist der eponyme Heros der Ionier, was im engeren Sinne die Ionien Kleinasiens, im weiteren Sinne die Bewohner des gesamten ionisch-attischen Sprachgebiets mit Euboia, Attika und einem Teil der Kykladen meinen kann."

[48] Hdt 7, 94; 8, 44.

[49] The depiction of the colonisation of Ionia proposed by Herodotus is extremely interesting, since on the other hand, the author stresses that the colonisation process started from the Athenian territory.

[50] Hdt 5, 66: [..] τῶν Ἴωνος παίδων Γελέοντος καὶ Αἰγικόρεος καὶ Ἀργάδεω καὶ Ὅπλητος [...]; later sources say that it was Ion who divided the population of Attica into four phyla; Strabo 8, 7, 1 (C 383): ὁ [Ἴων – J.K.] δὲ πρῶτον μὲν εἰς τέτταρας φυλὰς διεῖλε τὸ πλῆθος [...]. According to Plutarch (*Adv. Col.* 31) Ion, compared to Lycurgus, Numa, and Deucalion, taught the Athenians about religious matters.

[51] Hdt 8, 44: [...] Ἴωνος δὲ τοῦ Ξούθου στρατάρχεω γενομένου Ἀθηναίοισι ἐκλήθησαν ἀπὸ τούτου Ἴωνες. Ion's leadership of the Athenians, mentioned by Herodotus, may refer to conflicts with Eleusis, known from later sources (Paus. 7, 1,4), or with the Thracians under the rule of Eumolpos (Strabo 8, 7, 1 (C 383)).

[52] Hdt 7, 94.

[53] Hdt 1, 142–148.

[54] *Liber Suda*, s.v. *Ἡρόδοτος*; Bichler/Rollinger 2000, 111.

ticipation in the war against the Persians.[55] Consequently, Herodotus was likely to have access to the local traditions, taken mainly from the elites of Athens and Ionia. The fact that Ion makes such a rare appearance in *Histories* may mean that, for some reason, Herodotus did not find it appealing to refer to the Panhellenic genealogy, related e.g. in the *Catalogue of Women*. Let us note that he is equally reserved when mentioning other figures connected with this tradition – Hellen himself, and one of his sons, Dorus, appear only once in *The Histories*, in the same chapter.[56]

Herodotus' version is important for one more reason. Although the description of the Ionian colonisation includes the information that some of the settlers set off from Athens, it is also stated that the colonists were of various origins; the participants in this venture included the Abantes of Euboea, the Cadmeans and the Dorians of Epidauros. Those who set off from Athens reportedly did not take their women with them and later married the barbarian Carian women.[57] This is a very interesting interpretation of the colonisation of Ionia, which seems to combine two independent traditions. The Athenian tradition echoes in the fragments about the "noble birth" of the participants setting off from the Prytaneion (note, however, that Herodotus does not write *expressis verbis* that it was the Athenians who set off from the Prytaneion). On the other hand, naming other tribes as colonists who supposedly organised their campaigns independently from Athens seems to be reminiscent of the colonisation myths functioning in individual Ionian *poleis* in Asia Minor. Therefore, it can be concluded that with regard to the colonisation of Ionia, *Histories* relate information from various traditions, and Herodotus himself rarely mentions Ion or other figures connected to the Panhellenic genealogy (e.g. Hellen, Dorus). In the fragments of *Histories* that do mention Ion, he is presented as the eponymous hero and reformer attached to the territory of Attica. His connections with Ionia in Asia Minor are not mentioned, and he is not presented as the founder of any colonies.

Another author of key importance for this article is a different 5th-century writer connected with Athens – Euripides. His works include a tragedy called *Ion*, created at a very difficult time for the Athenian *polis*, in the final stages of the Peloponnesian War.[58] In several places, Euripides' version of the myth is markedly different from the information related in the previously mentioned sources. The tragedy follows the fate of Ion, the son of the god Apollo and Creusa, who is abandoned by his mother at birth. However, his divine father orders Hermes to fetch the child from the cave in which he was left and to bring him to Delphi, where he is raised and serves as a guard in the temple of Apollo.[59]

---

[55] Plut. *De Herod.* 862b; cf. Bichler/Rollinger 2000, 112.

[56] Hdt 1, 56.

[57] Hdt 1, 146: [...] τῶν ῎Αβαντες μὲν ἐξ Εὐβοίης εἰσὶ οὐ κἐλαχίστη μοῖρα, τοῖσι 'Ιωνίης μέτα οὐδὲ τοῦ οὐνόματος οὐδέν, Μινύαι δὲ 'Ορχομένιοί σφι ἀναμεμίχαται καὶ Καδμεῖοι καὶ Δρύοπες καὶ Φωκέες ἀπο δάσμιοικαὶ Μολοσσοὶ καὶ Ἀρκάδες Πελασγοὶ καὶ Δωριέες 'Επιδαύριοι, ἄλλα τε ἔθνεα πολλὰ ἀναμεμίχαται. Οἰδὲ αὐτῶν ἀπὸ τοῦ πρυτανηίου τοῦ Ἀθηναίων ὁρμηθέντες καὶ νομίζοντες γενναιότατοι εἶναι 'Ιώνων, οὗτοι δὲ οὐ γυναῖκας ἠγάγοντο ἐς τὴν ἀποικίην ἀλλὰ Καείρας ἔσχον, τῶν ἐφόνευσαν τοὺς γονέας.

[58] The dating of the staging of the play is controversial. Some historians attempt to set an exact date, e.g. 419, 414, or 413 BC, see Lesky 2006, 489–490. Others propose more cautious time periods, e.g. 412–408, see Łanowski 2006, 350. K. Zacharia (2003, 2–5) suggests that *Ion* was staged in 412.

[59] This information is included in the prologue, in the part spoken by Hermes: Eur. *Ion* 1–81. Let us add that the long prologue used by Euripides in *Ion* introduces the audience to a version of the myth modified by the writer. Euripides used the same device in his other plays as well, see Czerwińska 2013, 40.

In the meantime, Creusa has married Xuthus, but has been unable to give him a child. Together with her husband, she goes to Delphi, where Ion and Creusa meet (unaware of their kinship).[60] Xuthus, meanwhile, heads to the Oracle of Trophonius to seek advice on how to end their infertility, and the oracle mysteriously foretells a positive resolution.[61] The audience of *Ion* finds out the resolution in the prologue; Apollo intends to give his son to Xuthus.[62] From that moment onwards the plot moves towards the mutual recognition (*anagnorismos*) of the mother, Creusa, the father, Xuthus, and the son, Ion. First, the father and the son recognise each other when Xuthus (who has just been told the prophecy) leaves the temple and meets Ion. The recognition of Creusa and Ion and the explanation of the *peripetaia* take place at the end of the tragedy, when the mother and son meet at the foot of the altar. They both leave for Athens, and the whole play ends with the goddess Athena predicting that Ion's deeds, as well as those of his sons, will be famous.[63]

Even this very brief summary of the plot allows us to note that in fact Euripides' tragedy is the first source to offer a more extended narrative about Ion. The play's message is decidedly pro-Athenian; Euripides showed a similar attitude in his other works, but this does not mean that he was uncritical about the policies of the Athenian *polis*.[64] It seems justified to say that, at such a difficult moment in its history, Athens needed an ideological boost, a show of unity between the city and its allies in the Delian League.[65] Let us remember that *Ion* was staged several years after the failure of the expedition to Sicily, which severely lessened the power of the Athenian Empire.[66] This weakening was considerable enough for the *hegemon* of the Delian League to have increasingly serious problems with keeping a tight rein on his allies. Out of the Ionian allies, according to Thucydides, Chios and Erythrai began negotiations with Sparta.[67] Referring to the common ancestry of the Athenians and the Ionians was probably meant to strengthen the Athenians' sense of entitlement to control the Ionian territory. In Euripides' tragedy, Ion is shown as a descendant (through his mother Creusa) of the Athenian king Erechtheus, and therefore Erichthonius, born of the earth.[68] This is probably a reference to the already mentioned belief about the autochthonous origin of the Athenians, which is also brought up by Ion himself when he says that the Athenians are "not drawn from

[60] Eur. *Ion* 237–400.

[61] Eur. *Ion* 300, 404–409.

[62] Eur. *Ion* 69–71: δώσει γὰρ εἰσελθόντι μαντεῖον τόδε Ξούθῳ τὸν αὑτοῦ παῖδα, καὶ πεφυκέναι κείνου σφε φήσει.

[63] Eur. *Ion* 1261–1622.

[64] Lesky 2006, 313. Euripides praises Athens e.g. in one of the songs of the chorus in *Medea*, see Eur. *Med.* 824–865. The trilogy of plays consisting of *Alexandros, Palamedes*, and *Trojan Women* (the latter extant in its entirety) staged in 415 BC was probably also a protest against the Peloponnesian War: Czerwińska 2013, 40–41.

[65] Euripides expressed the greatness and fame of Athens through Hermes' words in the first lines of the prologue, see Eur. *Ion* 8–10: [...] ἔστιν γὰρ οὐκ ἄσημος πόλις, τῆς χρυσολόγχου Παλλάδος κεκλημένη [...].

[66] Rhodes 2009, 160.

[67] Thuc. 8, 5.

[68] Eur. *Ion* 265–270; this is a reference to the belief about the autochthonous origin of the Athenians: Lee 1997, 35–36; Zacharia 2003, 56–66.

foreign lineage".[69] At the same time, very importantly in the context of this article, Ion is for the first time connected *expressis verbis* with the colonisation of the territories in Asia Minor. In the prologue, a very characteristic term is used to refer to him – κτίστωρ Ἀσιάδος χθονός[70] – while at the very end of the tragedy, *nomen omen*, Athena shows Creusa the bright future of her descendants[71] – Ion's sons will give names to "land and people" (ἐπώνυμιοι γῆς κἀπιφυλίου χθονος λαῶν ἔσονται).[72] Although the text of the tragedy is damaged here, we can easily see that this is a reference to the ancient division of Athens into four phyla mentioned earlier.[73] The crux of the foretold power of Athens, which will also be connected with the colonisation of Ionia, is the following fragment, worth quoting *in extenso*:

> [...] In years to come, their children will build cities in the Cyclades islands and around the shores of the mainland and so give much power to my city. They will build colonies on the land opposite Europe and Asia. Those in Ionia will be called Ionians, taking the boy's name and they will earn great glory.[74]

This passage predicts the colonisation which would bring Athens great fame and power. Euripides' version makes a very clear connection between the colonisation and Ion and his sons. The mention in this context of the territories of Europe, Asia, as well as the Cyclades, clearly reveals the propaganda role of *Ion*, demonstrating the unity of the Athenian empire.[75]

Euripides' modification of the genealogical tradition is also very important in the context of the colonisation of territories in Asia Minor by Ion and his descendants. In the previous version of the myth, which can be found, for example, in the *Catalogue of Women*, Ion is Xuthus' son, which makes him Hellen's grandson (following this line we would find Deucalion and Pyrra, i.e. a purely human family tree). Linking Ion to the Panhellenic genealogy turned out to be insufficient for Euripides. In the variant proposed by the tragedian, Ion becomes a son of one of the most important gods of the Hellenic pantheon – Apollo.[76] As a result, the divine origin of Ion and the tribes descended from him sets them apart from and above the Panhellenic genealogy. This can be interpreted as an attempt to show the superiority of the Athenians and their allies in the Greek world; an impression that is strengthened by the fact that in *Ion*, Dorus, the eponymous founder of the Dorians (and so the Spartans, among others) becomes the younger brother of the main character.[77] In the version of the myth known from the *Catalogue of Women* and

[69] Eur. *Ion* 589–590: εἶναί φασι τὰς αὐτόχθονας κλεινὰς Ἀθήνας οὐκ ἐπείσακτον γένος. English translation by Robert Potter (The Internet Classics Archive).

[70] Eur. *Ion* 74.

[71] The suddenly appearing *deus* (in this case *dea*) *ex machina* in the final part of the tragedy is a device that Euripides uses to show a happy ending: Czerwińska 2013, 41.

[72] Eur. *Ion* 1577–1578.

[73] Eur. *Ion* 1579–1580.

[74] Eur. *Ion* 1582–1587. English translation by George Theodoridis (http://bacchicstage.wordpress.com/euripides/ion/; access September 2013).

[75] Mattingly 1999, 189.

[76] Plato relates the same version (*Euth.* 302c). Smarczyk (1990, 362) believes that making Apollo Ion's father was not Euripides' innovation, but a motif taken from an earlier tradition, e.g. from Sophocles' lost tragedy *Creusa*.

[77] Athena predicts the birth of a younger son to Creusa: Eur. *Ion* 1589–1590.

Herodotus' *The Histories*, Dorus is not Ion's brother (let alone a younger one) but uncle.[78] Moreover, in Euripides' account Dorus is the less important brother, as he is the son of Xuthus, not Apollo. This genealogical degradation of Dorus is quite telling in the context of the Peloponnesian War raging between Athens and Sparta.[79] The reason why Apollo specifically was made Ion's father may be the fact that the god, called ἀρχηγέτες and πατρῷος, was worshipped as a protective deity of cities and the god of colonisation.[80] Bernhard Smarczyk claims that this is the context in which Apollo appears in *Ion*.[81] It should be noted that in *Euthydemus*, Plato also relates the information about the Ionians worshipping Apollo as their protective deity.[82]

It seems possible that, in the difficult situation Athens was facing at the end of the 5th century BC, Euripides wanted to popularise the myth about Ion among the Athenians.[83] It is very difficult to prove whether he succeeded or not. However, we should also mention an interesting inscription found on Samos, and first published in the *Bulletin de correspondance hellénique* in 1884, which reads: *῞Ορος τεμένους ῞Ιωνος Ἀθενέθεν*.[84] The text, as well as the finding place, are very intriguing; the dating of this find and its authorship are just as important. With regard to the date, the *BCH* editors laconically call the inscription *une inscription archaique*. J.P. Barron believes that it was probably created in the Hellenistic period.[85] He also cites another inscription with the same wording, which he in turn dates to the 5th century BC. It is difficult to determine when exactly it was created. J. Hall believes that inscriptions of this type appeared on Samos around 440 BC.[86] However, we must agree with Barron that the content of this inscription is in keeping with the ideology of the Athenian domination, expressed, among others, in Euripides' *Ion*.[87]

In conclusion, a well-confirmed opinion that the Ionian colonisation was an Athenian initiative can be found quite late, in sources from the 5th century BC, especially its

[78] Ps.-Hes. *Cat. Mul.* F 9 = Plut. *Quaest.conv.* 747f; Hdt 1, 56.

[79] Zacharia 2003, 55; Łanowski 2006, 350.

[80] Roscher (ed.) 1890, 438–441.

[81] Smarczyk 1990, 363.

[82] Plat. *Eut.* 302c.

[83] We can find an analogy to confirm the claim that Euripides wanted to popularise the myth about Ion when we study the writer's biography. Towards the end of his life, Euripides left Athens and went to Macedonia, to the court of King Archelaos (who ruled in 413–399 BC). The tragedian's biographer, Satyros of Callatis, who wrote in the Hellenistic period, states that Euripides wrote a play entitled *Archeloas* in honour of his host (see Satyros, *Vita Euripidi* 21–25). One of the play's topics was the genealogical tradition describing the beginnings of the Temenids (Argeads) who ruled Macedonia, and Archelaos was presented as Temenos' son (see Harder 1985, 131). In doing so, Euripides made him the *de facto* founder of the Macedonian dynasty. What is most important from our point of view is the assertion that before the play was written, Archelaos had not been perceived as the founder of the Macedonian royal house; the earlier tradition, recorded in Herodotus' *Histories,* credited Perdiccas (cf. Sprawski 2012, 17–18). Although the version related in *Archelaos* did not take in Macedonia, and Caranus is presented as the founder of the Temenid dynasty in later sources, such as Theopompus of Chios and Plutarch (cf. Theopompus, *FGrH* 115 F 393, Plut. *Alex.* 2; see Sprawski 2012,18–19), the stories told in *Ion* could have been received better.

[84] *BCH* VIII (1884), 160.

[85] Barron 1964, 37–38.

[86] Hall 1997, 55.

[87] Barron 1964, 47–48.

second half. In *The Land of Ionia,* a book devoted mostly to archaeology, Alan Greaves is right on the mark when he notes that stories about the Athenian colonisation of the Ionian territories reveal who the Ionians were according to the Athenians.[88] Of course, such a belief could have existed earlier, although claims that it had been strong before the 5th century BC receive very weak backing from the sources. The popularisation of the myth may therefore be connected not with the period of building political cooperation between Athens and the Ionian cities, but rather with the period of the Athenians' struggle to keep their Empire in the second half of the 5th century. At that time, with Athens facing a difficult political situation, a need arose to emphasise the connections between the Athenians and the Ionians. Works in which this was reflected were written by authors connected with Athens; writers such as Thucydides or Euripides used their talent to support Athens in a very challenging period of time. Presenting the Athenians as the colonists of Ionia may be interpreted not only as a measure to emphasise their antiquity and ties with Ionia, but also as an attempt to add splendour to Athenian history and strengthen the imperial pride. Such measures perfectly correspond with the fragment of Salustius' *Bellum Catilinae* quoted at the very beginning, whose author believed that its very talented writers raised the status of Athens' history from great to the greatest.[89]

Bibliography

Barron, J.P. (1964): Religious Propaganda of the Delian League, *JHS* 84: 35–48.

Bichler, R., Rollinger, R. (2000): *Herodot*, Hildesheim–Zürich–New York.

Bremmer, J. (1997): Myth as Propaganda – Athens and Sparta, *ZPE* 117: 9–17.

Burkert, W. (1995): *The Orientalizing Revolution – Near Eastern Influence on Greek Culture in the Early Archaic Age*, Cambridge (Mass.)–London.

Crielaard, J.-P. (2009): The Ionians in the Archaic Period. Shifting Identities in a Changing World, in: T. Derks, N. Roymans (eds.), *Ethnic Constructs in Antiquity-the Role of Power and Tradition*, Amsterdam: 37–84.

Czerwińska, J. (2013): *Innowacje mitologiczne i dramaturgiczne Eurypidesa. Tragedia, tragikomedia*, Łódź.

Dräger, P. (1997): *Untersuchungen zu den Frauenkatalogen Hesiods*, Stuttgart.

Engels, J. (2010): *Die Sieben Weisen – Leben, Lehren und Legenden*, München.

Hammond, N.G.L. (1973): *Dzieje Grecji*, trans. into Polish by A. Świderek, Warszawa.

Hirschberger, M. (2004): *Gynaikōn Katalogos und Megalai Ēhoiai – Ein Kommentar zu den Fragmenten Zweier Hediodeischer Epen*, München–Leipzig.

Fowler, R.L. (1999): The Authors Named Pherecydes, *Mnemosyne* 53: 1–15.

Greaves, A. (2010): *The Land of Ionia*, Oxford.

Hall, J. (1997): *Ethnic Identity in Greek Antiquity*, Cambridge.

Hall, J. (2002): *Hellenicity – Between Ethnicity and Culture*, Chicago.

Harder, A. (1985): *Euripides' Kresphontes and Archelaos. Introduction, Text and Commentary*, Leiden.

[88] Greaves 2010, 223.

[89] Sal. *Bell. Cat.* 8.

Hirschberger, M. (2004): *Gynaikōn Katalogos und Megalai Ēhoiai – Ein Kommentar zu den Fragmenten Zweier Hediodeischer Epen*, München–Leipzig.
Hunter, R. (2005): *Introduction*, in: R. Hunter, *The Hesiodic Catalogue of Women: Constructions and Reconstructions*, Cambridge–New York: 1–5.
Huxley, J. (1973): The Date of Pherecydes of Athens, *GRBS* 14: 137–143.
Jacoby, F. (1947): The First Athenian Prose Writer, *Mnemosyne* 13: 13–64.
Keaney, J.J. (1992): *The Composition of Aristotle's Athenaion Politeia: Observation and Explanation*, New York–Oxford.
Lamboley, J.-L. (2007): Migration and Greek Civilization, in: A.C. Isaacs (ed.), *Immigration and emigration in historical perspective*, Pisa: 55–64.
Lardinois, A. (2006): Have we Solon's verses?, in: J.H. Block, A. Lardinois (eds.), *Solon of Athens. New Historical and Philological Approaches,* Leiden–Boston: 15–36.
Lee, K.H. (1997): *Euripides Ion with an Introduction, Translation and Commentary by K.H. Lee*, Warminster.
Lesky, A. (2006): *Tragedia grecka*, Polish trans., Kraków (original – *Die tragische Dichtung der Hellenen*, Göttingen 1956).
Łanowski, J. (2006): Wstęp – Ijon, in: Eurypides, *Tragedie*, vol. 2, trans. and commentary by J. Łanowski, Warszawa: 350–354.
Masaracchia, A. (1958): *Solone*, Firenze.
Mattingly, H.B. (1999): *The Athenian Empire Restored: Epigraphical and Historical Studies*, University of Michigan.
Miller, T. (1997): *Die griechische Kolonisation im Spiegel literarischer Zeugnisse*, Tübingen.
Morris, I. (2009): The Greater Athenian State (478–404 BC), in: I. Morris, W. Scheidel (eds.), *The Dynamics of Ancient Empires*, Oxford: 99–177.
Mülke, Ch. (2002): *Solons politische Elegien und Iamben (Fr. 1–13; 32–37 West) – Einleitung, Text, Übersetzung, Kommentar*, München–Leipzig.
Pergnigotti, S. (1998): *I Greci nell'Egitto Della XXVI Dinastia*, Imola.
Podbielski, H. (2005): Hezjod, in: H. Podbielski (ed.), *Literatura Grecji starożytnej*, vol. 1, Lublin: 185–231.
Rhodes, P.J. (1993): *A Commentary to Aristotelian Anthenaion Politeia*, Oxford–New York.
Rhodes, P.J. (2009): *Historia Grecji – okres klasyczny – 478–323 p.n.e.*, Kraków.
Roscher, W.H. (ed.) (1890): *Ausführlisches Lexicon der griechischen und römischer Mythologie*, vol. 1, Leipzig.
Sakellariou, M. (1958): *La migration grecque en Ionie*, Athènes.
Smarczyk, B. (1990): *Untersuchungen zur Religionspolitik und politischen Propaganda Athens im Delisch-Attischen Seebund*, München.
Snell, B. (1943): *Leben und Meinungen der Sieben Weisen*, München.
Sprawski, S. (2012): Perdikkas i kozy – w poszukiwaniu protoplasty rodu Argeadów, in: S. Sprawski (ed.), *Człowiek w antycznym świecie*, Kraków: 11–35.
West, M. (1985): *The Hesiodic Catalogue of Women – Its Nature, Structure and Origins*, Oxford.
Zacharia, K. (2003): *Converging Truths: Euripides' Ion – and the Athenian Quest for Self-Definition*, Leiden.

ELECTRUM * Vol. 20 (2013): 23–36
doi: 10.4467/20800909EL.13.002.1431

Greeks and non-Greeks in the City of Emporion and the Construction of Their Different Identities

Adolfo J. Domínguez
Universidad Autónoma de Madrid

Abstract: The Greek city of Emporion is one of the few Greek *emporia* which ultimately became a *polis*. Consequently, the city had to adapt the previously held structures of an *emporion* to cope with the new circumstances which being a *polis* required; thus its urban space, territory, population, laws, government had to be modified in the conversion from one situation to another. Furthermore, this change had to be fulfilled in the midst of a non-Greek environment, which obviously had consequences in the development of Greek identity within the city. Fortunately, in the case of Emporion we have both archaeological and literary evidence (although not very abundant) to observe these processes. The aim of this paper is, consequently, to consider this evidence in order to see how interactions worked in Emporion itself as well as in the surrounding region in different historical moments and how those interactions contributed to shaping several interrelated identities within the Greek city, which also became a strong point for building the identity of the non-Greek peoples in that region of north-eastern Iberia.

Key words: Emporion, Greek colonisation, Iberia, Iberians.

It is generally accepted that the Greek city of Emporion in north-eastern Spain became a true Greek *polis*, perhaps in the 5th century BC (Domínguez 2004b, 157–171). However, its "official" name, Emporion, clearly reveals its origins as an *emporion*. Whether this *emporion*, known to everyone as "the" *emporion,* had a previous name (Cypsela? Pyrene?) is something we cannot say at present.

Excavators date the origin of the Greek *emporion* to around 580 BC after an earlier period when Greek products increased following their first appearance in the last quarter of the 7th century BC. Similarly, the excavations emphasise the close relationship between this first *emporion* and Massalia (Aquilué 1999, 217–330). The fact that later traditions shifted between the Phocaean and the Massaliot origins of Emporion can be interpreted in various ways: either the sources are not precise, or the Emporitans wanted to create their own identity by breaking ties with Massalia and establishing a Phocaean identity (Domínguez 2004a, 429–456); the Phocaean identity is questioned by some authors mainly on the basis of archaeological evidence and an analysis of the city of Elea (Gassner 2003, 275). This is not, however, the place to reassert or add additional information to support the existence of this Phocaean identity, similar to that existing between other cities that were considered foundations of the same mother city, beyond the similarities or differences in their archaeological records. Identity is socially constructed and operates on different levels, depending on the interests or dominant forces at any given time. A Massaliote identity is compatible with a Phocaean identity, as in Massalia, but for minor centres, such as Emporion, a Phocaean and Emporitan identity may have been preferred to accepting a Massaliote identity. In any case, the issue of identities in Emporion has also recently been addressed by some authors (Demetriou 2012, 24–63), although with results somewhat different to those suggested in this paper.

But let us return to Emporion. The transition from *emporion* to *polis* must have been due to a significant increase in population, the need for a larger territory and hence the need to create a political organisation appropriate to the new situation. Archaeological evidence reveals an area of about 3 or 4 ha south of the former *emporion*, its northern and southern limits marked by at least two sanctuaries from the mid-6th century BC onwards (Dupré 2005, 103–123; Aquilué *et al.* 2008, 192–194). Its three- or fourfold increase in size can only have been produced by an influx of population, which may have reached Emporion after the capture of Phocaea by the Persians (Domínguez 2006, 476), a phenomenon which I would argue is also attested in Massalia itself (Domínguez 2012, 61–82).

The fact that newcomers considered themselves inheritors of the earlier settlement is shown by the name given to the future city, Emporion, and also by references to the site of the original *emporion* as the old city (*palaia polis*) (Strabo 3.4.8). Its successor was the recently founded new settlement, today known as Neapolis. As was common in other Greek establishments of the western Mediterranean, the Greeks had to negotiate their settlement with local populations (Lomas 2006, 174–196). This can be seen both in the archaeological record and in the later literary tradition.

I shall summarise here my previous analysis of the Emporitan funerary record and the main data acquired (Domínguez 2004a, 429–456). Firstly, bearing in mind Jones's warnings, also recalled by Lomas (Jones 1997, 122; Lomas 2006, 186), concerning "the difficulties of mapping ethnic divisions onto material culture," from the 6th century BC onwards we can still distinguish the tombs occupied by the natives from those occupied by Greeks. The first, cremations, usually with weapons and gradually with some imported wares, belong to a tradition well known in north-eastern Iberia from the Early Iron Age and also in the Emporitan region itself (Sanmartí 1992, 77–108). So it is not unreasonable to suggest that they belonged to the indigenous population that had settled in the Emporion area before the Greeks, and remained in the area. The Greek tombs, mainly burials, had less sumptuous grave offerings, and are not difficult to identify.

The location of these cemeteries around the Greek city would, on its own, suggest the coexistence of the two populations. However, we also have literary information about Emporion. Strabo's description of the city is sometimes a little confused, but is based on eyewitness accounts by Emporitan witnesses given to Greek authors of the late 2nd and early 1st centuries BC who visited Iberia and wrote about it (Poseidonius, Artemidorus). We must now reconsider the information from our sources, mainly Strabo and Livy.

> The Emporitans formerly lived on a little island off the shore, which **is now** called Old City, but they now live on the mainland. And their city is a double one, for it has **been** divided **into** two cities by a wall, because, in former times, the city had for neighbours some of the Indicetans, who, although they maintained a government of their own, wished, for the sake of **security,** to have a common wall of circumvallation **with the** Greeks, with the enclosure in two parts – **for** it **has been** divided by a wall through the centre; but in the course of time the two peoples united under the same constitution, which was a mixture **of both** Barbarian and Greek laws – a thing which **has** taken place in the case of many other peoples (Strabo 3.4.8; translation H.L. Jones, Loeb Classical Library).

Strabo describes three phases in the urban and political development of Emporion: first, occupation of the island; second, occupation by Iberians and Greeks of a common area, albeit one separated by a wall; third, a common structure with mixed Greek and barbarian laws. Perhaps an element of confusion, maybe provoked by Strabo himself, was the cause of the use of the term *dipolis*, which seems to have been interpreted awkwardly by Strabo. We can accept that the formation of the *polis* of Emporion, created as a result of the consolidation of the former *emporion* probably after the arrival of new Greek population, may have included some of the indigenous population, who, as we have seen, also shared the use of funerary areas. However, archaeology does not confirm the existence of any double wall at this time, which we could place between the second half of the 6th century and early 5th century BC; indeed, the oldest remains of fortifications in Emporion date to the late 5th century BC (Sanmartí/Nolla 1986, 159–191). It has also been suggested – and is not unlikely – that before the 4th-century BC wall was constructed and the entire southern part of the Greek city reorganised, some (or many) natives may have lived around the existing extra-urban sanctuaries (Sanmartí 1988, 99–137; 1993, 87–101). This situation would be no more than a continuation of the existing situation in the original *emporion* extended to the later Greek city. Was the dividing wall referred to by Strabo real, or a theoretical creation to justify a process of political integration of different communities? So far, archaeology has not provided an answer to this question.

It is difficult to know how this archaic situation lasted until the time of Strabo (or his sources) because the author asserts that Emporion "is" a dipolis (the verb is in the present tense) divided by a wall. It is likely that the present tense used by Strabo refers to the situation between the late 2nd century and the beginning of the 1st century BC, when there were actually two cities separated by a wall, but this situation cannot be projected back to the time when the Greek city was founded. Strabo possibly combined data from various periods; in this context the integration of indigenous people with the Greeks is the key, because it seems to be something that the Emporitans themselves accepted as a matter of fact. However, Strabo tried to find material evidence by introducing the issue of the common wall but separated by an intermediate wall, a situation that could only have existed in a given period, namely between the second half of the 2nd century and the mid-1st century BC.

We must now add Livy's account, which largely relies on the eyewitness account of Cato. Livy narrates his campaign, although he also introduces later data into his story.

> Even at that time Emporiae consisted of two towns separated by a wall. One was inhabited by Greeks from Phocaea, whence came the Massilienses also, the other by the Spaniards; but the Greek town, being entirely open to the sea, had only a small extent of wall, of less than four hundred

> paces in length, while the Spaniards, who were farther back from the sea, had a wall three miles around. A third class of inhabitants, Roman colonists, was added by the deified Caesar after the final defeat of the sons of Pompey, and at present all are fused into one mass, the Spaniards first, and later the Greeks, having been received into Roman citizenship (Livy 34.9.1; translation E.T. Sage, Loeb Classical Library).

The key to Livy's text is given in the first two words, "*iam tunc*," because Livy, who undoubtedly knew what Emporion was like, in describing it as a *dipolis* tried to take this situation back to Cato's days, although at the same time projecting the future of the city by alluding to the establishment of Roman colonists. However, from the passage by Livy and the subsequent account it seems that the Iberian city is somewhat distant from the Greek city. The mistrust between them, although this may well reflect the situation of open war existing when Cato landed, can hardly be reconciled with Strabo's description of the two groups' coexistence. Moreover, archaeology does not confirm the existence in the immediate area around Emporion of a native city with a circuit wall of 3000 paces (4.4 km), and attempts to locate it have so far proved fruitless. Consequently, some scholars believe that this native city simply did not exist before the Romans arrived (Pena 1988, 20–27).

Therefore, the data gathered from the literary sources suggest that Greek and Roman authors have included different kinds of events in their accounts. In particular, they have projected back in time Emporion's character as a *dipolis*, which existed at a very precise time, between the second quarter of the 2nd century and the mid-1st century BC. It was then that the Greek city, whose population included a considerable proportion of natives, coexisted with the Roman establishment, first military and then civilian, which also had a significant native presence, and according to some scholars even a dominant one (Pena 1989, 219–248).

This was an actual *dipolis*, with the two constituent units separated by walls. This situation is described by Strabo in the present tense, although this present was not Strabo's, but that of the sources. However, he projected this character of *dipolis* back to the origins of the city as a prelude to the integration of Greek and indigenous communities, something that already seem to have happened in the original *emporion*. Strabo does not know of the new legal status granted by Rome to Emporion in the time of Caesar. On the other hand, Livy, who also knows that Emporion was a *dipolis* – which, as we have seen, was a result of Roman action – puts it back to the time of Cato's landing. However, his description of Emporion at that time, undoubtedly taken from the consul's historical writings, mentioned a large indigenous *oppidum*, far from the sea and with a perimeter of 3000 paces. Livy says that Cato sited his camp 3000 paces from Emporion (34.13.2) and the subsequent battle was against the *Emporitani Hispani* (Livy 34.16.4) (Nolla 1984, 150–157). It is not unlikely that Livy, combining information from different sources, believed that the native *oppidum* rose in the place where, a few years after Cato's campaign, the Roman camp appeared. This would, at the beginning of the 1st century BC, be the origin to the Roman walled city. However, the perimeter of this was only 2 km, and what may have been an internal conflict in Emporion between supporters and opponents of the Roman presence may have been interpreted as the existence of a double city (Ruiz de Arbulo 1998, 539–554). Portions of a new wall of Roman date (2nd century BC) and massive character (3.40 m thick) have been recently discovered (2012). It enclosed a surface bigger than the later Roman city and its quite possible that the Greek city was also incorporated within it. This wall would confirm the existence of a Roman military installation, long suggested, although we had no data so far (Castanyer *et al.* 2013, 25–27). While it is soon to properly assess the significance of this wall, there is no doubt that it provides more insight to why later writers, such as Livy and Strabo, insist that during a period in its hisotry Emporion has been a *dipolis*. The presence of the *Emporitani Hispani* that fought Cato could also suggest the existence of an indigenous rural population living in Emporion's territory.

The literary sources, although contributing some information of interest, do not completely resolve some of the problems of Emporion, such as the relationship between Greeks and natives in the area during the first centuries of the city's life. As mentioned above, perhaps the most important fact is the co-existence of Greeks and natives and the creation of a "mixed" political system that included both populations. While the first phenomenon seems to correspond to the earliest days of the Greek presence, it is more difficult to know when such a mixed system of Greek and barbarian laws could have been developed. It is tempting, though, to place this occurrence after the urban reform that took place in the Greek city in the early 4th century BC, and which would coincide with the period when the necropolis known as Martí, located on the western side of the Greek city, was used (Almagro 1953, 29–127; Pena 1988, 18) and which I referred to, albeit briefly, on another occasion (Domínguez 2004a, 438).

This cemetery was to the west of the Greek city, in the space between it and the hill later occupied by the Roman city; 140 burials and 32 cremations have been excavated, apart from an unknown number of tombs plundered before scientific excavations began. Although this cemetery may have originated as early as the 5th century BC, the 4th century BC is the period best represented. The wealth of this cemetery is not particularly great and there are numerous children's burials in Iberian amphorae of difficult cultural affiliation (Greek or native?). Many of the cremations consist of a hand-made urn, but beyond that specific characteristic of the ritual itself, the homogeneity of the grave goods must be stressed because they consist of five cases (three burials and two cremations) of Attic squat-lekythoi (Fig. 1). I think that the choices of both cremation ritual and hand-made vases to contain the ashes are conscious ones that relate to the manifestation of a particular identity (namely, native). But the restrained wealth of the grave-goods – typical of Greek, but not indigenous, cemeteries – is another sign of the converging customs of the two ethnic components of 4th-century BC Emporion (Almagro 1953, 29–127; Miró 2006, 93–95).

Although it is possible that these native inhabitants come, for the most part, from Emporion's hinterland, Iberian peoples from other parts of the Iberian territory may have come to Emporion and eventually settled in the city as a result of trade led by the Emporitans. This trade between Emporion and the Iberian territories, near and far, may have led to the arrival and settlement of Iberian peoples in Emporion, who may have contributed to the mixed nature of its population but apparently did not question the Greek supremacy. It seems that with the passage of time, and despite having become a *polis* that even minted its own currency (Domínguez 2004b, 164–165), Emporion never lost its character as a trading post, as shown by the evidence mentioned here. Even at the beginning of the 2nd century BC Livy still emphasised this character when he highlighted

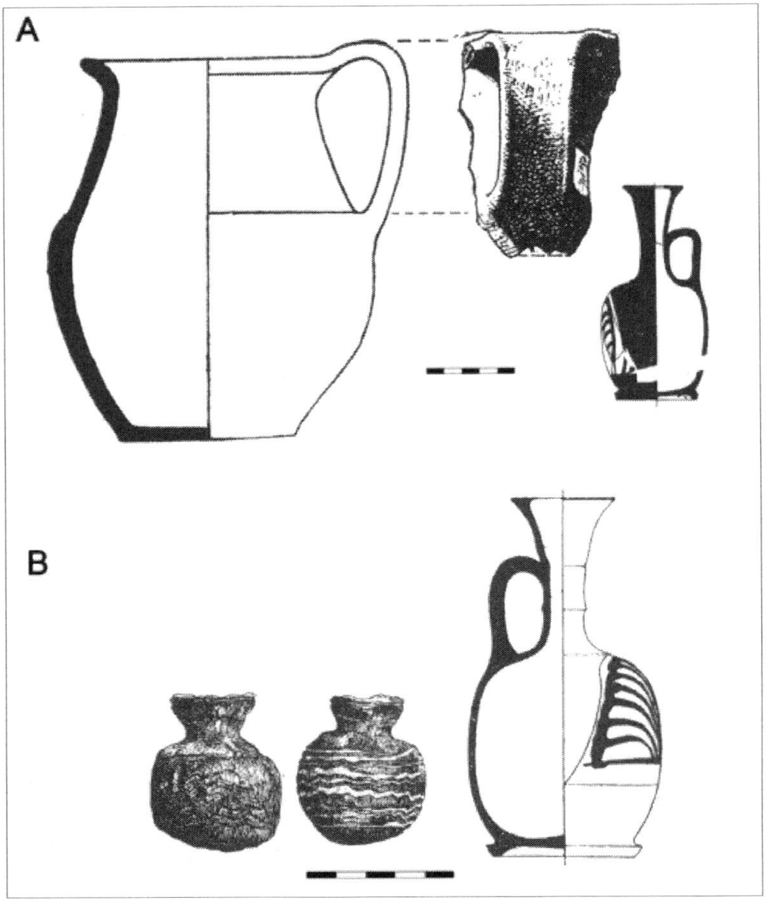

Figure 1. Two tombs of the Martí cemetery: A: Cremation Martí 20; B: Inhumation Martí 103 (After Almagro 1953)

the natives' interest in trading the products of their fields with the Emporitans for goods that reached the city by sea (Livy 34.9.9).

In addition to its own agricultural territory, Emporion certainly created (Plana 1994; Sanmartí 1995, 157–174) an important area of economic influence around it (Domínguez 1986, 193–199), whose operation has gradually become better known (Ruiz de Arbulo 2002/2003, 161–202). Apart from Ullastret, which presents problems of a somewhat different nature, it is perhaps the site of Mas Castellar at Pontós that tells us most about the relationship of the native hinterland with Emporion. This town is about 20 km from Emporion as the crow flies. Although it already had contact with Emporion, more intense relations between the Greek city and this Iberian fortified town began during the second half of the 5th century BC, as imported pottery shows. From the beginning of the 4th century BC the walls of this town were gradually dismantled while life went on in it, and Greek pottery arrived. It was probably abandoned around 375 BC (or even later, according to the latest estimates), and soon afterwards, from the late 3rd century BC, another quarter was occupied, although we only know of its final stages. It seems that the main purpose of this Iberian settlement was to produce cereals and, above all, store them in underground silos, a process that continued even when no other traces of occupation can be detected (Pons 2002, 587–594; Asensio/Pons 2004/2005, 199–211; Pons 2010, 105–118). Demolition of the town's walls was probably connected with a new economic and legal situation, encouraged by Emporion, which was undergoing rapid economic development at this time (Plana 1998, 61–64). Mas Castellar is only one of many native towns around the Emporitan plain in which silos have been found, as well as obvious signs of economic contacts with Emporion (Pons *et al.* 2001, 145–156; Bouso 2002, 210–215; Plana 2012, 165–168).

Touched upon earlier was the difficulty of linking the material evidence with the creation of identities, but it is worth mentioning a type of pottery that appears closely linked to the indigenous world related to Emporion and that may thus be a defining feature of Indiketai, which is, as we shall see, the name the written sources give to these natives. This is grey pottery with decorative motifs painted in white, clearly modelled on Greek pottery, first of Ionian and later Attic type, but also displaying motifs of native origin. Its distribution is concentrated in the native towns directly linked to Emporion, with few pieces outside that zone (Fig. 2); one of the main centres of production seems to have been the centre of Ullastret. This is seen as proof of a genuinely Indiketan production, not found outside its territory (Martín 1988, 47–56). It seems to have emerged in the mid-5th century BC (or even before) and from the first quarter of the 4th century BC became the only painted pottery from this Iberian area. Its production continued until the mid-3rd century BC, but later pieces exhibit much poorer decorations (Maluquer de Motes *et al.* 1984, 47–53). In any case, the distribution of this kind of pottery in the area directly linked to Emporion is interesting; it is found in all those native villages that stored surplus grain and received imported Attic pottery, sometimes of high quality.

Without doubt, these native villages are part of the trading network that Livy describes so accurately, and its end from the second quarter of the 2nd century BC coincides with the new situation fostered by Rome in the area, whose big beneficiary was Emporion itself. It is tempting to identify these populations, so near and closely linked with Emporion, as the ancestors of those *Emporitani Hispani* against whom Consul Cato fought soon after his landing at Emporion (Livy 34.16) in a place still unknown but close to the city. This explains the flight of many of its inhabitants to Emporion itself, where the consul accepted their surrender (Livy 34.16.5). It is also reasonable to assume that this unique concept, *Emporitani Hispani*, may be the Latin rendering of the term that we find in Greek to refer to local people, Indiketai, which would constitute the bulk of the rebels against Rome in 195 BC (Nolla 1984, 154). If the sources of Avienus' *Ora Maritima* for the part devoted to the north-eastern coast of Iberia are in fact archaic, we should find here the first definition of these people (*vv.* 523–525); likewise, they are mentioned by Strabo when he describes the north-eastern coasts of Iberia (Strabo 3.4.1) and, more specifically, when he refers to the creation of the Emporitan *dipolis* (Strabo 3.4.8). Only Stephanus of Byzantium (*s.v.*) mentions the existence of a city, *Indike*, from which the Indiketai would take their name. Others call this *Blaberoura*, a term that has been identified, correctly, with the damp character of the region where Emporion was

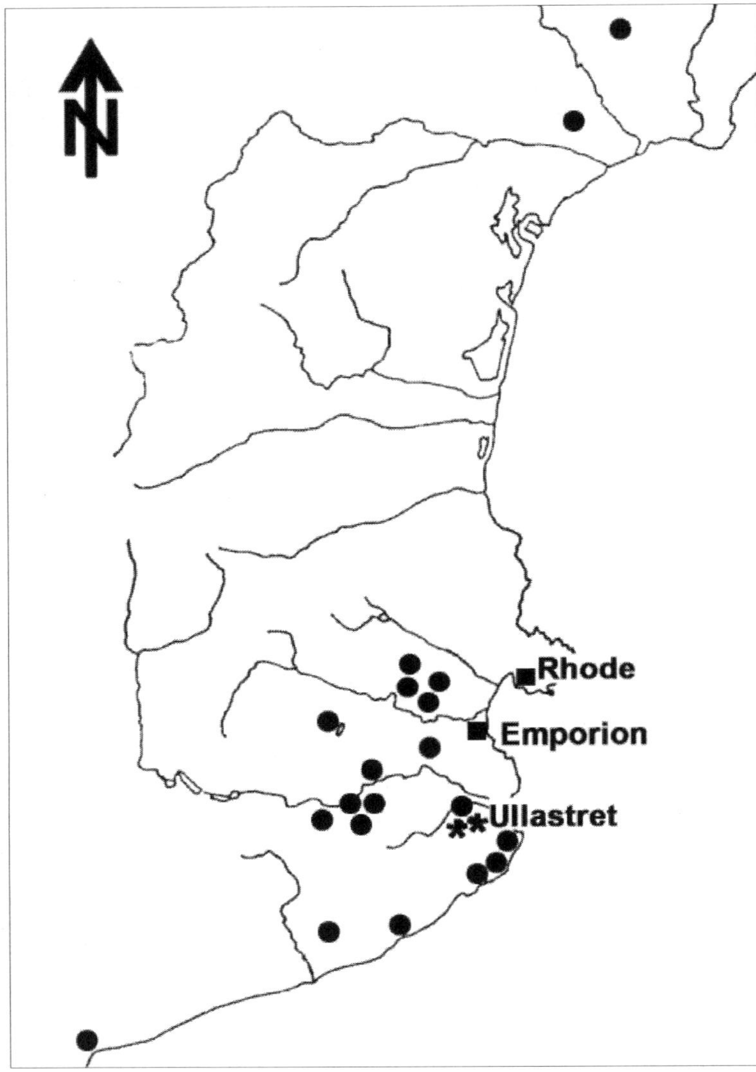

Figure 2. The distribution of "Indiketan" white-painted pottery (Redrawn after Martín 1988)

founded (Pericay 1950, 151–173) even before recent investigations revealed this fact in all its complexity (Rovira/Sanmartí 1983, 95–110; Marzoli 2005).

This name, Indiketai or Indigetes, could in its Greek and Latin versions predate the existence of a city or, as suggested by Stephanus of Byzantium, be derived from the place-name. In either case, the name is confirmed by the Iberian coinage with the ethnic Untikesken which began to be minted from the early 2nd century BC (García-Bellido/Blázquez 2002, 1, 50). This was after Rome had pacified the area and given the natives of the territory a certain political identity, perhaps encouraging their settlement near the ancient Greek city (Pena 1988, 11–45), which, in reality, was already a mixed Greek-

Iberian city. While the indigenous political body of Emporion (Untika-Indika) coined only bronze asses with a helmeted figure on the obverse and a series of figures on the reverse (rooster, lion, Pegasus, bull) (García-Bellido/Blázquez 2002, 2, 387–396), the Greek political entity continued to mint its traditional silver coinage with the Greek legend *Emporiton*, but with a progressive loss of artistic quality until at least the 80s or 70s BC (Campo 1998, 46–49; García-Bellido/Blázquez 2002, 2, 128); the iconographic relationship of the Iberian and Greek coinages is obvious and they were perhaps even complementary, the Iberian bronze coin serving as currency for small transactions in contrast to the Greek currency, which was coined only on silver. From the mid-1st century BC onwards, and after the creation of the *municipium*, only bronze coinage was issued, with the legend *Municipium Emporiae* being a clear continuation of the bronze currency of Untikesken rather than the silver currency of Emporion (García-Bellido/Blázquez 2002, 2, 138–141; Ripollés 2012, 131–138). The minting of the asses of Untikesken depended, like other contemporary currencies, on the interests of Rome, which gave the indigenous community in Emporion its own personality, perhaps not in the ancient Greek city, but alongside it, within or next to the Roman *praesidium* to the west of the Greek city. If so, as some scholars have suggested (Pena 1988, 11–45), we should regard Rome as the true creator of an indigenous political structure (*oppidum*) fashioned from the populations that lived in Emporion's area of influence before Cato's invasion, and were referred to in Livy as *Emporitani Hispani*.

From the time when it was founded as a simple *emporion*, and as a result of its primary character, Emporion shared the same environment as the natives. It was they who allowed the first Greek settlement and the transformation of the small peninsula which had for generations served as a point of exchange with foreign traders in a Greek settlement. Surely it was they too who permitted the occupation of the area south of the inlet that served as a harbour to allow the expansion of the city from the mid-6th century BC. The presence of cemeteries that can be characterised as Greek or indigenous in the same area, although in specific spaces, also suggests the proximity to Greek and native residential areas. Furthermore, the commercial interests of Emporion, in addition to possibly affecting the hinterland of the city, were felt over a wide coastal strip along the eastern shores of the Iberian Peninsula, as attested by Greek pottery (Domínguez 2003, 201–204) and also other evidence. The Emporitans seem to have been primarily responsible for the marketing of Iberian products destined for the city itself, but also for other parts of the Western Mediterranean.

The development of Emporion as a *polis*, perhaps as early as the 5th century (coinage, walls), does not imply a break with the native world, but, on the contrary, shows a growing relationship with this world. The Iberian peoples of that time lived (and were buried) in the Greek city; around the city wall and the shrines that existed in the south of the city a quarter grew up that housed people who used the Iberian language and writing but used Greek and Greek-style pottery. And perhaps some of these natives, and even people from other backgrounds, performed administrative functions, at least if any of the transactions recorded on the Pech Maho lead strip took place in Emporion itself.

As pointed out previously, it is tempting to link the reorganisation of Emporitan's urban layout in the early 4th century BC with the integration of the indigenous population living in the immediate vicinity of the city into the Greek community, giving rise to a common political structure (*politeuma*) that combined Greek and barbarian laws, as mentioned by Strabo. It is certainly a process that had its roots in the previous century, with the progressive association of the hinterland with the Emporitan economy. The increase of Greek imports into native towns around the Emporitan plain (Ullastret, Mas Castellar de Pontós) during the second half of the 5th century BC, and the perhaps related creation of a specific Indiketan identity (could the white-decorated grey pottery be a marker of this?), may have been favoured by the role of indigenous people living around Emporion who acted as intermediaries and included people from other parts of the Iberian territories. The political integration of these people within the *polis* would be a recognition of the interdependence of Greeks and natives, and the economic boom is demonstrated by strong "investment" in public works (walls, shrines); the 4th-century cemeteries show, alongside the maintenance of various funerary traditions (burial for the Greeks, cremation for the natives) a remarkable similarity in grave goods. The sharing of the same funerary space suggests that they also shared the same urban space.

The situation of people living in the areas surrounding Emporion, Indiketai, was not, however, comparable to that of the natives who had been integrated into the *polis*, since they seem to have been somewhat dependent on Emporion. A possible exception was Ullastret, which in any case seems to mark the southern limit of direct Emporitan influence (Martín/Plana 2001, 39–52), and whose features and historical development show its unique character (Martín *et al.* 2010, 89–104). The major agricultural surpluses generated in the Indiketan area were marketed by Emporion in a similar way to that witnessed by Livy in the early 2nd century BC. But Emporion did not lose sight of the rest of the Iberian area. Undoubtedly there were many points touched by Emporitan trade during the 4th century BC, although the discovery in Emporion of amphorae made in Campello (in today's province of Alicante) identifies at least one of those points; besides, Emporitan ships exchanged their products in ports in southern Italy for commodities from these areas (Sanmartí 1995, 31–47) and Attic pottery, which was experiencing strong demand in the city, in the native *hinterland*, and generally throughout the Iberian world during the first half of the 4th century BC. An example of this boom is shown by the native town of Ullastret, where, in all the houses dated to this period, several red-figure and black-glaze Attic vases were found (Picazo 1977, 131–133).

Throughout this period Emporion remained the centre of economic transactions involving indigenous people. Certainly Cato's campaign of 195 BC was a time of change, since while the Greek city, where people of native origin still lived, backed the consul, the native territory opposed Rome, perhaps because of the discriminatory treatment that the Romans had previously given the various territories. The rapid end of the war provoked a new process of integration, in which perhaps some of the territory's population, already displaced by the war, eventually settled near the Greek city. They were given political status by Rome, enabling them, among other things, to mint bronze currency with the legend "Untikesken." There is no doubt that the Greek city and this new native entity maintained close contacts, and this is possibly the picture that Strabo described, though not uncontaminated by data from the oldest period of the city, as in Livy's account.

The final period of the integration of the Greek and native populations, with the addition of Roman settlers, came with the creation of the *municipium*. Even at this stage monumental inscriptions began to appear, imitating the Latin characters, but in Iberian

Figure 3. Monumental inscription in Iberian script from Emporion

script and using various noble materials, including marble, used for Roman inscriptions (Almagro 1952, 63–69); these inscriptions were certainly made in the same workshops as the Latin inscriptions (Mayer/Velaza 1993, 667–682; Aquilué/Velaza 2000, 277–289), and in one of them we can read the Latin *nomen* Cornelius transcribed into Iberian script (*Kornele*) and even the Roman *praenomen* Lucius or Marcus (*[Lu]ke* or *[Mar]ke*) (Fig. 3) (Almagro 1952, 63–64; Untermann 1990, 19–20 [C.1.1]; Mayer 2012, 127). In any case, this inscription and others similar to it (Untermann 1990, 21–23 [C.1.2 to C.1.4]) show the prestige attained by the Iberian language and script in the city of Emporion in late Republican and early Imperial times (Velaza 2009, 160–161).

Emporion had to negotiate its Greek and Phocaean identity with natives from the start; its survival and even the urban flourishing it experienced in the 5th century and especially 4th century BC show that it succeeded. The principal mechanism consisted of integrating elements of the native environment at various times, possibly the elite but perhaps also people from other Iberian territories in the peninsula. In this process the main aspects of Greek life were preserved, perhaps because they were regarded as a prestigious element. This allowed the Greek character of Emporion to survive, probably in much the same way as Massalia, so highly praised by some ancient authors (Livy 37.54.21; Strabo 4.1.5). Similarly, we can still observe the Emporitan population's strength and even its pride in its Greek identity in the ambitious building programme that took place from the first half of the 2nd century BC, and which involved rebuilding the walls, constructing new sanctuaries and refurbishing older ones, the construction of an agora with a monumental stoa and even constructing Hellenistic-style houses, some of them decorated with mosaics with Greek inscriptions (Ruiz de Arbulo 1998, 539–554; Kaiser 2000; Aquilué 2012b, 30–32; Santos 2012, 69). However, while this programme was being carried out in the "Greek side" of the city, to the west of it a contiguous Roman city was developing. A few years later, the political integration of these two political bodies into a *municipium* presumably marked the end of the autonomy of the Emporitans' former *polis* and, consequently, the end of the process we have been analysing.

BIBLIOGRAPHY

Almagro, M. (1952): *Las inscripciones ampuritanas griegas, ibéricas y latinas*, Barcelona.

Almagro, M. (1953): *Las necrópolis de Ampurias*. Vol. I. *Introducción y necrópolis griegas*, Barcelona.

Aquilué, X. (ed.) (1999): *Intervencions arqueológiques a Sant Martí d'Empúries (1994–1996). De l'assentament precolonial a l'Empúries actual*, Gerona.

Aquilué, X. (ed.) (2012a): *Empúries. Municipium Emporiae*, Roma.

Aquilué, X. (2012b): Topografía y evolución urbana, in: X. Aquilué (ed.), *Empúries. Municipium Emporiae*, Roma: 25–38.

Aquilué, X., Velaza, J. (2000): Nueva inscripción ibérica ampuritana, *Palaeohispanica* 1: 277–289.

Aquilué, X., Castanyer, P., Santos, M., Tremoleda, J. (2008): Intervencions arqueológiques a Empúries (L'Escala, Alt Empordà) als anys 2006 i 2007, in: *Novenes Jornades d'Arqueologia de les comarques de Girona*, Olot: 185–209.

Asensio, D., Pons, E. (2004/2005): La troballa d'un crater àtic de figures roges en el jaciment ibèric del Mas Castellar (Pontós, Alt Empordà), *Quaderns de Prehistoria i Arqueología de Castelló* 24: 199–211.

Bouso, M., Gago, N., Pons, E. (2002): Els camps de sitges de Mas Castellar, in: E. Pons (ed.), *Mas Castellar de Pontós (Alt Empordà). Un complex arqueològic d'època ibèrica (Excavacions 1990–1998)*, Gerona: 165–215.

Campo, M. (1998): La moneda griega y su influencia en el contexto indígena, in: *Historia Monetaria de Hispania Antigua*, Madrid: 19–49.

Castanyer, P., Santos, M., Tremoleda, J. (2013): Noves troballes a Empúries, *Auriga* 68: 22–27.

Demetriou, D. (2012): *Negotiating Identity in the Ancient Mediterranean. The Archaic and Classical Greek Multiethnic Emporia*, Cambridge.

Domínguez, A.J. (1986): La función económica de la ciudad griega de Emporion, in: *VI Colloqui Internacional d'Arqueologia de Puigcerdà*, Puigcerdà: 193–199.

Domínguez, A.J. (2003): Archaic Greek Pottery in the Iberian Peninsula. Its Presence in Native Contexts, in: B. Schmaltz, M. Söldner (eds.), *Griechische Keramik im kulturellen Kontext*, Münster: 201–204.

Domínguez, A.J. (2004a): Greek identity in the Phocaean colonies, in: K. Lomas (ed.), *Greek Identity in the Western Mediterranean. Papers in Honour of Brian Shefton*, Leiden: 429–456.

Domínguez, A.J. (2004b): Spain and France (including Corsica), in: M.H. Hansen, T.H. Nielsen (eds.), *An Inventory of Archaic and Classical Poleis*, Oxford: 157–171.

Domínguez, A.J. (2006): Greeks in the Iberian Peninsula, in: G.R. Tsetskhladze (ed.), *Greek Colonisation. An Account of Greek Colonies and Other Settlements Overseas*, vol. 1, Oxford: 429–505.
Domínguez, A.J. (2012): The 1st Century of Massalia: Foundation, Arrival of Migrants and Consolidation of a Civic Identity, in: A. Hermary, G.R. Tsetskhladze (eds.), *From the Pillars of Hercules to the Footsteps of the Argonauts (Colloquia Antiqua 6)*, Leuven: 61–82.
Dupré, X. (2005): Terracotas arquitectónicas prerromanas en Emporion, *Empúries* 54: 103–123.
García-Bellido, M.P., Blázquez, C. (2002): *Diccionario de cecas y pueblos hispánicos.*Vol. I. *Introducción*; vol. II. *Catálogo de cecas y pueblos*, Madrid.
Gassner, V. (2003): *Materielle Kultur und Kulturelle Identität in Elea in spätarchaisch-frühklassischer Zeit*, Wien.
Jones, S. (1997): *The Archaeology of Ethnicity: Constructing Identities in the Past and Present*, London.
Kaiser, A. (2000): *The Urban Dialogue: An Analysis of the Use of Space in the Roman City of Empúries, Spain*, Oxford.
Lomas, K. (2006): Beyond Magna Graecia: Greeks and Non-Greeks in France, Spain and Italy, in: K.H. Kinzl (ed.), *A Companion to the Classical Greek World*, Oxford: 174–196.
Maluquer de Motes, J., Picazo, M., Martin, A. (1984): *Corpus Vasorum Antiquorum. Espagne. Musée Monographique d'Ullastret. Fasc. I*, Barcelona.
Martín, A. (1988): Algunes precisions més sobre la ceràmica ibèrica indiketa decorada amb pintura blanca, *Fonaments* 7: 47–56.
Martín, A., Plana, R. (2001): El Nord-Est català en època ibèrica i l'entitat territorial de l'oppidum d'Ullastret, in: A. Martín, R. Plana (eds.), *Territori polític y territori rural durant l'Edat del Ferro a la Mediterrània Occidental*, Gerona: 39–52.
Martín, A., Codina, F., Plana, R., de Prado, G. (2010): Le site ibérique d'Ullastret (Baix Empordà, Catalogne) et son rapport avec le monde colonial méditerranéen, in: H. Tréziny (ed.), *Grecs et Indigenes de la Catalogone à la Mer Noire*, Aix-en-Provence: 89–104.
Marzoli, D. (2005): *Die Besiedlungs- und Landschaftsgeschichte im Empordà von der Endbronzezeit bis zum Beginn der Romanisierung*, Mainz.
Mayer, M. (2012): La Epigrafía, in: X. Aquilué (ed.), *Empúries. Municipium Emporiae*, Roma: 126–131.
Mayer, M., Velaza, J. (1993): Epigrafía ibérica sobre soportes típicamente romanos, in: J. Untermann, F. Villar (eds.), *Lengua y Cultura en la Hispania Prerromana. Actas V Coloquio sobre Lenguas y Culturas Prerromanas de la Península Ibérica*, Salamanca: 667–682.
Miró, M.T. (2006): *La ceràmica àtica de figures roges de la ciutat grega d'Emporion*, Barcelona.
Nolla, J.M. (1984): La campanya de M.P. Cató a Empúries el 195 a.C. Algunes consideracions, *Revista de Girona* 30: 150–157.
Pena, M.J. (1988): Hipòtesis noves sobre Empúries a partir de l'analisi de les fonts literàries, *Fonaments* 7: 11–45.
Pena, M.J. (1989): Ampurias. Les débuts de l'implantation romaine, *DHA* 15: 219–248.
Pericay, P. (1950): Sobre los nombres de Indica, la ciudad hispana junto a Emporion, *Emerita* 18: 151–173.
Picazo, M. (1977): *Las cerámicas áticas de Ullastret*, Barcelona.
Plana, R. (1994): *La chora d'Emporion: paysage et structures agraires dans le nord-est catalan à la période pre-rómaine*, Paris.
Plana, R. (1998): El poblament indiqueta i la chora d'Empúries, in: R. Buxó, E. Pons (eds.), *El graner de l'Empordà. Mas Castellar de Pontós a l'edat del Ferro*, Gerona: 61–64.
Plana, R. (2012): La présence grecque et ses effets dans le Nord-Est de la péninsule Ibérique (VIIe-début du IVe siècle av. n. è), *Pallas* 89: 157–178.
Pons, E. (ed.) (2002): *Mas Castellar de Pontós (Alt Empordà). Un complex arqueològic d'época ibèrica (Excavacions 1990–1998)*, Gerona.
Pons, E., Fuertes, M., Gago, N., Bouso, M. (2001): Les sitges dels assentaments de Mas Castellar de Pontós i les del territori, in: A. Martin, R. Plana (eds.), *Territori polític y territori rural durant l'Edat del Ferro a la Mediterrània Occidental*, Gerona: 145–156.

Pons, E., Asensio, D., Fuertes, M., Bouso, M. (2010): El yacimiento de Mas Castellar de Pontós (Alt, Empordà, Girona): un núcleo indígena en la órbita de la colonia foce de Emporion, in: H. Tréziny (ed.): *Grecs et Indigenes de la Cataloge à la Mer Noire*, Aix-en-Provence: 105–118.

Ripollés, P.P. (2012): La numismática, in: X. Aquilué (ed.), *Empúries. Municipium Emporiae*, Roma: 131–138.

Rovira, J., Sanmartí, E. (1983): Els orígens de l'Empúries precolonial i colonial, *Informació Arqueològica* 40: 95–110.

Ruiz de Arbulo, J. (1998): La evolución urbana de Emporion en época tardorrepublicana. La complejidad de una tradición, in: *De les estructures indigenes a l'organitzacio provincial romana de la Hispania Citerior*, Barcelona: 539–554.

Ruiz de Arbulo, J. (2002/2003): Santuarios y Fortalezas. Cuestiones de indigenismo, helenización y romanización en torno a Emporion y Rhode (s. VI–I a.C.), *Cuadernos de Prehistoria y Arqueología de la Universidad Autónoma de Madrid* 28–29: 161–202.

Sanmartí, E. (1988): Datación de la muralla griega meridional de Ampurias y caracterización de la facies cerámica de la ciudad en la primera mitad del s. IV a.C., *REA* 90: 99–137.

Sanmartí, J. (1992): Las necrópolis ibéricas en el área catalana, in: *Congreso de Arqueología Ibérica: Las Necrópolis*, Madrid: 77–108.

Sanmartí, E. (1993): Els íbers a Emporion (segles VI–III a.C.), *Laietania* 8: 87–101.

Sanmartí, E. (1995): Recent Discoveries at the Harbour of the Greek City of Emporion (L'Escala, Catalonia, Spain) and in its Surrounding Area (Quarries and Iron Workshops), *PBA* 86: 157–174.

Sanmartí, E., Nolla, J.M. (1986): Informe preliminar sobre l'excavació d'una torre situada a ponent de la ciutat grega d'Empúries, in: *Protohistoria Catalana. 6è Colloqui Internacional d'Arqueologia de Puigcerdà*, Barcelona: 159–191.

Sanmartí, E., Castanyer, P., Tremoleda, J., Santos, M. (1995): Amphores grecques et trafics commerciaux en Méditerranée occidentale au IVᵉ s. av. J.-C. Nouvelles données issues d'Emporion, in: P. Arcelin, M. Bats, D. Garcia, G. Marchand, M. Schwaller (eds.), *Sur les pas des Grecs en Occident. Hommages à André Nickels*, Paris: 31–47.

Santos, M. (2012): Arquitectura doméstica, in: X. Aquilué (ed.), *Empúries. Municipium Emporiae*, Roma: 69–84.

Tréziny, H. (ed.) (2010): *Grecs et Indigènes de la Catalgone à la Mer Noire*, Aix-en-Provence.

Untermann, J. (1990): *Monumenta Linguarum Hispanicarum.* III 2. *Die Inschriften*, Wiesbaden.

Velaza, J. (2009): Escritura, autorrepresentación y poder en el mundo ibérico. *Cultura Escrita y Sociedad* 9: 144–167.

ELECTRUM * Vol. 20 (2013): 37–56
doi: 10.4467/20800909EL.13.003.1432

Seleukid Settlements: Between Ethnic Identity and Mobility*

Omar Coloru
Università di Pisa

> Go noiselessly by, stranger; the old man sleeps among the pious dead, wrapped in the slumber that is the lot of all. This is Meleager, the son of Eucrates, who linked sweet tearful Love and the Muses with the merry Graces. Heavenborn Tyre and Gadara's holy soil reared him to manhood, and beloved Cos of the Meropes tended his old age. If you are a Syrian, Salam! If you are a Phoenician, Naidius! If you are a Greek, Chaire! And say the same yourself.
>
> Meleager of Gadara, I cent. BC, *Greek Anth.* 7.419, English trans. W.R. Paton

Abstract: The present paper deals with the population of the Seleukid settlements in order to address issues about the settlers' mobility and ethnic identity. By surveying the available evidence, this study aims in particular to understand the role played by non-Greek populations in the Seleukid Empire, trying to go beyond the thesis of an apartheid-like regime in which those ethnic groups would be socially as well as politically isolated from the Greco-Macedonian settlers.

Key words: Seleukid Empire, Ethnic Identity, Hellenism, Jews, Mobility, Macedonian.

In his celebrative portrait of the deeds accomplished by Seleukos I, Appian (*Syr.* 57) states that the king had founded many towns throughout his vast empire. From this particular point of view, the figure of Seleukos emerges not only as the continuator of Alexander the Great, the builder king *par excellence*, but also as a competitor of the Macedonian conqueror. Just as many of the so-called *poleis* founded or attributed to Alexander were often nothing but forts and guard posts, the first Seleukid settlements cannot all be classed under the label of city.[1] In many cases, moreover, a pre-existing site was simply

* I would like to express my gratitude to Alexander McAuley (McGill University) for a critical reading of the manuscript and for giving valuable comments which improved the quality of this contribution. Any mistakes are of course my responsibility alone.

[1] For a discussion on the idea of *polis* applied to the Hellenistic colonisation, see Grainger 1990, 63–66.

renamed in order to limit the high expenses that the foundation of a settlement on virgin soil entailed. However, it is unquestionable that Seleukos and his successors, especially his son Antiochos I, put special care into populating even the farthest corners of their empire and creating a network of settlements in strategic areas in order to enforce the royal presence on the territory, develop urbanisation, and strengthen communication between the Mediterranean and Central Asia. Laurent Capdetrey[2] has recently produced an in-depth study on the administration of the Seleukid Empire in which a great deal of attention is given to the role of colonisation policies as a means of territorial control and definition of the royal space. In the last two decades, the subject of Hellenistic foundations has received fresh and extensive attention especially thanks to the volumes by Getzel Cohen *The Hellenistic Settlements*,[3] which offer an exhaustive survey of the Hellenistic colonies from Greece to Central Asia.

As for the Seleukids, we see that in the first phase the settling of colonists concerned Asia from the Middle East to Bactria, and then, after the defeat and death of Lysimachos at the battle of Kouroupedion in 281, large parts of Asia Minor were added to the Seleukid empire to populate. While under the two first Seleukid kings the colonisation process was remarkably intense, it tended to decrease subsequently for various reasons such as territorial losses and stabilisation of the control over a certain area until its end, possibly after the reign of Antiochos IV.[4] Accordingly, the colonisation programme followed by the Seleukids involved despatching groups of settlers all over the Empire. This contribution aims to present a few reflections on the ethnic composition of the Seleukid colonies, their mobility and their role within the empire.

Kings and cities

In such a vast and heterogeneous empire the colonisation process followed different patterns depending on the area. A regional study is beyond the scope of this paper, so I will limit myself to the remark that the Seleukids adopted several methods in order to populate a colony. While on the one hand the kings would settle soldiers and veterans who served in their armies, on the other they sent colonists to these new settlements by taking them from other cities inside or outside the kingdom. Sometimes, as in Babylon and Uruk, an indigenous town received settlers to form a new community. In some cases the new settlement resulted from the synoikism of two or more local villages to which a certain number of colonists of different origin was added.

The well-known inscription from Magnesia on the Meander *I. Magnesia* 61 provides us with a basic idea of the procedures which lay behind the colonisation process when a city was involved in sending colonists for the new settlements. The inscription is a copy of an official letter sent from the assembly of Antioch in Persis (nowadays

[2] Capdetrey 2007.

[3] Cohen 1995; Cohen 2006, and Cohen 2013. For the set of problems concerning the Hellenistic colonisation, Briant (1982a and 1982b) still offer important and stimulating reflections.

[4] Cohen 1978, 32 clearly distinguishes two phases, the first one going from Seleukos I to Antiochos II, and the second from Antiochos III to Antiochos IV.

Bushir) to the city of Magnesia concerning the recognition of the festival of Artemis Leukophryene. The first part of the letter recalls the ties of kinship (*syngeneia*) between the two cities, as in the past Magnesia had sent a group of colonists to Antioch during the reign of Antiochos I. Despite its celebrative and summarising character, the section of the document from *ll.* 15 to 20 gives us the following information: in the first place, the king despatches an embassy to the city which was asked to send the colonists, then the matter is put to a vote and approved by the local assembly in the form of a decree, and afterwards the city proceeds to the selection of the individuals to be sent to the colony. Eventually, the departure of the colonists is accompanied by sacrifices and religious ceremonies. We do not know how the colonists actually reached the settlement: one can image a caravan led by royal agents or envoys from the recipient city accompanying the group to its new destination.

Likewise, the inscription does not tell us if the council could oppose the request of the king, or if the debate mentioned in the document was just a formality which the city had to follow without having any real freedom of decision. In fact, the style of the decree conveys the image of a council performing its activities in the framework of an independent and democratic process, but this turns out to be a misleading impression. It is likely that it emerged from the status of the cities in their relations with the Seleukid kingdom: according to the classification elaborated by Capdetrey,[5] Magnesia actually belonged to the category of the subject cities, thus the request for colonists was in all probability an order concealed under the veil of the language register in use for official communication between the king and the cities.[6]

Our sources generally mention the colonists by region or ethnic group, while only in a few cases are we informed of their exact place of origin. Among the cities sending colonists is Miletos, which at the end of the 3rd century provided settlers for Seleukeia/Tralleis in Karia.[7] More problematic is the case of a group of individuals from Ephesos sent to Seleukeia on the Eulaios/Susa,[8] whose presence has been inferred by Le Rider on the basis of coin types struck in the local mint showing the identification of the Iranian goddess Nanaia with the Ephesian Arthemis.[9] Perinthos in Propontis could have provided settlers for the homonymous colony of Perinthos in Syria.[10] Seleukos I moved part of the Greco-Macedonian community of Babylon to the new capital of Seleukeia on the Tigris.[11] Magnesia on the Maeander, on the other hand, was involved in the colonisation of Antioch near Pisidia, possibly Seleukeia on the Eulaios/Susa,[12] Antioch in Persis,[13] as

[5] Capdetrey 2007, 191–224. A different kind of classification is adopted by Ma 2002a, 150–174.

[6] Ma 2002a, 179–242.

[7] Cohen 1995, 265–268.

[8] The Eulaios corresponds to the River Kerkha. On Susa under Seleukid rule, see Martinez-Sève 2010a, 41–66.

[9] Le Rider 1965, 281.

[10] Cohen 2006, 124.

[11] Contrary to what is affirmed by classical sources such as Diodoros of Sicily, Clancier 2012, 303–304 has shown that the population transfer to Seleukeia on the Tigris concerned only the Greco-Macedonian residents in Babylon, and not the Babylonians.

[12] Robert 1969, 330.

[13] Cohen 1995, 279; Martinez-Sève 2009, 130–131.

we have seen, and settlements in Bactria.[14] Although the evidence is quite limited, cities outside the control of the Seleukids seem to have taken part in their colonisation efforts. As far as one can infer from the explicit reference to kinship ties, it seems that Samos was involved in the foundation of Antioch on the Maeander by Antiochos I.[15] The Athenian Soteles was the chief of the Seleukid garrison on the island of Ikaros (Failaka) in the Persian Gulf.[16] Athens actually represents an exception in the Seleukid colonisation process, because the sources are generally silent or suspiciously celebrative about Athenian participation to the foundation of settlements, as in the case of the claim by John Malalas concerning the presence of Athenians among the founding population of Antioch on the Orontes.[17] In fact, the highest praise a town could receive was being defined as *eugenis*, i.e. "of noble origins." This nobility was acquired if the city could demonstrate that it was a colony of one of the Greek communities traditionally considered to be colonisers, such as the Achaeans, Arcadians, Ionians, Spartans, and of course the Athenians.[18] Among the settlers of Antioch, Libanius (Or. 11.91) enumerates the Cretans, the Argives, the Cypriots, and the descendants of two demi-gods as Herakles and Triptolemos.[19] Although it is more than plausible to assume that individuals from continental Greece – especially those serving in Seleukos' armies – took part in the foundation of Antioch, caution should be employed with regard to the information by Libanius and Malalas. Invoking *eugeneia* was a common expedient in praise literature concerning towns, not to mention the great number of foundation legends which were embellished or outright fabricated by many other towns in order to enjoy the privileges following their status of high antiquity and nobility.

Settling within an Imperium Macedonicum

We are usually taught that the Macedonians formed the core of the colonisation policy led by the Seleukids. This is true, even though this statement, so often repeated, may in time flatten our perception of the issue. According to the plans of Seleukos I, the empire

---

[14] Bernard 1987, 103–110; Martinez-Sève 2009, 134.

[15] Cohen 1995, 250–253. On the decree of Samos see Habicht 1957, n. 65, *l.* 19. The founder of Antioch on the Maeander was, according to Steph. Byz. s.v. *Antiocheia in Caria*, "Antiochos son of Seleukos," thus it could be either Antiochos I or III. I agree with Cohen in thinking that Antiochos I is the most probable, as at the times of Antiochos III Seleukid control over Karia was considerably weakened. For mythical kinship ties between Greek cities, in particular for Samos and Antioch on the Maeander, see Patterson 2010, 148–149.

[16] Gatier 2007, 75–79. For a discussion of the Seleukid activity in the Persian Gulf, cf. Martinez-Sève 2010a, 58–63.

[17] The Athenians and the Macedonians settled in Antioch were taken by Antigoneia: Malalas 8.201; cf. Grainger 1990, 37–39; Cohen 2006, 27, 81.

[18] Robert 1973b, 202–203. On the contrary, Briant (1982b, 277–278) is more inclined to believe that despite the rhetorical use of the information made by Libanios, the participation of Aetolian, Cretan and Euboian colonists in the foundation of Antioch may be historically reliable. The presence of Cypriots at the earliest stages of the foundation of Antioch is quite probable, especially when considering the proximity of the island to the Syrian coasts. A new study about the foundation myths of Antioch is in preparation by Alexander McAuley (personal communication).

[19] See also Strabo 16.2.5; Malalas 8.201. For a commentary on the sources, see Cohen 2006, 81, 86.

had to reflect the nature of his monarchy. Being a Macedonian was one of the basic conditions justifying his right to rule over an empire founded on Macedonian sovereignty. However, his son and successor Antiochos I was the product of the intermarriage of Seleukos I with the Bactrian princess Apama, and it is quite interesting that Babylonian documents referring to Antiochos I attribute the ethnic *Makaduna*[20] to the only Seleukos. Nevertheless, his father was conscious of the political potential of his son's mixed origins, and it is no mere coincidence that he appointed him viceroy in the Upper Satrapies, where his twin Macedonian and Iranian origin could be useful to catalyse loyalty from two representative components of the population of the eastern Seleukid provinces.[21] Moreover, the Seleukids continued to practise intermarriage with the other Iranian royal houses of Pontos, Kappadokia, Kommagene, Armenia, and Media Atropatene, and one of the sons of Antiochos III – possibly the future Antiochos IV – had the Iranian name of Mithradates.[22]

Several colonies or simple forts all over the empire were populated by Macedonians who served in the Seleukid armies in order to form a network of settlements loyal to the king.[23] From this point of view, Northern Syria became a New Macedonia where cities and territory were renamed after Macedonian places such as Beroia, Edessa, Europos etc. on the basis of similarities in the geographical features of the homeland.[24] The anecdote recorded by the historian Nymphis of Herakleia,[25] which shows Seleukos suffering from homesickness and wanting to spend his last years in Macedonia, is anything but a reflex of the political project of control of the imperial space elaborated by the king. We find witnesses of Macedonian settlers in regions spanning from Asia Minor to Bactria. The vestiges of Macedonian identity can be seen in the presence of Macedonian institutions such as the *peliganes*, the elder council,[26] attested at Seleukeia on the Tigris, Laodikeia by the Sea, Babylon,[27] and quite probably also Susa.[28] In this regard, the definition of the

[20] See Marten Stol and Van der Speck's philological commentary on the preliminary online edition (last update 2008) of the Antiochos' Cylinder from Borsippa, *col.* 1.5, http://www.livius.org/cg-cm/chronicles/antiochus_cylinder/ antiochus_cylinder2.html. See also the transcription and translation in Kuhrt, Sherwin-White 1991, 71–86.

[21] Coloru 2009, 146–155.

[22] For Seleukid intermarriages with the Pontic house, see McGing 1986, 21–25, 32, 38; Kappadokian kings, see Diod. 31.19.6–7, App. *Syr.* 5; Armenia, Pol. 8.23.5; dynasty of Kommagene, see Facella 2006, 215–217; house of Media Atropatene, cf. Strabo 11.13.1–2. For Mithradates – Antiochos IV, see Mittag 2006, 34–36.

[23] Sartre 2001, 269–275.

[24] On the Seleukid foundations in Northern Syria, see Leriche 2003a, 117–146; on Europos, see Leriche 2003b, 171–191.

[25] Nymphis via Memnon of Herakleia, *FGrH* 434 F 1.

[26] For the *peliganes*, see Sarakinski 2010, 31–46, who offers a good review of the issue and shows that in the Hellenistic settlements of Asia this title was not a mere honorary one, but indicated a group of city officials in charge of the civic and political administration of the city on the king's behalf.

[27] Pol. 5.48.8–12 attests the *peliganes* in Seleukeia on the Tigris by the end of the 3rd century BC; as for the other cities, our sources date back to the 2nd century BC, which does not imply that this institution was not already active in the past. For the *peliganes* at Laodikeia by the Sea, see *IGLS* IV 1261, *l.* 22; a cuneiform tablet broken into several fragments known as the *Bagayasha chronicle* recording events occurred in Babylon in the 130s BC mentions the *peliganes*: Van der Spek 2006, 272, 284–288.

[28] Gatier 2013, 205–210.

lemma *peliganes* by the lexicographer Hesychios (s.v. *Peliganes*) is worth noting, as it says that among the Syrians – i.e. the Seleukid kingdom – the term refers to the *bouletai*, the councillors. These examples bring further confirmation of the Macedonian imprint given to the administration and civic life in a number of settlements of the Seleukid East. However, the overwhelming presence of Macedonian settlers in the Seleukid foundations as attested by the sources can be deceiving. One must not forget that they did not form the only community of the new colonies, nor did all the individuals labelled as "Macedonian" actually belong to that geographical area or ethnic group, but they could have been soldiers who served in regiments armed in the Macedonian style,[29] so that this term became a sort of supranational ethnic. Alexander already had young autochthonous men called the *Epigonoi* trained in the Macedonian style.[30] In Egypt a native soldier could become Macedonian after obtaining a promotion: this is the case of the Egyptian Dionysios, son of Kephalas, whose ethnic shifted from "Persian" to "Macedonian."[31] Discussing the attitude of the Lagid dynasty towards its Egyptians subjects, J. Bingen says that "Ptolemy assumed the Macedonian royal diadem, but also the pharaonic crown of Upper and Lower Egypt; and this inaugurated the ambiguous relationship between the king and a new bicultural Egypt, which was no longer a satrapy in a foreign empire, even though the king had his capital in Alexandria, a non-Egyptian city."[32] In addition, it is doubtful that the population from Macedonia continued to emigrate *en masse* after the reign of Seleukos I (and maybe that of Antiochos I) when the empire had reached stability, not to mention that the Antigonid kingdom of Macedonia would not have easily let its subjects quit the country to reinforce the population of an opponent state. If we once again have to cite the parallel of the Ptolemaic kingdom, new demographic studies show that the flow of Macedonian immigration to Egypt was irregular, while the number of Greek immigrants stopped in the years following the battle of Raphia.[33]

Other Hellenic groups equally managed to bring forth their contributions in order to create the perception not only of a New Macedonia but also of a New Greece. Once again, the sources concerning Magnesia on the Maeander allow us to contrast this view. In the first instance, we have to mention the wide range promotion the city made at the end of the 3rd century for having the Festival of Artemis Leukophryene recognised by all the Greek cities and communities from Greece to Persis.[34] The easternmost – at that time[35] – Seleukid settlements were invited to take part in this Pan-Hellenic festival by sending athletes: the section of the inscription (*ll.* 101–111) listing the cities which agreed to recognition of this festival is fragmentary, but we can still read the names of such well-known sites as Seleukeia on the Tigris (ll. 101–102) and Seleukeia on the Eulaios/Susa (ll. 108–109), together with other toponyms such as Apameia on the Sellas

[29] Cf. Kuhrt/Sherwin-White 1993, 53–57; Billows 1995, 208; Capdetrey 2012, 335–336.

[30] On the *Epigonoi* and the integration of Asian troops in the Macedonian army, see Curt. 8.5.1; Plut. *Alex.* 47.6 and 71.1; Diod. 17.108.1 and 17.110.1–2; Just. 12.4.2–10; Arr. *Anab.* 7.6.1, 7.23.1–4.

[31] Boswinkel-Pestman 1982, 51–63.

[32] Bingen 2007, 243.

[33] See Fischer-Bovet 2008, 56–78; Fischer-Bovet 2011, 135–154.

[34] *OGIS* 233; *I. Magnesia* 13; Rougemont 2012, no. 53.

[35] By the middle of the 3rd century and despite the campaign by Antiochos III in the Upper Satrapies (209–204), the Seleukid provinces in Central Asia were lost.

(*ll.* 103–104), Seleukeia on the Erythrean Sea (*ll.* 105–107) and Seleukeia on the Hedyphon (*ll.* 110–111).[36] The lacunae prevent us from knowing whether or not the invitation ever reached important centres like Laodikeia in Media (Nehavand), but we can say that all these settlements were certainly considered integral parts of the network connecting the cities of the Greek world.[37] More interesting is the influence exerted by the settlers of the Maeander valley in Bactria. Polybius[38] related that during the peace treaty (206) between Antiochos III and Euthydemos I, the latter showed that he and the Seleukid ambassador Teleas were originally from the same town, Magnesia. It is unlikely that Euthydemos himself was born in Magnesia, but his ancestors were, and handed down this memory to their descendants. Setting apart the diplomatic stratagem of invoking common origins in order to create an atmosphere of mutual comprehension, this episode is significant because it shows that the king was not only appealing to a generic feeling of ethnic identity but, more specifically, to a civic identity,[39] which was still strong even if the new generations of colonists were miles away from the homeland and had never directly experienced it. Moreover, the settlers from the Maeander valley also influenced the artistic representation of the local fluvial god Oxus, as attested by the votive offering made to this deity by an individual bearing the Iranian name of Atrosokes. Placed on a small pedestal, the little statue of the god Oxus is represented as the satyr Marsyas playing a double flute: now this iconography has its roots in the Maeander Valley, where Greek mythological tradition holds that the musical competition between Apollo and Marsyas took place.[40] Thus, the Bactrian landscape is reinvented in order to adapt to the cultural identity of the Magnesians and the representation they have of their native country. At a linguistic level, analysis of documents written in Greek coming from the Upper Satrapies has shown that the language underwent the same evolution which took place at the same time in Asia Minor, which means that this phenomenon would hardly be possible if the contacts between the two extremes of the Seleukid Empire had been scarce.[41]

Colonists from Ionian cities were sent both to neighbouring regions such as Karia (Milesians at Seleukeia-Tralles) and Phrygia (Laodikeia on the Lykos), but also to Susiana, where a group of Ephesians was possibly present in Susa, bringing with them the cult of the Ephesian Artemis. Greek families from Syria were possibly settled in Bactria, where a noticeable frequency of personal names containing the theonym *Helios-* is

[36] Apameia on the Sellas/Seleias was located in Mesene on the River Sihlu (nowadays Sihl) north of Wasit, see Potts 2002, 355. Seleukeia on the Hedyphon can be located at Ja Nishin c. 80 km SE of Ahwaz, while the River Hedyphon should correspond to the Jarrahi, cf. Potts 1999, 393–395. The town was taken by Hyspaosines and became one of the capitals and mints of the kingdom of Characene. Seleukeia on the Erythrean Sea was founded on the Persian Gulf, probably in the Seleukid satrapy known as Districts of the Red Sea, cf. Sherwin-White/Kuhrt 1993, 20. A few lines of the inscription (*ll.* 118–119) mention two more cities, Alexandreia and Antioch, the location of which is lost. The former could be the Alexandreia/Antioch in Characene, which later became Spasinou Charax.

[37] Cf. Ma 2003, 24–25; Honigman 2007, 125–140.

[38] Pol. 11.34.1.

[39] Mairs 2010, 180.

[40] Bernard 1987, 103–115; Coloru 2009, 152, 277–278.

[41] Bernard/Bopearachchi 2002, 237–278; on the Seleukid colonisation in Central Asia, cf. Bernard 1994, 473–511; Capdetrey 2007, 76–81; for a survey on the ethnic composition of the settlers in Bactria, cf. Coloru 2009, 150–153.

attested:[42] Syria was in fact the region where the solar cult was extremely popular, in both the Hellenistic and Roman periods.[43]

In Bactria some official documents of the administration are dated to the month of *Loos*, which is a Northern Greek variant – possibly from the region of Thessalonica – of the month name *Oloos*.[44] On onomastic grounds, it seems that settlers from Northern Greece had been present at Ai Khanum/Eucratidia in Bactria: Kineas, the founder of the town, has a typical Thessalian name, as does the Lysanias buried in the necropolis outside the city walls, while the rich citizen Triballos who financed the restoration of the gymnasium keeps in his name the memory of the relations his ancestors had with the Thracian tribe of the Triballians.[45] According to Diodoros (33.4a), the Thessalians were also settled in the Syrian town of Sizara, which was renamed Larisa in their honour.[46] A parchment discovered in Afghanistan mentions the town of Amphipolis, which was probably located in the Balkh oasis.[47] This toponym was frequent in Northern Greece, and had already been employed by the Seleukids to rename the settlement of Tapsakos on the Euphrates.

An exclusive population?

Our sources show that the indigenous populations were not subject to long-distance mobility. Compared to the Greco-Macedonian colonists, autochthonous settlers tended to cover shorter trajectories which were generally limited to the borders of their place of origin. The inhabitants of Al-Mina were probably transferred to the close colony of Seleukeia in Pieria,[48] while Lydians formed part of the population of Thyateira.[49] The same Antioch on the Orontes had among its settlers Syrian communities from Antigoneia.[50] Sometimes they did not move at all, as in the case of the synoikism of pre-existent Karian settlements which was at the basis of the Seleukid foundations of Antioch on the Maeander, Nysa and Stratonikeia in Karia. The reason for this short-distance mobility is that the kings needed to use these individuals in the immediate vicinity to populate their new settlements with an experienced work force at a small cost.[51] On the other hand, a Thracian settlement could have existed in Persis or in Central Asia, even if the sources about these military colonies are controversial to the point of precluding any

42 Robert 1973a, 443. Between Bactria and Northern India this class of personal names is represented by Heliokles, Heliodotos, Heliodoros, Heliophilos, cf. Coloru 2009, 152; on Heliophilos, see Fussman 1985, 37–38, 41; Falk/Bennett 2009, 200–202.

43 Iossif/Lorber 2009, 19–42.

44 Bernard/Rapin 1994, 275–278.

45 Robert 1968, 418–420; Coloru 2009, 150.

46 Cohen 2006, 117–119.

47 Clarysse/Thompson 2007, 277.

48 Cohen 2006, 128.

49 Cohen 1995, 238.

50 Downey 1961, 80; Cohen 2006, 81.

51 Briant 1982a, 90–91.

reliable conclusion.[52] The only attested exception we have is the transfer of 2000 Jewish families from Babylon and Mesopotamia, which were resettled by Antiochos III in Lydia and Phrygia and received an allotment of royal land.[53] In this case, however, the transfer was an expedient measure for enforcing Seleukid authority by integrating a foreign community loyal to the king thanks to the bestowing of the land in an area which had had troubles with the recognition of Seleukid power. Heavier mobility expenses seem to have been invested mainly in the long-distance transfer of the Greco-Macedonians, because they were meant to reinforce the Hellenic element of the settlements (and their loyalty to the royal house) throughout the empire.

At this point, a question that naturally arises is the integration of the non-Greek population within the Seleukid settlements. Though our knowledge is still fragmentary, it is possible to make some hypotheses by examining a few examples taken from the available evidence of different regions of the empire. Babylon hosted a Greek community which under Antiochos IV received a reinforcement of settlers, along with the new dynastic name of Epiphaneia together with a constitution taken from the model of nearby Seleukeia on the Tigris. This new *politeuma* governed by an *epistates* had its own council of the *peliganes*. The cuneiform tablets defined this community by the Greek term *politai* and their assemblies were held in the theatre. The Babylonians, on the other hand, kept their own administrative system led by a governor (*shatammu*) and the council of the functionaries involved in the administration of the town temples (*kinishtu*), which met in the House of Deliberation in the Junipers Garden.[54] It is also possible that some of the Hellenised Babylonians took part in the activities of the Greek community or even became part of the body of citizens. As Clancier points out, "Rien n'indique que ses limites éthniques [of the polis] aient été absolument infranchissables."[55]

The Babylonian Ardi-Bēlit was also called by his second name Aristeas, and could write in Greek; another Babylonian bearing a double name, Marduk-eriba/Heliodoros, gave his son only the Greek name of Erotios:[56] this onomastic evolution may suggest a progressive assimilation to Hellenic culture, even if it is not possible to evaluate how deep this process was. Anyway, the juxtaposition of the Greco-Macedonian and Babylonian administration came to an end after Antiochos IV had promoted Babylon to the rank of polis: by then, Greeks and Babylonians met together in the theatre which had become Babylon's centre of the political life, where communications from the royal power were relayed to the city.[57] In the provincial centre of Larsa in southern Mesopotamia, the Greco-Macedonian nobility was quite probably involved in the administration of the Ebabbar temple.[58] Although the astronomical diaries point to certain conflicts – some of which emerged in moments of political instability[59] – the documentary and archaeological evidence shows a substantial integration between Greeks and Babylonians. The

---

52 Dumitru 2011, 364–367.

53 Jos., *AJ*, 12.148–153; bibliography and discussion of the issue in Capdetrey 2007, 164–166.

54 On the role played by the Babylonian elites under Seleukid rule, see Clancier 2012, 297–326.

55 Clancier 2012, 324.

56 Boiy 2004, 290.

57 Clancier 2012, 322–324.

58 Monérie 2012a, 343–346.

59 Cf. Van der Spek 2009, 111.

Greek district of Homera, which the akkadian sources simply call *ālu eššu*, i.e. the new town, was located in the north-eastern corner of Babylon, but it was not isolated from the rest of the city.[60] As is known, Seleukid kings and high officials performed rituals and made offerings in the Esagila. Private religious practices of Greek individuals within the context of local temples were also attested in other Mesopotamian towns such as Kutha (40 km south of Seleukeia on the Tigris), where Kebros son of Troilos offered a certain number of slaves to the god Nergal.[61] Archaeological evidence for temples built according the Hellenic architectural canons has not yet been found, and it is possible that the indigenous shrines sufficed in meeting the religious needs of the colonists. This fact has interesting parallels with the situation observable at Ai Khanum, where both the Greek and the local populations frequented the temple of Zeus/Mithra, built in a Near Eastern style and conception. The only element providing a link to the Greek presence was the colossal statue of the god sculpted following the model of the Zeus by Phidias at Olympia but also presenting elements of syncretism with Iranian religion.[62] At Uruk the local governor Anu-uballit received the Greek name of Nikarchos from King Antiochos II. On the other hand, during the reign of Antiochos III the chief of the officers of Uruk (*rab ša rēš āli ša Uruk*), also called Anu-uballit, took the Greek name of Kephalon and married one Antiochis, daughter of Diophantos, a prominent member of the Greco-Macedonian community. While Anu-uballit/Nikarchos was the only one in his family bearing a Greek name, the brother of Anu-uballit/Kephalon, as well as nine members of the family – children, grandchildren and great-nephews – had Greek names.[63]

In Susa, during the reign of Antiochos I an Iranian may have been an officer at the local mint because of the presence of Aramaic letters in the control monogram,[64] while another Iranian, Aribazos, had a military office (*strategos*) in Kilikia between the reigns of Antiochos II and Seleukos II.[65]

Beginning from the reign of Antiochos IV, the representation of indigenous gods became more widespread – both under their local iconography and in a syncretistic form mixing Hellenic and indigenous characters – in the Seleukid coinage from the area stretching between Kilikia and Phoenikia.[66] Luwian deities such Sandan and Athena Margasia, the Semitic Atargatis and Ba'al Hadad, can therefore be observed, while the coinage from the Seleukis region privileges Hellenic representations because of the dense implantation of Greco-Macedonian colonists. However, one cannot state with conviction that the Hellenic imagery is to be interpreted univocally as a reference to a Greek deity or to an *interpretatio graeca* of a local god.[67] This phenomenon may find an explanation in the progressive shrinking of the Seleukid borders, especially after the treaty of Apamea, which as a consequence caused local identities to emerge and become more

60 Van der Speck 2009; Clancier 2012, 322; Monérie 2012b, 359.

61 Monérie 2012b, 359–360.

62 Coloru 2009, 20, 269, 277; Martinez-Sève 2010b, 199–201; Mairs 2013, 93–111.

63 Monérie 2012a, 330–343.

64 Kritt 1997, 127–130; Houghton/Lorber 2002, 165.3d.

65 *P. Petrie* 2.45 and 3.144 = *FGrH* 160. See also Capdetrey 2007, 244–245.

66 Wright 2009/2010, 193–206.

67 Wright 2009/2010, 200.

important for the preservation of the kingdom.[68] Actually, it was under the reign of Antiochos IV that the city of Tarsus in Kilikia was granted the right to strike an autonomous bronze coinage bearing on the reverse a representation of the god Sandan.[69] Likewise, it was Demetrios I who allowed Mallus to depict Athena Magarsia, the indigenous goddess worshipped at the close shrine of Magarsus, on the reverse of the silver coinage struck in the city.[70] Compared to the case of Tarsus, the coinage of Mallus is worth noting because the representation of the local deity appears on a silver royal series, and not in the local bronze coinage whose circulation was more limited.

As we have already seen, ancient historians tell us that the population of the capital of Antioch on the Orontes was composed of Macedonians, Greeks from Aeolis, Argolis, Crete, Cyprus, Euboea and, it goes without saying, autochthonous and non-Greek population.[71] According to Strabo (16.2.4), this ancient metropolis comprised four quarters built in different times and divided by walls, so that Antioch could be considered a Tetrapolis.[72] Seleukos I ordered the construction of the first quarter to settle the inhabitants of Antigoneia, who were not only Greco-Macedonians but quite probably Syrians, although we do not have any information about the way the different ethnic groups were organised inside this first settlement. The second quarter was created by the multitude of the *oiketores*. Regarding this term, Cohen is right in saying that the answer is bound to remain open, although he is inclined to identify them with the native Syrians.[73] The description by Strabo seems to describe a sort of suburb which was formed just outside the walls of the first settlement, to which it was added possibly between the reigns of Antiochos I and Antiochos II. If the term is to be translated as "local inhabitants," this does not imply that the royal authority intended to isolate Syrians from the Greco-Macedonian population, especially because we do not know if those *oiketores* were all natives or included Greek colonists who could not be settled inside the older settlement. Moreover, if we bear in mind that for a Hellenistic historian such as Polybius[74] this term simply meant "colonist," I think that we should take the information by Strabo for what it is, that is to say a generic group of settlers of different origins who established in that area. The third block was the work of Seleukos II, while the fourth, which was not originally walled, was created by Antiochos IV and named Epiphania after his royal epithet.

According to Flavius Josephus, the Jewish community of Antioch had received citizenship rights from Seleukos I.[75] This story has correctly been viewed with scepticism by modern historians, even if in another passage the same Josephus states that the Jewish community enjoyed citizenship rights under the successors of Antiochos IV,[76] which sounds more plausible as at that time the policy of the Seleukids towards the Jews became more favourable. Josephus also states that Seleukos granted the Jews of Antioch

[68] Wright 2009/2010, 199.

[69] Wright 2009/2010, 196.

[70] Houghton/Lorber/Hoover 2008, no. 1618–1619.

[71] For the details and the bibliography see the considerable amount of data provided by Cohen 2006, 80–93. See also Capdetrey 2007, 60–69.

[72] Downey 1961, 69, 71, 78–79; Cohen 2006, 81–82, 89, 93.

[73] Cohen 2006, 86.

[74] Pol. 3.100.4, but see also the precedent in Thuc. 2.27 and 3.92.

[75] Jos. *C. Ap*. 2.39; *AJ* 12.119.

[76] Jos. *BJ*, 7.43–44.

the right to receive a sum of money instead of the usual oil ration in order to buy purified oil according to the Jewish law.[77] The attribution of these privileges to the reign of Seleukos is without doubt a means by which to imbue them with an illustrious past. Involvement in typical civic activities, such as that of the gymnasium as well as the free distribution of supplies, clearly suggests that a certain number of Antiochene Jews may have enjoyed the rights of citizenship,[78] which were partly adjusted to meet the Jewish religious beliefs. Downey[79] assumed that a kernel of truth was detectable in the sense that Jews lived according to their traditions and institutions, but could have enjoyed a form of isopolity. However, I do not agree with his assertion that the Jews could not become citizens in their own right because this would equate to a transgression of the precepts of their religion. This is, in my opinion, taking the Jewish world as a monolith.[80] Individuals bearing Jewish names are present among the list of the ephebes at Iasos in Karia as well as at Cyrene.[81] A Jew from Alexandria boasted to having received an *appropriate paideia*, which may imply that he received an ephebic education.[82] Sources from the Diaspora, on the other hand, attest to Jews attending performances in the theatres and taking part in athletic activities.[83] If we have to take an example from a later context, the family of the apostle Paul was granted Roman citizenship despite being Jewish and monotheist. Antiochos IV decided to grant Jerusalem a *politeia* on the demand of the high priest Jason, who in addition established a *gymnasium* and an ephebate. The new citizens were given the name of *Antiochenes in Jerusalem*.[84] The ethnic composition of this *politeuma* and its political status is still a matter of scholarly debate among those who are inclined to think that it was formed by inhabitants of Jerusalem who obtained the right to organise themselves as a Greek polis, while other scholars deny this.[85] Cohen has suggested that the Antiochenes were individuals from Antioch/Ptolemais/Akko who already resided in Jerusalem before the Hasmonean revolution.[86] This may be partly true, but having to resort exclusively to a foreign community in order to create the body of citizens of Antioch/Jerusalem would diminish the significance of the act of Jason. He aimed, on the one hand, to win the favour of Antiochos,[87] to whom he was indebted for obtaining the high-priesthood, and on the other to find a way of integrating Jewish traditions based on the laws of the Torah in the framework of Hellenic civilisation and institutions.[88] The same Jason and his brother Menelaus had changed – and they were

[77] Jos. *AJ* 119–120.

[78] Sartre 2001, 80.

[79] Downey 1961, 80.

[80] For the Jewish approach to Hellenism, see Gruen 1998, especially 1–33. Under the Hasmonean dynasty, Jonathan and Simon were granted the rank of *philoi*, see 1 *Macc*. 10.16; 13.36.

[81] Robert 1946, 90–108.

[82] Gruen 2002, 123–124.

[83] Gruen 2002, 124–127.

[84] 2 *Macc*. 4.9; Jos. *AJ* 12.239.

[85] A detailed discussion of the issue may be found in Sartre 2001, 339–343; Cohen 2006, 231–233.

[86] Cohen 1994, 243–259; 2006, 231–232.

[87] It is in this light that we should interpret the episode of the envoy by Jason of *theoroi* bearing offerings for Melqart-Herakles to the penteteric games in Tyre, where the king himself was present, cf. 2 *Macc*. 4.18–20.

[88] Interesting views will be found in the PhD thesis by Andrade 2009, 60–70. The work will be soon published by Cambridge University Press.

not alone in doing so – their former Hebrew personal names[89] to adopt names recalling Greek mythology and the epic tradition. Moreover, in the same period, the legend began to circulate about the kinship ties of the Jews with the Spartans through Abraham:[90] this fact highlights the attempt of the Hellenised Jews to follow the practice of finding illustrious ancestors by taking them from the traditional Hellenic groups involved in the archaic colonisation process. Despite the accusations (2 Macc. 4.12) made against Jason of having forced the youths of the priestly families to attend the activities in the gymnasium, it is probable that some of those families spontaneously agreed. As Sartre pointed out,[91] the reform led by Jason would not have had such wide support if it had aimed to suppress the Torah. In this regard, the absence of popular reaction during the priesthood of Jason is also remarkable. Without the participation of the inhabitants of Jerusalem, it would be difficult to understand why the author of 2 *Maccabees* considered the foundation of the gymnasium to be such an act of impiety against the temple and a danger to the unity of the Jewish community if it had only concerned a group of foreign residents. In several cities – especially Sardeis – the participation of the Jewish communities in funding and providing military service is a sign that they could enjoy an important role inside the civic body, even if the extent of the civic rights they enjoyed is difficult to appreciate.[92] To summarise, different approaches to Hellenism existed inside the Jewish communities,[93] and it would not be surprising that some of them could enjoy citizenship, as the evidence we have cited seems to suggest. We do not have any source which can support the idea that some Jews "could probably become eligible for full citizenship by renouncing their faith and worshiping the city gods."[94] This view seems a better fit for the accounts of Christian martyrdoms than the complex reality of the Seleukid Empire, which was all but a confessional state.

In the Seleukid Empire, other non-Greek groups could receive citizenship, as attested by the well-known decree of *sympoliteia* between Smyrna and Magnesia on the Sipylos[95] concluded in the framework of the Third Syrian War (246–241). Magnesia revolted against Seleukos II, waging a war against Smyrna, which on the other hand remained loyal to the king. Eventually, the two opponents came to an agreement favourable to Smyrna and Seleukos which consisted in the absorption of Magnesia into the Smyrnaian territory. The Persian garrison under the command of Omanes in the fort of Palaimagnesia was also included in the treaty and obtained the citizenship of Smyrna.[96] Acting on behalf of Seleukos, Smyrna obtained a considerable increment of its territory, but also strengthened the loyalty of the Magnesians and their soldiers towards the king thanks to the bestowing of citizenship.

[89] Jos. *AJ* 12.239. Jason's Jewish name was Joshua, which could phonetically recall the Greek one, while Menelaus' former name was Onias.

[90] 2 *Macc*. 5.9. For a letter allegedly sent by a Spartan king named Areus to the high priest Onias, in which kinship between Spartan and Jews through Abraham is stated, see 1 *Macc*. 12.19–23; the same claim is to be found in a letter from Jonathan to the Spartans, see 1 *Macc*. 12.1–18. See Andrade 2009, 63.

[91] Sartre 2001, 343.

[92] Gruen 2002, 129–130.

[93] Cf. the important remarks by Sartre 2001, 316–370.

[94] Downey 1961, 116.

[95] OGIS 229; *I. Magnesia am Sipylos* 1.

[96] *I. Magnesia am Sipylos* 1C, *ll*. 104–108.

Hyrcanis in Lydia[97] was an ancient Achaemenid settlement populated by an Iranian community from Hyrcania. In the opinion of Cohen, the town received Macedonian colonists under the reign of Antiochos I.[98] What is noteworthy here is that from then on the inhabitants adopted the double ethnic of Macedonian Hyrcanians. The first attestation of this practice during the Hellenistic Age dates from the beginning of the second century BC,[99] while more evidence is available from coins of the Imperial period when the double ethnic Macedonian Hyrcanian alternates with Hyrcanian alone. Does this double ethnic refer to integration between Macedonians and Iranians, or did it just have a geographical connotation? Epigraphic evidence seems to attest the only presence of Macedonians even in the iconographic representation of the town,[100] and we have to wait until the Roman period to see the emergence of two individuals bearing an Iranian name, Bagoas.[101] However, as Briant has suggested, the presence of a double ethnic should demonstrate that the pre-existing Iranian population had been integrated into a new context marked by a "politique double."[102] In Lydia, possibly in the Mesogis range, there was also another community bearing a double ethnic, the Mysomakedones,[103] but whether it is the Seleukids, the Attalids or both who should be credited for the creation of this settlement has not been established.

Going beyond the paradigm of segregation?

This brief survey did not mean to be exhaustive, but rather intended to raise questions regarding ethnicity in the Seleukid settlements by taking a few examples which could provide some direction for discussion. It is important to point out that the heterogeneous nature of the Seleukid Empire as well as the patchy state of the documentation prevent us from arriving at univocal responses. The Macedonian identity was of course an important factor of unity, even if the Seleukid royal family was de facto a mixed one from the beginning and from subsequent intermarriages with members of Iranian royal houses that continued throughout the history of the dynasty: this fact did not pose particular problems of support to the settlers of Macedonian origin, as the ethnic identity and rights of the children born from mixed marriages were patrilineal. The Macedonian presence is particularly attested in key areas of the empire (Northern Syria, Central Asia and Asia

[97] Cohen 1995, 209–212. The site is now occupied by the modern Halitpaşaköy.

[98] Cohen 1995, 209–211. The attribution to Antiochos I is based on the finding of a dedication in honour of Zeus Seleukeios.

[99] Decree from Amphissa honouring the physician Menophantos son of Artemidoros, cf. Robert 1948, 16–18; Tataki 1998, 469. For other epigraphical attestations of this ethnic, see Robert 1948, 16–26; Tataki 1998, 470.

[100] Robert 1948, 19–20; local coinage bears the representation of a Macedonian shield and the town is possibly represented wearing a *kausia* in the base of the colossal statue for Tiberius at Pozzuoli, cf. Billows 1995, 179.

[101] TAM V, 2, 1322: Markos Antonios Bagoas (*l.* 4) and Markos Antonios Bagoas son of Melissos (*ll.* 6–7).

[102] Briant 1985, 173.

[103] Cohen 1995, 220–222. The site of the settlement is still unknown. Other examples of double ethnic are those of Dokimeion, Peltai and Blaundos in Phrygia, see Robert 1973b, 201–202.

Minor). But we have also seen that a certain number of individuals defining themselves as Macedonians were soldiers who assumed this ethnic for serving in Macedonian-styled units, they were actually Greeks or even indigenous. This seems to show that Macedonian identity became an ethnic and ideological construct more than a widespread reality and, even if in the first phase of the Seleukid period the high officers and aristocracy belonged to that ethnic group, Capdetrey[104] has rightly pointed out that at least from the 2nd century BC being Macedonian was no longer an essential prerequisite for pursuing a career in the upper echelons of the Seleukid hierarchy. Mobility tied to the foundation of settlements is attested in almost every corner of the Empire. The populations of the settlers included individuals coming from the Greek cities of Asia Minor, the Aegean and East Mediterranean Islands and continental Greece, but in this particular case our evidence is too scant or sometimes suspect because of the common practice among recent settlements of invoking illustrious founders from old Greece in order to ennoble their status and obtain privileges. Colonists from Greece took part in the founding of some settlements; however, our sources do not allow us to understand the extent of their contribution or whether or not it was limited to a specific period. Foreign soldiers from different parts of the Mediterranean world were certainly present in the empire, but we should also maintain a distinction among soldiers which stayed only temporarily and those who were implanted on a more permanent basis and later became part of the local communities.[105] Our sources show that the Greeks of Asia Minor gave a significant contribution to the population of several Seleukid settlements. This fact possibly results from the relatively more abundant evidence, which also conveys the overall impression of a mobility within, rather than without, the Empire.

The issue concerning the role played by indigenous populations inside the Seleukid settlements is even more difficult to detect, as the evidence is both patchy and still limited to certain areas. Thus, we should try to take an interpretative model and see how the available data fit in. To this end, we could start by quoting a comparison that Van der Spek has made considering the relations between Greeks and Babylonians: in the Roman Empire citizenship was used as an imperial strategy, while in the Seleukid kingdom

> a universal 'Seleucid citizenship' did not exist: instead, there were many cities with as many constitutions and forms of citizenship. The kings communicated with subject communities in their respective languages and according their traditions. In diplomatic contacts with the Greek cities, the kings developed a discourse which suited the Greek traditions, in Babylon they acted as a traditional Babylonian king, in Jerusalem they dealt with the temple authorities. [...] Some kings may have furthered the Greek type of citizenship in some parts of the empire, but – in contrast to what we know from Rome – this citizenship was always tied to the city, not to the empire.[106]

The multiple approaches that the Seleukids employed towards their subjects[107] alone could suffice to dispel the idea that non-Greek populations lived under the rules of an Apartheid-like state.[108] Just to compare a few examples of segregation in South Africa

---

[104] Capdetrey 2007, 389–392.

[105] On the role of the garrisons in the Hellenistic cities, see Chaniotis 2002, 99–114; Ma 2002b, 115–122.

[106] Van der Spek 2009, 114.

[107] Capdetrey 2012, 329.

[108] The term was employed by Van der Spek (2004, 393–408; 2009, 113) about the condition of Babylonians under Seleukid rule. Clancier (2012, 322–324) has criticised the idea of the existence of an

during Apartheid to what we can infer from the Seleukid state, there is no evidence for indigenous peoples being prevented from having access to quarters inhabited by the Greco-Macedonian population and vice-versa, and there were not spatial barriers which suggest the existence of a ghetto in the modern sense of the term; intermarriage was practised at different levels of society including the royal family; in several cases, non-Greek groups were granted citizenship by the cities or, as happened in Jerusalem during Jason's priesthood, the king patronised the creation of a civic body following the Greek model but mostly composed of Jews. Despite the lack of an entity similar to a national system of education, the access to Greek education and literacy was not impeded; rather, we can imagine that it was encouraged, especially when we bear in mind the fact that not only was a knowledge of Greek a way of obtaining social promotion, but bilingual individuals were also an important resource for the administration. If linguistic intermediaries between the Greco-Macedonian functionaries and non-Greek population were necessary in the Ptolemaic kingdom,[109] they were all the more vital in a multilingual empire like the Seleukid one.[110]

While one cannot talk about a segregation policy, it is nonetheless correct that the most important charges were entrusted to members belonging to the Greco-Macedonian aristocracy, while posts in the royal administration were assigned to non-Greeks in a few cases sometimes dictated by extraordinary contingencies. The local elites were in general left in charge of the administration of the native structures such as the temples in Babylonia and Jerusalem.[111] In this regard, religion seems to have represented a place of intercultural encounter between the indigenous and Greco-Macedonian peoples which turned out to be a means of integration. On the other hand, the degree of participation of non-Greek settlers in civic life cannot be determined because the evidence is too sparse, even if a few sources seem to indicate that this may sometimes have taken place. However, the lack of shared citizen rights is not to be interpreted necessarily as an intentional policy of segregation: inscriptions usually provide us with a description of matters concerning the civic life of the *polis* leaving aside the groups which were not involved, nevertheless the non-Greek settlers could have been free to administer their community according to their laws as long as they kept their loyalty to the king and paid taxes to the royal treasury through the intermediation of their representatives. Moreover, Cohen[112] has rightly drawn our attention to the fact that even for Greco-Macedonian settlers the most important element in the preservation of their ethnic identity was not the organisation of the colony according to the system of the *polis*, but rather the presence of structures relevant to the practice of Greek cultural values such as the gymnasium, the theatre or the market place.

apartheid, showing that the sumero-akkadian elite enjoyed a privileged position under the Seleukids. On the concept of dominant ethno-class, see Briant 1982a–b; Briant 1996, 362–366. See also the views of Capdetrey 2007, 389–392.

[109] Torallas Tovar 2010, 17–46.

[110] On documents written in Greek in the archives of Mesopotamian temples, see Clancier 2005, 85–104; Monérie 2012a, 337–339.

[111] See the important conclusions by Capdetrey 2007, 390–392.

[112] Cohen 1994, 256–257. For a fresh view on the role of Hellenism in the East, cf. Traina 2002; Traina 2005.

The issue is inevitably bound to remain open, but I would abandon the model of ethnic segregation, which seems to be excessively shaped by episodes drawn from our recent contemporary history. It is paramount to remember that the term "isolation" applied to the autochthonous or non-Greek communities inside the Hellenistic foundations should not be taken immediately as a synonym of "ghettoisation." The populations of the settlements, especially the major cities, resulted from the juxtaposition of different ethnic groups, the most visible of which was that represented by the Greco-Macedonians. This prominence could sometimes cause conflicts with non-Greek settlers, but the policy followed by the Seleukids was not marked by a systematic plan of submission or isolation of the other ethnic groups, as this would entail the constant danger of revolts and social instability. The cooperation with the local elites was vital in order to assure the loyalty of the subjects towards a dynasty ruling a Macedonian empire within a multiethnic context.

Bibliography

Andrade, N.J. (2009): *"Imitating Greeks": Being Syrian in the Greco-Roman World (175 BCE–275 CE)*, PhD dissertation, University of Michigan.

Bernard, P. (1987): Le Marsyas d'Apamée, l'Oxus et la colonisation séleucide en Bactriane, *Studia Iranica* 16: 103–115.

Bernard, P. (1994): L'Asie Centrale et l'Empire séleucide, *Topoi* 4(2): 473–511.

Bernard, P., Bopearachchi, O. (2002): Deux bracelets grecs avec inscriptions grecques trouvés dans l'Asie Centrale hellénisée, *JS*: 237–278.

Bernard, P., Rapin, Cl. (1994): Un parchemin gréco-bactrien d'une collection privée, *CRAI*: 261–294.

Billows, R.A. (1995): *Kings and Colonists: Aspects of Macedonian Imperialism*, Leiden–New York–Köln.

Bingen, J. (2007): *Hellenistic Egypt: Monarchy, Society, Economy, Culture* (edited and introduced by Roger S. Bagnall), Berkeley–Los Angeles.

Boiy, T. (2004): *Late Achaemenid and Hellenistic Babylon*, Leuven.

Boswinkel, E., Pestman, P.W. (1982): *Les archives privées de Dionysios, fils de Kephalas: textes grecs et démotiques*, Leiden.

Briant, P. (1982a): Colonisation hellénistique et populations indigènes. I. La phase d'installation, in: P. Briant, *Rois, tributs et paysans. Études sur les formations tributaires du Moyen-Orient ancien*, Paris: 227–262 (= *Klio* 60 (1978), 57–92).

Briant, P. (1982b): Colonisation hellénistique et populations indigènes. II. Renforts grecs dans les cités hellénistiques d'Orient, in: P. Briant, *Rois, tributs et paysans. Études sur les formations tributaires du Moyen-Orient ancien*, Paris: 263–279 (= *Klio* 64 (1982), 83–98).

Briant, P. (1985): Les Iraniens d'Asie Mineure après la chute de l'Empire achéménide. (À propos de l'inscription d'Amyzon), *DHA* 11, 166–195.

Briant, P. (1996): *Histoire de l'Empire perse*, Paris.

Capdetrey, L. (2007): *Le pouvoir séleucide. Territoire, administration, finances d'un royaume hellénistique (312–129 avant J.-C.)*, Rennes.

Capdetrey, L. (2012): Fondations, diasporas et territoires dans l'Asie hellénistique au IIIe siècle, *Pallas* 89: 319–344.

Chaniotis. A. (2002): Foreign Soldiers – Native Girls? Constructing and Crossing Boundaries in Hellenistic Cities with Foreign Garrisons, in: A. Chaniotis, P. Ducrey (eds.), *Army and Powering the Ancient World*, Stuttgart: 99–114.

Clancier, Ph. (2005): Les scribes sur parchemin du temple d'Anu, *RA* 99: 85–104.

Clancier, Ph. (2012): Le *šatammu*, l'assemblé de l'Esagil et les Babyloniens. Les notables de Babylone: du relais local à la marginalisation, in: Chr. Feyel *et al.* (ed.), *Communautés locales et pouvoir central dans l'Orient hellénistique et romain*, Nancy: 297–326.

Clarysse, W., Thompson, D.J. (2007): Two Greek Texts on Skin from Hellenistic Bactria, *ZPE* 159: 273–279.

Cohen, G.M. (1978): *The Seleucid Colonies. Studies in Founding, Administration, and Organization*, Wiesbaden.

Cohen, G.M. (1994): The 'Antiochenes in Jerusalem'. Again, in: J.C. Reeves, J. Kampen (eds.), *Pursuing the Text: Studies in Honor of Ben Zion Wacholder on the Occasion of His Seventieth Birthday*, Sheffield: 243–259.

Cohen, G.M. (1995): *The Hellenistic Settlements in Europe, the Islands, and Asia Minor*, Berkeley–Los Angeles–Oxford.

Cohen, G.M. (2006): *The Hellenistic settlements in Syria, the Red Sea Basin and North Africa*, Berkeley–Los Angeles–Oxford.

Cohen, G.M. (2013): *The Hellenistic Settlements in the East from Armenia and Mesopotamia to Bactria and India*, Berkeley–Los Angeles–Oxford.

Coloru, O. (2009): *Da Alessandro a Menandro. Il regno greco di Battriana*, Pisa–Roma.

Downey, G. (1961): *A History of Antioch in Syria: From Seleucus to the Arab Conquest*, Princeton.

Dumitru, A.G. (2011): Les Séleucides et les Balkans: les Thraces dans l'armée séleucide, in: A.G. Dumitru, M. Hauser, I. Feodorov, N.V. Sekunda (eds.), *Le livre. La Roumanie. L'Europe*, Bucarest: 349–376.

Facella, M. (2006): *La dinastia degli Orontidi nella Commagene ellenistico-romana*, Pisa–Roma.

Falk, H., Bennet, Ch. (2009): Macedonian Intercalary Months and the Era of Azes, *AcOr* 70: 197–216.

Fischer-Bovet, C. (2008): *Army and Society in Ptolemaic Egypt*, PhD dissertation, University of Stanford.

Fischer-Bovet, C. (2011): Counting the Greeks in Egypt: Immigration in the First Century of Ptolemaic Rule, in: C. Holeran, A. Pudsey (eds.), *Demography and the Graeco-Roman World: New Insights and Approaches*, Cambridge: 135–154.

Fussman, G. (1985): Nouvelles inscriptions Śaka (III), *BEFEO* 74: 35–42.

Gatier, P.-L. (2007): Sôtélès l'Athénien, *Arabian Archaeology and Epigraphy* 18: 75–79.

Gatier, P.-L. (2013): Des péliganes à Suse, *ZPE* 184: 205–210.

Grainger, J.D. (1990): *The Cities of Seleukid Syria*, Oxford.

Gruen, E.S. (1998): *Heritage and Hellenism: The Reinvention of Jewish Tradition*, Berkeley–Los Angeles–London.

Gruen, E.S. (2002): *Diaspora: Jews Amidst Greeks and Romans*, Cambridge, MA.

Habicht, Chr. (1957): Samische Volksbeschlüsse der hellenistischen Zeit, *MDAI(A)* 72: 152–274.

Holt, F.L. (1999): *Thundering Zeus. The Making of Hellenistic Bactria*, Berkeley–Los Angeles–London.

Honigman, S. (2007): Permanence des stratégies culturelles grecques à l'œuvre dans les rencontres inter-ethniques, de l'époque archaïque à l'époque hellénistique, *Pallas* 73: 125–140.

Houghton, A., Lorber, C.C. (2002): *Seleucid Coins: A Comprehensive Catalogue*, Part I, *Seleucus I through Antiochus III*, New York–Lancaster.

Houghton, A., Lorber, C.C., Hoover, O. (2008): *Seleucid Coins: A Comprehensive Catalogue*, Part II, *Seleucus IV through Antiochus XIII*, New York–Lancaster.

Iossif, P., Lorber, C.C. (2009): The Cult of Helios in the Seleucid East, *Topoi* 16: 19–42.

Kritt, B. (1997): *The Early Seleucid Mint of Susa*, Lancaster.

Kuhrt, A., Sherwin-White, S. (1991): Aspects of Seleucid Royal Ideology: The Cylinder of Antiochus I from Borsippa', *JHS* 111: 71–86.

Le Rider, G. (1965): *Suse sous les Séleucides et les Parthes*, Paris.

Leriche, P. (2003a): Peut-on étudier la Syrie séleucide?, in: F. Prost (ed.), *L'Orient méditerranéen de la mort d'Alexandre aux campagnes de Pompée*, Toulouse: 117–146.

Leriche, P. (2003b): Doura-Europos hellénistique, in: M. Sartre, A. Bousdroukis, F. Duyrat, J.F. Salles (eds.), *La Syrie hellénistique*, TOPOI supplement 4, Paris: De Boccard, 171–191.

Ma, J. (2002a): *Antiochos III and the cities of Western Asia Minor*, Oxford.

Ma, J. (2002b): "Oversexed, Overpaid and over Here": A Response to Angelos Chaniotis, in: A. Chaniotis, P. Ducrey (eds.), *Army and Powering the Ancient World*, Stuttgart: 115–122.

Ma, J. (2003): Peer Polity Interaction in the Hellenistic Age, *Past and Present* 180: 7–38.

Mairs, R. (2008): Greek Identity and the Settler Community in Hellenistic Bactria and Arachosia, *Migrations and Identities* 1: 19–43.

Mairs, R. (2010): The Places in Between: Model and Metaphor in the Archaeology of Hellenistic Arachosia, in: S. Chandrasekaran, A. Kouremenos, R. Rossi (eds.), *From Pella to Gandhara: Hybridisation and Identity in the Art and Architecture of the Hellenistic East*, Oxford: 177–187.

Mairs, R. (2013): The 'Temple with Indented Niches' at Ai Khanoum: Ethnic and Civic Identity in Hellenistic Bactria, in: R. Alston, O.M. Van Nijf, C.G. Williamson (eds.), *Cults, Creeds and Identities in the Greek City after the Classical Age*, Leuven–Paris–Walpole, MA: 85–117.

Martinez-Sève, L. (2009): Les Grecs en Orient: portraits croisés, in: P. Rouillard (ed.), *Portraits de migrants, Portraits de colons*, vol. 1, Paris: 129–140.

Martinez-Sève, L. (2010a): Suse et les Séleucides au IIIe siècle avant J.-C., *Electrum* 18: 41–66.

Martinez-Sève, L. (2010b): À propos du temple aux niches indentées d'Aï Khanoum: quelques observations, in: P. Carlier, Ch. Lerouge-Cohen (eds.), *Paysage et religion en Grèce antique*, Paris: 195–207.

McGing, B. (1986): *The Foreign Policy of Mithridates VI Eupator King of Pontus*, Leiden.

Mittag, P.F. (2006): *Antiochos IV. Epiphanes. Eine politische Biographie*, Berlin.

Monérie, J. (2012a): Notabilité urbaine et administration locale en Babylonie du sud aux époques séleucide et parthe, in: Chr. Feyel *et al.* (ed.), *Communautés locales et pouvoir central dans l'Orient hellénistique et romain*, Nancy: 327–352.

Monérie, J. (2012b): Les communautés grecques en Babylonie (VIIe–IIIe s. av. J.-C.), *Pallas* 89: 345–365.

Patterson, L.L (2010): *Kinship myths in ancient Greece*, Austin.

Potts, D.T. (1999): *The Archaeology of Elam: Formation and Transformation of an Ancient Iranian State*, Cambridge.

Potts, D.T. (2002): Five Episodes in the History of Elymais, 145–124 B.C.: New Data from the Astronomical Diaries, *Cahiers de Studia Iranica* 25: 349–362 (Republished in: D.T. Potts, *Mesopotamia, Iran and Arabia from the Seleucids to the Sasanians*, Farnham–Burlington, VT).

Robert, L. (1946): Un corpus des inscriptions juives, in: L. Robert, *Hellenika: recueil d'épigraphie de numismatique et d'antiquités grecques*, vol. 3, Paris: 90–108.

Robert, L. (1948): Hyrcanis, in: L. Robert L., *Hellenika: recueil d'épigraphie de numismatique et d'antiquités grecques*, vol. 6, Paris: 16–26.

Robert, L. (1968): De Delphes à l'Oxus. Inscriptions grecques nouvelles de la Bactriane, *CRAI*: 416–457 (= L. Robert, *Opera Minora Selecta*, vol. 5, Paris: 510–551).

Robert, L. (1969): *Laodicée du Lykos, le Nymphée*, Québec–Paris.

Robert, L. (1973a): Sur des inscriptions de Délos, in: *Études déliennes publiées à l'occasion du centième anniversaire du début des fouilles de l'École française d'Athènes à Délos* (*BCH* suppl. 1), Paris: 435–489.

Robert, L. (1973b): De Cilicie à Messine et à Plymouth, avec deux inscriptions grecques errantes, *JS*: 161–211.

Rougemont, G. (2012): *Inscriptions grecques d'Iran et d'Asie Centrale* (*Corpus Inscriptionum Iranicarum* II,1,1), London.

Sarakinski, V. (2010): Peliganes: The State of the Question and Some Other Thoughts, *Macedonian Historical Review* 1: 31–46.

Sartre, M. (2001): *D'Alexandre à Zénobie: Histoire du Levant antique (IVe siècle av. J.-C.-IIIe siècle ap. J.-C.)*, Paris.

Sherwin-White, S., Kuhrt, A. (1993): *From Samarkand to Sardis: A New Approach to the Seleucid Empire*, London.

Tataki, A.B. (1998): *Macedonians abroad. A Contribution to the Prosopography of Ancient Macedonia*, Athens.

Torallas Tovar, S. (2010): Linguistic Identity in Graeco-Roman Egypt, in: A. Papaconstantinou (ed.), *The Multilingual Experience in Egypt, from the Ptolemies to the Abbasids*, Farnham–Burlington VT: 17–46.

Traina, G. (2002): Hellenism in the East: Some Historiographical Remarks, *Electrum* 6: 15–24.

Traina, G. (2005): Notes on Hellenism in the Iranian East (Classico-Oriental Notes, 6–8), *Iran & the Caucasus* 9: 1–14.

Van der Spek, R.J. (2004): Ethnic Segregation in Hellenistic Babylon, in: W. van Soldt, R. Kalvelagen, D. Katz (eds.), *Ethnicity in Ancient Mesopotamia. Papers read at the 48th Rencontre Assyriologique Internationale, Leiden, July 1–4, 2002*, Leiden 393–408.

Van der Spek, R.J. (2006): The Size and Significance of the Babylonian Temples under the Successors, in: P. Briant, F. Joannès (eds.), *La transition entre l'empire achéménide et les royaumes hellénistiques*, Paris: 261–307.

Van der Spek, R.J. (2009): Multi-ethnicity and Ethnic Segregation in Hellenistic Babylon, in: T. Derks, N. Roymans (eds.), *Ethnic Construct in Antiquity*, Amsterdam: 101–115.

Websites: Stol M., Van der Speck, R.J., The Antiochus Cylinder (2): http://www.livius.org/cg-cm/chronicles/antiochus_cylinder/antiochus_cylinder2.html.

Wright, N.L. (2009/2010): Non-Greek Religious Imagery on the Coinage of Seleucid Syria, *Mediterranean Archaeology* 22/23: 193–206.

ELECTRUM * Vol. 20 (2013): 57–76
doi: 10.4467/20800909EL.13.004.1433

Ptolemaic Foundations in Asia Minor and the Aegean as the Lagids' Political Tool

Tomasz Grabowski
Uniwersytet Jagielloński, Kraków

Abstract: The Ptolemaic colonisation in Asia Minor and the Aegean region was a significant tool which served the politics of the dynasty that actively participated in the fight for hegemony over the eastern part of the Mediterranean Sea basin. In order to specify the role which the settlements founded by the Lagids played in their politics, it is of considerable importance to establish as precise dating of the foundations as possible. It seems legitimate to acknowledge that Ptolemy II possessed a well-thought-out plan, which, apart from the purely strategic aspects of founding new settlements, was also heavily charged with the propaganda issues which were connected with the cult of Arsinoe II.

Key words: Ptolemies, foundations, Asia Minor, Aegean.

Settlement of new cities was a significant tool used by the Hellenistic kings to achieve various goals: political and economic. The process of colonisation was begun by Alexander the Great, who settled several cities which were named Alexandrias after him. The process was successfully continued by the diadochs, and subsequently by the following rulers of the monarchies which emerged after the demise of Alexander's state. The new settlements were established not only by the representatives of the most powerful dynasties: the Seleucids, the Ptolemies and the Antigonids, but also by the rulers of the smaller states. The kings of Pergamum of the Attalid dynasty were considerably active in this field, but the rulers of Bithynia, Pontus and Cappadocia were also successful in this process.[1] Very few regions of the time remained beyond the colonisation activity of the Hellenistic kings.

The Ptolemaic colonisation, besides displaying some characteristics which had a lot in common with the activities of other Hellenistic kings, was also characterised by sig-

[1] Generally, for the new settlements, founded or refounded in the Hellenistic period see Tscherikover 1927; Cohen 1995, 2006. Seleucid colonies: Cohen 1978; Attalid: Hansen 1971; Allen 1983, in Macedonia: Papazoglou 1988; Ptolemaic: Cohen 1983; Mueller 2006 (focuses on situation in Egypt); local kings and dynasts in Asia Minor: Kobes 1996, 205–230.

nificant differences, which were emphasised by scholars. It is better to address the diverse character of the Ptolemaic colonisation itself, which resulted from the differences in the cultural-economic relationships between Egypt and the foreign properties of the dynasty. As is commonly known, the Ptolemies established only one *polis* in Egypt, which was a real city as understood by the Greeks, that is Ptolemais Hermiou, founded by the dynasty's creator, Ptolemy I. Apart from Ptolemais Hermiou, there still existed only two *poleis* in the state on the Nile (Alexandria[2] and Naukratis). The Lagids' circumspection in founding new *poleis* in Egypt probably resulted from the fact that the state's founder could encounter the extensive and effective system of executing his rule which could have easily been used while organising his own government. Introducing to this complex system a new element, which was *poleis*, was not only unnecessary, but even unfavourable. The extensive network of *poleis*, that is the institutions with their own organisation and autonomy, would have diminished the range of the direct rule of the dynasty. Given numerous opportunities to enrich themselves as well as make careers, the Greeks were still willing to arrive at the state on the Nile. The Ptolemies were able to create such attractive economic conditions for them that they forgot about the inconveniences resulting from the fact of living beyond the system of a *polis*. What is more, although from the Greeks' point of view the settlements founded by the Lagids were only villages, they offered the Greek lifestyle, but with the exclusion of the functioning of autonomic institutions, typical of the *polis*. The Greek-Macedonian newcomers also found the old Egyptian settlement principles in Egypt,[3] and at least in the main towns of the nomes, although they were not formally *poleis*, they could find conditions partly similar to those which were typical of the other cities of the Greek world. The situation must have looked different in the dynasty's foreign domains in the Mediterranean Sea basin, where the Ptolemies acted in the conditions determined by the more or less developed Greek settlement system and the competition of the other Hellenistic powers.

Particular settlements founded in the territory of Egypt were supposed to serve different functions, for instance Ptolemais Hermiou, situated in Thebaid, was meant to be the centre for administrative structures and settlement for the Greek immigrants. The settlements that come to the fore, however, are those whose purpose was to solve one of the urgent problems which the Ptolemies, similarly to the Seleucids, had to face – that is that of creating their own soldier recruitment bases. After the political map of the Hellenistic world had assumed its shape, it was only the Antigonids that could use the Macedonian recruitment base. The process of endowing the soldiers with ground in exchange for their performing military service had already been initiated by Ptolemy I.[4] The military aspects (acquiring combat elephants) besides those of a commercial character were also displayed in the dynasty's exploration and settlement activity, particularly in the case of

[2] For Alexandria and its institutions see Joquet 1948; Fraser 1972, I: 93–131; Cohen 2006, 357, 368–373; Huss 2011, 17–20.

[3] On the ancient Egyptian town planning, see Kemp 1977; 2009, 131–161; 404–414; Mueller 2006, 106–108.

[4] The origins of the cleruchies also prove the attractiveness of the conditions which were offered to the settlers, the majority of whom came from the territories which were not under the direct control of the Lagids. Bagnall (1984) listed that it was more than 2/3 cleruchies. As regards cleruchs and Ptolemaic settlement in Egypt, see Uebel 1968; Marrinan 1998, 15–80; Mueller 2006, 23–29, 60–64, 93–104; Serrati 2008, 472–475.

Ptolemy II, in the territories exceeding the southern borderline and reaching as far as the coast of the Red Sea.[5] The Lagids founded their settlements in almost every region they took control of except for Thrace. The first foundation in Cyrenaica had probably been undertaken by Ptolemy I.[6] The Lagids also conducted a very active colonisation campaign in Coele-Syria. The considerably dense network of Greek settlements in southern Syria was actually attributed particularly to the Ptolemies and their competitors in winning control over the territory, the Selucids. Some researchers implied that the Lagids founded a chain of fortified cities on the coast, to the east of the Jordan valley as well as in Idumea, which surrounded and protected the whole Coele-Syria.[7] Nevertheless, so far it has proved impossible to connect the dynasty with any settlement on the South Syrian coast since the closest situated, Ptolemais/Ake, was situated on the Phoenician coast.[8] A considerable number of Greek settlements appeared in the Jordan valley and further inland.[9]

Most of the settlements were founded by the Ptolemies just in Egypt, and they were a significant tool in achieving economic and financial success.[10] In this way, the Egyptian kings gained the means of pursuing great politics in the territory. This was the main object of interest of the main contenders in the political arena of the time, which was the eastern part of the Mediterranean Sea basin. The first representatives of the dynasty led a considerably large-scale foreign policy. For a long time researchers have been disputing over the objectives they were motivated by in the outer arena, particularly when leading overseas conquests in the Aegean Sea basin – in Asia Minor, in the islands of the

[5] Cf. Thompson 1969, 30–38; Dietze 1994; Sidebotham 1986; 1996; 2002; Burstein 1996; Huss 2001, 287–292, 366–367; Cohen 2006, 305–343; Mueller 2006, 151–157.

[6] Mueller 2006, 143–146.

[7] Rostovtzeff 1941, I: 347–349.

[8] It is interesting that the Ptolemies' activity reached much further towards the North. The ruins of the settlement founded in the mid-3rd century were discovered in Ras ibn Hani on the coast of northern Syria, in the very heart of the Seleucid domains. The considerable number of Ptolemaic coins as well as the inscription including the list of mercenaries in the pay of Egyptian rulers makes it plausible to view the Lagids as its founders: Cohen 2006, 51–52.

[9] Rarely did it happen that they were cities founded on "the raw root." They were more often local centres with their own history, which were refounded and gained new names after the settlement of the new colonisers. On the basis of the archaeological finds (mainly ceramics), attempts have been made to prove the continuation of the settlement from the times of the Persian domination. De facto, only a few cities founded in the Persian times survived in the Hellenic period, which left space for the Ptolemaic and Seleucid foundations – Mueller 2006, 51–52. The idea behind some of the settlements founded by the Lagids was to secure the safety of these territories against the attacks of the Arab desert nomads. A typical example of such a settlement was Brita, in "the Ammonites' country," the precise location of which remains unknown to this day. Most probably, it occupied the acropolis of Rabbat Ammon; however, even the latter of the proposed locations, 20 kilometres west of the present Amman, has its adherents among archaeologists. Cf. *P.Cairo Zen.* I, 59003; Cohen 2006, 237–239, with further literature. As regards the individual Ptolemaic settlements in Coele-Syria, see Schmitt 1995, 18, 90, 279; Sartre 2001, 120–122; Cohen 2006, 102–104, 237–239, 265–274, 290–299, 302–303 (with further literature).

[10] On the whole, it has been confirmed that there were 45 settlements founded (or renamed) by the Ptolemies in Egypt, of which as many as 30 were in Fayum. Mueller (2006, 58–59) rightly noticed, however, that the considerable disproportion between Egypt and the Ptolemaic dominions in Asia Minor and in the Aegean Sea may be, at least, partly misleading. We owe our knowledge of so many settlements in Egypt to the papyrus records, which other regions are deprived of.

region and in Magna Graecia. The key role in this discussion usually falls to the fragment of Polybius' *The Histories* (5.34) in which he characterises the foreign policy of the first Lagids. The Achaean historian writes that by possessing South Syria and Cyprus, the rulers of Egypt constituted a constant threat for the Seleucids. With the supporters on the coast of Asia Minor, from Hellespont to Pamphylia, they could influence the course of the events in the region, and ruling over such cities as Ainos and Maroneia, they could also hold Macedonia in check. Polybius concludes about the policy of the former Ptolemies: καὶ τῷ τοιούτῳ τρόπῳ μακρὰν ἐκτετακότες τὰς χεῖρας, καὶ προβεβλημένοι πρὸ αὑτῶν ἐκ πολλοῦ τὰς δυναστείας, οὐδέποτε περὶ τῆς κατ' Αἴγυπτον ἠγωνίων ἀρχῆς. διὸ καὶ τὴν σπουδὴν εἰκότως μεγάλην ἐποιοῦντο περὶ τῶν ἔξω πραγμάτων. Supported by an opinion of the ancient historiographer, it used to be thought that the Ptolemaic actions on the outside arena were motivated only by defensive purposes.[11] The whole activity of the Lagids was, inclusively, supposed to secure the safety of the country on the Nile. However, Polybius' intentions can also be interpreted as a way of merely emphasising that it was thanks to their active policy that the first Ptolemies managed to ensure the security of the most important part of their state, which was undoubtedly Egypt. The abovementioned passage appears together with the description of Ptolemy IV, and through displaying stark oppositions is expected to be evidence of the ruler's neglect of the outside problems. A historian from Megalopolis writes that that his predecessors had paid much more attention to foreign affairs than to the government of Egypt itself, whereas Ptolemy IV treated all this carelessly and tardily. We should remember that Polybius was not contemporary with the first Ptolemaic rulers and wrote all this from a long time perspective. After Ptolemy IV's death, grave danger loomed over the Lagids' monarchy in the form of the secret partition treaty which was made between Antiochos II and the Macedonian king Philip V, a problem that constituted an important part of Polybius' work. We do not know the whole contents of the treaty, and the ancient authors dealing with the information from it are not unanimous, in terms of not only the scope of the planned annexations, but also the division of the particular territories between the participants.[12] All in all, according to Polybius (3.2.8), it was planned to divide the whole of the Ptolemies' state. Antiochos is said to have assured himself South Syria and Phoenicia, while Philip claimed Egypt, Caria and Samos. In this passage, the Achaean historian might have only wanted to draw the readers' attention to the achievements and services of the predecessors of the – in his opinion – lazy and inefficient Ptolemy IV,[13] to emphasise that under his rule even the central part of the state had ceased to be safe.

[11] Cf. Rostovtzeff 1941, I: 29–30; 332–334; Will 1979/1982, I: 153–168; Errington 2008, 157–158. Economic factors also played a significant role in the Ptolemies' foreign policy; however, economic motifs (mainly trade relationships) cannot be overestimated in view of the steps taken by the kings of Egypt in the external arena. The direct political control was not necessary to apply in order to realise economic goals. The discussion concerning the problem was introduced by Will 1979/1982, I: 168–200.

[12] Apart from Polybius, the treaty is mentioned by App. *Mac*.4.1; Liv. 31.14.4–5; Just. 30.2.8; Porph. *FGrH* 260F 45; Hieronim, *In Daniel*. 11.13. There is a lot of literature behind the problem, and contemporary researchers have even – unconvincingly – tried to point out that it was a fabrication of ancient authors. Probably, however, both Antiochos and Philip planned only the annexation of the Lagids' dominions outside Egypt; cf. McDonald/Walbank 1937, 182–184, 205–207; Magie 1939; Schmitt 1964, 237–261.

[13] Cf. e.g. Plb. 5.62.7; 87.4.

However, in fact, the first Lagids' activity over the whole territory, which constituted the arena of the struggles of the contemporary world's powers, indicates that they were striving to gain hegemony in the Hellenistic world. This, obviously, could be achieved by using Egypt's natural resources, so taking particular care when it came to securing their interests in this country was self-evident, as only perfectly safe control over the country on the Nile could open the gates for large-scale politics. The Hellenistic world did not know the concept of the balance of power; however, in practice in the 3rd century such an equilibrium was achieved.[14] Remembering the role of victory in Hellenic ideology, it is difficult to ascribe a merely preventive character to the military operations that the Ptolemies conducted. The range of the Lagids' expansion in the 3rd century reached far beyond such needs. The Ptolemies' foreign policy could be rather defined as an amalgam of offensive and defensive actions, built on great ambitions as well as rational premises. None of the rulers of Egypt, also before the Lagids, could feel safe without creating an internal defence line. Ruling over South Syria was considerably important from the military point of view. The key resources for creating the sea power could be found in Cyprus as well as in South Syria and Asia Minor. It could be perfectly clear to the Ptolemies that maintaining a powerful fleet was of critical importance for their position in the world. Maintaining the influence over these territories opened access to the local recruitment resources. Last but not least, although together with the military expedition of Alexander the Great the borders of *oikumene* were considerably expanded, the heart of the Greek-Macedonian world still beat in Greece and in Asia Minor. The existence in the Aegean basin was also a matter of prestige, which for every power is of crucial importance. For different reasons, the aforementioned region played a key role in the Ptolemaic politics. The settlements founded by the Ptolemies in this region were an important means for achieving particular purposes.

To specify the aims which the Lagids wanted to realise by founding the new settlements and refounding the existing ones it is of considerable importance to establish the date when a particular settlement was made. Unfortunately, in most cases this is made difficult by the fragmentary character of the written sources, often deriving from a much later period. The inscriptions as well as the numismatic sources, although in a direct way proving the existence of a particular settlement, also rarely allow us to specify the precise date of the foundation.[15] In most cases, what remains is considering the foundation in the light of the geopolitical situation in the region and the politics of the Lagids, as well as an attempt at grasping a wider context. However, there is also a lack of well-preserved historiographic sources containing a constant narrative about the events of the 3rd century.

The Ptolemies founded settlements in nearly all the regions they took control of:[16] in the Troad (1), Ionia (1), Caria (1), Lycia (1), Pamphylia (1), Cilicia (2 or 3[17]), Cyprus (3),

[14] Cf. Braunert 1964; Klose 1972, 91–92; Schmitt 1974, 74–75, 84–86; Will 1979/1982: I, 154.

[15] For sources about Hellenistic settlements see Cohen 1995, 4–13.

[16] Thrace is an exception to the rule; at least there is a lack of information concerning the Ptolemaic settlements in this region. As regards the Ptolemaic presence in Thrace, see Bagnall 1976, 159–161; Huss 1976, 210–213.

[17] Philadelpheia in Cilicia might be the foundation of Antiochos IV, the king of Kommagene. What could be used against the hypothesis that the Lagids were the founders of this settlement was the fact that it was situated inland, whereas all the known Ptolemaic foundations in this region were located on the shore. However, the archeological finds in Meydancikkale confirming the presence of the Ptolemaic garrison in the

Crete (2), Greece and on the Aegean Islands (2) as well as in Cyrenaica (3), Coele-Syria (6) and in the region of the Red Sea (9).

The dynastic names of the founded or refounded settlements were of considerable importance. Among the cities founded by the Ptolemies beyond Egypt, we come across only five names, all of which have direct connotations with the dynasty: Arsinoe, Berenike, Philotera, Philadelpheia and Ptolemais.[18] Even the very nomenclature, regardless of the other premises, indicates that the greatest colonisation activity was displayed by the Ptolemies in the 3rd century.[19] Through the dynastic name the city constituted a visible symbol of the Ptolemaic ambitions and influences, which was particularly important in the regions in which the rivalry between the Hellenistic kingdoms was extremely strong. There existed two settlements with Ptolemaic names even in Aetolia, that is in the region which had never been under the Lagids' rule. The Ptolemies, however, undertook cooperation with the Aetolian League, which in the mid-3rd century became an important power in Greece.[20] The Ptolemies' attention was also attracted by the Aetolians' intense activity in the Aegean Sea. The above region remained in the centre of the Ptolemaic politics, and after the defeat of the Egyptian fleet at Andros circa 245 the position of the Lagids there was no longer as strong as before.[21] In the 250s and the 240s the Aetolian League was connected through a network of links with numerous communities of the Aegean Sea islands as well as Asia Minor coasts, among many others Chios, Delos, Tenos, Miletus, Smyrna and Abdera.[22] The Aegean Sean basin also witnessed at the time numerous pirate raids which were conducted by the Aetolian commanders on their own.[23] Finally, the Ptolemies provided the Aetolians with their support in the war with the Macedonian kings: Demetrius (probably) and Antigonos Doson (for sure), and even concluded a formal *symmachia* with the League.[24] It is very probable that it was just in Aetolia that the city of Ptolemais was established.[25] The case of the other city, that is that of Arsinoe/Konope, the name of which could be associated with the Lagid dynasty, is more disputable. It is very probable that it had nothing to do with the Ptole-

years circa 245–235 in the interior of Cilicia Trachea (Davesne/Le Rider 1989; Davesne 1998, 66) showed that the settlement of the Lagid settlements at a distance from the shore cannot be excluded, cf. Cohen 1995, 368–369.

[18] A much more considerable diversity in the nomenclature appeared in Egypt. As regards the toponyms of the Ptolemaic settlements, see Mueller 2006, 9–39.

[19] Compare, for example, only five settlements, all of them in Egypt, named *Kleopatris* or *Kleopatra*. This name was introduced to the Ptolemy family only after the marriage of Ptolemy V to Cleopatra, Antiochos III's daughter.

[20] As regards the development of the Aetolian League, see Grainger 1999, 29–129; Scholten 2000, 16–95.

[21] For the political situation in the Aegean, cf. Buraselis 1982, 164–179; Hölbl 2001, 50–51.

[22] *IG* IX 1^2 1.185; 1.191; *ISE* II 78; *FD* III 1.482; 1.483; Schmitt 1969: no. 564.

[23] Syll.^{3} 520; 521. Such raids were extremely profitable. In this period, there was an increase in the number of private dedications in Delphi, often very expensive and massive (*IG* IX 1^2 1.181; 200; 202; 203; 185; *Syll.*^{3} 514). One of the Aetolians, Nikolaos of Proscheion, even founded a festival bearing his name (*Nikolaeia*) at Delos, following in the footsteps of Macedonian and Egyptian kings, who had established their own festivals there (*IG* XI 2.287B.126–128).

[24] *P.Haun* 1.6.18; cf. Schwartz 1978, 98; Habicht 1980, 1–2. On the topic of the relations between the Lagids and the Aetolians, see Grabowski 2010; 2012.

[25] *Syll*^{3} 545.6; cf. Cohen 1995, 118–119.

mies. It might have been founded still at the time when Arsinoe II was Lysimachos' wife, before her return to Egypt and marriage to Ptolemy II.[26] The aforementioned cases were still not isolated ones in Aetolia: in the 3rd century on the map of this region appeared Lysimacheia, and the existence of Attaleia cannot be excluded either.[27] It is most probable, however, that none of those cities, including Ptolemias, was a royal foundation. They probably owed their foundation to the Aetolians, who in this way honoured the kings who maintained friendly relationships with them and supported them in various ways.[28] Such foundations or refoundations of the settlements under the dynastic name, conducted by the states which were on friendly terms with the kings, were not unusual in the Hellenistic world.[29] It was in this way that the close relationships between the two parties were confirmed, and the founders could count on the support of the kings, who, as is commonly known, willingly appeared in the role of *euergetai*. The Hellenistic foundations, even if they did not bear the name directly referring to a particular dynasty, did not have to be the token of their direct domination, nor the tool of organising the empire.[30] They were, however, of critical importance in terms of propaganda.

The rule of the Lagids over the particular territories of the Aegean Sea basin often lacked continuity. The range of their influences was subject to changes, and, due to the scarce basis of sources, it is difficult to determine the borders of the Ptolemaic dominions at a particular time precisely.[31] This also makes it difficult to date the cities founded or refounded by the kings of Egypt in this region. It was Ptolemy I Soter and Ptolemy II Philadelphos who played a decisive role in creating the Ptolemaic empire in the eastern part of the Mediterranean Sea basin. Interestingly, only one foundation – Ptolemias Hermiou in Egypt – can be attributed with any certainty to the former one.[32] As was rightly

---

[26] Strabo's account (10.2.22) seems to suggest that Arsinoe as Ptolemy II's wife was the founder. Researchers' opinions vary. Longega (1968, 33–35), Hammond/Walbank (1988, 236), Cohen (1995, 109), Scholten (2000, 65) believe that the foundation happened at the time of marriage between Lysiamchos and Arsinoe. Fraser (1954, 60) argues that it was when she was married to Ptolemy II. Mueller (2006, 57) proposes a hypothesis that its foundation might have been connected with the possible cooperation of Ptolemy II with the Aetolian League in the early period of his rule. But nothing, even records (though scarce) from times of the Chremonidean war, indicates that there were particularly close relationships between Ptolemy and the Aetolians, cf. Grabowski 2010, 201–205.

[27] Lysimacheia: Plb. 5.77; Liv. 36.11.7; Strabo 10.2.22, cf. Cohen 1995, 114–115; Attaleia: Allen 1983, 70.

[28] Longega 1968, 33–35; Hammond/Walbank 1988, 236; Cohen 1995, 34, 114, 119. For the relations between the Aetolians and Lysimachos, see Flacelière 1937, 80–82; Grainger 1999, 93; relations with Attalos I: Syll.[3] 523; Plb. 4.65.6; McShane 1964, 100–102; Hansen 1971, 46–49; Scholten 2000, 193–195.

[29] Cf., for example, Mantinea refounded as Antigoneia by the Achaean League (Plut. *Arat.* 45.6; Urban 1979, 157 n. 246; 179 n. 321; Cohen 1995, 123–125). The outcome of establishing close relationships by Ptolemy III with the Athenians was the establishment in Athens of a new *phyle* Ptolemias, *demos* Berenikidai (the name honoured Berenice II, Ptolemy III's wife). The cult of Ptolemy and Berenice was also established and the king's statue was erected on the Athenian agora and in Delphi; the king in turn financed the construction of a *gymnasion* called the Ptolemaion. Finally, from 224/23, the festival of *Ptolemaia* began to be held: *IG* II[2] 836; Paus. 1.5.5; 10.10.2; Steph. Byz., *s.v.* Βερενικιδαι.

[30] Mueller 2006, 58.

[31] For the Ptolemaic presence in this region, cf. Mastrocinque 1979, 66–106; Wörrle 1977; Jones/Habicht 1989; Kosmetatou 1997, 18–20; Behrwald 2000, 49–68; Sartre 2003, 59–62; Domingo Gygax 2005; Huss 2011, 150–178.

[32] *I. Philae* 166.

pointed out by K. Mueller, in comparison with the activity of the founder of the Seleucid dynasty, who was contemporary to Soter, the number of the founded settlements is modest. Mueller submitted for consideration the notion that Ptolemy I should be seen as the founder of still other settlements by providing convincing arguments in the case of Ptolemais in Cyrenaica.[33] Could one, however, associate him with one of the Ptolemaic foundations in Asia Minor, the Aegean or Cyprus known to us?

The longest-lasting dominion of the dynasty beyond Egypt was Cyprus, captured by Ptolemy I for the first time in 313 and finally in 295.[34] The island was very rich, among other things, in timber and tar, which were indispensable for developing the fleet. It was also of considerable importance for anybody who wanted to join the action on the Aegean Sea. During the fights between the *diadochoi* coalition and Antigonus I Monophthalmos, Ptolemy I also took up the action in Asia Minor and the Aegean Sea. As early as 314 Seleukos, who was acting on his behalf, undertook a military action on the coast of Ionia, where he unsuccessfully besieged Erythrai.[35] The first pieces of information about Ptolemy's interest in Caria came from this period too, although his intentions were limited at the time. Establishing cooperation with the local satrap, Asander, was aimed at winning a partner in the war with Antigonos Monophthalmos.[36] In the years 310–308, under the popular slogan of granting freedom to Greek cities, Ptolemy took up the action in Cilicia, Caria and Lycia and organised an expedition to Greece connected with the intense propaganda in the Aegean Sea, particularly in the Cyclades, which made a natural bridge between Greece and Asia Minor. He succeeded in capturing or winning the favour of some of the cities in Pamphylia, Caria and Lycia,[37] and the importance of the Aegean region for the Egyptian satrap was emphasised by choosing the island of Kos for his quarters. The Greek expedition proved less successful, although the Ptolemaic garrisons remained for a few years in Corinth, Sicyon and Megara.[38] Nevertheless, in the subsequent period Antigonos' success temporarily deprived Ptolemy of the control over Cyprus and almost certainly over the bases in Asia Minor.[39] After Antigonos' defeat at Ipsos, and then removing Demetrius I Poliorketes, Ptolemy I strengthened his influences in Lycia and probably in Pamphylia.[40] Eventually, as late as 287 he succeeded in taking

[33] Mueller 2006, 142–144.

[34] Diod. 19.62.3–6. Ptolemy temporarily lost control over Cyprus in the years 306–295/4 (Diod. 20.47–52). As regards the importance of Cyprus and its resources for the Ptolemaic fleet, see Hauben 1987a, 213–226; Mehl 1986, 216–234. Regarding the Ptolemaic rule in Cyprus, cf. Bagnall 1976, 38–79, 187–194; Mehl 1996, 234–260.

[35] Diod. 19.60.4.

[36] Diod. 19.62.2. On Asandros see Seibert 1969, 157–162; Mastrocinque 1979, 19–25.

[37] *I. Iasos* I.2; Diod. 20.27.1–2. Among the cities conquered by Ptolemy were Xanthos, Myndos, Kaunos, Phaselis, and probably also Iasos and Amyzon, cf. Bagnall 1976, 89–91; Wörrle 1977, 51; Mastrocinque 1979, 28–32; Robert/Robert 1983, 127–131: no. 6; Hauben 1987b, 3–5; Huss 2001, 173–174; Grainger 2009, 79–82.

[38] Diod. 20.37.1–2. As regards Ptolemy's expedition to Greece, see Bakhuizen 1970, 122–128; Huss 2001, 173–178; Grabowski 2008, 38–44.

[39] Cf. Will 1979/1982, I: 140; Meadows 2006, 460–461. The doubts concerning the loss of Lycia were expressed by Wörrle (1977, 52–53).

[40] Lycia: Wörrle (1977) *contra* Meadows (2006, 461–468) opts for Ptolemy II as the one who established the Ptolemaic rule in Lycia. Pamphylia: Bagnall 1976, 111–113; Huss 2011, 160–161.

over the lead in the League of the Islanders, which became the main tool of Ptolemaic politics in the Aegean Sea.

Ptolemy II Philadelphos, Ptolemy I's successor, succeeded at the beginning of his reign in expanding his rule in Asia Minor. The inscriptions confirm a number of successful attempts in Ionia, Caria, Lycia, Pamphylia, Cilicia and Samos.[41] The Chremonidean War (267–261) and the Second Syrian War (roughly 260–253) brought serious disturbances for the Ptolemies in the Aegean. The battle near Kos upset the Lagids' domination in the sea, although Philadelphos managed to retain a number of important bases.[42] However, for the benefit of the Seleucids, he lost his influences and a number of dominions in Cilicia and Pamphylia as well as Ionia. The Third Syrian War brought the restoration of the Ptolemaic influences in Asia Minor. The famous inscription from Adulis by the Red Sea lists among the territories won by Ptolemy III, among others, Ionia, Pamphylia, Cilicia and even Hellespont and Thrace.[43] The epigraphic sources also confirm the Ptolemaic presence there, but they cannot give the constant picture of the events. As a matter of fact, it seems that, except for Pamphylia,[44] the borders of the dynasty's dominions remained more or less long-lasting until the end of the 3rd century and, together with the disturbances connected with the death of Ptolemy IV and the beginning of the reign of Ptolemy V, the twilight of the Ptolemaic Empire in the eastern part of the Mediterranean Sea basin.

Among the Ptolemaic settlements commonly known to be in Asia Minor and in the islands in the eastern part of the Mediterranean Sea, only two – Arsinoe in Cilicia, near Nagidos, and Arsinoe in Cyprus, near Palaipaphos – are certain to have been new foundations.[45] Moreover, in the case of Ptolemais/Lebedos in Ionia as well as Ptolemais in Caria and Arsinoe/Marion in Cyprus, it is justified to assume that the new settlers might have been brought there.[46] According to the sources, the other five settlements can definitely be

---

41 Syll³ 390; *I. Strat.* 1002; *SEG* 1, 363; 28, 60; *TAM* II, 1; Robert/Robert 1983, 118–124: no. 3; 127 r . 5: cf. Bagnall 1976, 89–102; Wörrle 1978; Jones/Habicht 1989, 335–337; Hölbl 2001, 38; Sartre 2003, 59–60. Theocritus (*Id.* 17.86–90) summed up Ptolemaic possessions at the end of 270s, and in Asia Minor he names Cilicia, Lycia, Pamphylia and Caria.

42 For the dating of the battle of Kos, see Buraselis 1982, 146–151; Hammond/Walbank 1988, 595–599 – ca. 255 BC, *contra* Reger 1985 – ca. 261 BC. In this period the League of the Islanders ceases to be proved in the sources. To some extent, Ptolemy managed to restore his prestige in the Cyclades in the 450s, cf. *IG* XI 4.1038; 1043; Jos. Flav. *Ant. Jud.* 12.93.

43 *OGIS* 54.

44 Plb. 5.73.3–4; 77.1; cf. Huss 1976, 190.

45 Strabo 14.6.3; inscription from Arsinoe in Cilicia with commentary: Jones/Habicht 1989; Kirsten/Opelt 1989.

46 Ptolemais/Lebedos – towards the end of the 4th century. Antigonos Monopthalmos undertook the action of relocating the inhabitants of Lebedos to Teos, however, he never concluded his plan. Around 290 Lysimachos relocated the Lebedians together with the Kolophonians to Ephesus, which was refounded by him under the name of Arsinoe. The Ptolemies probably allowed the Lebedians to return to the rebuilt Lebedos: Paus. 1.9.7; 7.3.5; *I. Magn.* 53. 79–81; *RC* 3–4, cf. Cohen 1995, 188–191; Ager 1998/2000; Ma 2000, 72 n.71. Ptolemais in Caria was initially a *deme* of Kaunos: *SEG* 12, 463. Marion was destroyed by Ptolemy I in 312 BC and its people were relocated to Paphos: Diod. 19.79.4. Later on, it was probably Ptolemy who refounded the destroyed city as Arsinoe, cf. Cohen 1995, 134–136. Strabo (14.3.6) informs about rebuilding Patara by Ptolemy II and giving it a new name – Arsinoe. We do not know, however, what the rebuilding consisted in, cf. Cohen 1995, 329–330.

regarded as refoundations.[47] However, on the given assumptions it is difficult to arrive at any conclusions concerning the methods of foundation preferred by the Ptolemies since, in the case of the other seven ones, we do not possess appropriate information to allow us to determine with full certainty the way in which the settlement was established. It is also necessary in this case to pay attention to the already existing system of settlement in Asia Minor and the Aegean. As a matter of fact, the Ptolemies adjusted their settlement activity to the situation they encountered.[48] In the aforementioned regions the Greek colonisation had already developed before, and each of the regions varied in the Hellenic period. In some of them the existing settlements were more or less dispersed, and they differed from one another as far as the level of urbanisation is concerned.[49] Nothing indicates that the Ptolemies strove for unification of their dominions in terms of administration and politics; however, granting dynastic names to the founded or refounded settlements in all the foreign dominions favoured unification in the name of the dynasty.[50] The settlements bearing the name referring directly to the dynasty also included a propaganda message and constituted clear evidence of the Ptolemies' presence in a particular region. One of the most important aims of founding new settlements in Egypt was intensification of the land exploitation. In the case of the dominions in the Aegean it was political aims that dominated. Economic factors were of secondary importance; however, some of the settlements were located in the areas providing valuable natural resources, e.g. Arsinoe in Pamphylia, which was located near the forests from which timber for ship building was obtained.[51] It was similar in the case of the settlements in Pamphylia, Cilicia and Cyprus, that is in the regions rich in timber useful in ship building.

Fleets played a key role in the rivalry of Hellenic powers. As early as 314, Antigonus I Monopthalmos initiated armaments in the sea on a large scale.[52] As a result, his fleet became the mightiest power in the eastern part of the Mediterranean Sea. Such a state of affairs was maintained until the battle of Ipsos in 301 or even later. It took Ptolemy I several years to strengthen his position in the sea as well as to remove Antigonos' successor, Demetrius Poliorketes. Ptolemy I's most important achievements for building Ptolemaic thalassocracy was reinforcing his rule in Cyprus, capturing Coele-Syria, winning control over the League of the Islanders and gaining the centres of support on the coast of Asia Minor. It was of crucial importance for the Ptolemaic empire to maintain the communication routes between the dominions. Moreover, the logistics of the rivalry between the great Hellenic powers demanded a strong presence in the Aegean. Therefore, one of the most important tasks of the settlements founded by the Lagids was to support the dynasty's actions. Together with the other controlled cities, the colonies

[47] Arsinoe/Methana (*IG* IV 72; 76; XII 3.466), Arsinoe/Koressos (cf. Robert 1960, 146–160; Cohen 1995, 137–138), Arsinoe/Patara (Strabo 14.3.6), Arsinoe/Rithymna (cf. Le Rider 1966, 240–245; 1968, 231–234), Ptolemais/Larissa (cf. Robert 1982: 319–333, *contra* Cook 1988: 15).

[48] Mueller 2006, 83.

[49] Alcock 1994, 177–181, 187–189; Mueller 2006, 53–55.

[50] Mueller 2006, 84.

[51] Strabo 14.5.3. Strabo's account refers to the times of Cleopatra VII, but her predecessors surely used local forests.

[52] Diod. 19.58.1–4.

constituted convenient bases for the Ptolemaic fleet.[53] The importance of the coasts of Lycia, Pamphylia and Cilicia was emphasised by the fact that in the sea basin stretching along over six hundred kilometres down the coasts between Cyprus and Rhodes there are no islands which could be used as military bases. Taking control over those territories, or at least their seaside parts, was thus necessary. Taking into account the conditions of sailing in ancient times, winning control over those territories meant securing the sea route to the Aegean region. This was because each ship had to sail down the southern coasts of Asia Minor. The importance of the Lycian bases was additionally stressed by the fact that on the stretch between Myra and Patara it was difficult to encounter any springs of drinking water and that the shape of the coast in many places hindered or even prevented reaching the shore.[54] As early as 309, Ptolemy realised that Lycia constituted an important stopover for the expeditions from Egypt through Cyprus to the Aegean region and Greece. Therefore, most of the Ptolemaic foundations functioned as ports at the same time. A similar role was played by the settlements founded on the Aegean Sea islands, that is Keos in Crete and Arsinoe/Methana in the Argolid, which was considered to be of considerable importance. The strategic importance of Cilicia was also connected with the rivalry between the Lagids and the Seleucids. The route which was of great importance for the latter led through this territory. It connected the western Asia Minor provinces with the central part of the monarchy, that is Syria. Therefore, what can be observed in this region is unusual colonisation activity on the part of the Seleucids.[55]

Another factor which was also taken into account by the Ptolemies while founding the cities was that of the military recruitment resources of a particular region. Apart from the cleruchs, it was the mercenaries that were the second basic source of recruits. It is known, for instance, that the Cilicians provided the garrison crews in Egypt and in Cyprus, and that a close-knit group of Creteans settled down in Egypt.[56] Besides the Hellens, who constituted a predominant part of the mercenary units, among many others the inhabitants of Lycia and Pamphylia were willingly recruited. It was an important element in the politics of the kings of Egypt to maintain the influence or found settlements in the territories from which, for example from Crete, the mercenaries were particularly eager recruits.[57]

The interesting thing is that in such an important basin as the Aegean Sea there were relatively few Ptolemaic settlements; as a matter of fact, there were not more of them than in the particular regions of Asia Minor. Certainly, part of the answer to the question concerning the reasons for this phenomenon might be the natural conditions, which were unfavourable for establishing new settlements.[58] Neither can the possibility be ruled out that due to the Ptolemies' control over the League of the Islanders, the Lagids did not

[53] This aspect also accounts for the concentration of the Ptolemaic settlement on the coasts. Only in Caria and Lycia did the dynasty's influence reach further inland. Cf. Bagnall 1976, 106; Mastrocinque 1979, 43–47.

[54] Keen 1993, 72–73.

[55] Cf. Cohen 1978, 16; 1995, 55–56.

[56] Launey 1949/1950, I: 476–481; II: 1068–1072.

[57] Research into the ethnic composition of the mercenaries was conducted by Launey (1949/1950, I) and, despite numerous reservations, it still remains the most important point of reference. For soldiers from Pamphylia, cf. Bagnall 1976, 111; Brandt 1992, 87–91.

[58] Mueller 2006, 158.

feel the need to found their own settlements. The League as well as the other Ptolemaic bases were sufficient to maintain the influence in the Aegean Sea. Moreover, the Ptolemaic settlements existed in a few key places, that is in Crete, Keos and the Peloponnese (Arsinoe/Methana).

The majority of the Ptolemaic settlements were founded in the first period of the dynasty existence, both in Egypt and beyond. It was rightly pointed out that since the first Ptolemies were considerably effective in the process of colonisation, in the subsequent period there was no need to found any new settlements.[59] In the case of the territories constituting the Ptolemies' overseas empire in the eastern part of the Mediterranean Sea, the natural turning point was marked by the turn of the 2nd century, which saw the collapse of the Lagids' rule in the territories beyond Egypt. Most often it is Ptolemy II Philadelphos who is considered to have been the founder of the settlements established by the Lagids, which refers to all the regions of the dynasty's activity.[60] However, we should note that, in the case of Asia Minor, the region of the Aegean Sea, it is only with respect to the two settlements (Arsinoe/Patara, Arsinoe in Cilicia near Nagidos) that such a thesis can be supported by irrefutable, direct source information.[61] The other settlements are associated with Philadelphos on the basis of the name of the settlement and the political situation. In recent times there has been strong opposition to the practice of associating the majority of the foundations with Ptolemy II.[62]

Due to Ptolemy II's activity in Caria, the foundation of Ptolemais is ascribed to him. The existence of this *polis* is confirmed by the two inscriptions, of which the former is dated to the year 205, and the latter, on the basis of the paleographic research, to a time "earlier rather than later Hellenistic."[63] In this case, however, it must be acknowledged that the foundation of this city might have fallen in the times of Ptolemy I, who was also conducting actions in Caria, or of Ptolemy III.

Ptolemais in the neighbouring Pamphylia is also associated with Ptolemy II on the basis of his policy, which was very active in this region. The political situation in Pamphylia in the 3rd century is exceptionally vague. For sure, towards the end of the 270s Pamphylia remained under Ptolemaic control.[64] However, we cannot rule out that the dynasty's rule there had already been initiated by Ptolemy I, since the character of the first *Pamphyliarches* is confirmed possibly in 281/280.[65] Although the Lagids lost Pamphylia during the Second Syrian War, they subsequently regained it during the Laodicean War (246–242/241).[66] However, right after Ptolemy III's death they lost control over it once more,[67] and never again regained it.

[59] Mueller 2006, 81. The new settlements were still sporadically being founded in Egypt in the 1st century BC. Mueller (2006, 82) points out that the refoundations might have been established until the 2nd–1st centuries BC.

[60] Cohen 1995, 417.

[61] Strabo 14.3.6; *SEG* 39, 1426; cf. Jones/Habicht 1989, 317–346; Kirsten/Opelt 1989, 55–66.

[62] Mueller 2006, 141, 158–159, 179.

[63] Bean 1953, 21–23 no. 5; *SEG* 12, 463; *I. Magn.* 59.

[64] Theoc. *Id.* 17.88–89.

[65] Huss 2011, 160; cf. Robert 1966a, 53–58; Bagnall 1976, 111–114.

[66] *OGIS* 54, *ll.* 13–14; cf. Bagnall 1976, 114.

[67] Bagnall 1976, 197 (based on numismatic sources); cf. Huss 1976, 190–191.

The foundation of Philotera in Lycia does not arouse any major doubts when it comes to associating it with Ptolemy II.[68] Philadelphos had a sister of this name, and, according to the information provided by Strabon (16.4.5), it was after her that one of the settlements by the Red Sea was named.

In the case of Berenice in Cicilia[69] there exist two possibilities: it was either the foundation of Ptolemy II or Ptolemy III. As regards the former, the point of reference is again his activity in southern Asia Minor, confirmed, among other things, by establishing Arsinoe/Patara or Arsinoe near Nagidos in Cicilia. As far as the latter is concerned, the name of the settlement, Berenice, was his wife's name.[70] However, it is not the name itself that should settle the matter since, as is commonly known, at least one settlement bearing such a name was established by Ptolemy II. It is worth noticing that yet one more aspect weighs in favour of Ptolemy III.[71] The Laodicean war commenced as a result of the internal turbulences in the monarchy after Antiochos II's death. There were two rivals aspiring to reach power: his once dismissed first wife, Laodike, together with their son Seleukos II and the second wife, Berenice, Ptolemy III's sister, acting on behalf of her child born of the relationship with the deceased king. The defence of his sister's interests, and in particular the interests of her child, who was the rightful heir to the throne, constituted a very convenient pretext for Euergetes to intervene. At the very beginning of the conflict, the Asia Minor dominions of the dynasty sympathised with Laodike. However, it was with Berenice's success that her expedition to Cilicia ended. Her forces captured Soloi and prevented Laodike's supporters from seizing the treasure, which was worth 1500 talents.[72] In the course of the subsequent military operations, Ptolemy III took control over considerable parts of the Seleucids' state. On the basis of the peace treaty, apart from the dominions in Ionia, Caria, Pamphylia, Cilicia and even remote Thrace, he also received Seleucia Pieria – his rivals' most important port and their gateway to the Mediterranean Sea.[73] Taking control over Seleucia Pieria was also strategically important in the context of Cilicia, and vice versa. Therefore, we cannot rule out the possibility that Ptolemy III, for the sake of strengthening his position in the only just regained territory, founded a settlement there.

Recognising Ptolemais/Lebedos and Ptolemais/Larisa as Ptolemy III's foundations is fully justified. It is not known when exactly the Lagids won control over Lebedos; however, around 267–262, together with the other cities in Ionia, it honoured Antiochus I. Most probably, the recondition of the city under the name of Ptolemias was accomplished by Ptolemy III, who during the Third Syrian War regained those territories for the dynasty.[74] It is likely that during his reign, which coincided with the Third Syrian War, for the first time the Lagids won control over Hellespont. However, they lost the

[68] Wörrle 1979, 104–105; Cohen 1995, 331; Mueller 2006, 141.

[69] Steph. Byz., *s.v.* Βερενικε, no 5; Stadiasmus 190 (= *GGM* I, 485).

[70] Ptolemy II: Cohen 1995, 365; Ptolemy III: Tscherikover 1927, 188.

[71] It is absolutely certain that Berenice Troglodytike was the foundation of Ptolemy II. There are much more certain or probable foundations by Ptolemy III which were named as Berenice: one in Syria, four in the Red Sea basin.

[72] *FGrH* 160 F1, col. II, *ll.* 2–16; cf. Piejko 1990.

[73] Plb. 5.58.10; Just. 27.2.9.

[74] *OGIS* 222; cf. Piejko 1991. Cf. Cohen 1995, 189–191 for other arguments, including portraits of the royal couple on the coins identified as Ptolemy III and Berenice II.

majority of Troad during the reign of Ptolemy IV. As early as around 230–220, in one of the Delphic inscriptions on the list of *theodorokei*, the city of Larissa appeared, probably returning to its original name, which had been changed into Ptolemais as a result of the refoundation.[75]

A particularly important place in the research into the Ptolemaic settlements falls to the numerous settlements named Arsinoe which appeared in the territory in question: Arsinoe/Methana in the Argolid, Arsinoe/Koressos at Keos, Arsinoe/Patara in Lycia, Arsinoe in Pamphylia, Arsinoe in Cilicia, two on Crete (Arsinoe/Rithymna and Arsinoe Lyktou) and three on Cyprus (Arsinoe/Marion, Arsinoe near Salamis and Arsinoe near Palaipaphos).[76] The foundation of all of them – or at least the considerable majority – is often attributed to Ptolemy II. It is connected with his policy of developing the fleet. In this logically proposed interpretation, the cities of this name were supposed to be the manifestation of the Ptolemaic *thalassocracy* and the influences of Arsinoe II. These settlements were, above all, ports which were used by the Ptolemaic fleet.[77] It has also been pointed out that the cities bearing this name were often situated in the regions rich in timber, which was used in ship building (Cyprus, Pamphylia).[78] There is every likelihood that the appearance of Arsinoe/Methana and Arsinoe/Koressos ought to be associated with the Chremonidean War.[79] Those two places were, in fact, of great strategic importance. Arsinoe/Methana, situated in Argolid on the protruding into the sea peninsula, allowed the sea traffic in the Saronic Gulf to be controlled. A Ptolemaic garrison was based there, and the city played the role of the port which was important for the Egyptian fleet.[80] The Ptolemaic epistates resided on Keos,[81] which possessed an excellent port. It goes without saying that Cilician, Lycian and Cretan Arsinoes were also of critical strategic importance.[82] As regards the last ones, there were attempts to associate their refoundations on the basis of the interest in the island on the part of the aforementioned ruler; however, it is more plausible to acknowledge them as the attainment of Ptolemy II.[83]

[75] Cook 1973, 219–222; Robert 1982, 319–333; Cohen 1995, 157–159. It was Cook (1988, 15) who expressed his reservations concerning associating Larissa with Ptolemais. As regards the permanence of the Ptolemies' rule in the region of Hellespont, see Plb. 5.78.6; cf. Bagnall 1976, 159–162; Robert 1982, 327–330. Huss (1976, 209) claims that Ptolemy IV did not control any of the cities in Troad.

[76] There were much more Ptolemaic settlements named Arsinoe (in Coele-Syria, Cyrenaica, Red Sea basin).

[77] So Cohen 1995, 35. For the importance of wood in Cyprus for the Ptolemaic fleet, cf. Strabo 16.6.2.

[78] Cohen 1995, 135, 335–336.

[79] Arsinoe/Methana: Heinen 1972, 131; Gill/Foxhall/Bowden 1997, 74; Mueller 2006, 65; cf. also Bagnall 1976, 135; Cohen 1995, 125 (they believe that the refoundation was made shortly after the death of Arsinoe II). Arsinoe/Koressos: Cherry/Davis/Matzourani 1991, 240; Cohen 1995, 137; Mueller 2006, 65.

[80] L. Robert (1960, 159) aptly compared Methana to Gibraltar. It is unclear since when it had been in the Ptolemaic hands, most likely since the Chremonidean War. Cf. also Meyer 1935, 1375–1379; Bagnall 1976, 135–136; Cohen 1995, 124–126; Gill/Foxhall/Bowden 1997, 68–76.

[81] *IG* XII 5.1061; cf. Bagnall 1976, 141–142; Huss 2011, 175.

[82] For the importance of Arsinoe/Patara as a naval base, cf. Robert 1960, 155. Arsinoe in Cilicia: Jos. Flav. *Ant. Jud.* 12.149; cf. Cohen 1995, 135; 335–336. Identification of Arsinoe Lyktou is not certain; most probably it was a port city: Le Rider 1966, 242; 1968, 230; Cohen 1995, 132.

[83] We do not know any settlement of the name of Arsinoe which, contrary to Ptolemy II, could be certainly regarded as Ptolemy IV's foundation. It cannot be ruled out that Ptolemy IV might have refounded Arsinoe Lyktou, which had earlier been founded by his grandfather (in 220–219 the city was destroyed by

There have been several counter-arguments raised against attributing all the settlements known as Arsinoe as well as the predominant majority of the other settlements to Ptolemy II. It has been pointed out that the dynastic toponyms are of lesser importance, the Ptolemaic rule on the territories was unstable, and there were permanent clashes of interest among the Lagids, Seleucids and Antigonids. The process of Ptolemaic colonisation in Asia Minor was meant to resemble a patchwork, within the framework of which the subsequent rulers added new settlements and refounded the old ones.[84] The argument concerning the lack of stability of the spheres of influence seems to be justified, except for Cyprus. Rule over the island since 295 had not been threatened for a long time. On the other hand, it cannot be ruled out that it might also explain the possibly weak activity of Ptolemy I in terms of founding or refounding settlements. In the reality of the epoch, which was filled with the diadochus wars, changing coalitions and the borders of influences, such activity might have been difficult to conduct beyond the territories where his rule was more stable (Egypt, Cyrenaica).

In the case of the settlements named after Arsinoe, however, the fact is that, apart from Ptolemy II's sister-wife, Arsinoe II Philadelphos, in the 3rd century there was only one important member of the dynasty by this name: Arsinoe III, Ptolemy IV's sister-wife.[85] The king in question did not pursue such active politics outside as his predecessors, which raises doubts concerning his settlement activity, although it cannot be ruled out. Ptolemy II proved himself to be a skilled organiser and a man of broad horizons as far as foreign policy was concerned, who extended his political and diplomatic influence as far as India and Italia.[86] One of the fields of Philadelphos's activity was religious policy. He played a decisive role in the organisation of the dynastic cult. It is not impossible that even the marriage to his sister was a part of Ptolemy's intricate religious policy in terms of the dynastic cult. Ptolemy II and Arsinoe II were united in matrimony, following Zeus and Hera's footsteps, which gave rise to the development of the cult of θεοὶ ἀδελφοί.[87] A significant role in the dynastic cult was also played by the separate cult of Arsinoe II. The queen's cult, both in the Egyptian and Greek forms, had very many aspects, one of which was her identification with Aphrodite.[88] Aphrodite was an Olympic deity, who, apart from Dionysius, enjoyed particular support from the Ptolemies. As Isis-Aphrodite, Arsinoe, followed by the other Egyptian queens, became the guarantor of the

Knossos: Plb. 4.53.3–54.3). Cf. Huss 1976, 154–156; Cohen 1995, 133, 139 *contra* Tscherikover 1927, 7 (Arsinoe Lyktou); Le Rider 1966, 140; 1968, 239 (Arsinoe/Rithymna); Bagnall 1976, 119, 201 (Arsinoe/Rithymna, more cautious).

[84] Mueller 2006, 158.

[85] There is no evidence that Arsinoe, Ptolemy I's mother, or Arsinoe I, Lysimachus' daughter and Ptolemy II's first wife played a significant role in the politics and ideology of the monarchy.

[86] *Corpus Inscriptionum Indicarum* I, 25; Liv. *per.* 14; Plin. *NH* 6.58; App. *Sic.* 1.2; Cass. Dio 10. frg. 41; Just. 18.2.9; Eutr. 2.15; cf. Lampela 1998, 32–56; Huss 2001, 301.

[87] It cannot be ruled out, however, that the remarks expressed explicitly or the allusions of this kind which were present in the Alexandrian poetry of the time (cf. Theoc., *Id.* 17.131–134) were an attempt made by the poets associated with the court to justify the steps taken by the ruler in the eyes of the Greeks (as it is commonly acknowledged), but that they reflected the actual intentions of the monarch. For this topic: Carney 1987, 430; Hazzard 2000, 89–90.

[88] Tondriau 1948, 16–18. On the cult of Arsinoe, see Fraser 1972, I: 197–198, 228–246; Plantzos 1991/1992; Hölbl 2001, 101–104; Barbantini 2008, 121–132.

dynasty's continuation. The role of Arsinoe-Aphrodite as a patron of sailors was particularly strongly emphasised. Kallikrates of Samos, commander of the Ptolemaic fleet, built the temple of Arsinoe-Aphrodite, also known as Arsinoe-Aphrodite-Zephyritis, on the Zephyrion peninsula, near Kanopos.[89] Ptolemy II managed to create the cult of the new goddess, who descended from the dynasty, and to popularise it in the eastern part of the Mediterranean Sea basin. The votive tablets with the name of Arsinoe, found in numerous littoral cities, can be used as evidence of the importance of the cult for the people of the time.[90] The feast of *Arsinoeia* was held on Thera, and the feast of *Philadelpheia* was organised on Delos.[91] Traces of the cult, certainly, can also be found in the cities named after her: e.g. the temple in Arsinoe in Cilicia and the altar dedicated to Arsinoe in Arsinoe/Marion.[92] It therefore seems that this is one more argument weighing in favour of Ptolemy II as the founder or refounder of the settlements named after his sister-wife. Not only was this a large-scale plan in terms of the strategic importance of the particular places, but it also functioned as a scheme immensely charged with religious and propaganda issues.[93]

The Ptolemaic colonisation in Asia Minor and in the Aegean thus had a few goals connected with the imperial policy of the dynasty. Apart from the strategic significance, which in the rivalry between the superpowers of the time and due to the vastness of the Ptolemaic empire was of critical importance, the settlements functioned as a means of control. In Ptolemy II's politics they additionally played a propaganda and religious role. They also constituted the proof of the power of the dynasty. The settlements founded as *polis*, through their contacts with the other cities of the Greek world, provided clear evidence of the Ptolemies' presence in a particular region, which, supported by the euergetism of the Egyptian kings, was an important weapon used in the fight for hegemony in the eastern part of the Mediterranean Sea basin.

BIBLIOGRAPHY

Alcock S.E. (1994): Breaking up the Hellenistic World: Survey and Society, in: L. Morris (ed.), *Classical Greece: Ancient Histories and Modern Archeologies*, Cambridge: 171–190.

Ager, S.L. (1998/2000): Civic Identity in the Hellenistic World: The Case of Lebedos, *GRBS* 39: 5–21.

Allen, R.E. (1983): *The Attalid Kingdom*, Oxford.

Bagnall, R.S. (1976): *The Administration of Ptolemaic Possesions outside Egypt*, Leiden.

Bagnall, R.S. (1984): The Origins of Ptolemaic Cleruchs, *BASP* 21: 7–20.

Bakhuizen, S.C. (1970): *Salganeus and the Fortifications on Its Mountains*, Groningen.

89 Posidip. frg. 12–13 Gow-Page. See Fraser 1972, I: 239–240, 568–569; Hauben 1983, 111–114.

90 *IG* XI.4.1303; XII.2.513; XII.3.462; 1386; XII.7. 99; 263–264; *OGIS* 34; Mitford 1961, 7–9, nos. 12–14; Robert 1966b, 175–211; Bruneau 1970, 544; Brun 1991, 101–102 no. 2; cf. Hölbl 2001, 104.

91 *IG* XII 3. 1343; Bruneau 1970, 528–530.

92 Segre 1937; Hermary 1988, 102; Jones/Habicht 1989, 318; Kirsten/Opelt 1989, 57–61.

93 Similarly Marquaille (2008, 59–60), who emphasised the importance of naming habits in Ptolemy II's policy.

Barbantani, S. (2005): Goddess of Love and Mistress of the Sea. Notes on a Hellenistic Hymn to Arsinoe-Aphrodite (P.Lit Goodsp. 2 I–IV), *AncSoc* 35: 135–165.
Barbantani, S. (2008): Arsinoe II Filadelfo nell'interpretazione storiografica moderna, nel culto e negli epigrammi del P.Mil.Vogl. VIII 309, in: L. Castagna, C. Riboldi (eds.), *Amicitiae templa serena. Studi in onore di Giuseppe Aricò*, vol. I, Milano: 103–134.
Bean, G.E. (1953): Notes and Inscriptions from Caunus, *JHS* 73: 10–35.
Behrwald, R. (2000): *Der Lykische Bund. Untersuchungen zur Geschichte und Verfassung*, Bonn.
Brandt, H. (1992): *Gesselschaft und Wirtschaft Pamphyliens und Pisidiens im Altertum*, Bonn.
Braunert, H. (1964): Hegemoniale Bestrebungen der Hellenistischen Grossmächte in Politik und Wirtschaft, *Historia* 13: 80–104.
Brun, P. (1991): Les Lagides à Lesbos: Essai de Chronologie, *ZPE* 85: 99–113.
Bruneau, P. (1970): *Recherches sur les cultes de Déelos à l'époque hellenistique et à l'époque impériale*, Paris.
Buraselis, K. (1982): *Das hellenistische Makedonien und die Ägäis*, München.
Burstein, S.M. (1996): Ivory and Ptolemaic Exploration of the Red Sea. The Missing Factor, *Topoi* 6: 799–807.
Carney, E.D. (1987): The Reappearance of Royal Sibling Marriage in Ptolemaic Egypt, *PP* 42: 420–439.
Chaniotis, A. (1993): Ein diplomatischer Staathalter nimmt Rucksicht auf den verletzten Stolz zweier hellenistischer Kleinpoleis (Nagidos und Arsinoe), *EA* 21: 33–42.
Cherry, J.F., Davis, J.L., Matzourani, E. (eds.) (1991): *Landscape Archaeology as Long-Term History. Northern Keos in the Cycladic Islands from earliest Settlement until Modern Times*, Los Angeles.
Cohen, G.M. (1978): *The Seleucid Colonies: Studies in Founding, Administration and Organization*, Wiesbaden.
Cohen, G.M. (1983): Colonization and Population Transfer in the Hellenistic World, in: E. van't Dack (ed.), *Egypt and the Hellenistic World. Proceeedings of the International colloquium, Leuven 24–26 May 1982*, Leuven: 63–74.
Cohen, G.M. (1995): *The Hellenistic Settlements in Europe, the Islands, and Asia Minor*, Berkeley–Los Angeles.
Cohen, G.M. (2006): *The Hellenistic Settlements in Syria, the Red Sea Basin, and North Africa*, Berkeley–Los Angeles.
Cook, J.M. (1973): *The Troad*, Oxford.
Cook, J.M. (1988): Cities in and Around the Troad, *ABSA* 83: 7–19.
Davesne, A. (1998): Reflexions sur l'histoire du site, in: A. Davesne, F. Laroche Traunecker (eds.), *Le Site de Meydancikkale. Recherches entreprises sous la direction d'Emmanuel Laroche (1971–1982)*, Paris: 63–67.
Davesne, A., Le Rider, G. (1989): *Le Trésor de Meydancikkale (Cilicie Trachée, 1980)*, Paris.
Dietze, G. (1994): Philae und die Dodekaschoinos in Ptolemäischer Zeit. Ein Beitrag zur Frage Ptolemäischer Präsenz im Grenzland zwischen Ägypten und Afrika an Hand der architektonischen und epigraphischen Quellen, *AncSoc* 25: 63–110.
Domingo Gygax, M. (2005): Change and Continuity in the Administration of Ptolemaic Lycia. A Note on P.Tebt. I 8, *BASP* 42: 45–50.
Errington, R.M. (2008): *A History of the Hellenistic World 323–30 BC*, Oxford.
Flacelière, R. (1937): *Les Aitoliens à Delphes. Contribution à l'histoire de la Grèce centrale au IIIe siècle av. J.-C.*, Paris.
Fraser, P.M. (1954): Two Hellenistic Inscriptions from Delphi, *BCH* 78: 49–67.
Fraser, P.M. (1972): *Ptolemaic Alexandria*, vol. I–III, Oxford.
Gill, D., Foxhall, L., Bowden, H. (1997): Classical and Hellenistic Methana, in: C. Mee, H. Forbes (eds.), *A Rough and Rocky Place. The Landscape and Settlement History of the Methana Peninsula, Greece*, Liverpool: 62–76.

Grabowski, T. (2008): Ptolemy's Military and Political Operations in Greece in 314–308 BC, *Electrum* 14: 33–46.
Grabowski, T. (2010): Związek Etolski w polityce greckiej pierwszych Ptolemeuszy, in: E. Dąbrowa *et al.* (eds.), *Hortus Historiae. Księga pamiątkowa ku czci Profesora Józefa Wolskiego w setną rocznicę urodzin*, Kraków: 191–216.
Grabowski, T. (2012): The Ptolemies versus the Achaean and Aetolian Leagues in the 250s–220s BC, *Electrum* 19: 83–98.
Grainger, J.D. (1999): *The League of the Aitolians*, Leiden.
Grainger, J.D. (2009): *The Cities of Pamphylia*, Oxford.
Habicht, C. (1980): Bemerkungen zum P. Haun 6, *ZPE* 39: 1–5.
Hammond, N.G.L., Walbank, F.W. (1988): *A History of Macedonia*, vol. III, Oxford.
Hansen, E.V. (1971): *The Attalids of Pergamon*, New York.
Hauben, H. (1983): Arsinoé II et la politique extérieure de l'Égypte, in: E. van't Dack, P. van Dessel, W. van Gucht W. (eds.), *Egypt and the Hellenistic World. Proceedings of the International Colloquium Leuven 24–26 May 1982*, Leuven: 99–127.
Hauben, H. (1987a): Cyprus and the Ptolemaic Navy, *RDAC*: 213–226.
Hauben, H. (1987b): On the Ptolemaic Iasos Inscription IGSK 28.1, 2–3, *EA* 10: 3–6.
Hazzard, R.A. (2000): *Imagination of a Monarchy: Studies in Ptolemaic Propaganda*, Toronto.
Heinen, H. (1972): *Untersuchungen zur hellenistischen Geschichte des 3. Jahrhunderts v. Chr. Zur Geschichte der Zeit des Ptolemaios Keraunos und zum Chremonideischen Krieg*, Wiesbaden.
Hermary, A. (1988): Le culte d'Aphrodite a Amathonte, *RDAC* 2: 101–109.
Hölbl, G. (2001): *A History of the Ptolemaic Empire*, London.
Huss, W. (1976): *Untersuchungen zur Aussenpolitik Ptolemaios' IV*, München.
Huss, W. (2001): *Ägypten in hellenistischer Zeit 332–30 v.Chr.*, München.
Huss, W. (2011): *Die Verwaltung des Ptolemaischen Reichs*, München.
Jones, C.P., Habicht, C. (1989): A Hellenistic Inscription from Arsinoe in Cilicia, *Phoenix* 43: 317–346.
Jouquet, P. (1948): Les Assemblees d'Alexandrie a l'epoque Ptolemaique, *BSAA* 37: 71–92.
Keen, A. (1993): Gateway from the Aegean to the Mediterranean. The strategic Value of Lycia down to the Fourth Century B.C., in: J. Borchardt, G. Dobesch (eds.), *Akten des II. Internationalen Lykien-Symposions, Wien 6–12 Mai 1990*, Wien: 71–77.
Kemp, B.J. (1977): The Early Development of Towns in Egypt, *Antiquity* 51: 185–200.
Kemp, B.J. (2009): *Starożytny Egipt. Anatomia cywilizacji*, Warszawa.
Kirsten, E., Opelt, I. (1989): Eine Urkunde der Gründung von Arsinoe in Kilikien, *ZPE* 77: 55–66.
Klose, P. (1972): *Die völkerrechtliche Ordnung der hellenistischen Staaten in der Zeit von 280 bis 168 v. Chr. Ein Beitrag zur Geschichte des Völkerrechts*, München.
Kobes, J. (1996): *Kleine Konige: Untersuchungen Zu Den Lokaldynasten im hellenistischen Kleinasien (323–188 v. Chr.)*, St. Katharinen.
Kosmetatou, E. (1997): Pisidia and Hellenistic Kings from 323 to 133 BC, *AncSoc* 28: 5–37.
Lampela, A. (1998): *Rome and the Ptolemies of Egypt. The Development of Their Political Relations 273–80 B.C.*, Helsinki.
Launey, M. (1949–1950): *Recherches sur les armées hellénistiques*, vol. I–II, Paris.
Le Rider, G. (1966): *Monnaies crétoises du V au I siècle av. J.-C.*, Paris.
Le Rider, G. (1968): Les Arsinoéens de Crete, in: C.M. Kray, G.K. Jenkins (eds.), *Essays in Greek Coinage Presented to Stanley Robinson*, Oxford: 229–240.
Longega, G. (1968): *Arsinoe II*, Roma.
Ma, J. (2000): *Antiochos III and the Cities of Western Asia Minor*, Oxford.
Magie, D. (1939): The „Agreement" between Philip V and Antiochus III for the Partition of the Egyptian Empire, *JRS* 29: 32–44.
Marquaille, C. (2008): The Foreign Policy of Ptolemy II, in: P. McKechnie, P. Guillaume (eds.), *Ptolemy II Philadelphus and his World*, Leiden: 39–64.

Marrinan, R. (1998): *The Ptolemaic Army: Its Organization, Development and Settlement*, University College London (Unpublished PhD Thesis).

Mastrocinque, A. (1979): *La Caria e Ionia Meridionale in Epoca Hellenistica (323–188 a.C.)*, Roma.

McDonald, A.H., Walbank, F.W. (1937): The Origins of the Second Macedonian War, *JRS* 27: 180–207.

McShane, R.M. (1964): *The Foreign Policy of the Attalids of Pergamum*, Urbana.

Meadows, A. (2006): The Ptolemaic Annexation of Lycia, SEG 27.929, in: K. Dörtlük *et al.* (eds.), *The IIIrd Symposium of Lycia. 7–10 November 2005, Antalya. Symposium Proceedings*, vol. 2, Antalya: 459–470.

Mehl, A. (1996): Militärwesen und Verwaltung der Ptolemäer in Zypern, *RCCM* 38: 215–260.

Meyer, E. (1935), Methana, *RE* XV, 2: 1375–1379.

Mitford, T.B. (1961): The Hellenistic Inscriptions of Old Paphos, *ABSA* 56: 1–39.

Mueller, K. (2006): *Settlements of the Ptolemies: City Foundations and New Settlement in the Hellenistic World*, Leuven.

Papazoglou, F. (1988): *Les villes de Macédoine à l'époque romaine*, Paris.

Piejko, F. (1991): Decree of the Ionian League in Honor of Antiochus I, ca 267–262 B.C., *Phoenix* 45: 126–147.

Piejko, F. (1990): Episodes from the Third Syrian War in a Gurob papyrus, 246 BC, *ArchPF* 36: 13–27.

Plantzos, D. (1991–1992): ΕΚΘΕΩΣΙΣ ΑΡΣΙΝΟΗΣ. On the Cult of Arsinoe Philadelphos, *Archaiognosia* 7: 119–133.

Reger, G. (1985): The Date of the Battle of Kos, *AJAH* 10: 155–177.

Robert, J., Robert, L. (1983): *Fouilles d'Amyzon en Carie*, vol. I, Paris.

Robert, L. (1960): Sur un décret des Korésiens au musée de Smyrne, *Hellenica* 11–12: 132–176.

Robert, L. (1966a): *Documents de l'Asie Mineure Méridionale. Inscriptions, monnaies et géographie*, Genéve–Paris.

Robert, L. (1966b): Sur un décret d'Ilion et un papyrus concernant ds cultes royaux, *AmStP* 1: 175–211 (= *id.*, *Opera Minora Selecta*, vol. VII, Amsterdam 1990: 599–635).

Robert, L. (1982): Documents d'Asie Mineure, *BCH* 106: 309–378.

Rostovtzeff, M. (1941): *The Social and Economic History of the Hellenistic World*, vol. I–III, Oxford.

Sartre, M. (2001): *D'Alexandre à Zénobie. Histoire du Levant antique IVe siècle avant J.-C. – IIIe siècle après. J.-C.*, Paris.

Sartre, M. (2003): *L'Anatolie hellénistique de l'Égée au Caucase (334–31 av. J.-C.)*, Paris.

Schmitt, G. (1995): *Die Siedlungen Palästinas in griechisch-römischer Zeit*, Wiesbaden.

Schmitt, H.H. (1964): *Untersuchungen zur Geschichte Antiochos' des Grossen und seine Zeit*, Wiesbaden.

Schmitt, H.H. (1969): *Die Staatsverträge des Altertums III. Die Verträge der griechisch-römischen Welt von 338 bis 200 v. Chr.* München.

Schmitt, H.H. (1974): Polybios und das gleichgewicht der Mächte, in: E. Gabba (ed.), *Polybe*, Genève: 67–93.

Scholten, J.B. (2000): *Politics of Plunder. Aitolians and Their Koinon in the Early Hellenistic Era, 279–217 B.C.*, Berkeley–Los Angeles.

Schwartz, J. (1978): Athenes et L'Etolie dans la politique lagide (à la lumière de P. Haun 6), *ZPE* 30: 95–100.

Segre, M. (1937): Il culto di Arsinoe Filadelfo nelle citta greche, *BSAA* 31: 286–298.

Seibert, J. (1969): *Untersuchungen zur Geschichte Ptolemiaos' I.*, München.

Serrati, J. (2008): Warfare and The State, in: P. Sabin, H. van Wees, M. Whitby (eds.), *Cambridge History of Greek and Roman Warfare*, vol. I, Cambridge: 461–497.

Sidebotham, S.E. (1986): Ports of Red Sea and the Arabia-India Trade, *MBAH* 5: 16–36.

Sidebotham, S.E. (1996): An Overwiev of Archaeological Work in Eastern Desert, *Topoi* 6: 773–783.

Sidebotham, S.E. (2002): From Berenike to Koptos. Recent Results of the Desert Route Survey, *Topoi Suppl.* 3: 415–438.

Thompson, L.A. (1969): Easter Africa and the Graeco-Roman World (to A.D. 64), in: J. Ferguson, L.A. Thompson (eds.), *Africa in Classical Antiquity. Nine Studies*, Ibadan: 26–59.

Tondriau, J. (1948): Princesses ptolémaiques comparées ou identifiées à des déesses, *BSAA* 37: 12–33.

Tscherikover, W. (1927): *Die hellenistischen Städtegrünfungen von Alexander dem Grossen bis auf die Römerzeit*, Leipzig.

Uebel, F. (1968): *Die Kleruchen Ägyptens unter den ersten sechs Ptolemäern*, Berlin.

Urban, R. (1979): *Wachstum und Krise des Achäischen Bundes. Quellenstudien zur Entwicklung des Bundes von 280 bis 222 v. Chr.*, Wiesbaden.

Will, É. (1979–1982): *Histoire politique du monde hellénistique (323–30 av. J.-C.)*, vol. I–II, Nancy.

Wörrle, M. (1977): Epigraphische Forschungen zur Geschichte Lykiens I, *Chiron* 7: 43–66.

Wörrle, M. (1978): Epigraphische Forschungen zur Geschichte Lykiens II. Ptolemaios II und Telmessos, *Chiron* 8: 201–246.

Wörrle, M. (1979): Epigraphische Forschungen zur Geschichte Lykiens III, *Chiron* 9: 83–111.

ELECTRUM * Vol. 20 (2013): 77–115
doi: 10.4467/20800909EL.13.005.1434

Die städtischen Eliten der Kolonien der syrischen Tetrapolis zwischen Seleukiden, Armeniern, Parthern und Römern*

David Engels
Université Libre de Bruxelles

Abstract: The following paper proposes, for the first time, an exhaustive overview over the situation of the late-Hellenistic local elites of the Syrian tetrapolis (Antiochia, Seleucia, Apamea, Laodicea), a first part concerning the late-Seleucid situation from the death of Antiochus IV onwards, a second one the movemented decades of the Armenian, Parthian and Roman Republican era. Both parts first analyse the general political situation of the Syrian elites on the basis of our literary and numismatical sources in order to sketch the interaction between the respective communal and the imperial level, then systematically discuss the prosopographical evidence.

Key words: Syria, Antiochia, Seleucia, Apamea, Laodicea, Seleucids, Parthians, Armenia, Elites, Colonies, Prosopography, Numismatics.

Einleitung

Nordsyrien stellte seit der Herrschaft der Seleukiden eines der wichtigsten strategischen Gebiete des antiken Mittelmeerraumes dar. Mit der Gründung der aus dem Stadtviereck Antiocheia-Seleukeia-Apameia-Laodikeia bestehenden syrischen Tetrapolis und des sie umgebenden Rings weiterer Siedlungen[1] unterlag die bis dahin weltpolitisch nur sekundär hervorgetretene Region einem massiven Hellenisierungs- und Urbanisierungsprozess, welcher das Gebiet zwischen Euphrat, Antitauros, Mittelmeer und Libanon in

* Vorliegender Beitrag ist im Rahmen eines von der Gerda Henckel-Stiftung finanzierten Forschungsprojekts zu antiken Eliten entstanden, welches von Peter Mittag und Boris Dreyer betreut wurde. Ihnen und den zahlreichen anderen Mitarbeitern sei an dieser Stelle herzlich für die angenehme Zusammenarbeit und die interessanten Forschungsanregungen gedankt.

[1] Neben der Tetrapolis, der man aufgrund seiner Bedeutung noch Arados hinzuzählen kann, sind als Städte zweiten Ranges Alexandreia-Issos, Beroia und Zeugma zu nennen, denen dann Nikopolis, Hierapolis, Chalkis, Gabala, Herakleia-ad-Mare und die Siedlungen bei Ras Ibn Hani und Ras el-Basit nachzuordnen sind. Zusätzlich sind noch Siedlungen wie Hamath („Epiphaneia“ seit Antiochos IV), Laodikeia-ad-Libanum, Emesa und Mariamme zu nennen. Vgl. hierzu die Analyse bei Grainger 1990, 120–136.

einen wichtigen Knotenpunkt wirtschaftlicher, politischer und militärischer Kontakte umwandeln sollte, in dem sich, als Resultat einer komplexen historischen Entwicklung, Laodikeia und Seleukeia zu den zentralen Hafenstädte Nordsyriens,[2] Apameia zum logistischen Zentrum des seleukidischen Heeres[3] und Antiocheia zur Hauptresidenz der Seleukiden entwickeln sollten;[4] vier Städte, zu denen man schließlich seiner Bedeutung halber Arados hinzuzählen kann. Die Gründung und großzügige Förderung dieser und anderer neuen Städte hatten allerdings nicht nur positive Folgen für die wirtschaftliche Integration und staatliche Kohäsion des Seleukidenreiches: Zum einen riefen Wachstum und Reichtum zumindest einiger dieser Poleis bei ihrer kommunalen Elite das zunehmende Bedürfnis hervor, ihre Angelegenheiten autonomer von der Zentralmacht und ihrem chronischen Bedarf nach Steuergeldern und Truppen zu regeln. Zum anderen zwang der außenpolitische Zerfall des Seleukidenreichs seit dem Tod Antiochos' III. die Poleis, das allmähliche Ordnungsvakuum auszufüllen und den mittlerweile auch außenpolitischen Handlungsspielraum zu nutzen, um Einfluß und Konkurrenzfähigkeit der eigenen Stadt wie auch die effektive Beherrschung des jeweiligen landwirtschaftlichen Umlands, der *Peraia*, langfristig zu sichern.

Den kommunalen Eliten kam hierbei also notgedrungen eine tragende Funktion bei der Umstrukturierung des syrischen Großraums vom Kerngebiet des seleukidischen Staates zu einer wichtigen Außenprovinz des römischen Reichs zu, wobei ihre aktive Einwirkung auf die verwickelten Ereignisse jener Zeit die große politische Eigenständigkeit dieser Führungsschichten beweist. Die folgende Untersuchung, welche erstmals einen Überblick über die spezifische Situation der lokalen Eliten in den seleukidischen Kolonien der Tetrapolis liefern soll, ist angesichts der Disparität der Quellenlage wie auch der Besonderheiten der betreffenden Übergangszeit zweigeteilt: In einer ersten Untersuchungsphase soll v.a. die spätseleukidische Zeit, also ab dem Tode Antiochos' IV., beleuchtet werden; in einer zweiten wird dann der Beginn der römisch-parthischen Zeit analysiert. Jeder dieser Teile ist in sich durch einen doppelten methodischen Zugang geprägt: In einem ersten Teilschritt soll durch gezielte Auswertung unserer sehr beschränkten historiographischen und numismatischen Zeugnisse versucht werden, die kommunale Perspektive der Krise des seleukidischen Syrien und der späteren Aufnahme der Tetrapolis ins römische Provinzialsystem nachzuzeichnen, um Interessensdivergenzen zwischen Poleis und Reich aufzuzeigen und die daraus hervorgehenden Abweichungen bei der Auffindung konkreter politischer Grundsatzentscheidungen und Krisenlösungen herauszuarbeiten. Nur in seltenen Fällen ist es allerdings möglich, in spätseleukidischer wie in frührömischer Zeit von der kommunalen Ebene auf das Niveau der lokalen Eliten selbst zu gelangen. In einem zweiten Schritt soll versucht werden, durch Auswertung unserer spärlichen prosopographischen Dokumentation einige Fallbeispiele zu kompi-

[2] Seleukeia war ursprünglich wohl als Hauptort Syriens gedacht, wie auch der Name und die Anlage der Königsgräber (Polyb. 4,48) zeigen. Laodikeias Wachstum litt teils unter der Besatzung Seleukeias durch ptolemaische Truppen, deren Einflußbereich bis wenige Kilometer vor Laodikeia reichte.

[3] Strabon 16, 2, 10 (C 752).

[4] Es ist hierbei natürlich nicht zu vergessen, daß das seleukidische Königtum wie das achaimenidische wesentlich ein „Wanderkönigtum“ darstellte und Antiocheia erst, als das Reich auf Syrien und Mesopotamien beschränkt war, die Rolle der ständigen Residenz spielte, die es vorher mit Ephesos oder Seleukeia-Tigris teilte. Vgl. Marinoni 1972; Held 2002.

lieren, um die Tätigkeit einzelner Mitglieder der städtischen Eliten Syriens und ihrer Funktion als Mittler oder Krisenfaktor zwischen Stadt und Reich zu rekonstruieren.

1. Von Antiochos IV zu Tigranes

1.1. Allgemeine historische Entwicklung

Ursprünglich verfügten die Städte der Tetrapolis als seleukidische Gründungen wohl nur über eine recht begrenzte innere Autonomie und unterlagen der engen Kontrolle der seleukidischen Verwaltung, welche durch Garnisonen wie auch königliche Statthalter vertreten war.[5] Nominell waren die syrischen Städte als gemäßigte Demokratien nach dem Vorbild der nur begrenzt autonomen makedonischen Städte verfaßt,[6] wenn es in der Realität wie auch in den zeitgenössischen alten griechischen Poleis wohl eher oligarchische Eliten waren, die das Regiment führten.[7] Städtische Magistrate in toto sind sowohl für Seleukeia-Pierien als auch für Antiocheia 246 belegt;[8] Seleukeia verfügte unter Seleukos IV. über Magistrate, Demen, Phylen, einen Sekretär und ein Bouleuterion;[9] Antiocheia erhielt 170 unter Antiochos IV. ebenfalls ein Bouleuterion;[10] und die städtischen Magistrate von Laodikeia trugen den makedonischen Namen *peliganes*[11] und zeigen, daß es makedonische Institutionen waren, die zumindest bei dieser Gründung Pate gestanden hatten. Alle drei Städte sahen in einer Inschrift der Zeit Antiochos' III. den *demos* ausdrücklich als lokalen Souverän an,[12] wie auch die noch zu besprechende Münzprägung Seleukeias und Antiocheias in den 140er Jahren belegt.[13]

Die politische Krise des Seleukidenreichs seit der Niederlage gegen die Römer und dem Vertrag von Apameia im Jahr 188 bewirkten allerdings eine zunehmende innere Schwächung des Reichs, welches sich, nach dem erneuten Höhepunkt außenpolitischer Macht unter Antiochos III., nun unversehens dem Verlust der transtaurischen Gebiete, massiven Kriegsentschädigungen, erzwungener Abrüstung und dem Zusammenbruch der neugeschaffenen iranischen Feudalordnung[14] gegenübersah. Auf lange Sicht hin konnte das Reich sich in Anbetracht seiner prekären militärischen, finanziellen und au-

[5] Letzterer ist z.B. für Seleukeia allerdings erst ab 186 belegt, vgl. *IGLS* III 1183 = *RC* 45 = Austin 176. Zur Verwaltung seleukidischer Städte vgl. Bikerman 1938; Orth 1977; Cohen 1978; Quass 1979; Grainger 1990; Rey-Cocquais 1991; Capdetrey 2007. Zur Zielsetzung der Gründung vgl. Brodersen 2001.

[6] Hierzu Papazoglou 2000.

[7] Jones 1940, 157–169.

[8] Vgl. *P. Gurob* = *FGrH* 160 F 1 mit der Schilderung verschiedener Institutionen, welche Ptolemaios III. 246 bei seinem Einzug in diese Städte begrüßten (Würdenträger, Satrapen, Garnisonskommandanten, Soldaten, Priester, Magistrate, Gymnasiasten etc.). Hierzu ausführlich Piejko 1990.

[9] *IGLS* III 1183 = *RC* 45. Zum Ausgangsschreiben des Königs s. weiter unten.

[10] Malal. 205.

[11] *IGLS* IV 1261; die Bezeichnung bezieht sich vielleicht auf einen Ältestenrat; hierzu Roussel 1942/1943 und Hatzopoulos 1998.

[12] Vgl. die bei Herrmann 1965 kommentierte Isopolitie-Inschrift von Seleukeia, Antiocheia und Laodikeia mit Teos (*SEG* 41, 1003–1005); hierzu Gawantka 1975, 120–125.

[13] *BMC*, 151–152.

[14] Hierzu Engels 2011a.

ßenpolitischen Lage nur noch ungenügend gegen die regionalen Autonomiebestrebungen durchsetzen, und diese Bestrebungen griffen allmählich auch auf die syrischen Städte über. Zwar unternahm Antiochos IV. durch eine verstärkte Hellenisierung und verwaltungsmäßige Homogenisierung der städtischen Zentren den Versuch einer Konsolidierung des geschwächten seleukidischen Reichs,[15] doch wird eben jener Reformversuch oft als Ursache oder zumindest Einleitung des weiteren Niederganges gesehen. Antiochos IV. hatte als erster seleukidischer König das tatsächliche Funktionieren einer großen, außen- wie innenpolitisch souveränen und zahlreichen oligarchischen Machtkämpfen ausgesetzten Stadt kennengelernt, da er mehr als 10 Jahre (188–178) als Geisel in Rom zubrachte. Diese Erfahrung scheint sein Stadtbild wesentlich geprägt zu haben, so daß er versuchte, dieses Beispiel zumindest auf den Hauptort seines eigenen Reich zu übertragen, indem er selbst als Kandidat für verschiedene kommunale Ämter in Antiocheia auftrat, unter welchen die Agoranomie und die Demarchie genannt werden,[16] und etwa auch ein Bouleuterion stiftete.[17] In dieser Hinsicht ist auch die Umbenennung zumindest einiger Städte des Reiches zu nennen,[18] welche wie im Falle Jerusalems allerdings vielleicht eher von den lokalen Eliten ausging als von einer königlichen Order; ob diese Reform aber letztlich auch verfassungsmäßige Umbildungen zur Folge hatte und somit ein gesteigertes Kommunalbewußtsein, kann nur vermutet, nicht aber bewiesen werden.

Die nunmehr einsetzende Phase seleukidischer Geschichte ist wesentlich bestimmt von immer größerer Autonomie der bedeutenderen Städte. Diese läßt sich zum einen sinnfällig durch das Privileg eigener Münzprägung demonstrieren, wobei hervorzuheben ist, daß die Prägung königlicher, städtischer oder völlig autonomer Münzen zwar oft als Resultat eines königlichen Privilegs und somit Zeichen eines gewissen Autonomiegewinns des jeweiligen Prägeortes interpretiert wird, der oft fehlende historische Kontext in den meisten Fällen aber eine präzisere Deutung unmöglich macht und daher zur Vorsicht mahnen sollte, da die „Gewährung" des Münzrechts oft sogar als oktroyierte Münzpflicht interpretiert werden kann.[19] Die diesbezüglichen Reformen Antiochos' IV. v.a. im Bereich der Kleingeldprägung sind an anderer Stelle umfassend dargestellt worden und brauchen hier nicht besprochen zu werden. Insgesamt läßt sich formulieren, daß die zweifellos gesteigerte Prägeautonomie ein angestiegenes kommunales Selbstbewußtsein und größere innere Manövrierfähigkeit der Eliten impliziert bzw. hervorrief, wie etwa erstmals im syrischen Raum für Arados deutlich wird, welches seit 243/242 Münzen mit Verweis auf eine 259 beginnende Ära schlug;[20] eine Ära, die vielleicht mit einer Ablösung der zur Zeit Alexanders belegten,[21] einheimischen Königsherrschaft zusammenhängt.[22]

[15] Das Thema ist ein weites Feld; auch ist die Regelung der Frage für uns nur von untergeordneter Bedeutung. Vgl. die neueste Darstellung bei Mittag 2006 (mit Literatur).

[16] Polyb. 26,1. Zum Polybios vs. Antiochos IV (Polyb. 26,1,5; 30,25,1) etwa Morgan 1990.

[17] Malal. 205 (s.oben); Lib. *or.* 11,25.

[18] Mittag 2006, 204–205 nennt als Kandidaten für Umbenennungen nur Ekbatana und Epiphaneia in Armenien; dazuzurechnen sind – vielleicht – drei weitere Epiphaneiai, Adana, Mopsuhestia, Kastabala und Ake-Ptolemais, sowie die Neugründung Antiocheia-Charax.

[19] Mittag 2006, 187.

[20] Seyrig 1951, 206–220; Milne 1938.

[21] Arr. 2,13,7.

[22] Die Dynastie scheint 218 verschwunden zu sein: Polyb. 5,68,7. Diese Münzprägung sollte nach längerer Unterbrechung 138/7 wieder aufgenommen werden (Seyrig 1951, 220) und stellte wohl den Preis für die Unterstützung Antiochos' VII. gegen Diodotos dar.

Was die spezifischen Anliegen der städtischen Eliten betrifft, läßt sich hieraus allerdings wenig Konkretes schließen; einige Ausnahmen natürlich ausgenommen wie die antiochenische Münzprägung der Zeit des Alexander Balas (149–147). Hier sind die wohl in Seleukeia geprägten, aber auch in Antiocheia gefundenen[23] Bronzemünzen mit der Legende ΑΔΕΛΦΩΝ ΔΗΜΩΝ[24] zu beachten, die von 149 bis 147 geprägt wurden und zeitlich mit den Epistateis Hierax und Diodotos[25] und der Herrschaft des Alexandros Balas[26] assoziiert wurden. Es ist zwar zweifelhaft, ob man diese Münzen als Indiz für einen „effort to introduce popular rule" interpretieren muß, wie manchmal vermutet wurde;[27] wahrscheinlich ist, daß diese Münzen eher an kommunale oder regionale Interessen als an monarchische Prärogative appellierten[28] und nicht nur einen rein propagandistischen Zusammenhalt syrischer Städte implizieren, sondern den Beginn einer auch institutionell festgelegten Zusammenarbeit bezeichnen, wobei unsicher bleiben muß, ob diese nur Seleukeia und Antiocheia umfaßte, wie Fundorte und Ikonographie des Doppelportraits nahelegen, oder die gesamte Tetrapolis, in welchem Falle man die Abbildung eher als Symbol einer Kollektivität sehen müßte.[29] Manchmal wurden diese Münzen gar als Beweis für einen „autonomen Bund" gesehen,[30] was wohl zu hoch gegriffen ist; bedenkt man aber das Übergreifen des zunächst kontinentalgriechischen Systems der Städtebünde auf den Orient, wäre es nicht erstaunlich, wenn auch die syrische Tetrapolis sich in Anbetracht der Schwäche der Zentralmacht dieser Tendenz angeschlossen hätte.[31] Der Verweis auf eine Entscheidung des syrischen *populus* wäre in diesem Fall ein Indiz für eine solche überregionale Zusammenarbeit, deren institutioneller Träger und Hauptinteressent natürlich die städtischen Eliten waren.

In den bald nach dem Tod Antiochos' IV. im Jahr 164 einsetzenden dynastischen Kriegen gelang es den kommunalen Eliten, durch geschicktes Taktieren zwischen den Parteien zunehmende Autonomierechte für ihre Städte zu erlangen. Schon immer war die Verleihung bestimmter Autonomierechte (Aphorologesia, Aphrouresia, Asylia, Autonomia, Demokratia, Eleutheria)[32] ein klassisches Element in der Definition der Beziehungen zwischen Reich und Stadt gewesen, wie sich v.a. am Beispiel Kleinasiens oder ausgewählter orientalischer Städte wie Arados (Asylierecht unter Seleukos II.)[33] nachweisen läßt, doch war hier der König generell die langfristig dominante Figur. Die Gewährung verschiedener Stufen von Autonomie wird aber v.a. in der 2. Hälfte des 2. Jh.s zum Regelfall, wie etwa durch die Fragmente der königlichen Korrespondenz erhellt wird. Arados löste sich schon recht früh von der seleukidischen Oberhoheit; Lao-

---

23 Grainger 1990, 157 mit Anm. 89.

24 Head 1911, 778–790; *BMC* 4 (Sel. 165 = 148/47 v. Chr.).

25 Diod. 32,9c; 33,3e 22; Poseid. in Ath. 6,252e.

26 Vgl. Downey 1961, 121.

27 Downey 1961, 121.

28 BMC 151ff.

29 So Bellinger 1949a, 60, Anm. 6; Downey 1961, 121.

30 Holm 1894, 569.

31 Freilich gilt es hier zu bedenken, daß die Entscheidung des syrischen *populus* offensichtlich nicht Seleukeia umfaßte, wie zu besprechen ist.

32 Allg. zu den verschiedenen Etappen städtischer Autonomie vgl. etwa Piatkowski 1991; Mastrocinque 1977; Seyrig 1939.

33 Strabon 16, 2, 14 (C 754).

dikeia wurde 110/09 durch Antiochos VIII. als heilig und Asylstadt erklärt.[34] Seleukeia schließlich erlangte in den 140er Jahren zunächst den Status einer heiligen und 138 einer Asylstadt;[35] im Jahre 109 wurde sie dann sogar offiziell für frei erklärt, entweder von Antiochos VIII., oder aber von Antiochos IX.,[36] wobei dies entweder als bloße Propaganda zu sehen ist, falls der jeweilige König die Stadt ohnehin nicht kontrollierte, oder aber, falls sich die Stadt im Besitz des Herrschers befand und somit einen seiner wenigen Stützpunkte ausmachte, ein zunächst inhaltsleeres Eingeständnis[37] des Königs bedeutete, daß er die Stadt als eigenständigen Bündnispartner anerkennen musste, um sich weiter ihrer Unterstützung zu versichern.[38]

Ein weiteres Anliegen der Poleis war die politische Kontrolle über ihr agrarisches Umland, die Peraia,[39] auf welchem sich durchaus weitere kleinere Städte befinden konnten, wie für Antiocheia belegt ist[40] oder sich in der Zugehörigkeit von Larissa zum Territorium Apameias zeigt.[41] Daß die Beteiligung der Städte an den seleukidischen Bruderkriegen daher nicht allein von ihrer jeweiligen Beziehung zu den Kriegsparteien bestimmt war, sondern häufig nur als Vorwand zum Austragen zwischenstädtischer Rivalitäten zur Ausdehnung der Peraia diente, beweisen einige Belege zu städtischen Privatkriegen. So ließe sich zum einen an die Auseinandersetzung zwischen Apameia und Larissa[42] denken, die entweder in den 140er Jahren, oder in den 80er Jahren stattfand,[43] und wesentlich von dem Wunsch Larissas bestimmt war, ein politisch von Apameia getrenntes Dasein zu führen. Ein weiteres, wenn auch vielleicht atypisches[44] Beispiel hierfür sind die Regelungen der seleukidischen Könige bezüglich Arados.[45] Arados übte spätestens seit 259 eine dominierende Rolle gegenüber seinem ländlichen Umland aus, da die Siedlungen Marathos, Gabala, Paltos, Balanaia und andere die 259 einsetzende aradische Ära verwendeten.[46] Dieser besondere Status wurde aber um 227 zurückgenommen,[47] wie die in den 220er Jahren einsetzende unabhängige Münzprägung der umliegenden Städte belegt,[48] die aber 218 wieder aufhört, was mit der Thronbesteigung Antiochos' III. und

[34] *I. Délos* 1551. Höchstwahrscheinlich war es in dieser Zeit, daß ein König Antiochos dem Tempel von Baitokaike den Besitz des dazugehörigen Dorfes sicherte und ihn mit Steuerfreiheit und Asylie bedachte (*RC* 70 = *IGLS* VI 4028 = *SEG* 30, 1665).

[35] *RC* 71 (S. 292 n. 3) = *OGIS* 257.

[36] Ehling 2008, 223.

[37] Grainger 1990, 170–171.

[38] Allg. zur Eleutheria Mastrocinque 1977.

[39] Allg. zur Peraia, vgl. Kolb 2004.

[40] Strabon 16, 2, 10.

[41] Athen. 4,176b–c (= Poseidonios, *FHG* III 253; *FGrH* 87 F 2).

[42] Athen. 4,176b–c (= Poseidonios, *FHG* III 253; *FGrH* 87 F 2).

[43] Jones 1971, 254.

[44] Vgl. Grainger 1990, 147, der die innenpolitische Aktivität Arados' zum einen mit seiner maritimen Sonderstellung angesichts der ptolemaischen Besatzung Seleukeias erklärt, zum anderen mit seiner phoinizisch geprägten Autonomietradition.

[45] Allg. zu Arados, vgl. Seyrig 1951; Duyrat 2000; Duyrat 2005.

[46] Für Grainger 1990, 145 ist dies ein Beweis, daß Arados im Besitz der Peraia war, während Rey-Coquais 1974, 157 von einer Amphiktyonie mit Zentralheiligtum in Baitokaike ausgeht.

[47] Strabon 16, 2, 12–15.

[48] Seyrig 1951; Seyrig 1971.

einer neuen Regelung in Verbindung gebracht werden könnte.[49] Unter Antiochos IV. kam es wieder zu Spannungen, welche in der Verwüstung der Peraia (und vielleicht die Neubenennung in Antiocheia-Pierien)[50] durch den König endeten.[51] Daß die Kontrolle des Umlands zumindest für Arados eine zentrale Bedeutung hatte, belegt die Bestechung des Kanzlers von König Alexandros Balas (150–146), Ammonios, welche dem Ziel diente, für 300 Talente Marathos offiziell eingliedern zu dürfen, mit der Folge, daß Marathos sich gezwungen sah, den Truppen des Königs den Einmarsch (erfolgreich) zu verwehren.[52] Ähnlich ist auch der Krieg Arados' gegen Marathos und Simyra zu verstehen,[53] der wohl 129 stattfand, als die Nachricht vom Tod Antiochos' VII. ein Machtvakuum hervorrief[54] und zu einer Erweiterung der aradischen Peraia führen sollte.[55]

Dieser fortgesetzte Machtverfall konnte sich allerdings auf lange Dauer für Handel und Sicherheit nur negativ auswirken, so daß das Übermaß an Autonomie den kommunalen Entscheidungsträgern ermöglichte, die seleukidische Partei aufzugeben und viel eher durch Zusammenwirken mit umliegenden hegemonialen Mächten die Lage zu stabilisieren. Hierbei gilt es zunächst zu betonen, daß von einer dynastischen Loyalität nur in begrenztem Maße gesprochen werden kann.[56] Schon seit Beginn der Dynastie lassen sich daher Beispiele zusammentragen, daß es den Poleis weniger auf die Herkunft des Herrschers ankam als auf seine schlichte Präsenz und Effizienz, welche oft mit der Furcht der griechischen Kolonisten vor Aufständen der aramäischen Bevölkerung des Umlands in Verbindung gebracht wird[57] und natürlich das Problem der „herrschenden Gesellschaft" im Seleukidenreich berührt.[58] Erwähnt werden mag hier die Revolte der Seleukis nach dem Tode Seleukos' I. im Jahre 280,[59] der festliche Empfang, den Seleukeia und Antiocheia Ptolemaios III. nach dem Tode Antiochos' II. 246 bereiteten[60] oder der Abfall Antiocheias 235 von Seleukos' II.[61] Immerhin gelang es den seleukidischen Königen im 3. Jh. trotz des gesteigerten Selbstbewußtseins zumindest der hauptstädti-

[49] Polyb. 5, 68, 7.

[50] Steph. Byz., *s.v.* Antiocheia 7.

[51] Porph. F 56.

[52] Diod. 33,5,1–6.

[53] Diod. 33,5.

[54] Strabon 16, 2, 14 (C 754).

[55] Strabon 16, 2, 12 (C 753).

[56] Vgl. etwa etwa Grainger 1990, 142 Anm. 26: „Loyalty to the dynasty is a historian's myth." In dieser Hinsicht wird oft die spontane Ermordung des römischen Gesandten Cn. Octavius aus Empörung über die erzwungene Tötung der Kriegselephanten in Apameia direkt nach dem Tod Antiochos' IV. als Zeugnis eines seleukidischen Patriotismus' erwähnt (Polyb. 31,2,9–11; App., *Syr.* 46; Zon. 9,25; Cic., *Phil.* 9,4); doch ist nicht auszuschließen, daß es sich einerseits um schlichte Empörung angesichts des Massakers handelte, andererseits um einen wesentlich lokal motivierten Widerstand, ließ die militärische Abrüstung doch auch einen wirtschaftlichen Niedergang des militärischen Zentrums Apameia befürchten. Ein anderer Fall ist etwa die seleukidische Selbststilisierung des aus Syrien stammenden Sklavenkönigs Eunus, doch stellt sich hier die Frage, inwieweit diese weniger dynatischem Patriotismus als vielmehr antirömischem Ressentiment geschuldet ist; vgl. Engels 2011b.

[57] Vgl. Grainger 1990, 147–148.

[58] Vgl. etwa Habicht 1958; Mehl 2003.

[59] *OGIS* 219.

[60] *P. Gurob*; s. oben.

[61] Jos., *Contra Ap.* 1, 206 (= Agatharkides, *FHG* III 196, frg. 19).

sche Bevölkerung,[62] die Lage zu beruhigen und sich ohne größere Auseinandersetzungen in den Besitz der syrischen Städte zu setzen, was beweist, daß es diesen weniger um dynastische Fragen ging als vielmehr um die Notwendigkeit, das durch die jeweiligen Krisen entstehende Vakuum durch Unterwerfung unter den jeweils vielversprechendsten König zu beenden.

Erst nach Einsetzen der Reichskrise nach dem Tod Antiochos' IV. sollte sich die Sachlage ändern, da die Ausdehnung der umliegenden Staaten einen Abfall vom Seleukidenreich als dauerhafte Alternative zu ermöglichen schien. Die Städte, bislang nur Verfügungsmasse der Zentralverwaltung, wurden nun angesichts des auf seinen syrischen Kernbestand geschrumpften Reiches notwendigerweise zu eigenständigen politischen Akteuren, welche aktiv in die spätestens seit Antiochos VII. ungebrochen einsetzenden Bürgerkriege eingriffen und Partei für einzelne Prätendenten ergriffen, so daß der Eindruck rechtfertigt ist, die Bürgerkriegskönige seien eher als Exponenten rivalisierender Städte und Stadtkonstellationen zu interpretieren. Antiocheia nahm hier natürlich eine Kernstellung ein. So zwang die Revolte Antiocheias zu Gunsten des makedonischen Prätendenten Andriskos den seleukidischen König Demetrios I. zum Verlassen der Stadt,[63] die sich bald danach dem Usurpator Alexandros Balas anschloss,[64] bevor sie kurzfristig das Diadem Ptolemaios VI. anbot, der es zugunsten Demetrios' II. ablehnte.[65] Nachdem Demetrios II. im Jahre 145 die aufsässige Bevölkerung der Stadt durch seine Söldner bedrängt hatte,[66] schlossen sich der von Chalkis ausgehenden Usurpation Antiochos' VI. neben Antiocheia auch Larissa und Apameia an,[67] während Seleukeia und Laodikeia zu Demetrios II. hielten.[68] Der spätere Seitenwechsel Larissas zeigt deutlich, daß die politische Parteinahme weniger von Loyalitätsdenken bestimmt war als von innerstädtischen Rivalitäten, so zwischen Seleukeia und Antiocheia, zwischen Laodikeia und Apameia, und zwischen Larissa und Apameia. In ähnlicher Weise sollte die Rückkehr Demetrios' II. und sein Krieg gegen Ägypten 128 Antiocheia, Apameia und Laodikeia erneut zum Abfall motivieren.[69] Hierbei sind sogar die Namen der Anführer der Revolte Laodikeias bekannt (Antipatros, Klonios und Aeropos); inwieweit die Revolte aber von den Eliten oder von der breiten städtischen Masse getragen wurde und sich gegen Demetrios II. oder Alexandros II. Zabinas richtete, ist unklar.[70] Die gewollte oder ungewollte Unterstützung diverser Parteien durch die syrischen Städte wurde dann zum Charakteristikum

[62] Umfassend Mittag 2000.

[63] Diod. 31,40a.

[64] Jos., *Ant.* 13,2,1.

[65] Diod. 32,9c; Jos., *Ant.* 13,4,7.

[66] 1. *Makk.* 11,44–51; Diod. 33,4.

[67] Diod. 33,4a; 1 *Makk.* 11,56.

[68] Seleukeia (Anwesenheit Kleopatra Theas): Diod. 33,28; Laodikeia (Anwesenheit Demetrios' II.): Jos., *Ant.* 13,7,1.

[69] Iust. 39,1,3; Diod. 34,25,22.

[70] Grainger 1990, 166 vermutet, daß der Aufstand gegen den Willen der Elite, welche zu Demetrios II. gehalten habe, durchgeführt wurde, mit Berufung auf Diod. 34,35,22, der von der Belagerung der Stadt, Alexandros II. Zabinas' Popularität bei der breiten Masse und der Vergebung des Königs für die Aufstandsführer spricht. Grainger 1997, 129 allerdings erklärt, die Revolte sei 125/3 zu datieren und habe sich gegen Alexandros gerichtet. Vielmehr kann aber vermutet werden, daß der Abfall lediglich die Unabhängigkeit der Stadt herbeiführen sollte, und Alexandros II. Zabinas durch Unterstützung der breiten Volksmassen ein Gegengewicht gegen die Autonomiebestrebungen der regierenden Oligarchie schaffen wollte.

der seleukidischen Geschichte von 113 bis 83, welche durch die pausenlosen Bürgerkriege geprägt wurde, die Antiochos VIII. Grypos gegen seinen Halbruder Antiochos IX. Kyzikenos führte, und die von den jeweiligen Nachkommen fortgesetzt wurden.

Diese offensichtliche Suche nach einem starken und fähigen Herrscher mag auch die wohl gerade Ende des 2. Jh.s häufigen Verfassungswechsel erklären, welche von einer oligarchischen Struktur hin zur Errichung von Kleinfürstentümern tendierten, sei es auf äußeren Druck hin, sei es aufgrund innerer Krisen. In dieser Hinsicht läßt sich an Beroia denken, welches 96 von Herakleon, dem Mörder Antiochos' VIII., besetzt und zum Kleinfürstentum ausgebaut wurde, welches auch Hierapolis und eine Stadt namens Herakleia umfaßte.[71] 88 befand das Gebiet sich in der Hand eines Dynasten mit Namen Straton, der angesichts des seleukidischen Niedergangs die parthische Karte ausspielte, so daß die zeitweise von Philippos I. gehaltene Stadt von Demetrios III. belagert wurde, bis sie von einem arabisch-parthischen Heer entsetzt wurde.[72] Noch 69 regierte in Beroia ein Dionysios, Sohn von Herakleon. Ganz ähnlich läßt sich daher auch das ansonsten kaum näher bekannte Dynastentum in Chalkis erklären, welches 92 n.Chr. erlosch und seinen Ursprung sicher in den spätseleukidischen Bürgerkriegen hatte.[73]

Der Grund dieser Ereignisse mag darin liegen, daß auch Syrien von den zahlreichen zeitgleichen sozialen Unruhen der mittelmeerischen Welt nicht verschont wurde[74] und der Zwiespalt zwischen den verarmten Volksmassen und den regierenden Eliten gerade in Zeiten außenpolitischer Unsicherheit das Aufkommen einzelner Führungspersönlichkeiten begünstigte, welche zwischen den Parteien vermittelten und einen klaren außenpolitischen Kurs steuerten. Gleichzeitig entsprach die Übernahme einer monarchischen Verfassung aber auch einfach dem Geist der Zeit, denkt man an die Errichtung oder den Ausbau der zahlreichen arabischen Fürstentümer an der syrischen Steppengrenze, wie etwa Emesa,[75] Palmyra, Petra und den Staat der Ituräer,[76] und bedenkt man die von Plinius zitierten nordsyrischen Stammesverbände, deren Territorium vor Beginn der Reichskrise zur Peraia der Tetrapolis-Städte gehörte.[77] Die Parteinahme für einzelne Bürgerkriegsparteien sollte dann bald einer offenen Anlehnung an die umliegenden Staaten weichen, wie im zweiten Teil unserer Untersuchung zu zeigen sein wird.

1.2. Zur Prosopographie

Während die bislang besprochenen Elemente überwiegend der literarischen und numismatischen Dokumentation zu verdanken sind, ist der epigraphische Befund leider sehr spärlich, was die Konstellation der lokalen Eliten in späthellenistischer Zeit angeht. Dies

[71] Athen. 4,153b–c (= Poseid. frg. 75 Edelstein/Kidd). Zweifel hieran allerdings bei Otto 1912.

[72] Jos., *Ant.* 13,14,3.

[73] Das Ende des örtlichen Dynasten belegt durch Head 1911, 778. Grainger 1990, 133 bringt den Dynasten in Verbindung mit dem arabischen Fürsten, welcher Diodotos Tryphon 145 bei der Einnahme der Stadt half (Diod. 23,4,1).

[74] Vgl. hierzu auch Grainger 1990, 167–168.

[75] Strabon 16,2,10 (C 753).

[76] Cf. Strabon 16,2,18 (C 755); vgl. Jones 1931.

[77] Plin., *HN* 5,81–82.

wird noch dadurch erschwert, daß zum einen die Nennung einer Stadt mit tetrapolischem Namen nicht nur auf Syrien, sondern auch auf eine der anderen zahlreichen Gründungen verweisen könnte, zum anderen, und das ist das Hauptproblem, die Nennung einzelner Bürger meist nur in einem außerseleukidischen Bereich und zudem noch dezidiert apolitischen Kontext geschieht.

Zunächst wären hier die wenigen bekannten städtischen Magistrate oder wichtigen politischen Akteure zu nennen. Aus Antiocheia kennen wir nur vier *agoranomoi* aus der Zeit zwischen Antiochos III. und dem Zusammenbruch des Reichs, sowie einen Oberpriester von 198/7.[78] Aus Seleukeia-Pierien sind in ähnlicher Weise ebenfalls nur die Namen von sechs *agoranomoi* bekannt, die über das 2. Jh. verstreut sind,[79] doch verfügen wir immerhin über das Glück einer inschriftlichen Auflistung der wichtigsten Priester Seleukeias aus der Zeit um 186,[80] welche uns gleichzeitig Einblick in die Personalstruktur des Königskults jener Zeit gewährt, deren Diskussion aber hier zu weit gehen würde.[81] Interessant ist, daß sich Noumenios, Sohn des Noumenios, Priester Seleukos' IV., vielleicht als Vater des gleichnamigen Noumenios[82] identifizieren läßt, der wahrscheinlich 165/4 ein militärisches Kommando (*praepositum*) für Antiochos IV. im Persischen Golf ausübte,[83] was die enge Verbindung zwischen städtischer und militärischer Elite nahelegen könnte.[84] Aus Laodikeia kennen wir dann einen Sarapis- und Isispriester der Zeit um 174 sowie drei *agoranomoi* des 2. Jh.s. Aus Apameia schließlich sind keine Magistrate bekannt, was bereits in sich aussagekräftig sein und den nur wenig autonomen Status der Stadt unterstreichen könnte.

Während unser Wissen um euergetische Aktivitäten städtischer Eliten in Syrien – sieht man von Hermogenes ab, der wohl in der Gründungszeit Seleukeias-Pierien den Fußbo-

---

[78] Die im Folgenden zusammen mit den Namen aufgeführten Ordnungszahlen und Abkürzungen verweisen auf Grainger 1997. Chairedemos (S), *agoranomos* von 213/2 (*SEG* 36, 1282); Iphitos, auf einem Gewicht als Verwalter für 212/1 oder 183/2 erwähnt (*IGLS* III 1071g); Dionysios 56 (S), *agoranomos* von 93/2 (*IGLS* III 1071d); Nikanor 1 (S), Sohn des Artemidoros, 65/4 (*IGLS* III 1071h); [Men]edemos, Hauptpriester in Antiocheia um 198/7. Allg. zum hellenistischen und römischen *agoranomos*, vgl. Foster 1970; Raschke 1974.

[79] Als *agoranomoi* belegt sind Delphion, 187/6 (*IGLS* III 1213a); Aristokles 4 (S), um 160/59 (*IGLS* III 1213b); Lyikonos um 158/7 (*IGLS* III 1213e, f); Eudoros 1 (S), 151/0 (*IGLS* III 1213g); Dionysios 65 (S), 150/49 (*IGLS* III 1213c, d); Zenobios 3 (S) 106/5 (*SEG* 41, 1536).

[80] *OGIS* 245. Allg. zum seleukidischen Königskult und der Einbindung der Eliten, vgl. Funck 1991; Debord 2003; Van Nuffelen 2004.

[81] Diogenes 2 (S), Sohn des Artemon, sowie Eukrates 1 (S), Sohn des Anaxion, beide Königspriester um 186; Hieron 4 (S), *keraunophoros* (S); Iatron 2 (S), *keraunophoros* (S); Kallikles (S), Sohn des Diogenes, Apollopriester in Daphne; Nikeratos 2 (S), Sohn des Nikeratos, Priester des Zeus Olympios, der Theoi Soteres, und Zeus' Koryphaios; Noumenios 4 (S), Sohn des Noumenios, Priester des Seleukos IV; Zenobios 2 (S), Sohn des Zenon, Apollopriester.

[82] Noumenios 2 (O).

[83] Plin., *HN* 6,15. Allerdings nennt Plinius nur „Antiochos", so daß Antiochos I.–IV. und VII. in Erwägung gezogen werden. Immerhin erscheint „Mesene" erst im 2. Jh. als offizielle Bezeichnung, und Antiochos' IV. Siege im Roten Meer wurden durch eine Münze (LeRider 1965, 309–311) gefeiert. Allg. vgl. auch bald Coşkun/Engels/Erickson, forthcoming.

[84] Vgl. Antiochos 12 (S), Sarapis- und Isispriester um 174; Apollodoros 26 (S), *agoranomos* zu Laodikeia um 145/4 (*IGLS* IV 1271a); Philodamos, *agoranomos* 106/5 (*IGLS* IV 1271b) und Zoilos 6 (S), *agoranomos* um die Wende zu 1. Jh. v. Chr. (*SEG* 36, 1292).

den eines dorischen Gebäudes stiftete[85] – so gering sind, daß diese Frage im Kontext des Übergangs in die römische Herrschaft behandelt werden soll, für welche die Quellenlage ein wenig ergiebiger ist, bleibt zu untersuchen, inwieweit der prosopographische Befund eine gewisse Mobilität der kommunalen Elite innerhalb des Reichs erkennen läßt. Die Verbindung zwischen Polis und König wurde, in Abwesenheit des Königs, meist durch Gesandte wahrgenommen,[86] welche sicherlich zur lokalen Elite zu zählen sind, durch ihre Mission beim König gleichzeitig aber auch sich und ihre Stadt diesem empfehlen konnten, so wie Konon, Zethos, Androkles und Artemidoros, die als Gesandte Seleukeias an Seleukos IV. um 186 fungierten.[87] Auch die umgekehrte Richtung ist denkbar. So ließe sich auch ein unbekannter *philos* Seleukos' III. nennen, den Antiochos III. zum Priester in Daphne bestimmte,[88] oder Aristolochos anführen,[89] ein verdienter Veteran Antiochos' III., der durch Seleukos IV. dem Epistates Seleukeias, Theophilos,[90] sowie den städtischen Magistraten und der Polis selbst empfohlen und, nach gebührender Feststellung seiner öffentlichen wie privaten Wohltaten für die Stadt, mit dem dortigen Bürgerrecht bedacht und durch das Aufstellen einer Bronzestatue im Bouleuterion geehrt wurde;[91] eine wahrscheinlich gängige Praxis, welche zum einen die städtische Bevölkerung Syriens regelmäßig mit neuen und zweifellos königstreuen Honoratioren auffüllte, zum anderen aber auch den Städten regelmäßig finanzkräftige Wohltäter sicherte.

Schließlich ist auf die Präsenz syrischer Bürger in außerseleukidischen Territorien zu verweisen. Hier stellt sich als methodologisches Problem die Frage nach der Zugehörigkeit der Betroffenen zur lokalen Elite, welche nur indirekt beantwortet werden kann, indem auf die Kosten der Reise von Syrien in die Ägäis verwiesen wird und die bezeichneten Aktivitäten als Symbol gehobenen sozialen Status' betrachtet werden. Diese Bemerkungen beziehen sich v.a. auf die Gegenwart solcher Personen in Athen, Delos, Rhodos und Milet. So läßt sich etwa an den Euergetismus des Aristokreon, Sohn des Nausikratos, aus Seleukeia denken, dem der Athener Demos 239/8 und nach 229/8 ein Ehrendekret widmete.[92] Auch beteiligten sich antiochenische Bürger an sozialen Aktivitäten wie Dionysios von Laodikeia, der als Mitglied eines Athener Vereins um 103/2 geführt wird,[93] oder Sosigenes von Apameia, der während des Archontats des Theokles ebenfalls Mitglied eines Athener Vereins war.[94] Die Zahl der Grabinschriften von Verstorbenen v.a. antiochenischer Herkunft ist sehr groß, erlaubt aber meist keine Datierung und weitere inhaltliche Auswertung im Sinne unserer Zielsetzung.

Ähnlich sind die Aktivitäten zahlreicher Syrer auf Delos zu nennen,[95] bestand hier doch eine nicht unbeträchtliche dauerhafte Diaspora, da einige Syrer sogar als Pächter

85 Hermogenes 4 (S) (*IGLS* III 1115).
86 Allg. zu Gesandten im Hellenismus vgl. Mosley 1973; Piccirilli 2001.
87 Grainger 1997, Konon 4 (S), Zethos (/), Androkles 2 (S), Artemidoros 30 (S); *IGLS* III 1183 = *RC* 45.
88 Savalli-Lestrade 1998, Nr. 24 (*IGLS* III 992 = *RC* 44).
89 Savalli Lestrade 1998, Nr. 43 (Holleaux 1942, 199–254 = *RC* 45).
90 Grainger 1997, 120 (O).
91 *IGLS* III 1183 = *RC* 45. Zum Antwortschreiben s.o.
92 *IG* II/III 785, 786, 814; Grainger 1997, 278 (S).
93 *IG* II/III 1335; Grainger 1997, Dionysios 64 (S).
94 *IG* II/III 1335; Grainger 1997, 581 (S).
95 Zu Fremden auf Delos vgl. Baslez 1983; Le Dinahet 1997; Mavrojannis 2002; Vial 2007.

bekannt sind.[96] Während zumindest fünf Syrer aus Antiocheia und Laodikeia im 2. Jh. die Aufsicht über gymnasiastische Übungen bei den Romaia oder Apollonia wahrnahmen,[97] und eine nicht unbeträchtliche Anzahl syrischer Epheben belegt ist, die sich freilich auf einige wenige Inschriften konzentrieren, verweisen unsere Belege v.a. auf den religiösen Bereich. In dieser Hinsicht mag man auch die verschiedenen seleukidischen Bürger zusammenstellen, welche auf Delos Weihungen v.a. für verschiedene orientalische Gottheiten vornahmen,[98] wobei v.a. die syrischen Götter[99] zu nennen sind, denen sich etwa ein Dutzend syrischer Bürger v.a. während der Wende vom 2. zum 1. Jh. verbunden fühlte.[100] Ähnlich fand auch Sarapis großen Anklang; belegt sind hier drei Subskriptionen zum Bau des Sarapeions, die ebenfalls der Jahrhundertwende entstammen.[101] Interessant ist, daß Syrer auch eine bestimmte Rolle bei der Organisation der orientalischen Kulte spielten, wobei hier meist Hierapolitaner als Priester des Kultes der syrischen Götter bekannt sind, und sich von 150 bis 112/1 nachweisen lassen.[102]

Wenn wir sonstige Aktivitäten wie Teilnahme bei musischen Wettbewerben auslassen,[103] mögen ferner die Verleihung fremden Bürgerrechts an explizit als seleukidische Bürger belegte Personen untersucht werden, wie die milesische an Dionysios (39),

[96] Lysias 3 (S), Sohn des Straton, aus Laodikeia, um 156/5 (*I. Délos* 1417).

[97] Karpon 3 (S), Sohn des Hera, aus Antiocheia, *pompostolos* auf Delos Ende des 2. Jh.s (*I. Délos* 2631); Herakleides 10 (S) aus Laodikeia, *hieropoios* der delischen Romaia 127/6 (*I. Délos* 2596), ferner die Antiochener Artemidoros 27 (S), Dositheos 1 (S) und Heliodoros 3 (S), welche 119/8 als *hieropoioi* gymnastische Übungen der Epheben bei den delischen Apollonia überwachten (*I. Délos* 2598).

[98] Als Ausnahme mag Soter (Grainger 1997, 583 (S)), Sohn des Thinoth[eos] aus Antiocheia gelten, der der Delischen Trias eine Weihung Ende des 2. Jhs. stiftete (*I. Délos* 2335).

[99] Zu den syrischen Göttern, vgl. Siebert 1968.

[100] Artemon 5 (S) von Antiocheia (*I. Délos* 2268, undatiert); Demetrios 16 (S), Sohn des Demetrios, der zwischen 118/7 und 90 eine Weihung für die syrischen Götter hinterließ (*SEG* 31, 731 = *I. Délos* 2256); Hermione 1 (S), Tochter des Demetrios von Antiocheia und Gattin eines weiteren Demetrios, Sohn des Demetrios, welche ihrem Gemahl zwischen 118/7 und 90 eine Statue im Heiligtum der syrischen Götter widmete (*I. Délos* 2266); Laodike 4 (S), Tochter des Xanthippos, aus Laodikeia, welche sich um 108/7 an einer Subskription für die syrischen Götter beteiligte (*I. Délos* 66); Sosibios 2 (S), Sohn des Aristios, aus Laodikeia, der dem Hagne Theos Weihung und Säule stiftete (*I. Délos* 2262 und 2270); Diokles 5 (S) und Hieron 1 (S), Söhne des Diokles, aus Hierapolis, die den syrischen Göttern einen Altar weihten (*I. Délos* 2276, undatiert); Sarapion 1 (S), Sohn des Asklepiodes, aus Laodikeia, der den syrischen Göttern um 100 eine Weihung hinterließ (*I. Délos* 2267); Heras 1 (S), Sohn des Diokles, aus Seleukeia, der 90/89 mit einem Römer eine Exedra der syrischen Götter finanzierte (*I. Délos* 2255).

[101] Etwa Paris 2 (S), Sohn des Nikandros, aus Seleukeia, der 118/7 eine Weihung für Sarapis stiftete, 112/1 die Portikus des Sarapeion subskribierte und im frühen 1. Jh. als Subskribent erscheint (*I. Délos* 2122; 2168; 2169; 2614); Heraios 1 (S), Sohn des Philostratos, aus Arados, Subskribent für das delische Sarapeion 94/3 (*I. Délos* 2621); Nikandros 2 (S), Sohn des Paris, aus Seleukeia, der im frühen 1. Jh. das Sarapeion subskribierte (*I. Délos* 2622).

[102] Hier v.a. Hierapolitaner wie etwa Nikon 2 (S), Sohn des Apollonios, wohl aus Hierapolis, um 150, Priester der syrischen Götter (hierzu bes. Siebert 1968); Marion, Sohn des Achaios, aus Hierapolis, 128/7 Priester der syrischen Götter (*I. Délos* 2257); Achaios, Sohn des Apollonios, der um 128/7 Priester der Hadat und Atargatis war (*I. Délos* 2226 of 128/7) und ihnen einen Tempel sowie mehrere Altäre stiftete; Sarapion 5 (S) und Seleukos 6 (S), Sohn des Zounodoros von Hierapolis, beide vor 118/7 Priester der syrischen Götter (*I. Délos* 2283 und 2247); Hermias 7 (S), Sohn des Soterichos, aus Laodikeia, 112/1 Verwalter des Tempels der syrischen Götter (*I. Délos* 2248).

[103] Kliodoros, Sohn des Kliodoros, aus Antiocheia, Sieger in einem Poesiewettbewerb im boiotischen Thespis (undatiert, *IG* VI 1762).

Sohn des Meniskos, aus Seleukeia, um 198/7.[104] Dorion (2) aus Antiocheia betätigte sich als Kavallerieoffizier auf Rhodos im 1. Jh., während Dromon in derselben Zeit der rhodischen Phyle Olympias eingeschrieben war. Soterichos von Antiocheia ist als Gymnasiarchos in Rhodos im 1. Jh. bekannt.[105]

Schließlich ist auf die königlichen *philoi* der Zeit zwischen dem Tod Antiochos' IV. und der Absetzung Philippos' II. Philorhomaios zu verweisen. Zwar hat uns eine Inschrift aus Teos aus der Zeit um 204/3 oder 197/6[106] die Information bewahrt, die Stadt habe den königlichen *philoi* dadurch eine Ehre erweisen wollen, daß sie den syrischen Städten Antiocheia, Seleukeia und Laodikeia das Bürgerrecht verlieh, was im Umkehrschluß suggeriert, daß alle königlichen *philoi*, selbst jene, die nachgewiesenermaßen nicht aus Syrien stammten, das Bürgerrecht jener Städte besitzen mußten, damit der Ehrenbeschluß von Teos sinnvoll und allumfassend war. Dies wiederum läßt die Vermutung zu, daß die Seleukiden selbst zu einem gewissen Zeitpunkt beschlossen haben mußten, ihren *philoi* jenes Bürgerrecht zu sichern. Viel läßt sich hieraus für die syrischen städtischen Eliten allerdings nicht schließen, da, wie gesagt, nur ein Bruchteil der *philoi* überhaupt aus Syrien stammte, und die genuin syrischen *philoi* es nicht unbedingt ihrer lokalen Aktivität verdankten, in den Freundeskreis des Königs aufzusteigen.

Es handelt sich hier zunächst um Philonides (I) von Laodikeia und seine Söhne Dikaiarchos und Philonides (II). Ersterer ist dank einer Athener Inschrift der Zeit um 175 als Freund Antiochos' III. und Seleukos' IV. und Vater der genannten Söhne überliefert.[107] Die beiden Brüder werden auf der delphischen Theorodoken-Inschrift in dieser Eigenschaft geführt,[108] während auf einer Inschrift des Jahres 168 nur Dikaiarchos aus Dank für seine Fürsprache den delphischen Theoren der Zeit Antiochos' III. gegenüber als Theorodok geführt wird;[109] vielleicht ein Zeugnis dafür, daß Philonides den Status des königlichen Freunds nach der Machtübernahme Antiochos' IV. verloren hatte. Einer der beiden Philonideis ist zudem wahrscheinlich mit dem aus dem Papryus Herculaneanum 1044 bekannten gleichnamigen epikureischen Philosophen Philonides identisch,[110] der durch seine umfangreiche Publizistik Demetrios I. zu seiner philosophischen Doktrin bekehren und großen politischen Einfluß erlangen sollte. Interessanterweise wurde Philonides daher zum Ansprechpartner seiner Heimatstadt Laodikeia, welche ihn mehrfach um Vermittlung bat, wobei Philonides selbst aktiv an der Formulierung der Anträge teilnahm.[111] In ähnlicher Weise bat er eine nicht bekannte politische Größe darum, Laodikeia zu verschonen,[112] was wohl im Kontext der Ermordung des Cn. Octavius in Laodikeia durch den Rhetor Leptines 162 zu sehen ist.[113] Ein Fragment des Papyrus mag

[104] Milet I,3,62.

[105] *IG* XII 1,127. Siehe Grainger 1997: Dorion 2 (S), Dromon 2 (S), Soterichos 3 (S).

[106] *SEG* 41, 1003–1005; hierzu Herrmann 1965 (Inschr. B 22–24; Inschr. D 92–94).

[107] *IG* II², 1236; Grainger 1997: Philonides I (/), Dikaiarchos: S. 87 (O); Philonides II (/); Savalli-Lestrade 1998, Nr. 47 (Philonides I), Nr. 50 (Dikaiarchos), Nr. 60 (Philonides II).

[108] Plassart 1921, col. IV, 78–80.

[109] *OGIS* 241.

[110] Grainger 1997, 113 (O); Savalli-Lestrade 1998, Nr. 72. Zum Forschungsstand: Crönert 1975; Habicht 1988; Savalli-Lestrade 1998, 47.

[111] *PHerc* fr. 62,6–7 und fr. 16,1–2 (Gallo). Der Anlaß ist leider unbekannt.

[112] *PHerc* fr. 32,5–8.

[113] Polyb. 31,2,4; 32,3,3; Diod. 31,29; App. *Syr*. 46.

nahelegen, daß Philonides im Alter zum *epistates* Laodikeias bestimmt wurde, doch ist die Lektüre umstritten.[114]

Sieht man von der Familie der Philonideis ab, welche von Antiochos III. bis Demetrios I. eine gewisse Rolle als königliche *philoi* spielte, ist aus der Folgezeit nur wenig Tangibles bekannt. Der Regierungszeit des Alexandros Balas entstammt die Notiz, daß der aus Apameia gebürtige Diodotos Tryphon zum *philos* aufstieg[115] und nach dem Fall des Ammonios zusammen mit Hierax, der mal als Syrer, mal als Ägypter gilt,[116] zum *epistates* Antiocheias bestimmt wurde.[117] In dieser Eigenschaft habe er die bereits erwähnten Münzen geprägt und dann nach dem Tod Balas' um 145 die Bevölkerung angestiftet, Ptolemaios VI. als König zu akklamieren,[118] bevor er schließlich die Usurpation Antiochos' VI. betrieb. Der Zeit Antiochos' VII. verdanken wir die Notiz auf einer delischen Statuenbasis, daß Krateros von Antiocheia als einer der *protoi philoi* des Königs galt.[119] Bei Eusebios ist er dann als Eunuch und Erzieher des Thronfolgers bezeichnet, bevor er nach der Rückkehr Demetrios' II. mit dem jungen Antiochos nach Kyzikos floh.[120] Als letzter sicherlich über ein syrisches Bürgerrecht verfügender *philos* ist aus der Zeit Antiochos' VIII. Herakleion von Beroia bekannt, der seinen König zu ermorden suchte,[121] bevor er – vielleicht – in Beroia eine Tyrannis errichtete.[122]

Dieser Liste hinzuzufügen wären dann noch, freilich aus einem anderen Blickwinkel, die arsakidischen *philoi* syrischer Abstammung, wie etwa Adaios, der in Dura Europos um 87 n.Chr. das Richteramt ausübte und durch seinen Namen vielleicht als Makedone zu identifizieren ist.[123]

2. Von Tigranes zu Augustus (84/3–27 v. Chr.)

2.1. Allgemeine historische Entwicklung

In einer zweiten Phase gilt es nun, die Übergangszeit vom Seleukidenreich zur römischen Herrschaft zu betrachten. Der historische Kontext ist allgemein bekannt; interessant ist allerdings zu betonen, daß wichtige Impulse zur Neuordnung der Verhältnisse in Syrien nicht ausschließlich von den äußeren Mächten, also den Parthern, Armeniern, Juden, Römern sowie den syrischen arabischen Stämmen ausgingen, sondern scheinbar wesentlich auch von den Städten selbst, was in Anbetracht der demokratisch verbrämten oligarchischen Verfassung der Gemeinden die politische Initiative der städtischen Eliten impliziert. Tatsächlich nämlich sollte die Parteinahme für einzelne Bürgerkriegsfakti-

114 Frg. 52a, 9–10.

115 Diod. 33,4a; Savalli-Lestrade 1998, Nr. 74. Zu Tryphon: Fischer 1972; Houghton 1992.

116 Syrer: Savalli-Lestrade 1998, Nr. 74; auch Grainger 1997, 94 (O); Ägypter: Grainger 1990.

117 Diod. 32,27,9c; 33,1,3.

118 Diod. 32,27,9c.

119 *I. Délos* 1547 = *OGIS* 256; Savalli-Lestrade 1998, Nr. 84.

120 Euseb., *Chron.* (arm.) p. 121,14–18 Karst; Porphyrius, *FGrH* 260 F 32,20.

121 Poseidonios, *FGrH* 87 F*24 = Athen. 12,540a–b; Savalli-Lestrade 1998, Nr. 91.

122 Strabon 16,2,7 (C 751).

123 Savalli-Lestrade 1998, Nr. 1 (Arsacides); vgl. auch 205.

onen nunmehr einer offenen Anlehnung an die umliegenden Staaten weichen.[124] So ist zwar überliefert, daß etwa die Städte Mesopotamiens, welche in der Zwischenzeit unter die Dominanz lokaler Dynasten geraten und unter parthische Oberhoheit gefallen waren, zwar die Rückkehr Antiochos VII. um 130–129 begrüßten und teils sogar tatkräftig unterstützten, wie die Revolte des Pitthides in Seleukeia-Tigris gegen die Parther beweist, von der Diodor spricht.[125] Nichtsdestoweniger aber ist auch bekannt, daß andere Städte kollektiv dem Seleukidenkönig in den Rücken fielen und die im Winterquartier befindlichen Truppen angriffen, da sie letztlich die parthische Herrschaft der erneuten seleukidischen Steuerlast bevorzugten.[126] Ähnliche Tendenzen griffen auch auf Nordsyrien über, bedenkt man den bereits erwähnten Fall Beroia. Ähnlich heißt es auch von Damaskus, es habe dem Nabatäerkönig Aretas III. seine Tore geöffnet, um den Arabern zu entgehen.

Diese Zerfallstendenzen, die zweifellos von den städtischen Eliten ausgingen, kulminierten dann im Dynastiewechsel von 87/6 oder 84/3: So heißt es bei Justin, der syrische *populus* habe in Anbetracht der ständigen Bürgerkriege beschlossen, eine auswärtige Macht zum Schutze Syriens herbeigerufen. Nachdem die Ptolemaier aufgrund der langjährigen Feindschaft und Mithridates VI. von Pontos aufgrund seines Kriegs mit Rom ausfielen, sei dann die Wahl auf den armenischen König Tigranes II. gefallen, da er sowohl mit Mithridates verwandt als auch ein Verbündeter der Parther war und daher größtmögliche Stabilität zu garantieren schien.[127] Schenkt man Justins Bericht Glauben – Appian und Strabo sprechen eher von einer militärischen Eroberung[128] –, ist die bereits diskutierte Frage berechtigt, ob der Verweis auf den *populus* sich auf einen gewissen Druck von unten bezieht und letztlich die populäre Zustimmung zur Besetzung des Landes belegt, oder aber vielmehr als Indiz für eine überregionale Versammlung der Magistrate der größeren syrischen Städte zu sehen ist und somit die Diskussionen dieses Gremiums mehr oder weniger getreu widerspiegelt. Dies ließe sich vielleicht auch mit anderen Indizien für eine engere Zusammenarbeit der Tetrapolis-Städte in Verbindung bringen, wie etwa der bereits erwähnten Isopolitie zwischen Seleukeia, Antiocheia und Laodikeia einerseits und Teos andererseits oder den von 149 bis 147 geprägten Bronzemünzen mit der Legende ΑΔΕΛΦΩΝ ΔΗΜΩΝ.

Daß Tigranes II. die Bedingungen richtig erfaßte, unter denen ihm der Zugriff auf Syrien gewährt wurde,[129] zeigt die artaxiadische Innenpolitik, die im wesentlichen die Tendenz der Seleukiden zur Gewährung größerer Autonomie der Städte[130] wie der Dynasten[131] fortzusetzen suchte, wenn auch offensichtlich nicht immer zur vollen Zufriedenheit der Syrer, die sich etwa bei Rom beklagten.[132] Antiocheia hatte bereits nach einer ersten Serie im Jahr 103[133] seit 92/1 autonome Bronzemünzen geschlagen; zeitgleich mit

[124] Vgl. zur generellen Tendenz Ehling 2003.

[125] Diod. 34/35,19.

[126] Iust. 38,10. Zum Kontext Wolski 1977.

[127] Iust. 40,1,1–4 (*ad externa populus auxilia concurrit peregrinosque reges sibi circumspicere coepit*).

[128] App., *Syr.* 48; Strabon 11,14,15 (C 523) und 16,2,8 (C 751).

[129] Zur Absetzung der letzten Seleukiden, vgl. Bellinger 1949a, 83; Koehler 1978; Mittag 2009.

[130] Allg. zur Tendenz Rigsby 1996, bes. 481–513.

[131] Inwieweit die Poleis ein härteres Zugreifen Armeniens erhofften, vgl. Grainger 1990, 188–190.

[132] Vgl. etwa Plut., *Luc.* 21,3.

[133] Newell 1917/1918, 107; vgl. Bellinger 1949a, 71 und 87–88.

der königlichen Prägung Demetrios' III., der sich in der Stadt aufhielt.[134] Die artaxiadische Besatzung bildete hier keinen Bruch; vielmehr finden wir für die nächsten 20 Jahre bis zur Regierung des Antiochos XIII.[135] gegen 70/69 eine kontinuierliche Prägung,[136] und das, obwohl Antiocheia faktisch zur südlichen Hauptstadt des armenischen Reichs und zur Residenz des Vizekönigs Magadates geworden war[137] und somit ebensosehr unter königlicher Kontrolle stand wie unter den Seleukiden.[138] Laodikeia, das 110/09 durch Antiochos VIII. als heilig und Asylstadt erklärt worden war,[139] erhielt im Jahre 82/1 durch Tigranes wohl die städtische Autonomie, wie die Übernahme einer neuen Ära nahelegt.[140] Auch Beroia erhielt im Jahr 81/80 die Autonomie,[141] während Apameia in dieser Zeit zunächst das Münzrecht erhielt bzw. jedenfalls erstmals ausübte, 76 dann als heilig erklärt und zum Asylort bestimmt wurde[142] und sich auf einen Privatkrieg mit Larissa einließ.[143] Nur Seleukeia verweigerte sich dem armenischen Zugriff[144] und verblieb also entweder längere Zeit in der Hand der letzten seleukidischen Könige oder bestand auf seiner im September 109 erlangten Unabhängigkeit. Im Jahr 104 folgte dann die erste Reihe autonomer Münzen,[145] die mit dem Abbrechen der königlichen Münzprägung um 92/89 denkbar kontrastiert.[146]

Die also bereits langangelegte Tendenz der syrischen Städte zu größerer Freiheit, welche etwa Forderungen wie innenpolitische Autonomie, Münzrecht, Steuerfreiheit und Besatzungsfreiheit umfaßt, erklärt dann auch die späteren Ereignisse, die zur Eingliederung ins römische Reich führten. Wie für die spätseleukidische Zeit ist auch für diese Jahrzehnte die Quellenlage zu den städtischen Eliten Nordsyriens trotz der eminenten wirtschaftlichen Bedeutung der Tetrapolis nicht einmal annähernd befriedigend, was wiederum dem Ausfall der epigraphischen Zeugnisse, dem Mangel archäologischer Daten und der nur spärlichen literarischen Überlieferung zuzuschreiben ist. Auf den Zusammenbruch der armenischen Hegemonie folgte, dank der Unterstützung von Politikern wie Lucullus oder Q. Marcius Rex, ein letztes seleukidisches Zwischenspiel, welches dann durch das Eintreffen des Pompeius endgültig beendet wurde – bezeichnenderweise mit der völkerrechtlich verbrämten, typisch hellenistischen Erklärung, daß eine Dynastie, die nicht stark genug sei, ihren Thron zu halten, keinen Anspruch auf Restitution besitze.[147] Die Gründe für die Entscheidung zur Annektion, die vielleicht

[134] Vgl. Newell 1917/1918, 117–118 und 124; Bellinger 1949a, 76.

[135] Ungewiß, ob Antiochos XIII die autonome Münzprägung beendete, vgl. Downey 1961, 138.

[136] Macdonald 1899–1905, III: 143–144; vgl. auch *RPC* I, S. 617.

[137] App., *Syr.* 48–49.

[138] Allg. zu diesem Problem Mittag 2009.

[139] *I. Délos* 1551.

[140] Seyrig 1950, 31; Grainger 1990, 174.

[141] Seyrig 1950.

[142] Seyrig 1950, 15–18.

[143] Athen. 4,176b–c (= Poseidonios, *FHG* III 253; *FGrH* 87 F 2). Die Datierung ist unsicher, da neben den 80er Jahren auch die 140er Jahre in Frage kommen. Vgl. Jones 1971, 254.

[144] Cic., *Verr.* 2,2,4,61.

[145] Bellinger 1949a, 71 und 87–88.

[146] Downey 1961, 134.

[147] Vgl. mit verschiedenen Akzenten: App., *Syr.* 49 und 70; *Mithr.* 106; Iust. 40,2,3–5; Plut., *Pomp.* 39,3.

durch einen formellen Rücktritt Antiochos' XIII verbrämt[148] und, wie noch zu sehen sein wird, vielleicht von den städtischen Eliten Antiocheias gefördert wurde, sind vielseitig: Sicherung der gerade wiederhergestellten Ruhe im Mittelmeer,[149] Gewährleistung eines unmittelbaren Aufmarschgebiets gegen die Parther,[150] wie die Expedition des Crassus wenige Jahre später zeigt, Schutz vor nomadischen Überfällen[151] und schließlich unmittelbare Erschließung des syrischen Wirtschaftsraums[152] nach dem Niedergang von Delos, das im Jahre 88 die Ermordung der italischen *negotiatores* sah und sowohl 88 wie auch 69 schwer verwüstet worden war.[153]

Doch auch Pompeius beabsichtigte keinesfalls, das heterogene Gebiet Syriens zentralistisch zu straffen, sondern setzte die Tendenz zur Gewährleistung kommunaler Autonomie in Kontinuität zu spätseleukidischen und armenischen Strukturen fort, um somit einen sicheren Rückhalt bei den städtischen Eliten zu gewinnen, die hier wie überall im Römischen Reich Träger der neuen Ordnung sein sollten. So wird allgemein angenommen und unkritisch wiedergegeben, daß Pompeius die Städte der Tetrapolis zu *civitates liberae* bestimmte, da bei Plinius Antiocheia und Seleukeia als *civitates liberae* bezeichnet werden,[154] obwohl unklar ist, inwieweit dieser Status, der wohl auf eine augusteische *formula provinciae* zurückgeht,[155] auch für die pompeianische Zeit gilt. Die Beweislage ist nicht ganz einfach, wie später anhand einer Konfrontation des numismatischen und literarischen Befunds zu zeigen ist. Nur soviel sei hier gesagt, daß keineswegs alle Städte der Tetrapolis und Phoiniziens[156] zusammen mit der Errichtung der Provinz um 64/3 auch die neue, pompeianische Ära übernahmen (deren Beginn zumindest für Antiocheia und Apameia im Herbst 66 mit der Niederlage des Tigranes koinzidierte).[157] Auch der Status der Städte scheint recht wechselhaft gewesen zu sein; und nicht nur Tigranes und Pompeius, sondern auch Caesar, Marc Anton und v.a. Augustus unternahmen schwerwiegende Eingriffe, welche sich in einer beständigen Neuformulierung des städtischen Autonomiestatus niederschlugen. Deutlich wird aber, daß die unter Tigranes erreichten Stadtrechte wohl nicht widerrufen wurden, so daß eine der offensichtlich wichtigsten Forderungen der städtischen Eliten an die Seleukiden wie die Armenier, nämlich eine größtmögliche innere und äußere Autonomie unter loser Unterordnung unter eine überregionale Schutzfunktion ausübende Hegemonialmacht, weitgehend erfüllt wurde. Was bedeutete nun diese Freiheit einiger Städte der Tetrapolis, und wie vereinbarte sie sich mit dem neuen Provinzstatus Syriens? Rein theoretisch impliziert die Vokabel der *civitas libera*[158] die völlige völkerrechtliche Unabhängigkeit, doch ist unstrittig, daß in Anbe-

---

148 Malal. 212,9–17; 212,20–213,1. Rücktritt: Downey 1951, 161 *contra* Bellinger 1949a, 85 Anm. 110.

149 Dobiaš 1931. Skeptisch dagegen Sherwin-White 1994, 260.

150 Vgl. Wirth 1983.

151 Gelzer 1984, 86 im Anschluß an Iust. 40,2,4.

152 Hatzfeld 1919, bes. 142 und 374f.; Sartre 2001.

153 Bruneau 1968.

154 Plin., *HN* 5,79.

155 Vgl. Magie 1950, II: 1335–1336 mit Anm. 17.

156 Seyrig 1954.

157 Allg. Seyrig 1950.

158 Vgl. allg. Bernhardt 1971; ders. 1980.

tracht der realen Machtverhältnisse und der strategischen Situation die freien Städte der Tetrapolis Rom in vielfacher Weise untergeordnet wurden.[159]

So dürfte die Freiheitserklärung zum einen von einem bilateralen Bündnisvertrag oder zumindest einer Einordnung in eine generelle *lex provincialis* begleitet worden sein, welche die außenpolitische Unabhängig faktisch zunichte machte. Und auch, wenn das Konzept der „Freiheit" eigentlich eine Befreiung von jeglicher Garnison (*aphrouresia*) impliziert, welche wohl auch tatsächlich gewährt worden zu sein scheint,[160] bewirkte die permanente Stationierung mehrerer römischer Legionen am Euphrat eine wirkungsvolle Einschränkung. Diese dürfte den Städten Nordsyriens allerdings durchaus willkommen gewesen sein, bedenkt man die offensichtliche Unfähigkeit der Tetrapolis-Städte zum Selbstschutz ihrer Interessen und somit die dauernde Forderung nach Ruhe und Schutz vor auswärtigen Übergriffen; eine Forderung, welche ja bereits zum Dynastiewechsel und zur Herbeirufung der Armenier geführt hatte und nun auch an die Römer herangetragen wurde: Bereits vor der offiziellen Einrichtung der Provinz, so überliefert Cassius Dio, sandte der Statthalter Ciliciens, Q. Marcius Rex, seinen Schwager und Legaten P. Clodius Pulcher nach Antiocheia, um hier den Bürgern die Hilfe Roms im Kampf gegen die „Araber" zuzusichern,[161] wohl im Kontext der Niederlage Antiochos' XIII.[162] Die Bedeutung dieser Schutzfunktion zeigte sich ferner daran, daß trotz der Neuordnung des Ostens fortgesetzte nabatäische Einfälle nach Syrien beklagt und dem Senat gemeldet wurden, welcher sich entschied, Syrien zur proconsularischen Provinz zu erheben und von 57 bis 54 dem A. Gabinius anzuvertrauen,[163] dem Urheber der *lex Gabinia*, welcher Pompeius sein Oberkommando im Piratenkrieg zu verdanken hatte. Doch auch nach Gabinius' Statthalterschaft sollten nomadische Einfälle ein ständiges Problem bleiben, das erst durch die augusteische Neuordnung eine gewisse Beruhigung fand, wenn auch unsere Quellen und die ältere Sekundärliteratur allzuoft von einem dichotomischen Griechen/Araber und Städter/Nomaden-Bild geprägt sind, welches sich zunehmend als anachronistisch erweist.[164] Daß die Römer auch überregional zumindest in einer Anfangsphase nicht als Unterdrücker, sondern wohlwollende Helfer angesehen wurden, zeigt sich daran, daß die unter parthischer Oberhoheit stehenden makedonischen Kolonien Nordwestmesopotamiens nicht nur eine von L. Afranius kommandierte Heeresabteilung des Pompeius auf seinem Zug durch den Osten unterstützten,[165] sondern später sogar den Truppen des Crassus ihre Mauern öffneten.[166]

---

159 Vgl. etwa Bojarski 1990; Musti 1999.

160 Man denke an Malalas 244, 15ff., der so umfassende Ausschreitungen zwischen Heiden und Juden 40 n. Chr. attestiert, daß kaum die Präsenz einer größeren Garnison anzunehmen ist, wenn auch unsicher ist, inwieweit dies auf die republikanische Zeit übertragen werden kann. Allg. hierzu auch Meeks/Wilken 1978. Die Freiheit von Garnisonierung betrifft natürlich nicht die Bürgerkriegsjahre, in denen die Tetrapolisstädte oftmals umkämpft und belagert wurden.

161 Cass. Dio 36,17,3.

162 Zur Frage nach Clodius' Verwicklung in die Aufstände gegen Antiochos XIII. und Philippos II: Koehler 1978, 61–69; Sherwin-White 1994, 259; Ehling 2003, 326–327; Mittag 2009, 183–184.

163 App., *Syr.* 51. Statthalter waren: Scaurus 62, Marcius Philippus 61–60, Lentulus Marcellinus 59–58, Aulus Gabinius 57–55, Licinius Crassus 54–53, Cassius Longinus 53–51, Calpurnius Bibulus 51–50.

164 Vgl. z.B. Rowton 1976.

165 Cass. Dio 37,5,5.

166 Cass. Dio 40,13,1; vgl. aber auch den Fall von Zenodotion bei Cass. Dio 40,13,2.

Was die innenpolitische Unabhängigkeit betrifft (*autonomia*), welche ja schon seit seleukidischer Zeit weitgehend gewährleistet war, so dürfte diese zumindest für Antiocheia psychologisch dadurch eingeschränkt worden sein, daß der Provinzgouverneur hier seinen Sitz bezog und somit die Stadtgeschäfte aus nächster Nähe verfolgte. Daß in der Kaiserzeit die kommunalen Münzen mit dem Namen des jeweiligen *legatus Augusti* versehen wurden, zeigt einmal mehr den Einfluß des Statthalters auf kommunale Belange.[167] Doch darf man die Auswirkungen dieses mehr oder weniger sanften Drucks des Statthalters und seiner Vertreter nicht überbewerten, bedenkt man, daß zumindest in Krisenzeiten genügend innerer Handlungsspielraum zu umfassenden Entschlüssen bestand und die Städte der Tetrapolis sich je nach Stimmung der Elite und Ausrichtung der römischen städtischen Diaspora einzelnen Bürgerkriegsparteien anschlossen. So durchzogen die Bruchlinien zwischen Cäsarianern und Republikanern auch Syrien, und die hohen Kontributionen, die zunächst C. Cassius Longinus,[168] dann Marcus Antonius einforderten,[169] bewirkten sogar eine zeitweise Hinwendung der syrischen Poleis zu den Parthern, die im Jahre 40 Syrien fast kampflos besetzen,[170] in Antiocheia offensichtlich recht beliebt waren, wenn man Cassius Dio Glauben schenkt,[171] und erst 38 vertrieben werden konnten. Der Principat des Augustus brachte hier wie im Rest des Reichs politische Stabilisierung und wirtschaftlichen Aufschwung, wenn auch die wechselhaften Statusbezeichnungen der Münzen zeigen, daß der Princeps hier wie überall Treue bzw. Abfall systematisch belohnte bzw. bestrafte. Daß die römische Provinzverwaltung generell als mildes Regime empfunden wurde und die langfristigen Tendenzen eher auf Integration als auf Sezession zielten, beweist jedenfalls etwa die (zunächst abschlägig beantwortete) Petition der südsyrischen Städte Gadara und Hippos, die nach der Friedensordnung des Augustus dem Reich des Herodes zugeteilt worden waren und in der Zeit um 22–20 darum baten, wieder in die Provinz Syrien aufgenommen zu werden.[172]

Schließlich suggeriert das Freiheitskonzept die Exemption von jeglicher Steuer (*aphorologesia*). Leider sind unsere Quellen zur Errichtung der Provinz zu spärlich, hier definitive Schlüsse für die Tetrapolis ziehen zu können. Allerdings ist immer noch kontrovers, inwieweit *libertas* auch unbedingt *immunitas* impliziert;[173] und selbst dann war nicht unüblich, daß der Bündnisvertrag mit Rom trotz genereller Steuerfreiheit diverse Verpflichtungen festschrieb[174] wie etwa die Übertragung der Hafensteuer an Rom,[175] so daß vermutet wird, daß Plinius' Verwendung des Begriffs der *civitas libera* zwar die Freiheit von direkten Steuern impliziert, nicht aber die von weiteren Verpflichtungen oder indirekten Steuern.[176] Insgesamt wissen wir jedenfalls, daß auch Syrien den Steu-

---

167 Grant 1946, 396–397.

168 Jos., *Ant.* 14,272.

169 App., *B.C.* 5,7.

170 Cass. Dio 48,25,1. Zum Kontext Wolski 1977; Engels 2008.

171 Cass. Dio 49,20,4.

172 Jos., *Ant.* 15, 354–359. Hierzu allg. Engels 2007.

173 Vgl. Dahlheim 1977, 262–263; Bernhardt 1980; unter Berufung auf App., *B.C.* 1,102,475 und 5,6; Suet., *Caes.* 25,1; Strabon 17,3,24 (C 839); *IG* XII Suppl. 11, S. 208; *GIBM* 792; *SGDI* 3504 für eine gemeinsame Verleihung in republikanischer Zeit (und *OGIS* 440 u.a. dagegen).

174 Vgl. etwa Cic., *Verr.* 2,4,21–23; 2,4,76; 2,5,50–51.

175 Staatsverträge 136–137; *portoria* zum eigenen Nutzen aber bei de Laet 1949, 91ff. und 351ff.

176 Bernhardt 1980, 199. Allg. zu den indirekten Steuern jetzt Günther 2008.

erpächtern nicht entging und, selbst wenn die gesamte Tetrapolis von direkten Steuern befreit war, genügend abwarf, um als eine der reichsten Provinzen des Imperiums zu gelten.[177] Als konkrete Steuern für Syrien insgesamt sind durch Cicero *portorium*, *vectigal* und *stipendium* belegt,[178] wobei letzteres auch bei Velleius Paterculus erwähnt wird;[179] inwieweit dies auf die Tetrapolis zu übertragen ist, ist unsicher. Einziges Indiz ist, daß Caracalla Antiocheia zwar zur Kolonie erhob, aber die bisherigen Tribute beibehielt (*salvis tributis*),[180] wobei sich *tributus* in Anbetracht der nicht unüblichen ungenauen Verwendung der Vokabel[181] durchaus auf indirekte Steuern beziehen kann,[182] doch mag dies auch auf eine kaiserzeitliche Statusveränderung verweisen. Frühestes Indiz für die generelle fiskalische Lage ist die Situation unter Gabinius, die die ersten tastenden Schritte der Verwaltung offenbart.[183] Dieser soll die Provinz rücksichtslos ausgebeutet haben, wenn man Cicero Glauben schenkt, der von Verhandlungen mit Tyrannen, zweifelhaften Geldgeschäften, Plünderungen (*direptiones*), Raub (*latrocinia*) und Mord (*caedes*) spricht.[184] Interessanterweise muß dieses Zeugnis aber insoweit abgeschwächt werden, als es gerade die von Cicero aufgrund seiner Affinitäten mit dem Ritterstand protegierten Steuerpächter waren, die am meisten über Gabinius klagten, welcher angeblich die Provinzialen, laut Cicero also Syrer und Juden, überproportional zu schützen suchte. Dieser Vermerk bezieht sich vielleicht darauf, daß die *immunitas* der Freistädte nur für die Bürger dieser Poleis galt, nicht aber für die Nicht-Bürger, wie etwa auch für Sizilien diskutiert wurde;[185] eine für das Verständnis der syrischen Situation sicherlich nicht unwichtige Frage, bedenkt man das oft nur auf die Griechen beschränkte Bürgerrecht dieser Gebiete. Gabinius gab den Städten ferner laut Cicero[186] die Möglichkeit, ihre Steuern direkt beim Personal der Provinzverwaltung während seines Besuchs in den Städten zu entrichten, nicht bei den Steuerpächtern. Auch verringerte er deren Amtsgewalt, änderte die Höhe von *stipendium* und *vectigal*, schloß neue Verträge mit den lokalen Dynasten, welche auch die Steuererhebung tangierten, und beseitigte die *custodiae*, also die mit der Erhebung des *portorium* beauftragten Zöllner. Wenn auch Rostovtzeffs Analyse, Gabinius habe offensichtlich das System der *publicani* durch eine zentralisierte proconsularische Steuererhebung ersetzen wollen,[187] sicherlich zu spekulativ ist,[188] so bestehen doch zahlreiche Indizien dafür, daß auch nach Beginn der römischen Herrschaft zwar nicht alles zum Besten bestellt war, Statthalter und städtische Eliten aber manchmal durchaus

[177] Cicero, *Sest.* 43, 94 spricht von den *pacatissimae et opulentissimae gazae*.

[178] Hierzu auch Rostovtzeff 1941 (1955), II: 777.

[179] Vell. Pat. 2,37,5 (...*Syria, quae tum primum facta est stipendiaria*).

[180] *Dig.* 50,15,8,5. Auf Malal. 246,16–19 und die hier im Zusammenhang mit den häufigen Erdbeben erwähnten Leiturgien der Ladenbesitzer der Kolonnadenstraße unter Caligula und Claudius soll hier nicht eingegangen werden; vgl. allg. Downey 1961, 196, Anm. 145.

[181] Vgl. Schwahn 1939, 10.

[182] Vgl. Bernhardt 1980, 203.

[183] Hierzu Sanford 1939/1940.

[184] Cic. *Sest.* 43; *prov. cons.* 4,9; Cass. Dio. 39,56.

[185] Carcopino 1905, 9ff.; ders. 1915, 212; Jones 1940, 321 Anm. 45.

[186] Cic., *prov. consul.* 5,10.

[187] Rostovtzeff 1941 (1955), II: 775–778.

[188] Sartre 2001, 128.

zum besseren Wohl der Steuerzahler zusammenarbeiten konnten.[189] Diese Möglichkeit schlägt sich auch in dem Bericht nieder, die antiochenische Bevölkerung habe dem römischen Staat zwei von Seleukos I. gestiftete Statuen aus Dank für die Statthalterschaft des M. Calpurnius Bibulus vermacht.[190]

2.2. Prosopographischer Befund

2.2.1. Antiocheia

Wie bereits erwähnt, erlauben unsere spärlichen Zeugnisse uns nur einen völlig unzureichenden Einblick in die Lage der syrischen Eliten zur Zeit der römischen Besetzung. Nur wenige prosopographische Ausnahmen sind hier zu nennen, und auch dies mit größter Vorsicht vor Verallgemeinerungen.[191] Beginnen wir mit Antiocheia,[192] einer zumindest zur Zeit des Plinius, wahrscheinlich aber schon zu der des Pompeius' rechtlich freien Stadt,[193] der Pompeius sich auch insoweit geneigt gezeigt hatte, als er ihr die von ihm oder Tigranes eingeforderten Geiseln zurückgab, ganz in seleukidischer Tradition das Heiligtum von Daphne durch Landzuweisungen förderte[194] und die Stadt zum Sitz des zunächst propraetorischen Statthalters bestimmte. Eine bei Porphyrios erhaltene antike Tradition berichtet gar, daß Pompeius sich von der Bevölkerung Antiocheias habe bestechen lassen, den letzten seleukidischen König, Antiochos XIII,, zu vertreiben.[195] Schenkt man dieser keineswegs sicheren[196] Überlieferung Glauben, kann diese Initiative nur von der wohlhabenden Elite ausgegangen sein, die sich von der römischen Herrschaft gleichzeitig Stabilität, Schutz und Autonomie versprach und hier einmal mehr ihren politischen Zusammenhalt signalisierte.

Ferner gilt es, die Münzprägung zu beachten: Seit 64/3 gab Antiocheia städtische Bronzemünzen mit der Aufschrift ΜΗΤΡΟΠΟΛΙΣ heraus und setzte hiermit die 69 unter Antiochos XIII. unterbrochene Tradition fort,[197] freilich nunmehr unter Verweis auf eine ins Jahr 66 rückdatierte pompeianische Ära. Erste Silbermünzen, deren Prägung bekanntlich meist der Hegemonialmacht, nicht der städtischen Verwaltung oblag, erscheinen erst 57 unter dem Proconsulat des Gabinius, imitieren aber interessanterweise die

---

[189] Daß es hierbei Gabinius gelang, eigenen Profit zu erwirtschaften (Cass. Dio 39,55,5 und 56,1), muß nicht unbedingt gegen die Vorteile seiner Neuordnung für die Steuerzahler sprechen. Zur Frage nach einer gemeinsamen Münzpolitik Gabinius' und Bibulus' während ihrer Statthalterschaften im Osten vgl. Sartre 2001, 129–130.

[190] Malal. p. 212,1–8; Lib., *or.* 11,116.

[191] In der Folge soll in das Zeugnis der Syrer auf Delos ausgeblendet werden, da infolge der veränderten politischen Umstände des 1. Jh.s. deren Zahl zu hoch anstieg, um hier in befriedigender Weise eine Übersicht zu erlauben, wie dies für die seleukidische Zeit der Fall war.

[192] Allg. vgl. zum Untersuchungszeitraum Mittag 2009.

[193] Plin., *HN* 5,79.

[194] Eutr. 6,11.

[195] Porph. von Tyros, in: Eus., *Chron.* 1, pp. 261f. Schoene = *FHG* III, 716, frg. 26. Vgl. auch Iust. 40,23,3–5; App., *Syr.* 49 und 70; *Mithr.* 106.

[196] Hierzu bereits Bevan 1902, II: 267.

[197] Seyrig 1950, 5–15. Allg. *RPC* I, Nr. 4201–4217.

seleukidischen Prägungen des Philipp I. Philadelphos (93–84).[198] Es handelt sich hier um eine im Römischen Reich wohl einzigartige Maßnahme, die keineswegs eine posthume Idealisierung des Seleukidenkönigs impliziert, sondern zum einen die Autonomie Syriens und seiner Traditionen unterstreichen, zum anderen eine ungestörte Fortsetzung des Handels durch Weiterprägung dieser sehr verbreiteten Stücke sichern[199] und, da die Münzen überbewertet waren, der Provinzkasse auch einen Bonus bescheren sollte.[200] Nicht nur Cassius,[201] auch Caesar hielt an dieser Praxis fest, doch ließ er die Silbermünzen mit seiner eigenen Ära (Beginn 1. Oktober 49) versehen,[202] welche zur antiochenischen Stadtära werden sollte. Diese Ära sollte einen entscheidenden Einschnitt in der Stadtgeschichte kennzeichnen: Als Caesar auf seiner Rückkehr von Alexandria Syrien besuchte, sandte er den Antiochenern, welche sich nach Pharsalos auf seine Seite geschlagen hatten,[203] einen Brief,[204] in dem er der Stadt gleich in der Anrede Heiligkeit, Asylie und Autonomie attestierte.[205] Wenn die Authentizität des Schreibens auch umstritten ist,[206] so schlug sich der generelle Gehalt der Statusfestsetzung in der autonomen städtischen Bronzemünzprägung nieder, deren Text ΑΝΤΙΟΧΕΩΝ ΤΗΣ ΜΗΤΡΟΠΟΛΕΩ ΙΕΡΑΣ ΚΑΙ ΑΣΥΛΟΥ ΚΑΙ ΑΥΤΟΝΟΜΟΥ lautet.[207] Inwieweit diese Aufzählung eine Statusänderung oder -bestätigung im Vergleich zur pompeianischen Zeit impliziert, muß dahingestellt bleiben;[208] denkbar ist auch, daß sich hier vielmehr kommunaler Stolz äußert, dessen Anlaß das von Caesar betriebene umfassende Bauprogramm war. Interessanterweise verschwinden allerdings unter Marc Anton, der auch erstmals sein eigenes Bild auf Münzen setzen ließ,[209] zeitweise die Epitheta *hieros* und *asylos*, was vielleicht ein Zeichen für eine erneute Statusänderung ist,[210] welche die Unterstützung des Cassius durch die Stadt bestrafen könnte,[211] wenn auch die Präsenz der Autonomie, des wichtigsten Stadtrechts, durchgehend belegt ist. In den offensichtlich recht positiv aufgenommenen[212] Jahren der parthischen Besatzung erscheinen *hieros* und *asylos* wieder auf den Münzen, doch verschwindet diesmal *autonomos*, während die seleukidische Ära wieder erscheint.[213] Nach der Rückkehr unter römische Herrschaft finden wir dann zunächst

[198] Bellinger 1951, 63–64; 1952, 55–57; Seyrig 1950, 5–15. Vgl. auch *RPC* I, Nr. 4108 mit S. 606–607 und Nr. 4124ff.; allg. Prieur/Prieur 2000, 1–5.

[199] Zur Verbreitung der Stücke vgl. Newell 1919, 81.

[200] Baldus 1987, 127; Mittag 2009, 188–189. Ob Gabinius das Silber durch Bestechung durch Aristobulos und Alexandros oder durch die von Ptolemaios XII. als Belohnung für seine Rückführung nach Alexandreia geschenkten Summen finanzierte, vgl. Mittag 2009, 189.

[201] Für Cassius, vgl. Bellinger 1944; Seyrig 1951; Bellinger 1951, 65.

[202] *RPC* I, Nr. 4127 (Caes. Jahr 3 = 47/46 v. Chr.); Nr. 4218 (Gegenpr. Kleopatra); Bellinger 1951, 65.

[203] Caes., *B.C.* 3,102,6.

[204] Laut Malal. 216,7–18 erreichte das Schreiben Antiocheia am 17. Juni 47 und wurde am 25. bekanntgegeben; am 27. betrat dann Caesar die Stadt.

[205] Malal. 216,15–17.

[206] Rigsby 1996, 498.

[207] Newell 1919, 69–113; Seyrig 1950, 5–15; Bellinger 1952, 55–57.

[208] Vgl. etwa Kolb 1996, der von einer Statusbestätigung ausgeht.

[209] *RPC* I, Nr. 4135; vgl. auch Prieur/Prieur 2000, 12.

[210] *RPC* I, Nr. 4222 und 4225; vgl. Newell 1919, 94; Downey 1961, 159.

[211] Cic., *fam.* 12,14,4 und 12,15,7; Cass. Dio 47,30,2.

[212] Cass. Dio 48,24,3–26,1 und 49,29,4.

[213] Newell 1919, 96–98; Bellinger 1952, 60–63; *RPC* I, Nr. 422 (Sel. 272 = 41/40 v. Chr.).

für kurze Zeit die Rückkehr zur vollen caesarischen Bezeichnung.[214] Doch finden sich recht schnell wieder Stücke, die ausschließlich die Autonomie aufführen.[215] Dies sollte sich auch in augusteischer Zeit nicht ändern.[216] Hier finden wir zunächst weiter imitierte seleukidische Silberstücke mit caesarischer Datierung,[217] dann, ab 21/20, erste silberne Tetradrachmen mit dem Bild des Augustus, wobei die caesarische Ära hier wie auch auf den Bronzemünzen nunmehr durch die Regierungsjahre des *princeps*, gezählt nach der Schlacht von Actium, ersetzt wird.[218] 17/6 erscheinen aber wieder Münzen mit dem Abbild Philipps I.[219] Gleichzeitig erscheinen seit 7/6 v. Chr. kleinere Bronzemünzen mit dem Namen des jeweiligen Legaten.[220]

So sehr in der Antike betont wurde, daß Antiocheia seit Pompeius die zweitgrößte (und nach Anschluß Alexandreias drittgrößte) Stadt des Römischen Reichs war,[221] so schlecht kennen wir namentlich zur Elite gehörige Personen. Daß eine reiche Verwaltungstradition bestand, ist allerdings kaum fraglich, bedenkt man etwa die bei Plutarch und Julian erwähnte Anekdote vom festlichen Empfang, welchen die Magistrate und Priester der Stadt dem Freigelassenen Demetrios von Gadara um 66 v. Chr. bereiteten.[222] Das Datum ist ein interessanter Hinweis: 67/66 Jahr hatte sich Philippos Philorhomais in den Besitz Antiocheias gesetzt,[223] 65/4 wurde er wohl von der Bevölkerung zugunsten des Antiochos XIII. vertrieben; 63 schließlich beendete Pompeius endgültig die seleukidische Herrschaft. Der bei Plutarch berichtete und auf 66 datierte *adventus* des Demetrios spiegelt also wohl noch die spätseleukidische oder Tigranes-zeitliche Verwaltungsstruktur wider und belegt somit die Existenz einer örtlichen Honoratiorenschicht, welche trotz seleukidischer Herrschaft in Demetrios von Gadara einen einflußreichen potentiellen Fürsprecher und *patronus* wahrnahm, dessen Interzession sie zugunsten der Orontes-Metropole erreichen wollte. Ähnlich wissen wir durch Malalas, daß Pompeius in einem Akt symbolischen Euergetismus' das verfallene Bouleuterion Antiocheias restaurieren ließ und die Antiochener – nicht ganz der Wahrheit entsprechend – als Nachfahren der Athener ehrte;[224] ein klares Zeichen für die von Rom intendierte Stärkung örtlicher Autonomie und ein Indiz für das kontinuierliche Funktionieren der Boule von der Seleukiden-

214 *RPC* I, Nr. 4224 (Caes. 9 = 41/40 v. Chr.).

215 *RPC* I, Nr. 4226–4228.

216 Z.Bsp. *RPC* I, Nr. 4237 (Caes. 21 = 29/28 v. Chr.) oder *RPC* I, Nr. 4240 (um 21 v. Chr.).

217 Newell 1919, 102–113; MacDonald 1904; Seyrig 1951, 213–214; *RPC* I, Nr. 4146 (Caes. 30 = 20/19 v. Chr.).

218 Newell 1919, 110–112; *RPC* I, Nr. 4269 (Act. 44 = 13/14 v. Chr.); Nr. 4159 (Act. 26 = 5 v. Chr.).

219 Newell 1919, 112–113.

220 Grant 1946, 397–400; Bellinger 1949b, nr. 1599; *BMC* 63 (Legat Silanus, 11–17 n. Chr.).

221 Jos., *Bell.* 3,2,4.

222 Plut., *Pomp.* 40, 1–5; Jul., *Misop.* 20. Allg. Bellemore 1995; zu Cato *Wussow 2004.*

223 Im Jahre 69 erzwang Lucullus die Evakuierung Syriens durch Tigranes und, dank der Unterstützung des Araberfürsten Samsigeramus, die Einsetzung Antiochos' XIII als König in Antiocheia (App., *Syr.* 49; Iust. 40,22). 67/6 kam es dann zu Auseinandersetzungen mit Philippos II Philorhomais, der durch den arabischen Fürst Aziz unterstützt wurde. Antiochos XIII wurde vertrieben und von Samsigeramus in Haft genommen (Diod. 40,1a–b). Vgl. Bellinger 1949a, 82–83; Ehling 2008.

224 Malal. 211,16–19. Zur ursprünglichen Zusammensetzung der antiochenischen Bevölkerung aus 5300 Athenern bzw. Makedonen sowie zahlreicher Juden, vgl. Jos., *Ant.* 12,119.

bis in die Kaiserzeit, wie etwa auch eine bei Malalas erhaltene Inschrift aus Tiberischer Zeit nahelegt, welche *boule* und *demos* der Stadt als Stifter einer Statue genannt habe.[225]

Leider kennen wir aus dem Untersuchungszeitraum namentlich nur zwei Paare von städtischen Magistraten aus Antiocheia: Zum einen Nikanor, Sohn des Artemidoros, und Apollonides, Sohn des Amphaïnetos (65/4 oder 47/6),[226] zum anderen Antiochos und Poplios (42/1),[227] vier *agoranomoi* also, deren Namen sich auf Bronzegewichten erhalten haben, die wir aber ansonsten keineswegs in einen präziseren Kontext einordnen können. Potentiell interessant ist jedenfalls die Erwähnung des „Poplios"; ein römisch klingender Name, der mehr Fragen aufwirft, als er beantwortet. So wurde zum einen betont, daß die Einnamigkeit impliziert, daß es sich um einen autochthonen, keineswegs römischen Bürger handelt, da im Bedarfsfall auch auf Gewichten sehr wohl die Tria Nomina verwendet werden konnte.[228] Zum anderen aber ist nicht auszuschließen, daß es sich bei Poplios um ein Mitglied der *gens Popilia* handeln könnte, oder der Name eine deformierte Wiedergabe des *praenomen* Publius darstellt. Dies hätte auf den ersten Blick nichts Erstaunliches, zeigen unsere Quellen doch die feste Anwesenheit nicht nur von *publicani*, sondern auch von *negotiatores*[229] spätestens im Jahr 48,[230] so daß ihre Teilnahme an der bürgerlichen Selbstverwaltung zumindest theoretisch möglich gewesen sein könnte, zumal 42/1 die Provinzialisierung weit fortgeschritten sein dürfte und der Bürgerkriegskontext eine stärkere Einbindung der Römer oder Italiker in den jeweiligen lokalen Kontext erleichtert haben könnte.[231] Ansonsten ist der epigraphische Befund leider völlig unergiebig, da selbst auf Delos, das uns so zahlreiche Aufschlüsse über die syrische Elite des 2. Jh.s gegeben hatte, die Verwüstungen der Mithridatischen Kriege mit einem fast gänzlichen Aufhören epigraphischer Zeugnisse außerdelischer Eliten einhergegangen ist.

Neben diesen Personen ist natürlich, schon bereits vor der Zeit des Pompeius, der bekannte Dichter Archias zu nennen, ein Bürger der Stadt Antiocheia und – wie man Ciceros Formulierung *Antiochiae – nam ibi natus est loco nobili*[232] entnehmen kann – Mitglied einer angesehenen Familie. Bedeutet diese etwas vage Formulierung nun aber auch, daß Archias Mitglied der städtischen Elite im engeren Sinne war und gar Amtsträger zu seinen näheren Anverwandten zählte? Die Frage ist schwer zu beantworten, bedenkt man, daß *nobilis*, wie Hellegouarc'h betont hat, auch lediglich die persönliche Herausgehobenheit des Betroffenen in seinem eigenen Milieu bezeichnen kann, etwa dem der Rhetoren.[233] Der Kontext des Plädoyers ist allbekannt,[234] es sei nur daran erinnert, daß Archias sich nach seiner Jugend in Antiocheia zunächst eine gewisse Zeit in Italien

[225] Malal. 233,4–9.

[226] *IGLS* III, 1071 B, h. Das Datum bezieht sich auf das 2. Jahr der pompeianischen oder der caesraianischen Ära.

[227] *IGLS* III, 1071 B, i.

[228] Sartre 1997, 159, Anm. 69 mit Verweis auf einen *agoranomos* aus Seleukeia von 191–192, Pompeius Simos (*IGLS* III, 1213, i).

[229] Caes., *B.C.* 3,102, 6. Vgl. auch Sartre 2001, 131 mit Verweis auf Poulsen 1938.

[230] Vgl. Sartre 1996 mit Hervorhebung vorkaiserzeitlicher römischer Gentilnamen in Antiocheia.

[231] Cass. Dio 48,24,7–26,2, demzufolge die Römer von Tyros die Stadt vor den Parthern retteten.

[232] Cic., *Arch.* 3.

[233] Hellegouarc'h 1963, 224.

[234] Coşkun 2010.

aufhielt, dann, unter dem Consulat von C. Marius und Q. Lutatius Catulus (102), nach Rom gelangte, wo er, obwohl er noch die *toga praetexta* trug, also höchstens 16 Jahre zählte, bei verschiedenen einflußreichen Familien empfangen wurde,[235] bevor er schließlich durch die Vermittlung des L. Licinius Lucullus das römische Bürgerrecht sowie den Namen A. Licinius Archias erhielt und 62 dann dem bekannten Prozeß unterzogen wurde.[236] Inwieweit Archias nun typisch oder untypisch für die Perspektiven und Interessen war, welche einem jungen Mitglied einer vornehmen Antiochener Familie gegen Ende des 2. Jh. zu eigen waren, darf wohl bezweifelt werden; immerhin verrät sein Lebenslauf sowohl die Mobilität jenes sozialen Milieus, das wir ja auch zumindest für das Ende des 2. Jh.s in so prominenter Weise auf Delos repräsentiert fanden, als auch die Tatsache, daß Antiocheia dem Talent des jungen Dichters offensichtlich nicht dieselben Entfaltungsmöglichkeiten bot wie Rom[237] – zwei Überlegungen, die natürlich in Anbetracht unserer völligen Unkenntnis der familiären Lage des Archias bloße Hypothesen bleiben müssen, immerhin aber durch die Klagen des Apollonius von Tyana über das niedrige intellektuelle Niveau der Stadt in flavischer Zeit eine gewisse Bestärkung finden.[238]

Die Frage nach den städtischen Eliten ist im Hellenismus natürlich untrennbar mit der Frage nach dem zeitgenössischen Euergetismus verbunden. Das Fehlen der epigraphischen Quellen wird bis zu einem gewissen Grade durch das Zeugnis von Malalas wettgemacht. So kennen wir immerhin noch aus spätseleukidischer Zeit Maron von Antiocheia, der nach Athen emigriert war, aber unter Antiochos Philopator, also zwischen 114 und 92,[239] seiner Stadt Antiocheia testamentarisch ein Heiligtum der Musen und eine Bibliothek hinterließ.[240] Aus augusteischer Zeit wissen wir dann von Sosibios, einem reichen Antiochener, der Augustus nahestand und mit ihm um 30 v. Chr. nach Rom zurückkehrte. Nach seinem Tod hinterließ er seiner Heimatstadt testamentarisch sein Vermögen unter der Bedingung, alle 4 Jahre im Oktober 30-tägige szenische und athletische Spiele sowie Wagenrennen zu organisieren[241] – eine Verpflichtung, welcher der örtliche Beamtenapparat sich offensichtlich nicht gewachsen fühlte, da schon unter Claudius der Kaiser eingreifen mußte.[242] Malalas, leider unsere einzige Quelle für das Antiocheia des gesamten Berichtszeitraums, bezeichnet Sosibios als συγκλητικός, was wohl nicht so zu verstehen ist, als sei Sosibios römischer Senator gewesen,[243] sondern ihn vielmehr als antiochenischen Bouleuten ausweist.[244]

---

[235] Cic., *Arch.* 3 nennt hier die *Aemilii, Caecilii Metelli, Licinii Crassi, Livii Drusi, Lutatii Catuli, Octavii* und die *Porcii Catones.*

[236] Zur Erwebung des römischen Bürgerrechts, vgl. Deniaux 1981, 133 und 137–138.

[237] Ähnlich auch Kolb 1996, 102.

[238] Philostrat., *Vita Apoll.* 1,16 und 6,38. Nicht auszuschließen ist, daß es sich hierbei um eine Rückprojizierung der Verhältnisse der Zeit des Philostratos, also der Severerzeit, handelt.

[239] Entweder Antiochos IX (114–95) oder X (95–92); Antiochos XII regierte nie in Antiocheia.

[240] Malal. 235,18–236,1.

[241] Malal. 224,22–225,2.

[242] Die Verwaltung dieser Hinterlassenschaft, welche 15 Goldtalente jährlich betrug, schien nicht einfach, was die Bewohner dazu bewog, Claudius im Jahr 43/44 um die Neuausrichtung der Spiele zu bitten (Malal. 248,27–249,27). Unter Commodus wurde dann das Kapital des Sosibios zum kaiserlichen Tresor geschlagen, der seitdem die Spiele verwaltete (Malal. 284).

[243] So Downey 1961, 168–169.

[244] Vgl. M. Heil, in *PIR*² ad S 772, p. 293.

Da unsere Zeugnisse fast ausschließlich den literarischen Quellen entstammen, ist kaum erstaunlich, daß sich nur euergetische Handlungen von offizieller, nicht privater Seite erhalten haben, und hier der Natur der Quellen gemäß lediglich Aktionen seitens der Römer attestieren,[245] deren aktive Bautätigkeit mal unter dem Aspekt der Romanisierung,[246] mal unter dem der Kompensation für den Verlust des Hauptstadtstatus,[247] mal unter dem der Sicherung der Zufriedenheit der Bevölkerung analysiert wurden.[248] So wissen wir bereits aus seleukidischer Zeit, daß Q. Marcius Rex (cos. 68) bei seinem diplomatischen Besuch bei Philipp II in Antiocheia in seiner Funktion als Proconsul von Cilicien 67 zwar einen *phoros* eintrieb,[249] gleichzeitig aber ein Hippodrom und einen Palast errichten oder renovieren ließ,[250] wobei manchmal vermutet wird, es handle sich hier um einen Beitrag zum Wiederaufbau der Stadt nach dem Erdbeben, das Antiocheia in der Regierungszeit des Tigranes verwüstet hatte,[251] vergleichbar etwa mit den reichen Spenden, welche Rhodos nach einer ähnlichen Naturkatastrophe 227 erhielt.

Nach der römischen Annektion trat dann Demetrios von Gadara als Euerget in Erscheinung; eine etwas schattenhafte, für Pompeius' syrische Neuordnung aber wohl kaum zu überschätzende Person, die als Freigelassener des Pompeius bezeichnet wird. Ob er bereits im Sklavenstand geboren wurde oder vorher vielleicht sogar der städtischen Elite Gadaras angehörte, ist unsicher; interessant ist jedenfalls, daß er sich ganz besonders um das Wohlergehen Antiocheias verdient machte, wie Plutarch und Julian betonen, welche seinen Empfang durch die Magistrate und Priester der Stadt beschreiben.[252]

Die Beschreibung der reichen Spenden Caesars, Agrippas, Augustus', Tiberius', Caligulas und anderer zum Bau fundamentaler städtischer Infrastruktur wie Theater, Tempel, Bäder, Thermen etc. mögen den Eindruck erwecken, Antiocheia habe vor der Provinzialisierung so gut wie keine städtische Infrastruktur besessen ; bedenkt man aber, daß Antiocheia innerhalb zweier Jahrhundert von insgesamt 8 zerstörerischen Erdbeben heimgesucht wurde (92, 65, 37 v. Chr.; 19 n. Chr., 37, 47, 53, 82–84)[253] und laut Iustin unter Tigranes 170.000 einem dieser Erdbeben zum Opfer fielen,[254] erscheinen die meisten bei Malalas, einem extrem späten Zeugen, erwähnten Bauten als bloße Renovierungsarbeiten oder Neubauten zerstörter Strukturen.[255] So wissen wir, daß Caesar bei seinem kurzen Aufenthalt in Antiocheia im Juni 47 sowohl eine Basilika (Kaisarion) als auch eine Bronzestatue der Tyche Roms, auf der Akropolis ferner Thermen und einen dazugehörigen Aquädukt, schließlich ein μον<ομ>άχιον (Amphitheater?) und ein The-

[245] Vgl. allg. hierzu Kolb 1996,109ff.; allerdings unter Überbewertung des Malalas.

[246] Downey 1961, 141 und 156.

[247] Sartre 2000, 500.

[248] Mittag 2009, 196–197.

[249] Zu den verschiedenen Deutungen Downey 1951, 154–155. Vell. Pat. 2,37,5 präzisiert, daß es sich nicht um eine reguläre Steuer handelte, da diese erst nach der Annektion eingesetzt wurde.

[250] Malal. 9,225, 7ff. Neuerrichtung: Downey 1961, 140–141. Renovierung: Bellinger 1949a, 84.

[251] Iust. 40,2,1.

[252] Plut., *Pomp.* 40,1–5.

[253] Sbeinati/Darawcheh/Mouty 2005.

[254] Iust. 40,2,1.

[255] So auch Downey 1961, 131, Anm. 57.

ater bauen ließ und außerdem das örtliche Pantheon renovierte und dessen Altar wieder aufstellte.[256] Auch Agrippa zeigte sich als bedeutender Bauherr.[257]

2.2.2. Seleukeia

Was nun Seleukeia-Pierien betrifft, einer schon in seleukidischer Zeit (109) mit der *eleutheria* beschenkten Stadt,[258] so machte Pompeius sie ebenfalls zur *civitas libera*,[259] letzteres laut Eutrop mit der Begründung, daß sie sich Tigranes widersetzt habe,[260] was auch bei Cicero belegt ist.[261] Leider wissen wir über Seleukeia noch erheblich weniger als für Antiocheia. Auf den vorrömischen Münzen findet sich neben der Stadttyche zunächst nur der Vermerk auf Autonomie und Heiligkeit. Aus unserem numismatischen Befund geht hervor, daß Seleukeia ab 84/83 keine Tetradrachmen mehr schlug, was mit der Abschließung vom Hinterland während der Herrschaft des Tigranes erklärt wurde.[262] Das Jahr 31 scheint dann eine gewisse Bedeutung für Seleukeia gehabt zu haben, da hier eine neue Ära begann, die allerdings die lokale Freiheitsära von 109 nicht ganz verdrängte. Doch auch die augusteischen Münzen tragen als Legende nur die Attribute ἱερὰ καὶ αὐτόνομος, so daß von einer Statusveränderung oder -bestätigung des Augustus auszugehen ist.[263] Augusteische Ära und Legende bleiben dann noch bis ins 2. Jh. erhalten, wie eine Münze des Jahres 157 n. Chr. zeigt.[264]

Erneut ist es ansonsten nur ein *agoranomos*, dessen Name sich erhalten hat, wenn auch der schlechte Zustand der Inschrift nur zeigt, daß es sich wohl um einen Einheimischen handelte, findet sich doch auf einer steinernen Form lediglich der Vermerk „[- - -]tiôn, Sohn des [- - -]iôn“ mit einem auf 24/3 v. Chr. verweisenden Datumsvermerk.[265]

2.2.3. Laodikeia

Was nun Laodikeia betrifft, so ist der Status der Stadt unter Pompeius in den Quellen widersprüchlich, wenn auch in der Forschung die Freilassung oft recht summarisch angenommen wird.[266] Die Münzprägung zeigt immerhin die Legende ἱερὰ καὶ αὐτόνομος und führt eine eigene Ära auf, die bis ins 34. Jahr geht, bevor sie von der caesarianischen abgelöst wird, deren erstes Jahr 48/7 ist, so daß die betreffende Ära auf 82/81 oder 81/80

[256] Malal. 216,19–217, 4.

[257] Malal. 222,15–22; 225,3–7.

[258] Zum Wert Mastrocinque 1977.

[259] Plin., *HN* 5,79; Eutr. 6,11; Strabon 16,2,8. Von Seleukeia flüchtete Pompeius auch nach Ägypten: Plut., *Pomp*. 77.

[260] Eutr. 6,11.

[261] Cic., *Verr*. 2,2,4,61. Vgl. aber Strabon 16,2,8. Diskussion bei Downey 1961, 137, Anm. 87.

[262] Seyrig 1950, 29; Sear 5887 (datiert nach 109/8).

[263] *RPC* I, Nr. 4328 (Jahr 114 = 6 n. Chr.)

[264] *BMC* 31 (Act. 188 = 157 n. Chr.)

[265] *IGLS* III 1214.

[266] Vgl. etwa Grainger 1990, 195.

verweist, also die Zeit des Tigranes,[267] wobei der hohe Münzausstoß mit dem Niedergang des eingeschlossenen Seleukeias erklärt wird.[268]

Parallel hierzu kennen wir aus Macrobius die Anekdote, daß der ansonsten unbekannte Andron von Laodikeia Anfang der 40er Jahre nach Rom gereist sein soll, um Caesar um die Freiheit (*libertas*) seiner Heimatstadt zu bitten, woraufhin ihn Cicero bat, im Falle des Erfolgs gleich auch um die Freiheit Roms nachzusuchen.[269] Es ist unsicher, ob es sich hier um eine individuelle Initiative oder um eine Auftragsreise handelt; auch ist es schwer, den Sinn der Anekdote zu verstehen. Entweder handelt es sich um einen Beweis dafür, daß Pompeius Laodikeia eben nicht weitgehende und mit anderen Städten der Tetrapolis vergleichbare Autonomierechte verlieh; oder aber es handelt sich um die Bitte um Rücknahme einer zwischenzeitlich verhängten Strafe. Immerhin wissen wir inschriftlich, daß Laodikeia im Oktober 48 eine neue Ära begann,[270] die klar auf Caesars Alleinherrschaft verweist; auf den Münzen erscheint dann manchmal sogar der Name Iulia Laodiceia,[271] wobei die alte Legende ἱερὰ καὶ αὐτόνομος nicht verschwindet.

Auch hier in Seleukeia sind es wieder die Namen einiger *agoranomoi*, die uns auf Gewichten begegnen; einige Stücke sind leider anonym,[272] andere informieren uns über die Amtsausübung des Polemon (zwischen 81 und 51),[273] Kynagos (36/5 v. Chr.),[274] Akamas (6/5 v. Chr.)[275] und Antipatros (23/4 n. Chr.),[276] ohne daß wir Weiteres sagen könnten.

Ein ansonsten in dieser Zeit seltener Einblick in euergetische Tätigkeiten der finanzkräftigeren Laodikeer findet sich in einer zwischen 88 und 60 datierten delischen Inschrift,[277] welche eine dem dortigen Isis-Heiligtum gestiftete Weihung eines namentlich unbekannten Laodikeiers beinhaltet und gleichzeitig auch Euodos aus Antiocheia erwähnt,[278] der zum achtzehnten Mal das Amt des Tempeldiener (*zakor*) ausübte.[279] Auch in Laodikeia manifestierte sich die augusteische Baupolitik, errichtete Augustus doch ein Theater, eine Statue seiner selbst, ein Tetrapylon mit Marmor und Mosaiken, das von einer Statue und 4 Bronzepferden gekrönt wurde,[280] während Herodes der Stadt einen Aquädukt spendete.[281]

---

267 *BMC* 7 (Tigr. 31 = 51/0 v. Chr.).

268 Vgl. Seyrig 1950, 28–29, der den hohen Münzausstoß damit erklärt, daß Laodikeia, während Seleukeia sich Tigranes verschloß, dessen Funktion als Hauptafen Nordsyriens übernahm.

269 Macr., *Sat.* 2,3,12.

270 *IGRR* III 1012; *BMC* 12 (Caes. 73 = 25/6 n. Chr.).

271 Vgl. allg. Seyrig 1950, 26–29; *BMC* 26.

272 *IGLS* IV 1271, B, c: 53/2 v. Chr.; B, e: 41/0 v. Chr.; B/g: 12/1 v. Chr.; B, j: 37/8 n. Chr.

273 *IGLS* IV 1271, B, d.

274 *IGLS* IV 1271, B, f.

275 *IGLS* IV 1271, B, h.

276 *IGLS* IV 1271, B, i.

277 Zu Syrern auf Delos, vgl. Rostovtzeff 1941 (1955), II: 680, 685, 1002, 1260–1261.

278 Auch bekannt aus *I. Délos* 2087, 21; 2160, 5; 2205, 6; 2212, 7; 2619,a,12.

279 *I. Délos* 2161.

280 Malal. 222,23–223,6.

281 Jos., *Bell.* 1,21,422.

2.2.4. Apameia

Betrachten wir schließlich Apameia am Orontes,[282] deren Freiheit weder unter den Seleukiden noch unter Pompeius belegt ist, was wohl damit zu tun haben könnte, daß Apameia als Heereszentrum des Seleukidenreichs fungierte und die innere Nord-Südroute kontrollierte, welche Palästina mit Syrien verband. Trotzdem scheint es, daß Pompeius die Burg der Stadt schleifen ließ[283] und somit vielleicht sowohl die Autonomie der Stadt betonen[284] als ihre strategische Bedeutung beeinträchtigen wollte. Nichtsdestoweniger gewann Apameia in der Zeit der römischen Bürgerkriege wieder an militärischer Bedeutung, wie die Belagerung der an Q. Caecilius Bassus gefallenen Stadt durch die Caesarianer belegt.[285]

In der Münzprägung lassen sich einige Indizien auf den Status der Stadt wiederfinden: Nach einer ersten Prägung autonomer Stücke, die unter Tigranes 76/6 beginnt und unter Antiochos XIII. 67/7 endet und die Bezeichnung ἱερὰ καὶ ἄσυλος führt,[286] beginnt die Münzprägung erst wieder im 7. Jahr einer ins Jahr 66 verlegten pompeianischen Ära unter Verweis auf dieselben Attribute wie in tigranischer Zeit.[287] Nach einigen Unterbrechungen und ikonographischen Veränderungen, u.a. während der parthischen Besatzung, während der die Seleukidenära wieder eingeführt wird,[288] kommt es dann zur Prägung von Münzen mit der Legende ἱερὰ καὶ αὐτόνομος, die auf eine Statusveränderung unter Marc Anton um 41/40 verweist, Beginn einer vielleicht mit dem Dank für den Widerstand gegen Q. Labienus verbundenen Ära.[289] Um 30/29 vermerkt die Legende der Münzen, wohl unter dem Einfluß von Actium, wieder nur ἱερὰ καὶ ἄσυλος.[290] Erst wesentlich später erscheinen dann Münzen mit dem Bild des Augustus und dem Verweis auf eine neue, augusteische Ära. 14/15 tragen die Münzen des Tiberius wieder die Seleukidenära, und nach der Erhebung in den Status einer Colonie unter Claudius erscheint eine neue Ära unter Verweis auf das Wort ἐλευθερίας.[291]

Was nun die Präsenz und Tätigkeit der städtischen Eliten Apameias betrifft, so wurde Diodotos Tryphon bereits in der ersten Bearbeitungsphase erwähnt; in spätseleukidischer und römischer Zeit gilt dann der stoische Philosoph Poseidonios von Apameia[292] (135–51) als berühmtester Sohn der Stadt,[293] wenn er auch der Nachwelt v.a. unter dem Beinamen seiner Wahlheimat, also Rhodos, bekannt ist, was nicht von ungefähr an den bereits erwähnten Archias erinnert. Leider sind wir nur ungenügend über sei-

[282] Allg. zu Apameia Balty/Balty 1977; Balty/Van Rengen 1993; Balty 2003.

[283] Jos., *Ant.* 14,3,2.

[284] Grainger 1990, 172 und 195.

[285] Strabon 16, 2, 10 (C 752–753); Cass. Dio 47,26,3 und 28,2.

[286] *BMC* 4 (Sel. 239 = 74/3 v. Chr.).

[287] *BMC* 15 (Pomp. 8 = 58/7 v. Chr.).

[288] *RPC* I, Nr. 4338 (Sel. 276 = 39/8 v. Chr.).

[289] Cass. Dio 48,25,1.

[290] *RPC* I, Nr. 4347 (Sel. 283 = 30 v. Chr.).

[291] Allg. Seyrig 1950, 15–20.

[292] Herkunftsort erwähnt bei Strabon 14,2,13; 16,2,10; Suda, *s.v.* Poseidonios.

[293] Vgl. auch die Aufzählung von Tryphon und Poseidonios in Strabon 16,2,10; eine Passage, die Engels 1999, 166 als Honoratiorenkatalog bezeichnet, wenn auch neben diesen beiden Personen keine weitere direkt aus Apameia zu stammen scheint.

ne Familienverhältnisse informiert; vermutet wird zwar zum einen eine „wohlhabende Honoratiorenfamilie“[294] – ein zweifellos aus dem Bildungsstand und den Reisen des Poseidonios abgeleitete Vermutung –, zum anderen, daß sich, „von seiner Familie [...] nur sagen [läßt], daß sie zur politischen Führungsschicht gehörte und in den Thronstreitigkeiten des untergehenden Seleukidenreiches wohl Partei für eine Linie der Dynastie nahm“,[295] was wohl aus dem politischen Engagement in Poseidonios’ Historien abgeleitet ist. Tatsächlich aber wissen wir nichts über Poseidonios’ Abstammung. Immerhin ist interessant, daß er in den 90er Jahren Bürger von Rhodos wurde, wenig später bereits Prytan im Inselstaat,[296] schließlich, um 87/86, diplomatischer Gesandter in Rom.[297] Ein politisches Engagement ist also unverkennbar, und hier schienen für Poseidonios trotz seiner sicherlich wohlhabenden Herkunft in Rhodos offenbar bessere Ausgangsvoraussetzungen vorzuliegen als in den ungleich größeren, aber politisch unsicheren Städten der Tetrapolis, über deren moralische Dekadenz er einige kritische Anmerkungen in sein Geschichtswerk einstreute.[298]

Leider sind uns aus Apameia bis in die Kaiserzeit namentlich keine örtlichen Magistrate bekannt; erst aus trajanischer Zeit stammt dann eine Inschrift des L. Iulius Agrippa, der Dexandros, seinen Urgroßvater erwähnt, welcher sicherlich bereits das römische Bürgerrecht besaß und später erster Priester des Herrscherkults der Provinz wurde,[299] auf dessen komplexe Organisation hier nicht eingegangen werden kann,[300] der aber als erster Beleg für die Schaffung eines syrischen *koinon* zu sehen ist.[301] Dexandros galt wohl seit 31/30 als *amicus et socius populi Romani*, wie es der Inschrift zufolge auch die auf dem Capitol verwahrten Bronzetafeln bestätigen sollen und empfing zusammen mit seiner Familie königliche Ehren. Ein Auszug (oder eine Kopie) des Dekrets befand sich in den Archiven von Apameia und wurde im Monat Xandikos eines unbestimmten Jahres erstellt. Ein fragmentarisch erhaltenes Dekret von *boule* und *demos* derselben Stadt ehrte dann Dexandros am 3. Tag vor Ende des Monats Peritios eines ebenfalls unbestimmten Jahres unter Verweis auf die vorher erwähnten Umstände. Der Stein ist leider dort, wo der präzise Inhalt der Ehren aufgeführt wird, zerstört, so daß wir auch über etwaige euergetische Aktivitäten nicht informiert sind.[302]

Im Jahre 6/7 umfaßte das städtische Territorium von Apameia immerhin 117.000 Bürger, also sicherlich eine halbe Million Einwohner, wie das in Berytus erhaltene Cen-

---

294 Engels 1999, 166.

295 Malitz 1999, 426.

296 Strabon 7, 5, 8 (C 316).

297 Plut., *Mar.* 45,7.

298 Poseidonios, *FHG* III, p. 263, Frg. 31 in Athen. 5,210e und 12,540b; *FHG* III, p. 258, Frg. 18 = *FGrH* IIA, p. 228, 87 F 10 in Athen. 5,210e–f und 12,540a–b.

299 Rey-Coquais 1973, Nr. 96 = *AE* 1976, 678.

300 Der syrische Kaiserkult teilte sich ursprünglich in die Eparchien Antiocheia (Tetrapolis), Tyros (Phoinizien) und Kilikien; nachdem Kilikien einen eigenen Kaiserkult entwickelte, kam die Kommagene hinzu, während sich die Region um Damaskus als eigene Eparchie von der phoinizischen abspaltete. Das Haupt des syrischen Kaiserkults residierte in Antiocheia. Hierzu Rey-Coquais 1973, Nr. 98. Dexandros mag verglichen werden mit Ariston, Sohn des Asklepiades von Arados, der Priester des noch lebenden Augustus wurde (*IGLS* VII 4012).

301 Hierzu etwa Deininger 1965, 87–88.

302 Vgl. Sartre 2001.

susdekret verrät, in welchem der Statthalter P. Sulpicius Quirinus den Q. Aemilius Q. f. Pal. Secundus[303] mit der Volkszählung betraut[304], doch leider gibt uns dies keinen weiteren Aufschluß über die Größe der örtlichen Verwaltung.

3. Zusammenfassung

Der meist von der epigraphischen Quellenlage abhängige prosopographische Befund zu den Eliten der seleukidischen Kolonien Syriens unterstützt die historiographische Kenntnislage in nur sehr unbefriedigendem Maße, so daß die Beantwortung der vier typischen Leitfragen antiker Elitenforschung – also das Verhältnis und die Erwartungshaltung zwischen der Elite und der übrigen Bevölkerung wie auch zwischen der Elite und dem König – weitgehend auf Basis der literarischen Texte und nur unzureichend erweitert durch den numismatischen Befund, beantwortet werden muß.

Dieses Problem wird noch durch die Frage nach der ethnischen Dimension von Elite erschwert, bedenkt man, daß lange Zeit die städtischen Eliten in sicherlich simplifizierender Weise mit der wohlhabenden griechischstämmigen Bevölkerung gleichgesetzt und in einen oft künstlichen Gegensatz zur sonstigen, unter dem Begriff „orientalisch" subsumierten Landbevölkerung gebracht wurden. Diese Sichtweise, die auf den ersten Blick auch von unseren literarischen, meist aus einem griechischen Blickwinkel vefaßten Quellen wie auch von der fast ausschließlich griechischen Onomastik des prosopographischen Befunds unterstützt wird, ist allerdings in dieser Schärfe nicht mehr aufrecht zu erhalten. Zum einen wissen wir, daß die seleukidischen Stadtgründungen bereits von Anfang an wesentlich kosmopolitischer angelegt waren, als ursprünglich vermutet, und nicht nur in Städten wie Antiocheia-Orontes oder Seleukeia-Tigris umfangreiche Viertel mit einheimischer Besiedlung bestanden, so daß der Gegensatz zwischen städtischen und ländlichen Interessen nicht (immer) mit dem zwischen griechischer und autochthoner Ethnizität übereinstimmt. Zum anderen zeigt der onomastische Befund des hellenistischen Ostens nur allzuoft die Möglichkeit, daß orientalische Bürger des Seleukidenreichs griechische Namen anzunehmen vermochten, bzw. ihre Kinder mit solchen griechischen Namen versahen. Bedenkt man zudem die sicherlich nicht seltenen Mischehen und die unbestreitbare Tatsache, daß die seleukidische Oberschicht trotz aller orientalischen Formen der seleukidischen Herrscherrepräsentation sich überwiegend griechischer kultureller Formen bediente, ist das Problem der Äquation von Elite und Ethnizität kaum befriedigend zu lösen. In dieser Hinsicht ist auch schwer zu eruieren, inwieweit die Herausbildung semitisch geprägter Kleinfürstentümer während des 1. Jh. v. Chr., die sich wesentlich im Machtvakuum der zwischen den hellenistischen Siedlungszentren gelegenenen Peraiai abspielte, als Folge oder vielmehr als Ursache der später in den Quellen zu beobachtenden Kontrastierung semitischer Land- und hellenisierter Stadtbevölkerung zu analysieren ist.

[303] Zuletzt Schäfer 2000, 100–101, Anm. 13.

[304] *CIL* III 6687 = *ILS* 2683 = *AE* 2006, 1579.

3.1. Erwartungen der lokalen Eliten an die übrige Bevölkerung

Die Erwartung der Elite an die Bevölkerung ist von der inneren Zusammensetzung dieser Führungsschicht untrennbar. Hier zeigt unser Befund (mit möglicher Ausnahme des „Poplios" in nachseleukidischer Zeit) ausschließlich eine griechische Onomastik, welche nahelegt, daß, wenn nicht das Bürgerrecht, so doch zumindest die Bekleidung von Magistratur oder wichtigen städtischen Positionen ausschließlich griechischsprachigen Personen offenstand. Freilich ist die seleukidische Onomastik, wie gesagt, in Anbetracht der Möglichkeit zur Annahme eines griechischen Namens durch nichtgriechische lokale Eliten eher kompliziert. Die Selbstdefinition der lokalen Eliten in seleukidischer Zeit ist nur schwer zu eruieren, doch suggeriert die Münzprägung der „Bruderstädte" eine gewisse, zumindest propagandistische Solidarität zwischen den einzelnen Städten der Tetrapolis, deren Gründung ja auch auf dieselbe Zeit und Herrschergestalt zurückging. Dies wird ebenfalls durch die gemeinsame kultische Verehrung der syrischen Götter auf Delos deutlich, welche nicht etwa auf die Bürger einer einzigen Stadt beschränkt ist. Diese Selbstdefinition läßt sich für das 1. Jh. durch die Aussage des Pompeius erweitern, die Antiochener seien Nachfahren der Athener; eine Aussage, deren Wahrheitsgehalt hier weniger zur Debatte stehen soll als vielmehr die hohe Wahrscheinlichkeit, Pompeius habe hier aus Artigkeit den Antiochenern ihre eigene Selbstwahrnehmung und – stilisierung entgegenhalten wollen. Freilich handelt es sich (trotz der Präsenz zahlreicher Antiochener in Athen) kaum um einen zentralen Aspekt der ethnischen Selbstdefinition Antiocheias als vielmehr den Wunsch, durch die Verbindung mit der Wiege antiker Demokratie und die Verdrängung des makedonischen Einflusses die Freiheit und Hellenizität der Stadt zu betonen. Dieser Wunsch paßt gut zusammen mit der rein griechischen Symbolik der Münzprägung wie auch mit der euergetischen Selbstdarstellung der Bürger innerhalb und außerhalb der Stadt während des 2. und 1. Jh., wie etwa in Athen oder auf Delos deutlich wird. Auch läßt sich diese Selbstdarstellung mit den immer wieder attestierten ethnischen Konflikten in Verbindung bringen, welche die Griechen der Tetrapolis wie im Jahre 40 n. Chr. mit der jüdischen Gemeinde innerhalb oder, wie zur Zeit des Clodius oder Gabinius, mit den räuberischen Arabern außerhalb der Stadt in Opposition brachten, wenn uns auch die konkrete Machtstellung von Personen wie den spätseleukidischen Araberdynasten Samsigeramus oder Aziz weitgehend unbekannt bleibt. Worauf die Bedeutung der lokalen Elite basierte, ist ungewiß; am wahrscheinlichsten scheint in Anbetracht unserer Quellen, welche Mitglieder der Elite auch als *philoi* der seleukidischen Könige attestieren oder, wie Moron und Sosibios von Antiocheia oder Dexandros von Laodikeia, meist im Zusammenhang mit euergetischen Tätigkeiten erwähnen, der Zugriff auf materielle Ressourcen, während dynastische Abstammung und sakrale Kultfunktion als wichtige Faktoren der Kennzeichnung von Elite nicht belegt sind, sondern höchstens als Formen der Auszeichnung erscheinen. In dieser Hinsicht sind natürlich auch Machtmittel und Handlungsspielräume kaum bekannt; immerhin suggeriert die Existenz des Bunds der „Bruderstädte" wie auch der Verweis auf den syrischen *populus* die Möglichkeit für die Elite, die städtischen Institutionen für ihre Zwecke zu nutzen, während der Bericht von der Bestechung des Pompeius durch die Antiochener wie auch die Anschuldigungen Ciceros gegen Gabinius nahelegen, daß auch der materielle Reichtum gezielt eingesetzt werden konnte.

3.2. Erwartungen der Bevölkerung an die lokalen Eliten

Die Erwartung der Bevölkerung an ihre Eliten ist eng verbunden mit der spezifischen Ausprägung ihrer Legitimation. In diesem Kontext muß die systematische Betonung der städtischen Autonomie auf der lokalen Münzprägung als Zeichen gesehen werden, daß auch die Legitimation der Elite in diesem Rahmen eher institutionell als etwa dynastisch oder charismatisch legitimiert werden mußte. Ähnlich sind auch euergetische Handlungen belegt, in welchen bedeutende Antiochener wie Maron oder Sosibios der Stadt Wohltaten wie den Bau einer Bibliothek oder die Ausrichtung von Spielen zukommen ließen; Handlungen, die ihr Status offensichtlich als nötig oder zumindest möglich erscheinen ließ. Freilich ist ungewiß, inwieweit diese Legitimationsbemühungen immer auch Akzeptanz fanden oder schufen; immerhin sind wir kaum über innerstädtische Unruhen informiert, wie sie etwa die Provinz Asia Ende des 2. Jh.s erschütterten. Was die Beziehung der ländlichen Bevölkerung zu den Eliten betrifft, so ist die Sachlage, wie bereits erwähnt, schwieriger zu bestimmen; immerhin zeigt die Genese zahlreicher Kleinstaaten an der Steppengrenze des Fruchtbaren Halbmonds, daß die politische Autorität der städtischen Eliten das von den Seleukiden hinterlassene Machtvakuum nicht ausreichend zu füllen vermochte; inwieweit dies aber auf einem ethnisch oder politisch begründeten Legitimationsdefizit beruhte und nicht vielmehr auf der militärischen Unterlegenheit der städtischen Milizen gegenüber beweglichen Reiterheeren, muß dahingestellt bleiben.

3.3. Erwartungen der lokalen Eliten an die Reichsadministration

Etwas besser informiert sind wir über die Erwartungen der lokalen Eliten der seleukidischen Kolonien Syriens an die Reichsverwaltung. So läßt sich etwa die Frage, ob die Existenz einer Hegemonialmacht als notwendig erachtet wurde, eindeutig mit „ja" beantworten, bedenkt man, daß die Städte der Tetrapolis nach dem Zusammenbruch der seleukidischen Herrschaft – an der sie selbst durch die Unterstützung verschiedener Prätendenten zeitweise in nicht unbedeutendem Maße beteiligt waren – selbst nach einer neuen Hegemonialmacht suchten, glaubt man Iustins Bericht, daß der syrische *populus* sich recht schnell auf Tigranes als Herrscher und Beschützer einigte. Ebenfalls in diese Richtung verweist die Nachricht, daß die spätere römische Verwaltung ihre Legitimität nicht nur aus dem Schutz vor Nomaden oder Parthern bezog, sondern auch aus der Unterstützung der hellenistischen „Kultur" gegenüber Assimilationsbestrebungen seitens autochthoner Kleinstaaten wie Judäa. In dieser Hinsicht ist allerdings interessant, daß die römische Zentralmacht trotz Provinzialisierung weiter das Bild eines Seleukidenkönigs auf die Tetradrachmen setzen ließ, um somit – ganz abgesehen vom zentralen Aspekt einer Gewährleistung der wirtschaftlichen Kontinuität – sowohl die fiktive politische als auch die regionale Eigenständigkeit der neuen Provinz zu betonen und den politischen Empfindlichkeiten der Bevölkerung oder/und der Eliten entgegenzukommen. Dergestalt fielen auch die Handlungen aus, welche der Hegemonialmacht zugestanden bzw. von ihr erwartet wurden: Neben dem erwähnten Schutz vor äußerer Bedrohung war es eine möglichst geringe bzw. möglichst gerechte Besteuerung, auf die einzelne Gouverneure wie Gabinius auch eingingen, sowie die Garantie größtmöglicher innerer Autonomie, die auch im Rahmen der Möglichkeiten gewährt wurde. Was schließlich die Kommunikation mit der Zentrale betrifft, so ist die seleukidische von der römischen Zeit zu trennen: Während unter seleukidischer Herrschaft die persönliche Präsenz des Königs in Syrien eine schnelle Interaktion zwischen Zentrale und Elite vereinfachte und durch die bewußte Eingliederung von Mitgliedern der Reichselite wie den *philoi* in die lokalen Eliten und umgekehrt beförderte, ist diese Zusammenarbeit in römischer Zeit durch die räumliche Distanz etwas erschwert. Hier sind dann sowohl persönliche Gesandtschaften nach Rom attestiert als auch wirkmächtige Zeremonien in Syrien selbst, wie etwa der prächtige Empfang, den eine Stadt wie Antiocheia sowohl einem einflußreichen römischen Freigelassenen wie Demetrios von Gadara als auch Politikern wie Caesar bereiten konnte (und der ganz in der Tradition der hellenistischen Zeit stand, wie der Empfang Ptolemaios' III. durch die Antiochener Elite im 3. Jh. beweist), und durch welche die Interaktion zwischen verschiedenen Ebenen von Macht und Verwaltung sinnfällig dargestellt und somit das Gleichgewicht zwischen den Instanzen neu ausgehandelt wurde. Ähnliches gilt für die aus Dank für die Statthalterschaft des M. Calpurnius Bibulus vermachten Statuen.

3.4. Erwartungen der Reichsadministration an die lokalen Eliten

Als Funktion, welche die lokalen Eliten erfüllen mußten, um den Erwartungen der Reichsverwaltung zu entsprechen, ist natürlich die Stabilisierung der jeweiligen Herrschaft und die Zusammenarbeit mit der Territorialverwaltung, sei es auf Satrapal-, sei es auf Provinzebene, zu erwähnen. Hinzu kommt dann natürlich auch, zumindest in seleukidischer Zeit, die Erwartung von Truppenstellung und die langfristige Sicherung oder gar graduelle Steigerung von Steuer- bzw. Zolleinkünften, was sowohl durch eine Förderung der wirtschaftlichen Aktivität durch Aufbau eines auf dem Modell der Stadt basierenden monetären Systems, als auch durch Beibehaltung bewährter, nur bedingt als im griechischen Sinn urban erscheinender Institutionen wie etwa des Jerusalemer Tempelstaats oder des mesopotamischen Wirtschaftsraums erreicht werden sollte. Daß die Erwartung von Loyalität nicht immer mit den Tatsachen übereinstimmte, zeigt etwa der positive Empfang, den nicht nur Ptolemaios III. und später Tigranes, sondern auch die Parther in Syrien gefunden zu haben scheinen, doch handelt es sich hier jeweils um eine atypische Reaktion auf eine Bürgerkriegssituation, der dann etwa der Empfang des Crassus in Carrhae wie auch der Wunsch einiger der Dekapolisstädte, lieber an die Provinz Syrien als an einen jüdischen Klientelstaat angegliedert zu sein, merklich widerspricht. Über den inneren Handlungsspielraum der Tetrapolisstädte sind wir nur ungenügend informiert. Sowohl in seleukidischer als auch in römischer Zeit scheint jedenfalls ein Minimum an Selbstverwaltung und Autonomie nicht nur begrüßt, sondern auch gefördert worden zu sein, denkt man an die Politik Antiochos' IV. wie auch an die euergetischen Maßnahmen der ersten römischen Machthaber; doch ist es schwierig zu bestimmen und auch im Lichte der Münzprägung nicht immer sicher, inwieweit das scheinbare graduelle Ansteigen der verschiedenen Autonomierechte mehr als reine Ehrentitel implizierte, die angesichts der weltpolitischen Lage recht belanglos bleiben mußten. Die Kommunikation mit der Zentrale geschah teils über Gesandtschaften wie die des Andron von Laodikeia nach Rom, teils durch direkte Interaktion mit dem Gouverneur oder seinen Vertrauten wie Clodius. Dabei ist klar, daß der seleukidische wie der römische Staat „akkulturierte“, in diesem Fall also hellenisierte Gruppierungen insoweit „bevorzugte“, als die hellenistischen Siedlungen größtenteils Autonomie erhielten und zum Ausgangspunkt nicht nur der wirtschaftlichen Erschließung Syriens wurden, sondern auch große städtebauliche Programme erfuhren, während die nicht in Polis-Form organisierten Landschaften allmählich dem Gutdünken lokaler Dynasten überlassen wurden (oder werden mußten), deren Anbindung an die Reichskultur sich unterschiedlich intensiv vollziehen konnte. Interessanterweise sollte die Romanisierung der Tetrapolis-Städte trotz eines reichhaltigen Bauprogramms recht langwierig ausfallen, da die innere Verwaltung mit wenigen Ausnahmen wie „Poplios“ in den Händen einer rein griechischen Bevölkerung blieb, und Bürger der Tetrapolis erst sehr spät auf Reichsebene belegt sind. Was letztlich die Belohnung der lokalen Eliten betrifft, so läßt sich in seleukidischer Zeit an die Aufnahme in die Ebene der *philoi* denken, in römischer Zeit dann an die Verleihung der *amicitia*, wie im Falle des Dexandros, zu der dann im 1. Jh., welches bereits außerhalb unserer Betrachtungsphase liegt, die Erhebung in den Ritter- und schließlich Senatorenstand kommen sollte. Über den Herrscherkult schließlich sind wir leider nur bruchstückhaft informiert, immerhin ist die Liste der Königspriester Seleukeias erhalten, wenn auch die Verbindung der genannten Namen zur städtischen Elite unklar bleibt; und die Nachricht, daß erwähnter Dexandros auch erster Priester des Kaiserkults werden sollte, zeigt wohl auch hier eine grundsätzliche Kontinuität.

Literatur

Baldus, H.R. (1987): *Syria*, in: A.M. Burnett, M.H. Crawford (Hgg.), *The Coinage of the Roman World in the Late Republic*, Oxford: 121–151.

Balty, J. (2003): A la recherche de l'Apamée hellénistique, in: *La Syrie hellénistique*, (*Topoi* Suppl. 4), Lyon: 211–222.

Balty, J., Balty, J.-Ch. (1977): Apamée de Syrie, *ANRW* II 8: 103–134.

Balty, J.-Ch., Van Rengen, W. (1993): *Apamea in Syria*, Brüssel.

Baslez, M.-F. (1983): Les étrangers à Délos. Formes et évolution de la vie de relation dans un sanctuaire panhellénique, *IH* 45: 165–169.

Bellemore, J. (1995): Cato the Younger in the East in 66 B.C., *Historia* 44: 376–379.

Bellinger, A.R. (1944): Crassus and Cassius at Antioch, *NC* ser. 7, vol. 4: 59–61.

Bellinger, A.R. (1949a): The End of the Seleucids, *TCAAS* 38: 51–102.

Bellinger, A.R. (1949b): *The Excavations at Dura-Europos, Final Report VI: The Coins*, New-Haven.

Bellinger, A.R. (1951): The Early Coinage of Roman Syria, in: P.R. Coleman-Norton (Hg.), *Studies in Roman Economic and Social History in Honor of A.C. Johnson*, Princeton: 58–67.

Bellinger, A.R. (1952): Notes on Some Coins from Antioch in Syria, *ANS–MN* 5: 1952, 53–63.

Bernhardt, R. (1971): *Imperium und Eleutheria. Die römische Politik gegenüber den freien Städten des Ostens*, Hamburg (Diss.).

Bernhardt, R. (1980): Die Immunitas der Freistädte, *ZAG* 29: 190–207.

Bevan, E.R. (1902): *The House of Seleucus*, 2 Bde., London.

Bikerman, E. (1938): *Institutions des Séleucides*, Paris.

Bojarski, W. (1990): La suprématie de l'État romain et l'autonomie des villes, *Eos* 78: 203–208.

Brodersen, K. (2001): „In den städtischen Gründungen ist die rechte Basis des Hellenisierens." Zur Funktion seleukidischer Städtegründungen, in: S. Schraut, B. Stier (Hgg.), *Stadt und Land*, Stuttgart: 356–371.

Bruneau, Ph. (1968): Contribution à l'histoire urbaine de Délos, *BCH* 92: 671–691.

Callataÿ, F. (2002): La production des tétradrachmes civiques de la Cilicie jusqu'à la Palestine, in: Chr. Augé, F. Duyrat (Hgg.), *Monnayages syriens*, Beirut: 71–91.

Capdetrey, L. (2007): *Le pouvoir séleucide. Territoire, administration, finances d'un royaume hellénistique (312–129 avant J.-C.)*, Rennes.

Carcopino, J. (1905): Les cités de Sicile devant l'impôt romain: Ager Decumanus et Ager Censorius, *Mélanges d'archéologie et d'histoire* 25: 3–54.

Carcopino, J. (1915): *La loi d'Hiéron et les Romains*, Paris.

Cohen, G.M. (1978): *The Seleucid Colonies*, Wiesbaden.

Coşkun, A. (2010): *Cicero und das römische Bürgerrecht. Die Verteidigung des Dichters Archias*, Einleitung, Text, Übersetzung und historisch-philologische Kommentierungen, Göttingen.

Coşkun, A., Engels, D., Erickson, K.: *Construction of Seleucid Royalty. Studies in the Politics and Propaganda of Antiochus I*, forthcoming.

Crönert, W. (1975): L'Epicureo Filonide, in: W. Crönert, E. Livrea (eds.), *Studi Ercolanesi*, Napoli: 39–61.

Dahlheim, W. (1977): *Gewalt und Herrschaft – Das provinziale Herrschaftssystem der römischen Republik*, Berlin–New York.

Debord, P. (2003): Le culte royal chez les Séleucides, *Pallas* 62: 281–308.

Deininger, J. (1965): *Die Provinziallandtage der römischen Kaiserzeit von Augustus bis zum Ende des dritten Jahrhunderts*, München–Berlin.

Deniaux, E. (1981): Civitate donati. Naples, Héraclée, Côme, *Ktèma* 6: 133–141.

Le Dinahet, M.-Th. (1997): Étrangers et commerçants à Délos: quelques enseignements des épitaphes, *REA* 99: 325–336.

Dobiaš, J. (1931): Les premiers rapports des Romains avec les Parthes et l'occupation de la Syrie, *Archiv Orientalni* 3: 215–256.

Downey, G. (1951): The Occupation of Syria by the Romans, *TAPA* 82: 149–163.

Downey, G. (1961): *A History of Ancient Antioch in Syria from Seleucus to the Arab Conquest*, Princeton.

Duyrat, F. (2000): Arados et la guerre de 333 à 37 avant notre ère, *RN* 155: 47–58.

Duyrat, F. (2005): *Arados hellénistique: étude historique et monétaire*, Beyrouth.

Dussaud, R. (1955): *La pénétration des Arabes en Syrie avant l'Islam*, Paris.

Ehling, K. (2003): Unruhen, Aufstände und Abfallbewegungen der Bevölkerung in Phönikien, Syrien und Kilikien unter den Seleukiden, *Historia* 52: 300–336.

Ehling, K. (2008): *Untersuchungen zur Geschichte der späten Seleukiden (164–63 v. Chr.)*, Stuttgart.

Engels, D. (2007): Die politische Geschichte des syrischen Hauran in hellenistischer Zeit, *BJb* 207: 175–210.

Engels, D. (2008): Cicéron comme proconsul en Cilicie et la guerre contre les Parthes, *Revue Belge de Philologie et d'Histoire* 86: 23–45.

Engels, D. (2011a): Middle Eastern ‚Feudalism' and Seleucid Dissolution, in: K. Erickson, G. Ramsay (Hgg.), *Seleucid Dissolution. The Sinking of the Anchor*, Wiesbaden: 19–36.

Engels, D. (2011b): Ein syrisches Sizilien? Seleukidische Aspekte des Ersten Sizilischen Sklavenkriegs und der Herrschaft des Eunus-Antiochos, *Polifemo* 11: 231–251.

Engels, J. (1999): *Augusteische Oikumenegeographie und Universalhistorie im Werk Strabons von Amaseia*, Stuttgart.

Fischer, Th. (1970): *Untersuchungen zum Partherkrieg Antiochos' VII. im Rahmen der Seleukidengeschichte*, München (Diss.).

Fischer, Th. (1972): Zu Tryphon, *Chiron* 2: 201–213.

Foster, B.R. (1970): Agoranomos and Muhtasib, *JESHO* 13: 128–144.

Funck, B. (1991): Herrscherkult der Seleukiden-Religion einer Elite oder Reichsideologie? Einige Bemerkungen zur Fragestellung, *Klio* 73: 402–407.

Gawantka, W. (1975): *Isopolitie. Ein Beitrag zur Geschichte der zwischenstaatlichen Beziehungen in der griechischen Antike*, München.

Gelzer, M. (1984): *Pompeius*, Stuttgart (ND 2. Aufl.).

Grainger, J.D. (1990): *The Cities of Seleukid Syria*, Oxford.

Grainger, J.D. (1997): *A Seleukid Prosopography and Gazetteer*, Leiden.

Grant, M. (1946): *From Imperium to Auctoritas. A Historical Study of Aes Coinage in the Roman Empire, 49 B.C.–A.D. 14*, New York.

Günther, S. (2008): *Vectigalia nervos esse rei publicae – Die indirekten Steuern in der Römischen Kaiserzeit von Augustus bis Diokletian*, Wiesbaden.

Habicht, Ch. (1958): Die herrschende Gesellschaft in den hellenistischen Monarchien, *VSWG* 45: 1–16.

Habicht, Ch. (1988): Zur Vita des Epikureers Philonides (P. Herc 1044), *ZPE* 74: 211–214.

Hatzfeld, J. (1919): *Les Trafiquants italiens dans l'Orient hellénistique*, Paris.

Hatzopoulos, M.B. (1998): Épigraphie et philologie: récentes découvertes épigraphiques et gloses macédoniennes d'Hésychius, *CRAI*: 1189–1218.

Head, B.V. (1911): *Historia Numorum. A Manual of Greek Numismatic*, London (2. Aufl.).

Held, W. (2002): Die Residenzstädte der Seleukiden: Babylon, Seleukia am Tigris, Ai Khanum, Seleukia in Pieria, Antiochia am Orontes, *JDAI* 117: 217–249.

Hellegouarc'h, J. (1963): *Le vocabulaire latin des relations et des partis politiques sous la republique*, Paris.

Herrmann, P. (1965): Antiochos der Große und Teos, *Anadolu* 9: 29–160.

Holleaux, M. (1942): *Études d'épigraphie et d'histoire grecques*, Bd. 3, Paris.

Holm, A. (1894): *Griechische Geschichte*, Bd. 4, Berlin.

Houghton, A. (1992): The Revolt of Tryphon and the Accession of Antiochos VI at Apamea, *SNR* 71: 119–141.

Jones, A.H.M. (1931): The Urbanisation of the Ituraean Principality, *JRS* 21: 265–275.

Jones, A.H.M. (1940): *The Greek City from Alexander to Justinian*, Oxford.

Jones, A.H.M. (1971): *The Cities in the Eastern Roman Provinces*, Oxford (2. Aufl.).

Kindler, A. (1983): The Status of Cities in the Syro-Palestinian Area, *INJ* 6–7: 79–87.

Koehler, H. (1978): *Die Nachfolge in der Seleukidenherrschaft und die parthische Haltung im römisch--pontischen Konflikt*, Bochum.

Kolb, F. (1996): Antiochia in der frühen Kaiserzeit, in: H. Cancik *et al.* (Hgg.), *Geschichte – Tradition – Reflexion. Festschrift für M. Hengel zum 70. Geburtstag*, Bd. 2, Tübingen: 97–118.

Kolb, F. (Hg.) (2004): *Chora und Polis*, München.

de Laet, S.J. (1949): *Portorium. Étude sur l'organisation douanière chez les Romains, surtout de l'époque du Haut-Empire*, Brügge.

Leder, S., Streck, B. (Hgg.) (2005): *Shifts and Drifts in Nomad-Sedentary Relaions*, Wiesbaden.

Le Rider, G. (1965): *Suse sous les Séleucides et les Parthes. Les trouvailles monétaires et l'histoire de la ville*, Paris.

MacDonald, G. (1899–1905): *Catalogue of the Greek Coins in the Hunterian Collection*, Glasgow.

MacDonald, G. (1904): The Pseudo-Autonomous Coinage of Antioch, *NC* 4: 105–135.

Magie, D. (1950): *Roman Rule in Asia Minor to the End of the Third Century after Christ*, 2 Bde, Princeton.

Malitz, J. (1999): Poseidonios von Rhodos, in: K. Brodersen (Hg.), *Große Gestalten der Antike*, München: 426–432.

Marinoni, E. (1972): La Capitale del regno di Seleuco I, *RIL* 106: 579–631.

Mastrocinque, A. (1977): L'eleutheria e le città ellenistiche, *AIV* 135: 1–23.

Mavrojannis, Th. (2002): Italiens et Orientaux à Délos, in: Chr. Müller, C. Hasenohr (Hgg.), *Les Italiens dans le monde grec*, Athen: 163–179.

Meeks, W.A., Wilken, R.L. (1978): *Jews and Christians in Antioch in the First Four Centuries of the Common Era*, Missoula.
Mehl, A. (2003): Gedanken zur „herrschenden Gesellschaft" und zu den Untertanen im Seleukidenreich, *Historia* 52: 147–160.
Millar, F. (1987): The Problem of Hellenistic Syria, in: A. Kuhrt, S. Sherwin-White (Hgg.), *Hellenism in the East*, London: 110–133.
Millar, F. (1993): *The Roman Near East 31 BC–AD 337*, Cambridge (Mass.).
Milne, J.G. (1938): The Coinage of Aradus, *Iraq* 5: 12–22.
Mittag, P. (2000): Die Rolle der hauptstädtischen Bevölkerung bei den Ptolemäern und Seleukiden im 3. Jahrhundert, *Klio* 82: 409–425.
Mittag, P. (2006): *Antiochos IV. Epiphanes. Eine politische Biographie*, Berlin.
Mittag, P. (2009): Zur Integration Antiocheias in den römischen Herrschaftsverband, in: H.-J. Gehrke, A. Mastrocinque (Hgg.), *Rom und der Osten im 1. Jh. v. Chr.*, Cosenza: 159–180.
Morgan, M.G. (1990): The Perils of Schematism: Polybius, Antiochus Epiphanes and the „Day of Eleusis", *Historia* 39: 37–87.
Mosley, D.J. (1973): *Envoys and Diplomacy in Ancient Greece*, Wiesbaden.
Musti, D. (1999): Città ellenistiche e imperium, *MediterrAnt* 2: 449–462.
Newell, E.T. (1917/18): The Seleucid Mint of Antioch, *AJN* 51: 1–151.
Newell, E.T. (1919): Pre-Imperial Coinage of Roman Antioch, *NC* 4th ser., vol. 19: 69–113.
Orth, W. (1977): *Königlicher Machtanspruch und städtische Freiheit*, München.
Otto, W. (1912): Herakleon, *RE* VIII,1: 511–512.
Papazoglou, F. (2000): Polis et souveraineté, *ZAnt* 50: 169–176.
Piatkowski, A. (1991): Eleutheria kai autonomia chez Polybe, *Klio* 73: 391–401.
Piccirilli, L. (2001): La diplomazia nella Grecia antica, *MH* 58: 1–31.
Piejko, F. (1990): Episodes from the Third Syrian War in a Gurob Papyrus, *APF* 36: 13–27.
Plassart, A. (1921): Inscriptions de Delphes. La liste des Theorodoques, *BCH* 45: 1–85.
Poulsen, F. (1938): Un portrait hellénistique du musée d'Antioche, *Syria* 19: 355–361.
Prieur, M., Prieur, K. (2000): *A Type Corpus of the Syro-Phoenician Tetradrachms and Their Fractions from 57 BC to AD 253*, London.
Quass, F. (1979): Zur Verfassung der griechischen Städte im Hellenismus, *Chiron* 9: 37–52.
Raschke, M.G. (1974): The Office of Agoranomos in Ptolemaic and Roman Egypt, in: *Akten des 13. Internationalen Papyrologenkongresses*, München: 349–356.
Rey-Coquais, J.-P. (1973): Inscriptions grecques d'Apamée, *AAAS* 23: 39–84.
Rey-Coquais, J.-P. (1974): *Arados et sa Pérée aux epoques grecque, romaine et byzantine*, Paris.
Rey-Coquais, J.-P. (1976): Inscription grecque découverte à Ras Ibn Hani, *AAAS* 26: 51–61.
Rey-Coquais, J.-P. (1978): Syrie romaine de Pompée à Dioclétien, *JRS* 68: 44–73.
Rey-Coquais, J.-P. (1991): Institutions hellénistiques des cités de Syrie et de Phénicie à l'époque romaine, in: *Ο ΕΛΛΗΙΣΜΟΣ ΣΤΗΝ ΑΝΑΤΟΛΗ. International Meeting of History and Archaeology, Delphi, 6–9 November 1986*, Athen: 407–416.
Rigsby, K.J. (1996): *Asylia. Territorial Inviolability in the Hellenistic World*, Berkeley–Los Angeles–London.
Rostovtzeff, M. (1955): *Gesellschafts- und Wirtschaftsgeschichte der hellenistischen Welt* (Dt. Übers. G. und E. Bayer), Bd. 2, Darmstadt.
Roussel, P. (1942/1943): Décret des Péliganes de Laodicée sur Mer, *Syria* 23: 21–32.
Rowton, M.B. (1976): Dimorphic Structure and Topology, *Oriens Antiquus* 15: 17–31.
Sanford, E.M. (1939/1940): The Career of Aulus Gabinius, *TAPhA* 70: 64–92.
Sartre, M. (1991): *L'Orient romain. Provinces et sociétés provinciales en Méditerranée orientale d'Auguste aux Sévères (31 avant J.-C. – 235 après J.-C.)*, Paris.
Sartre, M. (1996): Les progrès de la citoyenneté romaine en Syrie et en Arabie, in: A. Rizakis (Hg.), *Roman Onomnastics in the Greek East. Social and Political Aspects. Proceedings of the International Colloquium on Roman Onomastics, Athens, 7–9 September 1993*, Athen: 239–250.

Sartre, M. (1997): Vie municipale et intégration des notables dans la Syrie et l'Arabie romaines, in: *Colloque sur les élites provinciales dans l'Empire romain*, Wrocław: 153–173.

Sartre, M. (2000): Antioche: capitale royale, ville impériale, in: C. Nicolet *et al.* (Hgg.), *Mégapoles méditerranéennes: Géographie urbaine respective*, Rom: 492–501.

Sartre, M. (2001): Romains et Italiens en Syrie, in: O. Salomies (Hg.), *The Greek East in the Roman Context*, Helsinki: 127–140.

Savelli-Lestrade, I. (1998): *Les* philoi *royaux dans l'Asie hellenistique*, Genf.

Sbeinati, M.R., Darawcheh, R., Mouty, M. (2005): The Historical Earthquakes of Syria, *Annals of Geophysics* 48: 347–435.

Schäfer, N. (2000): *Die Einbeziehung der Provinzialen in den Reichsdienst*, Stuttgart.

Schwahn, W. (1939): Tributum und Tributus, *RE* VIIA, 1: 2–78.

Seyrig, H. (1939): Les rois séleucides et la concession de l'asylie, *Syria* 20: 35–39.

Seyrig, H. (1950): Sur les ères de quelques villes de Syrie, *Syria* 27: 5–50.

Seyrig, H. (1951): Aradus et sa pérée sous les rois séleucides, *Syria* 28: 206–220.

Seyrig, H. (1954): Les ères pompéiennes des villes de Phénicie, *Syria* 31: 83–80.

Seyrig, H. (1971): Séleucos III et Simyra, *RN* 13: 7–11.

Sherwin-White, A.N. (1994): Lucullus, Pompey and the East, in: *CAH*², vol. IX: 229–273.

Siebert, G. (1968): Sur l'histoire du sanctuaire des dieux syriens à Delos, *BCH* 92: 359–374.

Van Nuffelen, P. (2004): Le culte royal de l'empire des Séleucides, *Historia* 53: 278–301.

Vial, C. (2007): Économie et société à Délos au temps de l'indépendance, *Pallas* 74: 263–275.

Wirth, G. (1983): Pompeius – Armenien – Parther. Mutmaßungen zur Bewältigung einer Krisensituation, *BJb* 183: 1–60.

Wolski, J. (1977): Les Parthes et la Syrie, *Acta Iranica* 12: 395–417.

Wussow, S. (2004): *Die Persönlichkeit des Cato Uticensis. Zwischen stoischer Moralphilosophie und republikanischem Politikverständnis*, Diss. Düsseldorf.

ELECTRUM * Vol. 20 (2013): 117–141
doi: 10.4467/20800909EL.13.006.1435

Coloniam deducere. Colonisation as an Instrument of the Roman Policy of Domination in Italy in the 3rd and 2nd Centuries BC, as Illustrated by Settlements in the *Ager Gallicus* and Picenum

Maciej Piegdoń

Uniwersytet Jagielloński, Kraków

Abstract: This article is an attempt to present the role of colonisation in the Roman policy of expansion towards its Italian neighbours in the 3rd–2nd BCE and showing the effects of this phenomenon, as illustrated by settlements in the *Ager Gallicus* and Picenum. Information on the founded colonies in sources, appearing somewhat on the margins of accounts of military activities and diplomatic missions in Italy (*foedera*), but also connected with the internal policy conducted by Rome (grants of land), may indicate that colonisation complemented such activities. This complementary character of the process of colonisation in relation to other political, military, diplomatic, and internal activities seems to be an important feature of the Republic's activities.

Key words: Roman colonisation, Roman Republic, Ager Gallicus, Picenum, Roman conquest.

Roman colonisation during the Republic was a phenomenon that even ancient writers perceived as one of the fundaments of the Roman domination of Italy.[1] Contemporary historians are equally impressed, but there are also numerous controversies regarding its motives and reasons. The classical interpretation of the motives behind this process as military and strategic activities (E.T. Salmon is the main representative of this line of thinking[2]) has recently been criticised by various researchers who have tried to point

[1] *SIG* II[4], 543, 26; Livy XXVII, 10; App. *B.C.* I, 7; Toynbee 1965, I: 277–278; Salmon 1969, 51, 69; Sherwin-White 1973, 38–95; Ziółkowski 1994, 54–55; Bradley 2006, 161–162, 169–171; Laffi 2007, 13–88. Ancient writers suggest several definitions of a colony; see Livy VIII, 21; X, 217–211: *Nec qui nomina darent facile inveniebantur, quia in stationem se prope perpetuam infestae regionis, non in agros, mitti rebantur*; XXVII, 38, 5; Gell. *NA* 16.13, 8–9; Serv. *Ad Aen.* I, 12; Sic. Flacc. *De cond. agr.* 135, 20.

[2] Some ancient writers use military terminology in reference to colonies and colonists, e.g. Cic. *Leg. Agr.* 2, 73 (*propugnacula imperii*); Livy XXVI, 36, 12; XXVII, 50, 6; XXXI, 49, 6; XXXIV, 56, 8; XXXVI, 2, 9; XXXVII, 47, 2; Asc. *In Pis.* 3 C; Sic. Flacc. *De cond agr.* 135; Salmon 1969, 166, p. 9; Gargola 1995, 65–67; Pelgrom 2008, 333–335. Bispham (2006, 77–78), who – despite his criticism of some classical beliefs

out other aspects of the process. They often emphasise that other issues, including demographic and economic ones, should also be considered. Salmon himself did not reject them, either.[3] Salmon's classification of the colonies (*Priscae Coloniae Latinae*, *Coloniae Maritimae*, *Coloniae Latinae* and *Coloniae Civium Romanorum*), based mainly on the accounts of Livy, Velleius Paterculus and other Late Republic and Early Empire writers, has also sometimes been questioned.[4]

Identifying the reasons for Roman colonisation in the sources is not an easy matter, since we do not have access to a direct source that presents a planned and organised colonisation policy followed by the Republic. This raises the question of whether Rome could have had such a policy at all. On the one hand, it is not altogether possible to give a clear and positive answer to this question due to the source materials available to us. On the other hand, information on the founded colonies, appearing somewhat on the margins of accounts of military activities (war campaigns) and diplomatic missions in Italy (alliances and coalitions, so called *foedera*), but also connected with the internal policy conducted by Rome (grants of land) may indicate that colonisation complemented such activities. This complementary character of the process of colonisation in relation to other political, military, diplomatic, and internal activities seems to be an important feature of the Republic's activities.[5]

about colonisation – agrees with many of them, see Salmon 1969, 18–20; Gargola 1995, 58–64. Patterson (2006, 191, 194) emphasises that the officials founding colonies, the so-called *tresviri coloniae deducendae*, were meritorious Roman generals, usually consuls elected by the Assembly. The social structure of a Latin colony at Aquileia resembled a legion: there were the *equites*, *centuriones* and *pedites*: Livy XL, 34, 2. Aquileia sometimes used to be called the *claustrum Italiae*: Strabo 5.1.8.(214); Toynbee 1965, II: 150, 198, 284; Salmon 1969, 106; Bandelli 2003, 53–55, 59, 63. Previously, Ariminium used to be referred to by this term, see below.

[3] Salmon (1969, 112–113) emphasises a change in the motives behind founding colonies occurring from the mid-2nd century (the activity of the Gracchi brothers); Sherwin-White 1973, 9–10, 83–85. See Toynbee 1965, I: 179–189, 249–258; Ziółkowski 1994, 62–72; Oakley 2002, 19–22; Bispham 2006, 76–77; Bradley 2006, 169–171.

[4] Asc. *Pis.* 3 C proposes a different classification of colonies: *duo porro genera larum coloniarum quae a populo Romano deductae sunt fuerunt, ut* ***Quiritium aliae, aliae Latinorum*** *essent*. See Crawford 1995, 190: "La verità ché non abbiamo la minima idea di ciò che significasse il termine colonia populi Romani per il Romani della fina Repubblica"; Bispham 2006, 81–85. On the other hand, in the introduction to his *Roman Colonization under the Republic*, E.T. Salmon wrote: "In the great days of the Roman Republic, in the fourth, third and second centuries, the colonies sent out by the Romans were of two kinds. The one kind, the so-called Latin colonies (coloniae Latinae), were peopled by settlers who did not possess Roman citizenship; the other kind, the so-called citizen colonies (coloniae Romanorum), were peopled by settlers who did. Since both kinds of colonies were authorized and established by the Roman state, it may well be asked what determined the choice of one type rather than other on any given occasion" (1969, 15). See Salmon 1982, 63–67.

[5] Sherwin-White 1973, 76: "The Romans had another weapon in their armoury, the 'colonia civium Romanorum'"; Ziółkowski 1994, 49–79; Patterson 2006, 191–192; Piegdoń 2009, 128–129, 241–242. The only source account that provides continuous information about the colonies, dates, and circumstances of setting up colonies by Republican Rome is *Historia Romana*, written by Velleius Paterculus, which does not include all the foundations (from the capture of Rome by the Gauls in 390 to the foundation of the colony of Eporedia, whose date is very controversial), see Vell. Pat. I, 14–15; Laffi 2007, 247–259 (sources on colonisation). The time of founding colonies in a seized territory differed. Sometimes colonies were built soon after military operations were completed (or even while they were still being conducted), and in other cases several decades passed between the time of capture by Rome and the colony being founded, see Ziółkowski 2004, 140. It seems that there are several possible reasons for this. It depended, firstly, on the attitude of

Considering the objectives of Roman expansion, one of which was to obtain land for the growing population of citizens and allies, who could count on being granted limited or full citizenship, colonies were a realisation of this crucial reason for Roman imperialism.[6] Colonies were one of the instruments, next to organised or spontaneous *adsignationes viritanae*, which enabled Rome to transfer the *ager publicus* to their citizens and allies. The granted public land was divided into plots called *centuria* (centuriation), which were then divided into smaller *sortes*, separated by boundaries called *limites*.[7]

We should note one more aspect of Roman activities resulting, among others, in the foundation of colonies: the increasingly common tendency of contemporary researchers to emphasise Rome's role in transforming the Italian environment. By founding colonies, as well as smaller settlements (*fora*, *conciliabula* etc.), and by building roads with infrastructure, Rome was pursuing a close and subordinated urbanised civilisation, based on strong urban centres in mostly rural and pastoral Italy.[8]

Assessing the reliability of our sources (mainly the works of ancient historians) in connection to the process of colonisation, we should also remember that most of them were created towards the end of the Republic and during the Empire, and only very few fragments from earlier periods refer to the moment of founding specific colonies. Most

the conquered native people to Roman activities; secondly, on whether the region required, due to external danger, being guarded by placing a strong *claustrum* to protect Roman interests there. Various aspects of the Republic's internal policy were also important, such as the distribution of forces in the assemblies and the Senate, the support of influential officials, and demographic issues, which decided whether there was a sufficient number of people that could be sent out to a founded colony at a given moment. See Patterson 2006, 199–201 and below.

[6] Livy III, 1, 5; Dion Halic. 9, 59, 2; (Antium); App. *BC* I, 7; Sherwin-White 1973, 81–82 (Antium); Ziółkowski 1994, 67–69; 2004, 144–147, 159–160; Patterson 2006, 194–196. Many academic works have been devoted to identifying the reasons behind Roman imperialism, see Badian 1967; Harris 1992; Ziółkowski 1994, 72–79; 2004, 164–174; Edmondson 1993, 156–192; Brunt 2001, 288–323; Oakley 2002, 9–37; Rich 2002, 38–68; Cornell 2002, 139–170; Eckstein 2007, 567–589; Morley 2010, 14–37; Burton 2012.

[7] References to centuriation come from ancient sources, e.g. *Liber gromaticorum*; Hyginus' *Gromatici veteres*; Siculus Flaccus' *De condicionibus agrorum*; Frontinus' *De controversiis agrorum* etc. On centuriation, see Salmon 1969, 20–24; Brunt 1971, 294–296, Gargola 1995, 25–50; Patterson 2006, 189–199; Pelgrom 2008, 361–367.

[8] This was the case only in the regions which had not been affected by the process of intensive urbanisation, such as southern Italy, where Greek colonists were present, and partly Campania, Etruria and Apulia. Frequently, native settlements were transformed by the process of Romanisation into centres whose appearance, institutions, and buildings resembled their Roman and Latin neighbours, see Livy XXXVI, 3, 4–6; Salmon 1969, 70–81; Sherwin-White 1973, 77; Dench 1995; 1997, 43–52; Lomas 2003, 64–78. According to Patterson (2006: 210), the situation was different towards the end of the Republic: "In the process, the figure of the colonist became more ambiguous still – an upstanding soldier on the one hand, a threat to civic order on the other. The process was culminated with the atrocities of the triumviral period and Augustus' eventual abolition of colonial settlement for veterans in favour of cash donatives. Thereafter, colonisation in Italy was largely seen as a means of responding to urban crisis, reversing demographic decline, and demonstrating imperial favour in generosity. The main impetus of colonial settlement was now transferred to the provinces, where the combination of Romanised lifestyles and hard-handed behaviour towards local populations continued to alienate and attract the peoples of the empire in equal measure." Other activities which were supposed to increase dependence included building roads connecting settlements, both those founded by the Romans and native ones, see Laurence 2011. The process of transforming the territories captured by the Republic, as illustrated by Cisalpine Gaul, is described by Purcell 1990, 7–29. See Sherwin-White 1973, 8–9, 94–95; Laurence 2003, 95–110; Pelgrom 2008, 333–334.

frequently, the majority of our sources provide information about the colony's situation and the contemporary attitude towards colonisation (from the Late Republic and the Empire). For this reason, modern researchers frequently and justly accuse earlier sources of being anachronistic and unreliable.[9] Therefore, epigraphic and numismatic sources are an important addition to the accounts of ancient historians, which enable us to learn about various aspects (economic, social, religious etc.) of the functioning of certain Roman and Latin colonies. However, they date from different periods of the colonies' existence and constitute only a small percentage of all the documents of this kind created in the settlements. Similarly, archaeological sources (which help us pay attention to important aspects, such as the size of a colony and the population inhabiting it, the date of its foundation, and common features such as the presence of a forum, temples, and public buildings) are auxiliary.[10] It is therefore difficult to look for some principles or a possible colonisation policy of the Republic on the basis of inscriptions, coins, and archaeological sources.

The process of Roman colonisation underwent changes, and it is difficult to imagine that the colonies founded during the Early Republic (or even monarchy) were created on the basis of the same model/template (if there ever was one) as the ones founded in the 1st century. Early Rome, from the point of view of its size, policy, social issues, territory etc. was a state that faced different challenges and problems from the ones encountered in the 2nd–1st centuries BC.[11] However, the city's development in the 5th–1st centuries, in terms of its political system, administration, and law, was conducive to the gradual emergence of certain models of behaviour. Rome used such models when implementing its policy, one of the main aims of which was to subordinate Italy. It seems that the process of colonisation could also have undergone such changes, which gradually led to the model we know from available sources being worked out.[12] Since various types of transformations occurring in the Republic had an influence on the process of colonisa-

[9] Bispham 2006, 73–75, 78–83; Patterson 2006, 195.

[10] Bispham (2006, 81–92) mainly based his theories on an analysis of inscriptions and archaeological material from some colonies and on criticism of writers from the times of the Late Republic and especially the Empire. He also (Bispham 2006, 92–122) discussed cults in selected colonies on the basis of inscriptions. See Patterson 2006, 190–191; Laffi 2007, 247–259; Pelgrom 2008, 333–335.

[11] Bradley (2006, 167–171) strongly emphasises aspects of internal policy (conflict between the Patricians and the Plebeians) influencing the process of colonisation in the period of Early Republic. During the Early and Mid-Republic, the main challenge faced by Rome and its colonies was to capture important and strategic points of support in subjugated but usually hostile territories, giving the Roman state control over them. The colonies were also to become a reservoir of lands for Roman citizens and allies, including later generations (also towards the end of the Republic). See Salmon 1969, 13–18; Ziółkowski 1994, 50–72; Ungern-Sternberg 2005, 312–332. During the last century, colonies were also important for Roman generals fighting civil wars against one another. For them, colonies were important as strategic points during war campaigns, but the most crucial aspect was the possibility of awarding land to veterans, which was what foundations were for, see Keppie 1983; Patterson 2006, 202–208.

[12] Sherwin-White 1973, 3–37, 83–95. See Gargola 1995, 51–70; Oakley 2002, 18–19; Bradley 2006, 167–169; Pelgrom 2008, 358–360. The case of Greek colonies during the Great Colonisation is similar; we reconstruct their origins on the basis of various sources: archaeological, literary, and (less commonly) epigraphic. The majority of literary sources are from much later than the beginnings of the foundations, and frequently known foundation models are simply applied to much earlier times, cf. Hall 2011, 101–125.

tion implemented by Rome, the question arises of whether there were any common elements of the whole process during the existence of the Republic.

First of all, colonies in the 3rd and 2nd centuries BC were settlements created on Rome's initiative, and only the Republic decided if a colony would be founded, and whether it would be a Roman or Latin one. There are differences in comparison to the previous period of the 5th–4th centuries, when the decision to found a colony was also made by other Latin states (until Rome's war against the Latin League in 340–338 BC), sometimes together with Rome.[13] During the Early Republic, important and influential leaders of the Roman *gentes*, holding high military functions or offices, could also make decisions to found settlements for Roman citizens.[14]

After Rome's victorious war against the Latin League and the end of the rivalry between the Patricians and the Plebeians in the 4th century, only the Republic's institutions decided whether a colony would be founded.[15] The colonies created by Rome on conquered land, which became public land (*ager publicus*), can be divided into two categories: citizen colonies, i.e. those in which Roman citizens were settlers, and Latin colonies. The latter model was adopted by the Republic from the Latin League. Here, the settlers could be those who had the legal status of Latins; allies; Roman citizens after giving up their citizenship (*civitas optimo iure*) and accepting the Latin status;[16] and pacified native people (*incolae*), on whose lands such settlements were built.[17]

Citizen colonies, which the sources call *coloniae civium Romanorum* or *coloniae Quiritium*, were initially small settlements of three hundred people (with families?), which fell under the jurisdiction of Roman institutions and officials, but had their own magistrates and the Council of Decurions.[18] They were founded in the *ager publicus* in strategically important places, usually close to the coast, which led to the name *coloniae maritimae* mentioned in sources; their job was to prevent, or rather delay, any possible descent on the coast, which was regarded as a territory subordinate to Rome.[19] Colonists in such settlements were not recruited to Roman legions.[20] The creation of such posts may have been related to the fact that Rome had virtually no fleet to protect the coast,

---

[13] Salmon 1969, 40–54; Ziółkowski 2004, 121–124, 143–144; Bradley 2006, 171.

[14] Ziółkowski 2004, 108–111; Bradley 2006, 164–169. No doubt, in later times the interests of mighty and influential politicians could also decide whether a colony would be founded on a particular spot, or whether plots would be distributed among individual settlers, but all these decisions were made in the Senate or at an assembly. See below.

[15] Gargola 1995, 52–58.

[16] Ziółkowski 2004, 144–146.

[17] Generally Bradley 2006, 171–179. One example of the presence of native people (the Veneti, the Celts) was Aquileia: *CIL* V 8443; Livy XL, 34; Toynbee 1965, II: 146, 151; Salmon 1969, 101; Brunt 1971, 192; Bandelli 1988, 36–39, 42–46, 125–126; Pelgrom 2008, 354–358; Piegdoń 2009, 147–148. See Asc. *Pis.* 3; Tacit. *Hist.* III, 34. Settlers and colonists were often sent out to the territories whose population had been exterminated or deported, but also in place of or close to native settlements or smaller citizen settlements such as *fora*.

[18] *ILS* 5317, 1–2 (*lex de pariete faciundo* lub *lex Puteolana*); *CIL* X 1130, 1134, 5581, 5590 (censors in colonies), 6231; Cic. *Leg. Agr.* II, 92–93, 96 (pontiffs and augurs). See Toynbee 1965, I: 187; Salmon 1969, 71–75; Sherwin-White 1973, 87–94.

[19] Salmon 1969, 78 (as illustrated by the colony of Sena Gallica).

[20] Livy XXVII, 38, 3; XXXVI, 3, 5; Salmon 1969, 81. Attempts to conscript colonists during the Second Punic War (207) led to the *coloniae maritimae* appealing to plebeian tribunes.

nor ports in subordinated or influenced territories. Rome did not stop founding colonies, despite the fact that after the First Punic War it had a strong fleet and did not have to base its activities solely on ships provided by mostly Greek allies in Italy (*socii navales*); it still did not have proper ports for its fleet along the whole coast in its possession. After the First Punic War ended, the Roman fleet was depleted, and it was not Rome's main power during its expansion outside Italy.[21] The *coloniae maritimae* continued to be founded as a very convenient element of the Roman presence in an area. Such colonies were often founded as first settlements in freshly conquered territories, preceded the creation of larger and stronger Latin colonies, and were the *avant-garde* of the Roman presence in an area.

The Republic's view on such small colonies/garrisons changed only after the Second Punic War (218–201) and the crisis that affected Rome's relations with Latin colonies and other allies during the war against Hannibal. Unable to bear the burden imposed in connection with the military operations in Italy, some Latin colonies refused to provide supplies and soldiers in 209. After the Second Punic War, Rome punished the "defiant" colonies. The Republic's rulers also began to change their colonisation policy. Their war experiences led the Roman aristocracy to interfere more in the internal matters of their allies and to increasingly use Roman citizens as colonists; for over two decades they were to be the most privileged group when founding new colonies.[22] Starting in the mid-190s BC, the Republic started to found *coloniae civium Romanorum* for larger groups of citizens (2,000–3,000) and the settlers were supposed to receive much larger land grants (from 5 to 10 *iugera*). These colonies were also set up in strategically important places, but not necessarily in the vicinity of sea coasts, and could, importantly, provide Rome with military reinforcements. They were founded on important migration and trade routes, close to passes, rivers, coasts etc., and frequently several were founded at the same time (similarly to Latin colonies).[23] Individual colonial settlement at the time, organised by the state, also favoured Roman citizens, who were granted much larger

[21] Salmon 1969, 74; Lazenby 2012, 22, 70–71. Certainly, piracy was a problem which could have driven Rome to build such settlements; piracy was present in Italy, committed by the Ligurians on the Ligurian Sea, but also locally by the Etruscans on the west coast of Italy, and by the Illyrians, who were also active on the east coast of Italy, on the Adriatic. *Socii navales*: Badian 1958, 28–30.

[22] On the refusal of Latin colonies to support the Republic in 209, see Livy XXVII, 9; Salmon 1969, 82–91; Toynbee 1965, II: 90–91, 115–116; Ziółkowski 2004, 198. The increased interference of the Republic in the allies' affairs is emphasised by many modern historians: Badian 1958, 145–153; Toynbee 1965, II: 106–142; Sherwin-White 1973, 128–129 *contra* Jehne 2009, 145–147, 150. On changes in the Roman system of founding colonies for Roman citizens, see Smith 1954, 18–20; Badian 1958, 139–152; Toynbee 1965, II: 145–154, 198–199; Salmon 1969, 98–104; Wiseman 1971, 14–15; Sherwin-White 1973, 76–95; Piegdoń 2009, 141–143.

[23] After the Second Punic War the first citizen colonies were built at Puteola, Salernum and Buxentum in 195: Livy XXXIV, 45, 5–6. In the Roman colony of Saturnia, colonists received as many as ten *iugera* of land: Livy XXXIX, 55. In the colonies of Mutina and Parma the grants of land were five *iugera* at Mutina and as many as eight at Parma: *CIL* XI 826; Plin. *NH* II, 240; III, 115; App. *BC* III, 73, 298–301; Front. *Strat.* III, 14, 3–4; Toynbee 1965, I: 396; II: 147; Ewins 1952, 62, 63; Salmon 1969, 24, 104–105; Piegdoń 2009, 145–146. This is illustrated by Mutina and Parma, which protected the important passes through the Apennines, Abetone and Cisa, as well as the Latin colony Bononia in the vicinity of the Futa Pass: Ewins 1952, 55; Salmon 1969, 103, 105–106; Toynbee 1965, I: 281 n. 4, 486, 487; II: 144, 272; Harris 1971, 156. Pisaurum and Potentia were also founded close to the coast.

plots than the Latins and other Roman allies. One example is the settlement operation in the *ager Ligustinus et Gallicus* in northern Italy, undertaken by Rome in 173.[24] At the same time, the Republic started to abandon the idea of Latin colonies, fewer and fewer of which were founded.

Latin colonies, as mentioned above, were added to the system of citizen colonies when Rome, after the victorious war against the Latin League (340–338), took over the Latins' colonies and adapted this model of founding new settlements to its own goals. Latin colonies continued to be set up by the Republic for more than 150 years and became an important element of the Roman domination over the conquered areas, as well as a key factor which enabled Rome to solve demographic and economic problems.

Coloniae Latinae were also located in strategically important places, and usually at least two were founded in various parts of Italy, not necessarily close to one another (Placentia and Cremona on the banks of the Po River were exceptions). By founding large Latin colonies, Rome also solved the problem of "hunger" for land, sending the excess of the population, both citizens and allies, to such settlements. Roman citizens in these colonies had to give up their Roman citizenship, since from the legal point of view *coloniae Latinae* were completely separate bodies.[25] However, in return for large grants of land, sometimes as many as about a dozen or several dozen hectares (Aquileia, Bononia, Lucca),[26] the citizens who could not afford to support themselves in their homeland preferred to give up their citizenship and set off to other, more attractive, although sometimes dangerous, places. These colonies allowed the Republic to create strategic posi-

[24] Livy XLII, 4: *cum agri Ligustini et Gallici quod captum erat aliquantum vacaret, senatus consultum factum, ut is ager viritim divideretu Decemviros in eam rem creavit... Diviserunt dena iugera in singulos, sociis niminis Latini terna*; Ewins 1952, 59, 60, 61, 63, 65–66; Tibiletti 1965, 30; Toynbee 1965, II: 135, 198, 204–206. The colonists joined the *tribus* Pollia: Ewins 1952, 57, 60, 66. See Piegdoń 2009, 154–156.

[25] Salmon 1969, 74. A Roman citizen had to give up his citizenship; he did not lose it automatically, see Cic. *Dom.* 30, 78; *Caec.* 33, 98; Mouritsen 1998, 87–99. The presence of mostly Roman citizens in Latin colonies is confirmed by a passage from Cicero's speech *Pro Caec.* 98: *in colonias Latinis saepe nostri cives profecti.* A Roman citizen could not hold the *civitas optimo iure* and another citizenship at the same time. In order to receive the citizenship of another state, he first had to give up the *civitas optimo iure*: Cic. *Balb.* 11, 28: *Duarum civitatum civis noster esse iure civili nemo potest*; 12, 29: *Nos non possumus et huius esse civitatis et cuiusvis praetera. Ceteris concessum est*; Toynbee 1965, I: 179; Salmon 1969, 73–74. This does not mean, however, that a person who received the *civitas optimo iure*, and was originally not from Rome, did not feel connected to their birthplace, as illustrated by another fragment of Cicero's speech (*De Leg.* II, 5: *Omnibus municipibus duas esse censeo patrias unam naturae alteram civitatis. Ut ille Cato cum esset Tusculi natus in populi Romani civitatem susceptus est, itaque cum ortu Tusculanus esset, civitate Romanus, habuit alteram loci patriam alteram iuris... Sed necesse est caritate eam praestare qua reipublicae nomen universae civitatis est, pro qua mori et cui nos totos dedere et in qua nostra omnia ponere et quasi consecrare debemus. Dulcis autem non multo secus est ea quae genuit quam illa quae excepit*); Catull. 1: *unus Italorum*; Diod. Sic. XXXVII, 11; Gell. *NA* 11, 8, 1: *homo Romanus natus in Latio*; 17, 17, 1 (Q. Ennius); Badian 1958, 23–24. Sheidel (2006, 223) estimates that between 338 and 263 the Republic sent out 60,000–80,000 male settlers (excluding women and children), and between 200 and 177 another 40,000–65,000 settlers. On general information on Latin colonies, see Pelgrom 2008, 333–372.

[26] On grants of land in Bononia: Livy XXXVII, 57; Toynbee 1965, II: 234, 236–239; Salmon 1969, 23, 101; Brunt 1971, 191; Piegdoń 2009, 143. On the size of plots in Aquileia: Livy XL, 34, 2: *Tria milia peditum quinquagena iugera, centuriones centena, centena quadragena equites acceperunt*; Toynbee 1965, II: 236, 283; Pelgrom 2008, 343 n. 30; Piegdoń 2009, 147–148. On grants of land in Lucca: Livy XLI, 13: *Quinquagena et singula iugera et semisses agri in singulos dati sunt*; Salmon 1969, 104, 109, 187–188 n. 193; Toynbee 1965, II: 539–540; Brunt 1971, 193; Piegdoń 2009, 151–154.

tions, but also to people the conquered and hostile territories with its own citizens and allies. The aim of such settlements, whose community equalled that of a legion of the Roman army, was undoubtedly strategic. The settlements, similarly to the Roman *socii*, were also supposed to supply provisions and, most importantly, military reinforcements. The method of recruiting settlers for colonies, and the whole ritual of the settlers setting off under the command of the *tresviri coloniae deducendae*, who were former consuls and praetors, resembled the march of Roman troops off to war. The significance of these officials was not limited to the stage of founding the colony. Later, as patrons of the colony, they would intervene in Rome and arbitrate if there was a conflict of colonial settlers with the inhabitants of other colonies or native settlements.[27] Giving a lot of autonomy (their own offices, councils, bronze coins, military forces) to such colonies and their economic self-sufficiency meant that they did not pose a great burden to Rome but brought certain benefits.[28] Since many colonists had previously been Roman citizens, who had families, relatives, patrons, interests and various other affairs in Rome, the Republic allowed Latin colonists to marry Roman citizens (*ius conubium*), conduct legal business affairs with citizens in the city (*ius commercium*), participate in plebeian assemblies and vote (*ius suffragium*) and, with time, permitted colonial officials to receive full Roman citizenship (*ius civitatis per magistratum adipiscendae*).[29] Apart from this, settlers from the *coloniae Latinae* were granted some legal rights regarding inheritance from Roman

[27] The Latins supported the Republic with military reinforcements, as their presence in the *formula togatorum* is reported by Polybius (II, 24) and *FIRA* I² 8, 21, 50: *sociumque nominisque Latinis quibus ex formula togatorum milites in terra Italia imperare solet* [vide]; Sherwin-White 1973, 158 n. 2; Bispham 2007, 94. The practice of settling whole legions is also known from later accounts from the period of the Late Republic and Early Empire: Tacit. *Ann.* XIV, 27, 3; Hyg. 176, 11; Brunt 1971, 294–295. See Gargola 1995, 67–70; Pelgrom 2008, 337–354 (discussion on the actual size of the population in Latin colonies and critique of sources in connection to the number of colonists).

[28] On the financial support of Rome, see Livy XXVII, 9; XXIX, 15. Rome's biggest expense was most likely the foundation of a colony, which required certain funds for construction work and for providing for the colonists, who needed help to make a living in the initial period of their presence in a sometimes hostile and foreign territory. Another possible expense the state had to cover in a colony emerged if the colony was destroyed or considerably weakened by hostilities. In such circumstances, the Republic's interference was also necessary; its officials had to recruit new colonists (*supplementum*) and to provide financial support for the rebuilding of the colony. See below. On the role of the *tresviri coloniae deducendae* as arbiters, see Calderazzo 1997, 25–46.

[29] The Latin status (*Latinitas*) changed and transformed with regard to rights and duties during its existence in the times of the Republic and later: Gaius *Inst.* I, 96 (*Maius Latium* and *Minus Latium*). On the laws, see Cic. *Att.* 1, 1, 2; Asc. *Pis.* 3 C: *...id est ut petendo magistratus civitatem Romanam adipiscerentur*; Livy VIII, 14, 10: *conubia commerciaque et concilia inter se*; IX, 43, 23: *tribus populi... suae leges redditae conubiumque inter ipsos permissum*; XXIII, 22; XXV, 3, 16: *sitella lata est ut sortirentur ubi Latini suffragium ferrent*; XXXIV, 42, 5; Tac. *Hist.* III, 34: *adnexu conubiisque gentium adolevit floruitque* (this concerns Cremona, but it is difficult to say whether it referred to *conubium* between Roman citizens and Latin colonists, or *conubium* between native people and the colonists from Cremona, which is more likely); Caius *Inst.* I, 56, 57, 67, 79–80 (the Latins holding the *ius conubium*); Ulpian *Tituli* 5, 4; 9 (*ius conubium*); 19, 4 (*ius commercium*); Smith 1954, 20; Badian 1958, 20–24; Taylor 1960, 109; Toynbee 1965, I: 249–258; Salmon 1969, 51–69; Sherwin-White 1973, 96–118; Luraschi 1979, 160, 165, 168–173, 221–299, 301–329, 336–342; Gargola 1995, 51–70; Bispham 2007, 74–76. The "Latins" probably lost the right guaranteeing them the possibility of receiving the *civitas optimo iure per migrationem et censum* in the 2nd–1st century, perhaps on the basis of the *lex Iunia* of 122 or the *Licinia Mucia* of 95(?): Asc. *Pis.* 67; Sherwin-White 1973, 110–111; Luraschi 1979, 236–238. See Piegdoń 2009, 190–191.

citizens (these are probably the privileges referred to by the terms *ius Ariminiensis* or *ius duodecim coloniae*, which appear in sources with reference to Latin colonies).[30]

The model of Latin colonies worked well as an instrument of domination in Italy during the Roman conquest of the Apennine Peninsula in the 4th and 3rd centuries BC and during the First Punic War. However, the complications during the Second Punic War put a question mark over the trust in Latin colonies as well as allies in general. Numerous *socii* going over to Hannibal's side, as well as the refusal to supply Rome with provisions and military reinforcements by twelve Latin colonies exhausted by war, forced the Republic to re-think its colonisation policy in the early 2nd century BC. Its new main aim was mainly the creation of the *coloniae civium Romanorumi* for Roman citizens, who, following the example of Latin colonies, were given much bigger plots of land, while the settlers were more numerous compared to the *coloniae maritimae*. Even so, setting up Latin colonies was not completely abandoned in Italy in the first two decades of the 2nd century (two at Bruttium as well as Bononia, Aquileia, Graviscae and Lucca), and there were no attempts to change the status of the existing *coloniae Latinae*; on the contrary, they were strengthened after the chaos of the Second Punic War by sending in new settlers (*supplementum*) and rebuilding many of them from ruins.[31] From the mid-170s, no more Latin colonies were founded, and the frequency of creating new *coloniae civium Romanorum* was also smaller than before. The Latin legal status (*Latinitas*) was used by Rome in relations with the native people in Italy, who could be given such status, as illustrated by the *lex Pompeia de Transpadanis* of 89, which granted the *Latinitas* to over twenty native settlements in northern Italy loyal to Rome during the *bellum sociale*.[32]

Without doubt, colonisation was one of the tools of the Roman policy of domination in Italy in the 4th–3rd centuries BC; the Republic also used the instrument when conducting political and military operations against the inhabitants of Picenum and the *ager*

---

[30] This rather ambiguous type of status is only known from a reference in Cicero's speech *Pro Caecina* (35, 102), which read as follows: *...Sulla ipse ita tulit de civitate, ut non sustulerit horum nexa atque hereditates. Iubet enim eodem iure esse, quo fuerint Ariminenses; quos quis ignorat duodecim coloniarum fuisse et a civibus Romanis hereditates capere posse?*; Badian 1958, 24–25; Krawczuk 1960, 33–44; Toynbee 1965, I: 253–256; II: 533; Salmon 1969, 92–94, 106–108; Sherwin-White 1973, 102–104; Luraschi 1979, 225–299; Bispham 2006, 89. Perhaps it meant granting Latin colonists the right to inherit from Roman citizens, as suggested by the sources, see Cic. *Caec.* 98; Caius *Inst.* II, 101–102. See Luraschi 1979, 281–293; Piegdoń 2009, 191 n. 603.

[31] Aquileia: *CIL* I, 2, 621 = V 873; Livy XXXIX, 22; 54–55; XL, 34; 53; Piso *Historicorum Romanorum Reliquiae* frg. 35, Peter; Vell. Pat. I, 15; Strabo 5, 1, 8 (C 214); Plin. *NH* III, 126; Herodian VIII, 2; Ewins 1952, 56, 59; Toynbee 1965, II: 629; Salmon 1969, 106–107; Piegdoń 2009, 146–149. Lucca and Luna: Livy XLI, 13; XLV, 13; Vell. Pat. I, 15; Strabo 5, 1, 11 (C 217); Plin. *NH* III, 50. The matter of dating the foundations at Luna and Lucca is a very complicated historiographical problem: Toynbee 1965, II: 540, 655; Brunt 1971, 168, 192–193; Harris 1971, 149; Sherwin-White 1973, 78–79; Piegdoń 2009, 149–154. *Supplementum*: Livy XXXVII, 46, 9–11 (Placentia and Cremona); Ewins 1952, 57; Toynbee 1965, II: 144, 272; Salmon 1969, 101; Brunt 1971, 191; Luraschi 1979, 79–80; Piegdoń 2009, 140–141 and Livy XLIII, 17, 1 (Aquileia); Toynbee 1965, II: 57; Salmon 1969, 108; Piegdoń 2009, 149.

[32] Cic. *Att.* 1, 1, 2; Asc. *Pis.* 3; Strabo 5, 1, 1 (C 209); Plin. *NH* III, 138; Tac. *Ann.* XI, 23–24; Sherwin-White 1973, 158–159; Luraschi 1979, 144–145; Piegdoń 2009, 196–198.

Gallicus on the central Adriatic coast, which later belonged to Region V (present-day Marecchia) and Region VIII (Emilia).[33]

The Italian Adriatic coast played a very important role in Rome's policy. This strip of coast, inhabited by a mosaic of peoples, with big and strong Greek cities in the south, led by Tarent, was an appealing prospect for expansive Rome in the 4th–3rd century, and the Republic fought over it not just with the native people but also with Greek rulers, led by King Pyrrhus, who was interfering mainly on behalf of Greek *poleis*.[34]

Picenum, located on the Adriatic coast, inhabited by the tribes of Piceni, Picentines, and Praetutii (southern part of Picenum), with strong settlements such as Ausculum, and important cult centres such as Cupra and the Greek *polis* Ancona,[35] found itself within the sphere of the Republic's interest as early as the end of the 4th century. In the course of their military operations against the Etruscan Lucumoni and the Celts from Cisalpine Gaul, who, together with the Samnites, built a strong coalition against the Roman expansion (the Third Samnite War), the Romans also came into contact with the inhabitants of these territories.[36] For the inhabitants of the rich and fertile territories on the Adriatic coast the appearance of the legions was an important event, since these lands were frequently attacked by their Celtic neighbours from the north, the Senones, who had earlier (in the 4th century) captured some of their lands and settled there, posing a serious threat.[37] It seems that the difficult war situation forced both sides, i.e. the inhabitants of

[33] Polyb. II, 21, 7; Strabo 5, 2, 10 (C 227); 5, 4, 2 (C 241); Plin. *NH* III, 38–39; 109–111; VI, 218; Pomp. Mela *De chor.* II, 59; II, 65; Ptol. III, 1, 52; SHA *Gord.* IV, 6; *Liber coloniarum* II, 225–228 Lachmann; Thomsen 1947, 109–120; Antonelli 2003, 45–62; Riva 2007, 79–89. There are quite a number controversies concerning the border between northern Picenum, inhabited by the tribes of Picentines and Picenes and southern Picenum, inhabited by the Praetutii, see Thomsen 1947, 109–112. Determining the precise territory of the Senones in northern Picenum is also problematic, see Thomsen 1947, 112–116.

[34] Càssola 1972, 43–63; Bandelli 1985, 59–83.

[35] Cato frg. 43 Peter; Strabo 5, 2, 10 (C 227); 5, 3, 1; 5, 4, 2 (C 241); 5, 4, 13 (C 251); Plin. *NH* III 38–39; 70; 109–111; 139; VI, 218; Pomp. Mela *De chor.* II, 59; 65; 69; Ptol. I, 7; 69; III, 1, 52; Pseudo-Scylax 15; Avien. *or. mar.* 496–500; Silius Italicus *Punica* VIII, 424–445, 573–581; Eutrop. II, 8; SHA *Gord.* IV, 6; Steph. Byz. *s.v.* 'Ατρία; Speranza 1900; Percosi Serenelli 1990, 155–188; Naso 2002, 11–233. On literary sources on Picenum, see Thomsen 1947, 50–51; Fieconi 1996, 28–50; Naso 2002, 234–250; Antonelli 2003, 13–78; Luni 2004, 44–45; Riva 2008, 79–114; Sonocchia 2008, 49–76. The significance of Ausculum as the most important city in the region is emphasised by sources: Flor. I, 14; Fest. 235 Lachmann; Laffi/Pasquinucci/Gabba 1975, 11–56. Ancona, as a Greek colony, was founded by the ruler of Syracuse, Dionysius I the Elder: Naso 2002, 255–259; Braccesi 2007, 19–30. The Greek presence in the region was not restricted to Ancona, and Greek influences in the region had started in archaic times: Luni 2004, 51–54, 57–69; Braccesi 2007, 121–148. We should also mention such cities as Spina and Adria, which also had a strong Greek element. The significance of the cult centre at Cupra for the inhabitants of the region has been emphasised by: Mostardi 1977, 17–25, 39–73; Naso 2002, 234–250. These territories also experienced Etruscan, Illyrian (across the Adriatic), and strong Celtic influences: Toynbee 1965, I: 95–99; Colonna 1984, 95–105; Naso 2002; Luni 2004, 51–56; Riva 2007, 79–114.

[36] On the Third Samnite War, see Salmon 1967, 255–279; Harris 1971, 61–78; Ziółkowski 1994, 58–59; Oakley 2002, 11–12. Such a large coalition against Rome was unprecedented in the history of Roman expansion in Italy. On the Etruscan-Celtic cooperation in 299, see Polyb. II, 19, 1–4; Livy X, 10, 1. Some Umbrian settlements also joined the war, but their weak involvement, as well as the meagre help provided by the Etruscans to the Celtic-Samnite coalition, did not have much influence on the course of the war.

[37] Polyb. II, 17; 21, 7; App. *Gall.* 12; *Samn.* 6; Peyre 1979, 101; Fieconi 1996, 25–27; Kruta/Manfredi 1999, 136–143; Paci 2002, 86–93.

Picenum and the Roman Republic, to sign a treaty (*foedus*), perhaps in 299.[38] Rome must have been perceived by the Piceni as the lesser and more distant threat than the warlike Senones and their allies the Samnites.

Having expanded their rule along the River Tiber, the Romans had been present in the territories neighbouring Picenum from the east – Umbria to be precise – for well over a decade, and the Roman allies included the Umbrian settlements of Camerinum, Ocriculum (*foedus aequum*), and perhaps also Ravenna, located north of Picenum on the Adriatic coast. The Roman influence was also strengthened by the foundation of the Latin colony of Narnia on the bank of the River Nar in 299, which replaced the destroyed Umbrian settlement of Nequinum.[39]

Some of the tribes from Picenum participated actively in the battles during the Third Samnite War.[40] They mainly included the Senones from northern Picenum (later *ager Gallicus*) and the Praetutii from southern Picenum. However, the main war effort was sustained by the Romans on one side, and the Samnites and the Senones on the other. Undoubtedly, the Republic's alliance with the wealthy and numerous inhabitants of Picenum brought them many benefits: an ally who could provide military contingents[41] and whose lands separated Rome's enemies – the Samnites and the Senones – as well as access to the Adriatic Sea. If we consider the Roman efforts in Umbria too, also aimed at preventing dangerous coalitions between the Celts and the Samnites, it is clear that in order to conduct its policy of domination in Italy, the Republic used a range of instru-

[38] Livy X, 10, 12; Laffi/Pasqunucci/Gabba 1975, 15; Delplace 1993, 3–4; Luni 2004, 69–70. It is difficult to say what the character of Rome's alliance (*foedus*) with the inhabitants of Picenum was, since Livy's reference to this event is very brief. Badian (1958, 27) believes that the character of this alliance could have been similar to the treaties of Camerinum and Ocriculum, as it was signed when the Republic was facing a difficult moment during the Samnite War.

[39] On the treaties with Umbrian settlements, see *CIL* XI 5631 = *ILS* 432: *Imp. Caesari L. Septimio Severo... caelesti eius indulgentia in aeternam securitatem adque gloriam iure aequo foederis sibi confirmato Camertes p.p.*; Cic. *Balb.* 46: *cum Camertinum foedus dominium foederum sanctissimum atque aequissimum sciret esse*; 48: *Neque Iguvinatium neque Camertium foedere esse exceptum, quominus eorum civibus a populo Romano praemia virtutis tribuerentur*; Livy IX, 36, 1–14; 41, 20; Diod. XX, 35, 1–5; 44, 8–9; Pietrangeli 1943, 28; Badian 1958, 27; Toynbee 1965, I: 260, 263; Harris 1971, 99; Sherwin-White 1973, 121; Cornell 1995, 355–357; Bradley 2000, 107–109, 118–121; Burton 2012, 88–90, 191–192. Possibly, the *foedus* with Ameria and Iguvinum was the same. On the foundation of Narnia: Livy X, 10: *contra Umbros*; Plin. *NH* III, 113: *quod oppidum Nequinum antea vocitatum est*; Salmon 1969, 60, 63, 119; Harris 1971, 61, 68; Bradley 2000, 111–115. Staveley (1994, 421–422) claims that it was the foundation of colonies in the 4th–3rd century, including Narnia, that cut off communication between the Samnites and the allies from the north, see Toynbee 1965, I: 154–155; Bandelli 2002b, 24. Not all Umbrian tribes were allied with Rome; some of them joined the war against Rome with the coalition of the Samnites, Senones and Etruscans.

[40] Livy X, 11, 7–8; Bandelli 2002b, 23–24; 2008, 338; Luni 2004, 71–73. According to Livy, during the early stage of the war they informed Rome about the Samnite preparations for war and about the attempts to force the Picentes to leave the alliance with the Republic. Perhaps some of these attempts at a Samnite-Celtic coalition were successful, because Livy reports that the Praetutii were punished after the war with the confiscation of some of their lands, where the citizen colony of Castrum (Novum) and a Latin colony of Hadria/Hatria were built, and the inhabitants were given the status of *civitas sine suffragium*: Livy *Per.* 11, 8; Front. *De controv.* pp. 18–19 Lachmann; Laffi/Pasquinucci/Gabba 1975, 16; Bandelli 2008, 340–341.

[41] Perhaps the allies from Picenum fought on the Roman side in the battle of Ausculum against the King of Epirus, Pyrrhus, see Dion. Hal. XX 1 4–5; Bandelli 2008, 344–345.

ments, including a system of alliances (settlements in Umbria and Picenum), colonisation (Narnia) and using legions, even in the 4th and 3rd centuries.[42]

During the Third Samnite War, Rome was forced to fight on several fronts at once; although it was not a new phenomenon, this time the opponents did not fight separately, but formed a coalition conducting coordinated operations. The Republic had put a lot of effort into preventing its opponents from joining forces. The coalition consisted mainly of the Samnites and the Celtic Senones, as well as the Etruscans and the Umbrians, drawn into the conflict by the genius of the Samnite general Gellius Egnatius. The Samnite forces, despite a Roman buffer, managed to make their way north, where they conducted sabotage actions to embolden the other confederates to act against Rome and its allies. However, in the 4th–3rd centuries Rome's ability to mobilise an army was strong enough for the Romans not only to throw their main forces, i.e. the consular army, against the coalition of the Samnites and the Senones, but also to conduct a simultaneous operation against the Etruscans and the Umbrians.[43] A large part of the military operations occurred in the territory of Picenum's neighbours, Umbria and Etruria. The confederates even managed to defeat the consular army at Camerinum/Clusium in 296,[44] but the turning point of the war was the battle fought on the Umbrian fields at Sentinum in 295. The Samnite-Senonian forces were routed and the armies of their Etruscan and Umbrian allies were stopped by the sabotage actions of the Roman forces, which prevented them from joining up with the Samnites and the Senones. The Romans subjugated the territories of Etruria and Umbria within years of the victory at Sentinum.[45] The war against the Samnites continued until 290, but they were alone in their fight, since neither Celtic warriors nor Etruscans and Umbrians were able to engage in military activities.[46] When the war against the Samnites was over, the consul M'. Curius Dentatus subjugated the lands of the Umbrian Sabines in 290,[47] and some territories in northern Picenum were

[42] The lands of the allied Picentes were a buffer zone, which could stop Celtic invasions from Cisalpine Gaul, see Staveley 1994, 425. According to Pliny the Elder, the populous territories of Region V (i.e. roughly the lands belonging to the Picentes) provided Rome with considerable military contingents (*NH* III 110: *Quinto regio Piceni est, quondam uberrimae multitudinis: CCCLX Picentium in fidem p. R. venere*). See Strabo 5, 4, 2 (C 241–42); Dion. Hal. XX, 1, 4–5; Bandelli 2008, 338–339, 344–345.

[43] On the Republic's demographic and recruitment capacity during the Third Samnite War, see Livy X, 27, 10–11; *Per.* 11; Oakley 2002, 29; Suder 2003, 112–130; Ziółkowski 2004, 152–156, 161. On the Battle of Sentinum, see Salmon 1967, 265–270; Paci 2002, 81–93; Bandelli 2002a, 63–79. The significance of this clash has been emphasised by numerous modern theses and papers, e.g. a collection of articles published on the 2,300th anniversary of the battle, titled *Sentinum 295 a.C. Sassoferrato 2006. 2300 anni dopo la battaglia. Una città romana tra storia e archeologia. Convegno internazionale Sassoferrato 21–23 Settembre 2006* a cura di Maura Medri.

[44] Polyb. II, 19, 5 (Camerinum); Livy X, 25, 11; 27, 4 (Clusium); Salmon 1967, 266–268; Harris 1971, 69–70; Bradley 2000, 115–116. There are numerous controversies regarding the place of the battle of the coalition against the Romans in 296.

[45] On the Roman sabotage actions against the Etruscans and the Umbrians, see Livy X, 31; 34; 37; *Per.* 11 (Volsinii); Diod. XX, 35, 4–5; Salmon 1967, 268–269; Harris 1971, 74–78; Pallottino 1991, 129, 136; Bradley 2000, 116.

[46] Salmon 1967, 268–279.

[47] Livy XXVIII, 45; *Per.* 11; Vell. Pat. I, 14; Flor. I, 10; Harris 1971, 84; Pallottino 1991, 103; Bradley 2000, 116–117; Bandelli 2008, 340–341. On the division of the Sabines' lands, see Strabo 5, 3, 1 (C 228); Vell. Pat. I, 14; Plin. *NH* XVIII, 3, 18; Val. Max. IV, 3, 5; Front. *Strat.* IV, 3, 12; Toynbee 1965, I: 104, 377–387; II: 142; Ziółkowski 1994, 62, 63, 66.

captured; they had belonged to the Senones (*ager Gallicus*), who had taken them away from the native tribe.[48]

The military operations also affected the territories of southern Picenum, since some of the tribes (Praetutii) abandoned the alliance with the Republic and went over to the coalition's side.[49] Consequently, the Romans forced them into submission and captured some of their lands, on which two colonies were founded: the *coloniae civium Romanorum* of Castrum (Novum) and the Latin colony of Hadria, alias Hatria. We cannot say much about these foundations on the basis of written sources. Even the date and place of the foundation of Castrum (Novum) are not certain, because the accounts of Livy and Velleius Paterculus differ considerably. Livy states that the colony was founded in the same year as the colonies at Hadria/Hatria and Sena (Gallica), i.e. 290, and Velleius Paterculus claims that Castrum was built in 264, on the eve of the First Punic War, together with the Latin colony at Firmum. The place of the foundation is problematic since some historians, following the account of Velleius Paterculus, believe that Castrum (Novum) was founded in Etruria and corresponds with present-day Santa Marinella, while others, believing Livy's account to be more reliable, think that it was in Picenum, on the territory belonging to the Praetutii (present-day Giulianova).[50]

There are also serious doubts about the name of the Latin colony of Hadria or Hatria. It is mentioned in written sources as Hadria, but the abbreviation *HAT* appears on the legends of bronze coins (*aes grave*) minted in this colony. We are able to determine the status of this settlement on the basis of the facts that it minted its coins and had magisterial offices typical of Latin colonies, which can be recognised in epigraphic sources.[51]

The presence of the warlike Celts was not conducive to individual colonial settlement in the *ager Gallicus*, as the lives of unprotected settlers would be in danger. Rome, not wanting to endanger its citizens and allies, and wary of provoking the aggressive Cisalpine Celts (especially since it was on the eve of a war in the south against Tarent and its ally, the king of Epirus, Pyrrhus), restricted itself to selecting a small territory and allocating it to a civil colony of Sena Gallica. It was probably founded between 290/289 and 283.[52] Its garrison of three hundred men with their families was, naturally, incapable

[48] Delplace 1993, 25. It is difficult to say whether the Senones' lands in Picenum were captured by Rome right after the Third Samnite War or only in 283. See below.

[49] See above note 42.

[50] Livy, *Per.* 11, 6: *Coloniae deductae sunt Castrum, Sena, Hadria*; Vell. Pat. I, 14; Salmon 1969, 78–79, 119–120; Delplace 1993, 4; Bandelli 2002b, 27–30.

[51] *CIL* I² 40 = *ILLRP* 77 (consuls); *CIL* I², 2129a = *ILLRP* 545; *CIL* I², 2129b = *ILLRP* 545 (duoviri); Livy, *Per.* 11, 6: *Hadria*; XXVII, 10, 7: *Hadriani*; Salmon 1969, 62; Bandelli 2002b, 32–34; 2008, 350–351; Pelgrom 2008, 352 n. 30 (the colony's area is estimated at 30 ha). The colonists joined the tribus Maecia: *CIL* IX 5019 = *ILS* 5427 = *ILLRP* 304; Petraccia Lucernoni 1988, 186–187. On the repercussions of the events of 209 see above. The status of the Latin colony of Firmum can be determined in a similar way; see below.

[52] Polyb. II, 19, 12; Livy, *Per.* 11; XXVII, 38, 4: *ab supero mari Senensis*; Salmon 1969, 62, 78, 81; Càssola 1972, 43; Paci 2002, 82–83; Luni 2004, 73–74. The problem of dating the foundation of the colony at Sena Gallica results from confusion in the written sources. The Livy tradition cites the year 289, while Polybius seems to opt for the year 283: Toynbee 1965, I: 87, 149–150 n. 8, 154 n. 6, 155, 167; Salmon 1969, 176 n. 82, 180 n. 119; Harris 1971, 79–84; Paci 2002, 82–85. See Brunt 1971, 167; Bandelli 1988, 5, 8; 1999, 193; 2002a, 72, 74; Ziółkowski 1994, 62; Paci 2002, 92–93. The citizens settled at Sena were to belong to the *tribus* Pollia: Bandelli 1985, 59–83; 1988, 6; 2002a, 77 *contra* Harris 1971, 334, 339. On the discussion about

of stopping any serious act of aggression of the Celtic tribes from Cisalpine Gaul[53]. The colony of Sena Gallica, situated near the Adriatic coast, almost at the mouth of the River Sena, was supposed to be an outpost that would repel possible attacks of Illyrian pirates on the coast or pillaging attacks of small Celtic groups. Its importance was not just strategic – it was a modest but clear symbol of the Roman presence on the territories between the Rivers Aesis and Utens and on the Adriatic coast.

The breakdown of the coalition and the defeat of its members did not bring peace and quiet for the Republic. The factor which destabilised the situation in the region was the Cisalpine Celts. They interfered in the Italian matters on many occasions and posed a serious threat not only to their closest neighbours but also to tribes in central Italy and to the Roman imperial policy (*metus/tumultus Gallicus*).[54] In the 280s the Celtic tribes attacked several times, mainly in Etruria, spreading fear and fire among the Roman allies. The Republic tried to stop these Celtic attacks by sending legions and by building, through a system of alliances, a buffer zone to separate Roman lands from Celtic territories.[55]

In 284 at Arretium, the Senones inflicted a heavy defeat on the Roman legions, in which the consul L. Cecilius Metellus Denter was killed. Rome's response was almost immediate. In 283, legions under the command of the consul M'. Curius Dentatus completely sacked the territory inhabited by the Senones, and murdered or sold into slavery the majority of the people, so that only a handful managed to stay on their old lands. On the captured Senonian territory in Picenum, between the Rivers Utens in the north and Aesis in the south, the *ager Gallicus* was created, which remained undivided until 268, when the Latin colony of Ariminum was founded. The *ager Gallicus* was not divided immediately due to Rome's size – it did not have enough citizens and allies to people such a large area.[56]

However, exterminating the Senones did not put a stop to Gallic raids. In 283, the Senones' neighbours from the north, the Boii, invaded Etruria; after joining the Etruscan forces, they marched towards Rome. However, the Etruscans were routed, and the few Boii left alive withdrew after the defeat. The Boii made another attempt to attack the Roman territory, but they were defeated again and forced to sign a truce with Rome that held for over forty years,[57] which likely facilitated the Roman conquest of southern Italy.

---

the distribution of the settlers from Picenum in the tribes Velina and Quirinia, and from the *ager Gallicus* in the *tribus* Pollia, see Taylor 1960, 60–63; Toynbee 1965, I: 176–178, 225, 377–387.

[53] *CIL* I² 40 = *ILLRP* 77 (consuls); 2129a = *ILLRP* 545; 2129b = *IILRP* 545 (duoviri); Liv. *Per.* 11 6: *Hadria*; XXVII 10 7: *Hadriani*; Salmon 1969, 62; Bandelli 2002b, 32–34; 2008, 350–351; Pelgrom 2008, 352 n. 30 (the colony's area is estimated at 30 ha). The colonists joined the tribus Maecia: *CIL* IX 5019 = *ILS* 5427 = *IILRP* 304; Petraccia Lucernoni 1988, 186–187. The status of the Latin colony of Firmum can be determined in a similar way, see below.

[54] On the *tumultus italicus gallicusque* in the Roman policy, see Polyb. II, 22; Cic. *Philipp.* VIII, 2–3; Plut. *Marcell.* 3; Plin. *NH* III, 138; Gabba 1989, 207–208; Vishnia 1996, 22–23; Piegdoń 2009, 79–81.

[55] On the chronology of Celtic invasions, see Polyb. II, 19–20; Dion. Halic. 19, 13; Livy, *Per.* 12; App. *Gall.* 11; *Samn.* 6; Flor. I, 8; Eutrop. II, 10; Oros. III, 22; Corbett 1971, 656–664; Harris 1971, 79–84; Peyre 1979, 43–46; Dyson 1985, 24–27.

[56] Salmon 1969, 78; Ziółkowski 1994, 68–69; 2004, 160.

[57] Piegdoń 2009, 79–81.

The Republic was not only free to expand in the south of Italy, but was also able to secure its northern Italian border.[58]

Truce agreements with the Celtic tribes from Cisalpine Gaul and settlement and colonisation actions conducted by the Republic in the subordinated territories of Umbria, Etruria, and Picenum allowed the Romans to build a solid barrier protecting the territories of Roman Italy from Celtic interference from the north. After the war against the King of Epirus, Pyrrhus, and his allies from southern Italy, Rome began to move against the remaining independent tribes and settlements in Picenum and Umbria, whose lands separated Roman possessions. In the years 268–265, the Republic dealt with the northernmost and independent Umbrian tribes.[59] Earlier, perhaps already in 269, the independent inhabitants of Picenum had been dealt with. Sources inform us about the military campaigns of the Roman consuls, Q. Ogulnius and G. Fabius Pictor in 269 and P. Sempronius Sophus (Tib. Sempronius Gracchus?) and App. Claudius Russus in 268, who subjugated the inhabitants of Picenum.[60] Some of the defeated were deported south to Samnium, where they were settled near the Latin colony of Paestum (former Greek Poseidonia). The rest were given limited Roman citizenship (*civitas sine suffragium*), apart from Ausculum and perhaps the former Greek colony of Ancona, which maintained the previous alliance (*foedus*). In place of the displaced native people and the exterminated Senones, Rome founded (before the outbreak of the First Punic War) the Latin colonies of Ariminum in the *ager Gallicus* (near the Adriatic coast) in 268 and Firmum (present-day Fermo) almost in the middle of the old area of free Picenum in 264.[61]

In the northern part of the lands taken from the Senones, i.e. close to the territories of the Celtic tribes from Cisalpine Gaul, the large Latin colony of Ariminum was founded in 268 on the banks of the Rivers Arimnus (Marecchia) and Aprusa Crustumium (Ausa Conca).[62] The rulers of the Republic decided to found a Latin colony with special rights on the basis of the *ius Ariminensium* or *ius XII coloniarum*. Unlike small Sena, which had been built earlier, this colony was to withstand more effectively possible Celtic attempts at interfering south of their lands, towards the Adriatic coast, and in the newly conquered territories in Picenum (*ager Picenus*) in the vicinity of the Apennines.[63] It seems that the Roman initiative could have been related to plans for a new war in the

[58] Ibidem.

[59] Livy, *Per.* 15; Harris 1971, 84; Staveley 1994, 425; Bradley 2000, 117.

[60] *Act. Tr.*, Degrassi, 74f., 547; Livy, *Per.* 15; Dion. Halic. 20, 17; Front. *Strateg.* I, 12, 3; Vell. Pat. II, 14; Plin. *NH* XXXIII, 44; Flor. I, 14; Eutrop. II, 16; Zonar. VIII, 7; Broughton 1951/1952, 199–200; Laffi/Pasquinucci/Gabba 1975, 16; Delplace 1993, 4; Bandelli 2008, 348; Luni 2004, 74–75. However, there are no details of these activities of the 269 and 268 consuls.

[61] Strabo 5, 4, 13 (C 251); Pseudo-Scylax 11; Toynbee 1965, I: 224–225, 240–241, 300; II: 119; Laffi/Pasquinucci/Gabba 1975, 15–16. The Ligurian tribes in Cisalpine Gaul were similarly dealt with; they were displaced to Samnium in 180, 179 and 175: *CIL* IX 1445; Livy XL, 16; 17; 25–28; 41; 53; XLI, 12; 14; 18; XLII, 7–8, 22, 5–6; Flor. I, 20; Toynbee 1965, II: 279; Salmon 1967, 79, 310–311, 396; Brunt 1971, 189; Dyson 1985, 104–110. Deportation was, therefore, a frequently used tool in the Roman expansion policy in Italy.

[62] At the same time as Ariminum, another Latin colony was founded in the south of Italy – Beneventum in Samnium, on the spot of a former settlement of an Oscan tribe of the Hirpini – Maleventum: Livy, *Per.* 15; Vell. Pat. I ,14; Eutrop. II, 16; Toynbee 1965, I: 86; Salmon 1969, 63; Bandelli 2002a, 74.

[63] Strabo 5, 2, 9 (C 226); Ewins 1952, 54; Toynbee 1965, I: 281; II: 57; Bernardi 1985, 72–73; Ziółkowski 1994, 65. Ariminum became not only a *claustrum*, barring the Celts from entering Italy, but also an attack base

south (Sicily) against hitherto allied Carthage. It also cannot be ruled out that Rome wanted to ensure an advantageous position (*claustrum*) for its future activities against the Celts in Cisalpine Gaul. Despite the truce signed with the Boii in 282/281, Rome decided to send probably 6,000 settlers, both citizens and allies with families, to the area close to the old Etruscan settlement of Arimna.[64] The settlers received much bigger plots than the inhabitants of citizen colonies, which was supposed to compensate them for the loss of some of their citizens' rights (in the case of Roman citizens) and to ensure their survival in a place that was both unknown and far away from Rome. The inhabitants of Ariminum and subsequent colonies founded on the basis of the *ius XII coloniarum* (*ius Ariminensium*) received extensive advantages with regard to inheritance law and buying and selling regulations.[65] The distributed lands stretched between the River Aprusa Crustumium (Ausa Conca) in the south and the rivers of Utens or Utis in the southwest (Rubicon?).[66] This territory was probably subject to centuriation twice, first in 268, and later in 232. The colony itself was encircled by a wall of irregular shape, but quite strong, which confirms the defensive function of the settlement.[67] Unfortunately, we do not know who the *tresviri coloniae deducendae* were – their task was to prepare and select the spot for the settlement and to bring in the settlers.

Even less can be said about the colony at Firmum, mentioned above, which was undoubtedly a Latin colony. Its status is confirmed by bronze coins with the legend *FIR*; by inscriptions, which provide information about the offices typical for Latin colonies; and by literary texts, which indirectly indicate the colony's status. On the basis of archaeological data, researchers estimate the size of the colony at 10 to 12.5 hectares, and the community inhabiting Firmum at 2,500–4,000 families.[68]

---

for many of Rome's military actions in Cisalpine Gaul: Livy XXX, 18–19; Salmon 1969, 88–89; Bispham 2006, 90; Piegdoń 2009, 131–133.

[64] The heterogeneous origins of the people of Ariminum are confirmed by inscriptions: *CIL* VI 133; XI 379 = *ILS* 6664 and by Strabo 5, 1, 11 (C 216). See Toynbee 1965, I: 138 n. 2 and 3, 251 n. 3; Bandelli 1988, 12–17; Ziółkowski 2004, 180; Bispham 2006, 91; Bradley 2006, 173–174. Some historians believe there were 4,000 settlers, but it seems that the number 6,000 is closer to the truth; therefore, there could have been more than 18,000 and fewer than 24,000 settlers including families (multiplier: Caes. *BG* I, 29; Bandelli 1999, 192; Suder 2003, 126). See Ewins 1952, 54 n. 2; Bandelli 1988, 7; 1999, 193. This is why Ariminum was described by the term *claustrum*, as above.

[65] Cic. *Caec.* 35, 102: *...ipse ita tulit de civitate, ut non sustulerit horum nexa atque hereditates...*; *...a civibus Romanis hereditates capere posse...*

[66] Plin. *NH* III, 115: *Octava regio determinatur Arimino, Pado, Appennino. in ora fluvius Crustumium, Ariminum colonia cum amnibus Arimino et Aprusa, fluvius Rubico, quondam finis Italiae. ab eo Sapis et Utis et Anemo, Ravenna Sabinorum oppidum cum amne Bedese, ab Ancona CV, nec procul a mari Umbrorum Butrium*; Ewins 1952, 54; Cassola 1962, 210; Toynbee 1965, I: 85; II: 670–671; Brunt 1971, 167; Laffi 1987, 41; Oebel 1993, 54–74; Bonora 2000, 57–58. The Latin status of Ariminum is also confirmed by bronze coins minted in the colony, with the legend *ARIMN*, and inscriptions with offices typical of Latin colonies: *CIL* I^2 40 = *ILLRP* 77 (consuls); *CIL* I^2 2029a = *ILLRP* 545; *CIL* I^2 2029b = *ILLRP* 545 (duoviri); Salmon 1969, 86; Bandelli 2002b, 35; Bispham 2006, 108–110.

[67] Salmon 1969, 27; Chouquer/Favory 1983, 321.

[68] Vell. Pat. I, 14, 8: *At initio primi belli Punici Firmum et Castrum colonis occupata..*; *CIL* I^2 383 = *ILLRP* 593 (quaestors); Salmon 1969, 86; Polverini 1987, 19–31, 55–64; Bandelli 2008, 345, 348–349; Pelgrom 2008, 353 n. 30 (the area of the land distributed for the establishment of the colony is estimated at 10 ha!). The colonists joined the *tribus* Velina: *CIL* IX 5351 = *ILS* 6132 = *ILLRP* 593; Petruccia Lucernoni 1988, 186–187.

There is also little that can be said about the last colony founded in the 3rd century in the *ager Gallicus*, i.e. Aesis, also known as Aesium (present-day Iesi). We do not know the circumstances and reasons why it was founded even though there were already three Latin colonies in the *ager Gallicus et Picenum* – Hadria, Ariminum and Firmum – and two citizen ones – Sena Gallica and probably Castrum (Novum). All that has been established so far is the date of the foundation, i.e. probably 247, and the fact that it was a citizen colony. Aesis was built on the south border of the *ager Gallicus*, in the middle stretch of the River Aesis, which marked the southern border of the *ager Gallicus*, and quite far from the Adriatic coast.[69]

Aesis was not the last Roman colonial settlement initiative in the territories of the *ager Gallicus et Picenum*. After the deportation of most of the inhabitants of Picenum and the extermination of the Celtic Senones, there was still a considerable reservoir of free land to be peopled on the central coast of the Adriatic. Despite the foundation of three large Latin colonies (Hadria, Ariminum, and Firmum) and three smaller citizen colonies (Castrum Novum, Sena Gallica and Aesis), the area still offered considerable settlement possibilities. It seems that on the one hand the Romans found it hard to distribute such a large territory, and on the other hand there were conflicting opinions in Rome as to how and when the lands should be distributed. It is difficult to say what the possible dispute looked like, but it probably concerned the form of land division, i.e. whether to continue granting land to settlers in colonies, or to distribute it by grants to individual settlers. One argument for the first option was the danger related to the appearance in 236, i.e. after the truce ended, of the Boii and their allies *Gaesatae* at Ariminum. They did not threaten the colony, since as a result of internal conflicts instead of conquering the colony the two groups started to fight against each other, leading to their annihilation without Roman intervention (sic!).

However, in 232, the option of granting plots to individual settlers (*adsignationes viritanae*) won; one of its advocates was the plebeian tribune of 232, G. Flaminius Nepos. It was G. Flaminius, a *homo novus* on the Roman political scene, who passed the *lex Flaminia de agro Piceno Gallico viritim dividundo*. The pro-aristocracy historic sources (Polybius, Livy) considered him to be a populist and a political trouble-maker. In the opinion of the unsympathetic sources, the reason behind his postulate to divide and assign plots *viritim* was solely the desire to win over supporters.[70] It seems, however, that the initiative was not only an element of propaganda, but also an attempt to implement, albeit against the Senate, the Roman plan of putting the conquered lands to use. Most likely, the Senate, in accordance with the political and legal tradition, was going to carry out its own settlement project (perhaps a new colony or also *adsignationes viritanae*?), and consequently decide on its own what would become of the undistributed land. Meanwhile the tribune, who went on to cause a great deal of trouble for the establishment, completed his own project of distribution against the Senators' wishes during a plebeian

[69] Vell. Pat. I, 14, 8; Strabo 5, 2, 10 (C 227); Ptol. III, 1, 46; Toynbee 1965, I: 184; Salmon 1969, 180 n. 119–120; Harris 1971, 156; Bandelli 1988, 6; 2002a, 74; 2002b, 35–37; Oebel 1993, 89; Paci 2002, 90; Piegdoń 2009, 133.

[70] Polyb. II, 21; Cic. *Brut.* 14, 57; Livy XXI, 63; Val. Max. V, 4, 5; Toynbee 1965, I: 167; Bandelli 2002a, 77, 80; 2003, 50; Luni 2004, 79–83 (the extent of the distributed lands determined on the basis of inscriptions). See Toynbee 1965, I: 311–315.

assembly (*plebiscitum*). Naturally, this move won him the support and acclaim of the Roman *populus*, since it was probably carried out in the best interests of those without land. It seems that the objective of G. Flaminius Nepos' initiative was not only to win the people's favour; in actual fact it was supposed to replace wastelands with land cultivated by Roman citizens favoured by the tribune. It may seem like an absurd idea to people a front territory, between the Rivers Esino, Musone (in the north) and Chienti (in the south), with individual settlers (20,000–30,000 people), due to the danger faced by the settlers from the warlike Celtic neighbours from the north. However, the absurdity of this move is only apparent if we consider that the new settlers were not thrown onto a completely hostile territory but sent to an area which had been in Roman hands for over half a century and had been partially colonised before. Three colonies had been founded there (Sena Gallica, Ariminum, Aesis), which had put down roots and could provide protection for individual settlers. The new settlers joined the Roman *tribus* of the rural Pollia.[71]

The later activity of the plebeian tribune of 232 indicates that his interest in the affairs of the northern territories of Italy was not just a matter of trying to endear himself to the Roman people. Chosen as a consul or censor, he was successful in connecting the *ager Gallicus* to Rome by a road called the *Via Flaminia* in 223 or 220,[72] and actively participated in war campaigns against the Celts from northern Italy in 224–222, e.g. as consul he fought against the Insubres in 223.[73] His actions were always criticised and attacked by the Senate, but he disregarded the rules of the aristocratic class, supporting, for example, some efforts against the aristocracy. He was also the initiator of a law called the *lex Claudia de senatoribus* in 218, which was not welcome by the senatorial aristocracy, and he was probably able to count on the support of the emerging order of equites.[74]

Roman colonisation in the *ager Gallicus* made the Gallic tribes, especially the Boii, feel threatened by Rome. The Boii managed to ally themselves with their closest neighbours, the Insubres, as well as the Lingones and the Taurini, and to hire the mercenaries from across the Alps, the Gaesatae. In 225, a mighty Gallic army of 50,000 infantry and 20,000 cavalry invaded the south.[75] The great Roman victory over the Celtic forces at Telamon became a turning point in the history of the territories between the River Po and the Alps, as the Romans began to attack the Celtic and Ligurian tribes in the same

[71] Ewins 1952, 54; Taylor 1960, 96; Toynbee 1965, I: 177, 386–387; Forni 1989, 57; Bandelli 2002a, 78; Piegdoń 2009, 133–135.

[72] Toynbee (1965, I: 311–326) draws attention to the role of Roman aristocracy in ruling the Republic, including its considerable involvement in the distribution of the *ager publicus*, and emphasises the role of its outstanding opponents – M'. Curius Dentatus and G. Flaminius Nepos: Gabba 1979, 159–163; 1990, 70; Vishnia 1996, 25–34 *contra* Salmon 1969, 103. See Bandelli 1988, 22–24; 2002a, 76–78; 2003, 50; Brizzi 2002, 55–60; Ziółkowski 2004, 264–265, 269, 291–294; Ungern-Sternberg 2005, 316–322. The estimated number of settlers in the *ager Gallicus* is taken from Bandelli 1999, 194. See Oebel 1993; Vishnia 1996, 20.

[73] Polyb. II, 32–33; Livy, *Per.* 20; Plut. *Marcell.* 6; Dion 12, 50, 4; Càssola 1962, 218–228; Toynbee 1965, II: 265; Dyson 1985, 31; 97; Kruta/Manfredi 1999, 155–158; Piegdoń 2009, 85. Flaminius, against the Senate's wishes, held a triumph for his victory against the Insubres (sic!).

[74] Livy XXI, 63, 3: *...ne quis senator cuive senator pater fuisset maritimam navem quae plus quam trecentarum amphorarum esset haberet...*; Càssola 1962, 216–219; Toynbee 1965, I: 228; Wiseman 1971, 68; Ziółkowski 2004, 252–253; Ungern-Sternberg 2005, 316–322. The role of the emerging order of equites in the Republic's policy in the 3rd century is emphasised by Càssola 1962, 25–83.

[75] Polyb. II, 22–23; Plut. *Marcell.* 3–4; Brunt 1971, 185–186; McDonald 1974, 45–46; Harris 1992, 198–199; Luraschi 1979, 3; Dyson 1985, 29; Gabba 1990, 70.

year, which started a long period of conquest of Cisalpine Gaul.[76] With this victory it also seems that the fear of the Celtic threat, which had been at the back of Roman minds since the defeat at Allia, became a thing of the past. The fear of the *metus gallicus* was replaced by the desire to expel the hated enemy from northern Italy, especially since the conquest of Cisalpine Gaul meant new, very fertile territories for settlement and colonisation for the more and more numerous citizens and the takeover of the natural resources in the region.[77]

The victories and the conquest of northern Italy would probably not have been possible without the earlier Roman activity in Picenum and on the old territories of the Celtic Senones (*ager Gallicus*) and in Umbria. The territories became not only a place protected by Rome and its allies from Celtic invasions from northern Italy, but also an area for launching attacks against the Celts. If we also add the above-mentioned initiative of G. Flaminius Nepos, who built an important artery of the *Via Flaminia* in 223 or 220 connecting Rome with the already subordinated territories of Umbria and the *ager Gallicus* in northern Picenum and with the Adriatic coast,[78] we will be able to see the full range of Roman instruments for building their hegemony in Italy.

The most serious challenge to the Roman domination in Italy was, certainly, the Second Punic War, which shook the foundations of the Republic's power but did not break it. Over a decade of fights against Hannibal in Italy and on the other fronts of this war showed some cracks in the structure of the Roman hegemony in Italy. The destruction of war affected a considerable part of Italy, including territories on the central Adriatic coast. It was not the main front of military operations, but Hannibal's forces stayed in Picenum and nearby Umbria for some time after their victory at Lake Trasimene in 217, thoroughly destroying the lands, plundering, and murdering many of the inhabitants (probably settlers). The Republic kept military units in Picenum during the conflict, and the Latin colonies of Hadria, Ariminum and Firmum supported Rome by sending provisions and reinforcements.[79] The Latin colonies of Hadria/Hatria and Firmum were also casualties of the operations of the Carthaginian forces, as their territories were sacked.[80]

As has already been mentioned, the events of the Second Punic War had a great influence on the Republic's relations with its Italian allies and on the process of colonising

[76] Polyb. II, 31; Gabba 1990, 71: "È da qesto momento che i Romani si resero conto che l'eliminazione definitiva del pericolo gallico per l'Italia centrale era realizzabile soltanto con la conquista della Valle Padana, che le vittorie sui Galli dimostravano oramai possibile."

[77] Polyb. II, 31; Harris 1992, 199–200; Vishnia 1996, 23–24; Ziółkowski 2004, 194.

[78] *Via Flaminia*: *ILS* 84; Livy, *Per.* 20; Strabo 5, 1, 11 (C 217); Tac. *Ann.* III, 9, 1; Wiseman 1970, 124, 138, 140–144; Radke 1973, 1540–1575; Delplace 1993, 8; Laurence 2011, 21–23; Luni 2004, 83–85. Based on Livy's opinion (XXXIX, 2, 10), it is believed that the *Via Flaminia* ended at Ariminum. Not everybody agrees with this opinion: Felicioli 1987, 81–138.

[79] Polyb. III, 86, 8–11; 87; Livy XXII, 9, 1–5; XXIII, 14, 1–4; XXIV, 10, 1–5; 11, 1–4; 44, 1–5; XXV, 3, 1–7; XXVII, 43, 11–12; 44, 10–11; Strabo 5, 4, 13 (C 251); App. *Hann.* 9, 11; Eutrop. III, 18; Toynbee 1965, II: 10–11, 58, 526–527; Salmon 1969, 82–91; Alfieri 1986, 7–22; Delplace 1993, 8, 27–28. It is possible that the inhabitants of Ausculum, allied with Rome, took part in the battle of Cannae in 216: Livy XXIII, 14, 2–3 (vague mention of reinforcements from Picenum); XXIII, 32, 16–20 (recruitment of soldiers in Picenum); Silius Italicus *Punica* IV, 175; 176; V, 208; VIII, 438; IX, 273; X, 312; Laffi/Pasquinucci/Gabba 1975, 16–17. The Roman legions also crossed Picenum in 207, while marching against the Carthaginian troops under the command of Hasdrubal, Hannibal's brother, who was defeated by the Romans in the Battle of the Metaurus.

[80] Salmon 1969, 89.

Italy. Rome maintained its hegemony in Italy (defeated in the 4th and 3rd centuries), apart from Cisalpine Gaul. Gradually, at the beginning of the 2nd century, Rome abandoned the policy of founding Latin colonies in favour of Roman colonies of a new type, increasing the number of settlers in the new colonies and the plots granted. Interestingly, the new *coloniae civium Romanorum* also appeared in the *ager Gallicus*, i.e. in northern Picenum – Pisaurum (present-day Pesaro), as well as in the south of the region – Potentia (present-day Potenza). Information about the foundation in 184 of both of these citizen colonies indicates how great the size of the conquered area on the central Adriatic coast (Picenum and *ager Gallicus*) must have been, seeing as it was still possible to found colonies even after granting plots to settlers from six colonies and after completing individual settlement projects. Both colonies were founded at the same time, close to the Adriatic coast, a little over 100 kilometres apart.[81] The whole project was overseen by the same *tresviri coloniae deducendae*: Q. Fabius Labeo, M. Fulvius Flaccus, and Q. Fulvius Nobilior. These were meritorious and influential statesmen and generals.[82] The colonists, whose number is estimated at 2,000, received generous plots of land – six *iugera* per person.[83] The history of both colonies shows an active involvement of high-ranking Roman officials in the internal affairs of the *coloniae civium Romanorum*. In 174, the censor Q. Fulvius Flaccus persuaded the authorities of several colonies, including Potentia and Pisaurum, to make internal investments. At the censor's suggestion, a temple of Jove was built and a road paved at Pisaurum, as well as water being supplied to Potentia (an aqueduct was built?).[84]

Discussing the censors' initiatives in 174, Livy also mentions the censors' involvement in the matter of constructing defence walls and erecting buildings (shops?) in the area around the forum, e.g. in Auximum (present-day Osimo), another settlement

[81] Livy XXXIX, 44; Vell. Pat. I, 15; Salmon 1969, 104; Toynbee 1965, II: 145 ("*coastguard colonies*"!), 208; Harris 1971, 152; Moscatelli 1987, 395–402; Delplace 1993, 14; Luni 2004, 87–88. It is difficult to say whether the initiative to found both colonies on the Adriatic coast was connected with the situation in Macedonia, where Rome backed the younger son of Philip V, Demetrius, and pushed him to inherit the throne, and in Illyria (against Gentios), cf. Bandelli 1985, 68. The foundation of citizen colonies near the coast was not unusual in the 2nd century; apart from Pisaurum and Potentia in 177 the Latin colony of Luna was founded not far from the sea, cf. Salmon 1969, 104. Pisaurum may have been built on the spot where an earlier settlement had existed, and the colony's name is probably derived from the nearby river, cf. Braccesi 1984, 2–6. The colonists at Pisaurum were diverse socially and, interestingly, also ethnically; the Roman poet Q. Ennius, who had come from the Oscan town of Rudiae (the Salentines allied with Rome), was an inhabitant of Pisaurum or Potentia: Cic. *Brut.* 20; 78; *Arch.* 9; Gell. *NA* 17, 17, 1: *Quintus Ennius tria corda habere sese dicebat, quo loqui Graece et Oscae et Latine sciret*; Toynbee 1965, I: 192; II: 149 n. 1, 431, 667; Harris 1971, 159 n. 6, 175 n. 4, 177, 196; Braccesi 1984, 7; Luni 1988, 37–50.

[82] Toynbee 1965, II: 202; Braccesi 1984, 6–7. Delplace (1993, 16–18) identified the *tresviri coloniae deducendae*; cf. Broughton 1951/1952, 406.

[83] Livy XXXIX, 44; Toynbee 1965, II: 147; Salmon 1969, 24, 104–105, who estimates the number of colonists in both settlements on the basis of the number of colonists in other citizen colonies. Estimating the area of the colonies (23 ha at Potentia and 17 ha at Pisaurum) on the basis of archaeological research can also help to estimate the size of the community in both colonies, see Delplace 1993, 14, 23–24; Luni 2004, 88. Possibly, a *conciliabulum civium Romanorum* had existed there before the colony at Pisaurum was founded: Braccesi 1984, 7.

[84] Livy XLI, 27, 5–13. The censors' activities are described in detail by Delplace 1993, 19–23. See Toynbee 1965, I: 233 n. 1; II: 208 n. 2; Sherwin-White 1973, 84–85; Luni 2004, 89–90.

in the *ager Gallicus* in Picenum.[85] This is one of the first mentions (Livy) about this settlement, which was probably a citizen colony. There is some confusion resulting from the fact that other sources (Velleius Paterculus) date the colony's foundation to a later period, i.e. 157/156,[86] and some contemporary historians (E.T. Salmon) even to the times of the Gracchi brothers (128), whose agrarian reform could have also affected Picenum, as confirmed by inscriptions and the *Liber coloniarum.*[87] Auximum's citizen status is also confirmed by literary sources and, mainly, inscriptions, which mention offices typical for citizen colonies.[88] The colonists at Auximum were given as many as eight *iugera* of land.[89] Unlike Pisaurum and Potentia, Auximum was located farther from the Adriatic, similarly to Aesis founded in 247. The colony's location far from the coast may mean that factors other than strategic (economic and social) ones were decisive when Auximum was founded. The colonists joined the *tribus* Velina, as confirmed by the majority of inscriptions from the region.[90]

Founding Latin and citizen colonies and building settlements were not the only methods of subordinating and transforming the region of Picenum and the *ager Gallicus*. Colonial settlement organised by the state was most likely complemented by spontaneous settlement actions of the people, about which we have almost no information. Undoubtedly the colonies themselves were not the only settlements created on the lands which were being peopled. We should also remember smaller places, such as *fora, concialiabula, vici* etc., which were founded on those territories by Rome and its officials.[91] Together with colonies, they played an important role in the process of Romanisation of Picenum and the *ager Gallicus*. Colonies and smaller settlements of non-native population were connected with one another and with native settlements by a network of roads, many of which were built in the 3rd century, but the majority in the 2nd century, the prime example being the *Via Flaminia*.

[85] Livy XLI, 27, 5–13 (interpretations of Livy's fragment provided by Gentili 1955, 31; 56–62, 67; Toynbee 1965, II: 208 n. 2; Delplace 1993, 15); Plut. *Pomp.* 6. On belonging to Picenum, see Strabo 5, 4, 2 (C 241); Plin. *NH* III,13,111; Gentili 1955, 34–35.

[86] The problems related to the chronology of the foundation of the colonies at Pisaurum, Potentia and Auximum are discussed by Delplace 1993, 14.

[87] *CIL* I^2 719 = XI 6331; *Liber coloniarum*, p. 258 Lachmann: *Ausimatis ager limitibus Gracchanis per centurias est adsignatus*; Toynbee 1965, II: 209 n. 1, 241; Salmon 1969, 112, 113, 115, 118; Harris 1971, 150 n. 6; Delplace 1993, 28–29; Luni 2004, 90–92. The citizen colony at Auximum may have been built in place of an earlier settlement with the status of *forum*: Toynbee 1965, II: 208 n. 2.

[88] Hirtius *BC* 12; Plut. *Pomp.* 6; *CIL* IX 5839, 5841, 5843, 5849, 6384 (praetors); IX 5841, 5842 (aediles); IX 5823, 5828, 5843, 5855, 5856 (decurions); Gentili 1955, 43–44. See Bispham 2007, 101–103.

[89] Gentili 1955, 33.

[90] *CIL* IX 5830–5833, 5838, 5840, 5842 (Velina); Gentili 1955, 33. A few inscriptions name other *tribus* such as Claudia, Lemonia, and Collina. Auximum, like the whole of Picenum, played an important role as a place of recruitment in the 1st century, during the civil wars: Hirtius *BC* I, 12; 13; 31; Plut. *Pomp.* 6; Lucan *Phars.* II. On the reasons why Auximum was founded, see Salmon 1969, 112, 113–115, 118.

[91] Frayn 1993; Bispham 2007, 87–91.

BIBLIOGRAPHY

Alfieri, N. (1986): La battaglia del Lago Plestino, *Picus* 6: 7–22.

Antonelli, L. (2003): *I Piceni. Corpus delle fonti. La documentazione letteraria*, Roma.

Badian, E. (1958): *Foreign Clientelae 264 – 70*, Oxford.

Badian, E. (1967): *Roman Imperialism in the Late Republic*, Pretoria.

Bandelli, G. (1981): La guerra istrica del 221 a.C. e la spedizione alpina del 220 a.C., *Athenaeum* n.s. 59: 3–28.

Bandelli, G. (1985): La presenza italica nell'Adriatico Orientale in età repubblicana (III–I secolo a.C.), *Antichità Altoadriatiche* 26: 59–84.

Bandelli, G. (1988): *Ricerche sulla colonizzazione romana della Gallia Cisalpina: le fasi iniziali e il caso aquileiese*, Roma.

Bandelli, G. (1999): La popolazione della Cisalpina dalle invasioni galliche alla guerra sociale, in: *Demografia, sistemi agrari, regimi alimentari nel mondo antico. Atti del Convegno Internazionale di Studi (Parma 17–19 ottobre 1997)*, Bari: 189–215.

Bandellli, G. (2001): Roma e l'Adriatico fra III e II secolo a.C., *Antichità Altoadriatiche* 54: 17–42.

Bandelli, G. (2002a): Roma e l'Italia centrale dalla bataglia del Sentino (295 a.C.) al plebiscito di Gaio Flaminio (232 a.C.), in: *La bataglia del Sentino. Scontro fra nazioni e incontro in una nazione. Atti del Convegno di Studi Camerino-Sassoferrato, 10–13 giugno 1998*, Roma: 63–80.

Bandelli, G. (2002b): La colonizzazione medio-adriatico fino alla seconda guerra punica: questioni preliminari, *Quaderni di archeologia nella Marche* 11: 21–54.

Bandelli, G. (2003): Aquileia colonia latina dal senatus consultum del 183 a.C. al supplementum del 169 a.C., *Antichità Altoadriatiche* 54: 49–76.

Bandelli, G. (2008): Romani e Picenti dalla stipulozione del foedus (299 a.C.) alla deduzione di Firmum (264 a.C.), *Quaderni di archeologia nelle Marche* 14: 337–352.

Bernardi, A. (1985): Cremona, colonia latina a nord del Po, Cremona Romana, in: *Atti del congresso storico archeologico per il 2200 anno di fondazione di Cremona (Cremona, 30–31 maggio 1982)*, Cremona: 71–82.

Bishpam, E. (2006): *Coloniam Deducere*: How Roman was Roman Colonization During the Middle Republic?, in: G. Bradley, J.-P. Wilson (eds.), *Greek and Roman Colonization. Origins, Ideologies and Interactions*, Swansea: 73–160.

Bishpam, E. (2007): *From Asculum to Actium. The Municipalization of Italy from the Social War to Augustus*, Oxford.

Bonora, G. (2000): La centuriazione nell'Emilia orientale, in: *Aemilia. La cultura romana in Emilia Romagna dal III secolo a.C. all'età constantiniana*, Venezia: 57–63.

Bracessi, L. (1984): Lineamenti di storia pesarese in età antica, in: *Pesaro nell'antichità. Storia e monumenti*, vol. I, Venezia: 1–38.

Braccesi, L. (2007): Terra di confine archeologia e storia tra Marche, Romagna e San Marino, *ΑΡΧΑΙΟΛΟΓΙΚΑ archeologia, epigrafia, storia* 1, Roma.

Bradley, G. (2000): *Ancient Umbria. State, Culture, and Identity in Central Italy from the Iron Age to the Augustan Era*, Oxford.

Bradley, G. (2006): Colonization and Identity in Republican Italy, in: G. Bradley, J.-P. Wilson (eds.), *Greek and Roman Colonization. Origins, Ideologies and Interactions*, Swansea: 161–188.

Brizzi, G. (2002): La via Flaminia e la guerra annibalica, *Quaderni di archeologia nella Marche* 11: 55–60.

Broughton, T.R.S (1951/1952): *The Magistrates of the Roman Republic*, vol. I–II, New York.

Brunt, P.A. (1971): *Italian Manpower 225 B.C.–A.D. 14*, Oxford.

Brunt, P. (2001): *Roman Imperial Themes*, Oxford.

Burton, P.J. (2012): *Friendship and Empire. Roman Diplomacy and Imperialism in the Middle Republic (353–146 B.C.)*, Cambridge.

Calderazzo, L. (1997): Arbitrati romani in Cisalpina (197–89 a.C): problemi e status quaestionis, *Rivista di Studi Liguri*, Bordighera: 25–46.

Campagnoli, P. (1999): *La bassa valle del foglia e il territorio di 'Pisaurum' in età romana*, Imola.

Càssola, F. (1962): *I gruppi politici Romani nel III sec. a.C.*, Trieste.

Càssola, F. (1972): La politica romana nell'Alto Adriatico, *Antichità Altoadriatiche* 2: 43–63.

Chouquer, G., Favory, F. (1983): Cadastrations antiques de Campanie, du Latium méridional et de Romagne, in: *Cadastres et espace rural. Approches et réalités antiques*, Besançon: 318–321.

Colonna, G. (1984): Etruschi nell'*ager Gallicus*, *Picus* 4: 95–105.

Corbett, J.H. (1971): Rome and Gauls 285–280 B.C., *Historia* 20: 656–664.

Cornell, T. (1995): *The Beginnings of Rome. Italy and Rome from the Bronze Age to the Punic Wars (c. 1000–264 BC)*, London–New York.

Cornell, T. (2002): The End of Roman Imperial Expansion, in: J. Rich, G. Shipley (eds.), *War and Society in the Roman World*, London–New York: 139–170.

Crawford, M.H. (1995): La storia della colonizzazione romana secondo i Romani, in: A. Storchi Marino (ed.), *L'incidenza dell'antico. Studi in memoria di Ettore Leppore I. Atti del Convegno Internazionale, Anacapri 24–28 marzo 1991*, Naples: 187–192.

Delplace, Ch. (1993): *La romanisation du Picenum: l'exemple d'urbs Salvi*a, Rome.

Dench, E. (1995): *From Barbarians to New Men*, Oxford.

Dench, E. (1997): Sacred Springs to the Social War: Myths of Origins and Questions of Identity in Central Italy, in: T. Cornell, K. Lomas (eds.), *Gender and Ethnicity in Ancient Italy*, London: 43–52.

Dumitrescu, V. (1929): *L'età del ferro nel Piceno fino all'invasione dei Galli-Senoni*, Bucarest.

Dyson, S. (1985): *The Creation of the Roman Frontier*, Princeton.

Eckstein, A.M. (2007): Conceptualizing Roman Imperial Expansion under the Republic: An Introduction, in: P. Erdkamp (ed.), *A Companion to the Roman Army*, Oxford: 567–589.

Edmondson, J. (1993): *Instrumenta Imperii*: Law and Imperialism in Republican Rome, in: B. Halpern, D.W. Hobson (eds.), *Law, Politics and Society in the Ancient Mediterranean World*, Sheffield: 156–192.

Ewins, U. (1952): The Early Colonisation of Cisalpine Gaul, *PBSR* 20: 54–71.

Felicioli, D. (1987): Il problema della Flaminia originaria in teritorio marchigiano, in: *Atti e memorie 88–91 (1984–1986). Le strade nelle Marche. Il problema nel tempo Atti del convegno Fano, Fabriano, Pesaro, Ancona (11–14 ottobre 1984)*, Ancona: 81–138.

Fieconi, A. (1996): *In Appenninis Alpibus. Circoscrizioni antiche e medievali tra Marche e Umbria,* Ancona.

Forni, G. (1989): La tribu Velina degli aquilesi, *Antichità Altoadriatiche* 35: 51–81.

Fortini, P. (1981): *Cupra Maritima origini, storia, urbanistica*, Ascoli.

Fortini, P. (1995): *Cupra Marittima*: aspetti di vita economica di una città romana del *Picenum* attraverso l'esame dell' *instrumentum domesticum*, in: *Civiltà contadina e civiltà marinara nella marca meridionale e nei rapporti tra le due sponde dell'Adriatico. Atti del 7° Seminario di studi per il personale direttivo e docente della scuola*, Cupra Marittima: 39–170.

Frayn, J. (1993): *Markets and Fairs in Roman Italy. Their Social and Economic Importance from the Second Century BC to the Third Century AD*, Oxford.

Gabba, E. (1979): Caio Flaminio e la sua legge sulla colonizzazione dell'agro gallico, *Athenaeum* LXVII: 159–163.

Gabba, E. (1989): Rome and Italy in the Second Century, in: *CAH*², vol. VIII: 197–244.

Gabba, E. (1990): La conquista della Gallia Cisalpina, in: *Storia di Roma*, vol. II: *L'impero mediterraneo. La republica imperiale*, Torino: 69–78.

Gargola, D.J. (1995): *Lands, Laws & Gods. Magistrates & Ceremony in the Regulation of Public Lands in Republican Rome*, Chapel Hill–London.

Gentili, G.V. (1955): *Auximum (Osimo). Regio V – Picenum*, Roma.

Hall, J. (2011): *Historia Grecji archaicznej ok. 1200–479 p.n.e.*, Kraków.
Harris, W.V. (1971): *Rome in Etruria and Umbria*, Oxford.
Harris, W.V. (1992): *War and Imperialism in Republican Rome 327–70 B.C.*, Oxford.
Humbert, M. (1978): *Municipium et civitas sine suffragio. L'organisation de la conquête jusqu'à la guerre sociale*, Rome.
Jehne, M. (2009): *Diplomacy in Italy in the Second Century BC*, in: C. Pilers (ed.), *Diplomats and Diplomacy in the Roman World*, Leiden–Boston: 143–171.
Keppie, L. (1983): *Colonisation and Veteran Settlement in Italy, 47–14 B.C.*, Rome.
Krawczuk, A. (1960): *Kolonizacja sullańska*, Wrocław.
Kruta, V. (1981): Les Sénons de l'Adriatique d'après l'archéologie (prolégomènes), *Études celtiques* 18, 7–38.
Kruta, V. (1992): Materiali senonici del Piceno e arte celtica, in: *La civiltà picena nelle Marche. Studi in onore di Giovanni Annibaldi Ancona 10/13 luglio 1988*, Maroni (Regioni Marche): 388–401.
Kruta, V., Manfredi, V.M. (1999): *I Celti in Italia*, Milano.
Laffi, U. (1987): L'amministrazione di Aquileia in età romana, *Antichità Altoadriatiche* 30: 39–62.
Laffi, U. (2007): *Colonie e municipi nello stato romano*, Roma.
Laffi, U., Pasquinucci, M., Gabba, E. (1975): *Asculum I*, Pisa.
Laurence, R. (2003): Territory, Ethnonyms and Geography. The Construction of Identity in Roman Italy, in: R. Laurence, J. Berry (eds.), *Cultural Identity in the Roman World*, London–New York: 95–110.
Laurence, R. (2011): *The Roads of Roman Italy. Mobility and Cultural Change*, London–New York.
Lazenby, J. (2012): *Pierwsza wojna punicka*, Zasole.
Lomas, K. (2003): Roman Imperialism and the City in Italy, in: R. Laurence, J. Berry (eds.), *Cultural Identity in the Roman World*, London–New York: 64–78.
Luni, M. (1988): Popolamento e sistemazione agraria nell'ager Pisaurensis, *Picus* 8: 37–50.
Luni, M. (2004): *Archeologia nelle Marche. Dalla preistoria all'età tardoantica*, Firenze.
Luraschi, G. (1979): *Foedus Ius Latii Civitas – Aspetti constitutionali della romanizzazione in Transpadana*, Padova.
McDonald, A.H. (1974): The Roman Conquest of Cisalpine Gaul (201–191 B.C.), *Antichthon* 8: 44–53.
Morley, N. (2010): *The Roman Empire. Roots of Imperialism*, New York.
Moscatelli, U. (1987): La viabilità litoranea tra Potentia e Sacrata in età romana, in: *Atti e memorie 88–91 (1984–1986). Le strade nelle Marche. Il problema nel tempo Atti del convegno Fano, Fabriano, Pesaro, Ancona (11–14 ottobre 1984)*, Ancona: 395–402.
Mostardi, B.F. (1977): *Cupra*, Ascoli.
Mouritsen, H. (1998): *Italia Unification. A study in Ancient and Modern Historiography*, London.
Naso, A. (2002): *I Piceni. Storia e archeologia delle Marche in epoca preromana*, Milano.
Oakley, S. (2002): The Roman Conquest of Italy, in: J. Rich, G. Shipley (eds.), *War and Society in the Roman World*, London–New York: 9–37.
Oebel, L. (1993): *Flaminius und die Anfänge der römischen Kolonisation im Ager Gallicus*, Frankfurt am Main.
Paci, G. (1998): Pisaurum: sui magistrati della colonia, *Picus* 18: 246–252.
Paci, G.F. (2002): Consequenze storico-politiche della bataglia di Sentino per i popoli a nord del fiume Esino, in: *La bataglia del Sentino. Scontro fra nazioni e incontro in una nazione. Atti del Convegno di Studi Camerino-Sassoferrato, 10–13 giugno 1998*, Roma: 81–94.
Pallottino, M. (1991): *A History of the Earliest Italy*, London.
Patterson, J.R. (2006): Colonization and Historiography: The Roman Republic, in: G. Bradley, J.-P. Wilson (eds.), *Greek and Roman Colonization. Origins, Ideologies and Interactions*, Swansea: 189–218.
Pelgrom, J. (2008): Settlement Organization and Land Distribution in Latin Colonies before the Second Punic War, in: L. de Ligt, S. Northwood (eds.), *People, Land, and Politics. Demographic Developments and the Transformation of Roman Italy 300 BC–AD 14*, Leiden–Boston: 333–372.

Percosi Serenelli, E. (1990): La "civiltà picena", in: *Dalla rivoluzione neolitica all'età dei metalli. Atti del 2° Seminario di studi per personale direttivo e docente della scuola*, Cupra Marittima: 155–190.
Petraccia Lucernoni, M.F. (1988): *I Questori Municipali dell'Italia Antica*, Roma.
Peyre, C. (1979): *La Cisalpine gauloise du IIIe au Ier siecle avant J.-C.*, Paris.
Piegdoń, M. (2009): *Galia Przedalpejska. Studia nad rzymską obecnością w północnej Italii w III–I w. p.n.e.*, Kraków.
Pietrangeli, C. (1943): *Ocriculum (Otricoli)*, Roma.
Polverini, L. (1987): Fermo in età romana, in: L. Polverni, N.E. Parise, S. Agostini, M. Pasquinucci (eds.), *Firmum Picenum I*, Pisa.
Purcell, N. (1990): The Creation of Provincial Landscape: The Roman Impact on Cisalpine Gaul, in: T. Blagg, M. Millet (eds.), *The Early Roman Empire in the West*, Oxford: 7–29.
Radke, G. (1973): *Viae publicae Romanae*, *RE S.*XIII: 1415–1686.
Rich, J. (2002): Fear, Greed and Glory: The Causes of Roman War-Making in the Middle Republic, in: J. Rich, G. Shipley (eds.), *War and Society in the Roman World*, London–New York: 38–68.
Riva, C. (2007): The Archaeology of Picenum: The Last Decade, in: G. Bradley, E. Isayev, C. Riva (eds.), *Ancient Italy. Regions without Boundaries*, Exeter: 79–113.
Salmon, E.T. (1967): *Samnium and the Samnites*, Cambridge.
Salmon, E.T. (1969): *Roman Colonisation under the Republic*, Lund.
Salmon, E.T. (1982): *The Making of Roman Italy*, London.
Scheidel, W. (2006): The Demography of Roman State Formation in Italy, in: M. Jehne, R. Pfeilschifter (eds.), *Herrschaft ohne Integration? Rom und Italien in republikanischer Zeit*, Stuttgart: 207–226.
Sherwin-White, A.N. (1973): *The Roman Citizenship*, Oxford.
Smith, R.E. (1954): Latins and Roman Citizenship in Roman Colonies: Livy 34, 42, 5–6, *JRS* 44: 18–20.
Sonocchia, S. (2008): Le fonti classiche greche e latine sui Piceni, *Quaderni di archeologia nelle Marche* 14: 49–76.
Speranza, G. (1900): *Il Piceno dalle origini alla fine d'ogni sua autonomia*, vol. I, Ascoli.
Staveley, E.S. (1994): Rome and Italy in the early third century, in: *CAH*^{2}, vol. VII, 2: 420–456.
Suder, W. (2003): *Census populi. Demografia starożytnego Rzymu*, Wrocław.
Taylor, L.R. (1960): *The Voting Districts of the Roman Republic*, Roma.
Thomsen, R. (1947): *The Italic Regions from Augustus to the Lombard Invasion*, Copenhagen.
Tibiletti, G. (1965): La romanizzazione della Valle Padana, in: E. Gabba, P. Tozzi (eds.), *Storie locali dell'Italia romana*, Pavia: 27–36.
Toynbee, A.J. (1965): *Hannibal's Legacy. The Hannibalic War's Effects on Roman Life*, vol. I–II, London.
Ungern-Sternberg von, J. (2005): The End of the Conflict of the Orders, in: K.A. Raaflaub (ed.), *Social Struggles in Archaic Rome. New Perspectives on the Conflict of the Orders*, Oxford: 312–332.
Vishnia, R.F. (1996): *State, Society and Popular Leaders in Mid-Republican Rome 241–167 B.C.*, London–New York.
Wiseman, T.P. (1970): Roman Republican Road-Building, *PBSR* 38: 122–152.
Wiseman, T.P. (1971): *New Men in the Roman Senate, 139 B.C.–A.D. 14*, Oxford.
Ziółkowski, A. (1994): Podbój Italii przez Rzym. Motywy i mechanizmy, in: J. Wolski, A. Kunisz (eds.), *Starożytny Rzym we współczesnych badaniach*, Kraków: 49–80.
Ziółkowski, A. (2004): *Historia Rzymu*, Poznań.

ELECTRUM * Vol. 20 (2013): 143–162
doi: 10.4467/20800909EL.13.007.1436

Corinth after 44 BC: Ethnical and Cultural Changes

Marcin N. Pawlak
Uniwersytet Mikołaja Kopernika, Toruń

Abstract: A few months before his death, Caesar decided to establish a Roman colony on the spot where Corinth, destroyed in 146 BC, used to lie. The population of Roman Corinth was ethnically and socially diverse from the very beginning. This, however, does not change the fact that the city was a Roman colony, whose official name was *Colonia Laus Iulia Corinthiensis*. With time, natural demographic processes started to take place, which on the one hand increased the original diversity, and on the other hand reinforced the strongest element of this diversity, i.e. Greekness. In this article, the author tries to answer the often-asked question about the circumstances in which Corinth – a Roman colony – started to be perceived as a hellenised city. What exactly does the "hellenisation" of Corinth mean and how does it show?

Key words: Roman Greece, Roman Corinth, "Hellenisation" of Roman Corinth.

A few months before his death, Caesar decided to establish a Roman colony on the spot where Corinth, destroyed in 146 BC, had once lain.[1] For some time, the dictator had been implementing his plan of building Roman points of support along the coast of western Greece, which was a strategically important site, ensuring control over the routes connecting Italy, Greece, Macedonia and Asia Minor. After Caesar's death, the execution of the slightly modified plan was continued by Augustus, on whose initiative the colony at Patras was founded on the Peloponnese. The Roman practice of setting up colonies had a long tradition. It has been noted that in the Romans' eyes, the colonies were a window display of the Roman way of life, a tool for spreading Latin culture, and a way to win over and integrate the local elites.[2] Colonies were also tasked with protecting the Roman order in case it was violated.[3] A specific civilisational mission ascribed to colonies by his-

[1] Caesar was not the first Roman statesman to become interested in Corinth and its territory, turned into *ager publicus* in 146 BC. The *lex agraria* of 111 BC indicates that a part of Corinth's territory was divided into plots with the intention to sell them: *CIL* I² 585; Romano 2003, 280; 2005, 26–27.

[2] Rizakis 2004, 72–73.

[3] Rizakis 1997: *passim*. On the moral, military, and economic reasons for establishing colonies by the Romans, see Rizakis 2004, 72–73.

torians was obvious in the underdeveloped west, whereas in the east, with its centuries-long tradition of urban life, it proved to be much more problematic.

The first colonists probably arrived in the Peloponnese shortly before Caesar's death. None of the ancient writers recorded their number. The information about 3,000 colonists which sometimes appears in the literature on the subject is a guess based on Appian's mention of exactly 3,000 colonists being sent out to the colony at Carthage, also set up on Caesar's initiative. It was therefore assumed that an identical number of colonists participated in both colonisation campaigns. Naturally, such symmetry is possible, but it must be remembered that Appian's information concerns only Carthage, and Corinth is not mentioned.[4] The majority of historians assume that the number of colonists may have varied between 1,500 and 3,000 people.[5]

Ancient writers provide quite detailed information about the social status of the colonists. Strabo, who visited Corinth in 29 BC and so could have met the first generation of colonists, wrote that the majority of them were freedmen. He also added information about the motives behind Caesar's decision. Supposedly, he decided to set up the colony in the place where the Greek city of Corinth had lain due to the excellent geographical location. The dictator was therefore taking into consideration the future economic growth of the colony. The economic growth was dependent not only on geographical location but also on enterprising and resourceful people, and freedmen were the most economically active element of Roman society.[6] Freedmen did not constitute the whole of the colony's population, as Strabo also noted. Plutarch's account tells us that the colonists also included some veterans.[7] M.H. Walbank does not rule out the possibility that Plutarch passes on the information he had about the colonists sent out to Carthage, who included mostly veterans, to the colonists sent out to Corinth.[8] It is well known, however, that Plutarch was very familiar with the elites of Corinth and kept in touch with them, so he could have easily obtained information about the first colonists and their social background. Veterans most likely participated in establishing the colony, although they were not a very numerous group.

Strabo's information about freedmen being the majority among the colonists sent out to Corinth was confirmed by the findings of a prosopographic study, conducted by A. Spawforth, on the social background of Corinth's elites in the period from the colony's foundation to Nero's times. Spawforth based his analysis on numismatic and epigraphic sources, in particular the unique collection of Corinthian coins signed by the *duoviri*, whose names were placed on the coins. The analysis covered 40 people. On the basis of onomastic terms, Spawforth concluded that the majority of the Corinthian *duoviri* [uncertain cases are not included] were people connected with the milieu of Roman *negotiatores* operating in the east (14 persons), followed by people of freedman origin (9 persons), representatives of local elites from other Peloponnesian cities (4 persons),

[4] App. *Pun*. 136.

[5] Romano 2010, 171. See Brunt 1971, 261, according to whom the colonies founded in the times of Caesar and Augustus had a population of 2,000–3,000.

[6] Strabo 8.6.23.

[7] Plut. *Caes*. 57.8.

[8] Hoskins Walbank 1997, 97.

and finally veterans' family members (3 persons).[9] In reality, however, the presence of people of freedman origin among the Corinthian elite must have been larger than this list suggests. The first two groups overlapped, since people connected with the Roman *negotiatores* were mainly also freedmen, representing the interests of their patrons in the new colony. Clearly, during the early history of the colony, there were no representatives of local elites from Greek cities, who started to appear in Corinth only under Claudius (see below). Trying to reconcile Plutarch's account about the presence of veterans among the colonists with the results of his own research, Spawforth concluded that the veterans' families did not achieve a good enough economic position to ensure joining the city's absolute elite. This explanation is likely, although we must also remember the opinions of all the historians who emphasise that Corinth, unlike nearby Patras, was not a military colony.[10]

Other historians independently arrived at conclusions similar to Spawforth's with regard to the makeup of the Corinthian elite. Even before Spawforth's article was published, H.A. Stansbury pointed out the existence of two groups among the Corinthian elite, clearly discernible in the source material, namely wealthy freedmen and businessmen.[11] A. Rizakis also highlighted the presence of freedmen in Corinth, but pointed out that some of them could have arrived in the city after the colony had been officially founded. As freedmen from influential families of Roman politicians and *negotiatores*, and also Roman citizens, they could count on quicker integration, social and political promotion, and receiving plots of land, which was difficult in Greek cities and required a special decision of the local authorities.[12] B.W. Millis posed questions about the freedmen's origin, whether they were Greeks from the East, or perhaps Greeks Romanised in Italy, or Romanised Greeks who, as a result of their activity in the East, became re-Hellenised.[13] Ultimately, he concluded that the majority of the freedmen were of Greek origin, but were comfortable in both the Greek and Roman world due to their earlier experiences.

There are no obvious answers to Millis's questions. We could even be contrary and say that each of the questions also contains an answer. The first colonists included freedmen of Greek origin, which is indicated e.g. by the Greek *cognomina* of some elite members. Cn. Babbius Philinus, who generously supported the city in Augustus' times, used to be a slave lovingly called Philinus, or "Darling," before he was given freedom and Roman citizenship.[14] Freedmen such as him arrived together with the other colonists from Italy, so they knew Roman customs and norms, but at the same time their Greek origin made them susceptible to the influence of Greek culture. As the city grew, freedmen from all corners of the eastern part of the Mediterranean world started to arrive. Their knowledge of Roman culture and lifestyle may have been smaller than that of the freedmen sent from Italy. However, regardless of their familiarity with Roman culture,

[9] Spawforth 1996, 167–182.

[10] Recently, this issue was analysed by Millis 2010a, 20.

[11] Stansbury 1990.

[12] Rizakis 1996, 43.

[13] Millis 2010a, 22–23. G. Bowersock (1965, 67–71) already described the colonists in Corinth as the *Greek returning home*.

[14] Rizakis/Zoumbaki 2001, 273–274 (COR 111).

they were all legally Roman citizens, and by virtue of their resources, contacts, and enterprise they quickly started to play a leading role in the colony. Finally, people holding Roman citizenship but not of servile origin also played a role among the first colonists, as illustrated by L. Aeficius Certus, *duovir* in 43/42 BC, or M. Insteius C.f. Tectus, *duovir* between 43/42 and 37/36, and again in 34/33 BC, a close collaborator of Mark Antony, who were both Italics.[15]

It can be assumed that the first colonists sent out to Corinth were a very diverse group, in terms of both social and ethnic background, although the Greek element was strongly represented. With time, natural demographic processes started to take place, which on the one hand increased the original diversity, and on the other reinforced the strongest element of this diversity, i.e. Greekness. As D. Engels observed, until the 19th century no city could survive without an influx of new people. The death rate in cities was higher than the birth rate, and the difference was closed by immigrants, who migrated to cities for various reasons, but usually economic.[16] The phenomenon must have occurred on a large scale in Corinth, where there were few original colonists, while the necessity e.g. to build public buildings created demand for workforce. It is likely that many poor Greeks from the Peloponnese or other regions of Greece, tempted by the promise of earning money, moved to Corinth.[17] Some of them stayed in the city permanently, but did not become Corinthian citizens, belonging to the category of *incolae*. A buoyant trade and economic centre such as Corinth could not function without such people. With time, the more enterprising and braver, as well as luckier, *incolae* could be granted Roman citizenship and become inhabitants of Corinth with full rights. Such cases were probably rare, but we should not overlook them. Some of the *Claudii* present in Corinth could have been former *incolae*, who obtained citizenship during the reign of the Julio-Claudian dynasty.[18] The Corinthian *Flavii* and *Aelii*, who owed their naturalisation to the Flavian and Antonian dynasty, could have been a similar case.[19]

The population of Roman Corinth was ethnically and socially diverse from the very beginning. However, this does not change the fact that the city was a Roman colony, whose official name was *Colonia Laus Iulia Corinthiensis*.[20] Official documents were published in Latin, official titles were Latin, and the city apparatus was a copy of the Roman one, with *duoviri* as equivalents of consuls. Members of the most important priestly colleges also had the same names as their Roman equivalents, i.e. pontiffs and augurs. Typically Roman buildings were erected in Corinth, such as a basilica and an amphitheatre.[21] This is where *munera gladiatora* and *venationes*, i.e. hunts for wild animals, were organised.[22] The official name of the colony included the word *Corinthiensis*. Its begin-

[15] Engels 1990, 68; Rizakis/Zoumbaki 2001, 249 (COR 10); 330–331 (COR 320).

[16] Engels 1990, 74–76. S. Alcock (1997b, 103) draws attention to the depopulation of Greece probably caused by migration to urban centres.

[17] Engels 1990, 69.

[18] Stansbury 1990, 252; Rizakis 1996, 45; 2007, 193.

[19] Rizakis/Zoumbaki 2001, 314–318 (*Flavii*), 250–252 (*Aelii*).

[20] Hoskins Walbank 1997, 95–130.

[21] The amphitheatre in Corinth was the only building of this kind on the Peloponnese: Di Napoli 2010, 258–259.

[22] The gladiator fights in Corinth were mentioned e.g. by Dion of Prusa (Dio 31.121). See also Apul. *Meth*. 10–18.

ning referred to the old name of the Greek city, but the ending, *-ensis*, indicated that the colony had new citizens, who wanted to be called the *Corinthienses*, not the *Corinthii*, which was the Latin name for the old inhabitants of Corinth.[23]

* * *

An interesting reflection on the inhabitants of Roman Corinth can be found in the work of a tireless traveller and searcher of Greek antiquities, Pausanias, who visited the city in the second half of the 2nd century. He said repeatedly that the present inhabitants of Corinth were immigrants, descendants of the colonists sent by Caesar, who had nothing in common with the old inhabitants of the Greek city. Although he called the inhabitants of Corinth "Peloponnesians," he also added that they were the newest inhabitants of the peninsula.[24]

Favorinus, who wrote earlier than Pausanias, had a somewhat different opinion on the cultural identity of the Corinthians. The rhetor and representative of the Second Sophistic was particularly revered in Corinth, whose inhabitants asked him to leave Ephesus and live among them. Although Favorinus declined, the city authorities decided to dedicate a statue to him. Soon afterwards, in unclear circumstances, Favorinus lost the favour of Emperor Hadrian and the liking of the Corinthians. During his third stay in the city, he saw that his statue had been pulled down and only an empty base was left. He then made the famous speech, *Korinthiakos*, in which he defended the destroyed statue, and indirectly himself, against the aspersions cast on him by the fickle Corinthians. In a passage from the speech, Favorinus referred to Corinth's cultural identity:

> But if someone who is not a Lucanian, but a Roman, not one of the masses but of the equestrian order, who has emulated not only the language but also the sensibility and the manner and the dress of the Greeks … in order to achieve this one thing above all else, namely both appear and to be Greek, then should this man not deserve to have a bronze statue set up by you? Yes, he even deserves one in every city – by you, on the one hand, because he, though the Roman, has been thoroughly **Hellenised, just as your very own patrimonial city has been**…, and, on the other hand, by all the Greek cities, because he pursues philosophy and has both aroused many of the Greeks to join him in the pursuit of philosophy and has caused not a few of the barbarians. Why, it seems he has been equipped by the gods for just such a purpose.[25]

Thus, Favorinus voiced the opinion that the Roman colony which Corinth had become in 44 BC became a Hellenised, Greek city after 150 years of existence. As a representative of the Second Sophistic and propagator of the Greek renaissance, Favorinus was enthusiastic and sympathetic to all manifestations of the strength of Greek culture.

Favorinus' opinion about Corinth is also substantiated by the fact that the city was admitted to the Panhellenion, i.e. an organisation gathering Greek cities. Corinth joined such old Peloponnesian cities as Argos, Epidauros, Methana, or Sparta.[26] J. Oliver concluded that Corinth's accession to the Panhellenion proved that the Roman colony was

---

[23] Broneer 1941, 388–390; Stansbury 1990, 119. Cf. Engels 1990, 69.

[24] Paus. 2.1.2; 5.1.2; 5.25.1. On Pausanias' attitude to Corinth and its inhabitants, see Hutton 2005, 147–149, 166–173.

[25] Favorinus, *Korinthiakos* 25 (trans. L.M. White).

[26] Spawforth/Walker 1985, 80.

officially declared a continuator of Greek Corinth by Emperor Hadrian.[27] This is a very bold conclusion, but that does not change the fact that Roman Corinth must have been under strong Greek influence, which ultimately led Favorinus to formulate the quoted opinion about the city being Hellenised. In this article, the author tries to answer the often-asked question about the circumstances in which Corinth – a Roman colony – started to be perceived as a Hellenised city. What exactly does the "Hellenisation" of Corinth mean, and how is it manifested?

* * *

According to Greek and Roman writers, Corinth was razed to the ground by the soldiers of Lucius Mummius in 146 BC. The complete destruction of the city walls and buildings was described e.g. by an anonymous epitomator of Livy's work, by Diodorus Siculus, by Velleius Paterculus, and by Pausanias.[28] As a matter of course, the destroyed city must also have been depopulated. This is referred to by Strabo, who stated that Corinth was deserted for a long time, and the situation changed only with the arrival of the Roman colonists in 44 BC.[29] Ancient writers put a lot of effort into convincing their readers that the old Greek city had disappeared off the face of the earth in 146 BC. To some extent, Cicero stood apart. Remembering his journey to Greece as a youth, he mentioned that in Corinth he had seen and spoken to people he called the *Corinthii*.[30] Archaeological studies conducted in recent decades have allowed us to revise many parts of the picture painted by the ancient writers. It is thought today that some buildings in this Greek city survived almost untouched and only required minor repairs.[31] This is confirmed by Pausanias, according to whom the most noteworthy curiosities of Roman Corinth were the remnants of archaic times.[32] We can suspect that the soldiers of L. Mummius, preoccupied with plundering the city, did not have enough time to completely destroy the city. The city walls and the most important public buildings were most likely razed.[33] It is also increasingly difficult to believe the image of a completely abandoned city. The presence of people in Corinth during the transition period (i.e. 146–44 BC) is confirmed by excavated amphorae from the eastern part of the Mediterranean world, but also from Italy, as well as coins and inscriptions.[34] These inhabitants, sometimes referred to as squatters, did not come to the city directly after the Roman forces had withdrawn, but only at the end of the 2nd century BC.[35] Most researchers believe that they were not descended from the former inhabitants of Corinth, although it must be said that there is no unanimity on the subject.[36] Regardless of all difficulties over interpretation, it is clear that the vision propagated by ancient writers, of a destroyed and abandoned Corinth where colonists arrived in 44 BC, was not necessarily a fact. In 146 BC, Corinth

[27] Oliver 1978, 191.

[28] *Perioch.* 52; Diod. Sic. 32. 27; Vell. Pat. 1.13.1; Paus. 7.16.7, 9. See Wiseman 1979, 491–494.

[29] Strabo 8.6.23.

[30] Cic., *De leg. Agr.* 2. 87; *Tusc. disp.* 3. 22. 53.

[31] Wiseman 1979, 494–496.

[32] Paus. 2.2.6.

[33] This is pointed out by Gebhard/Dickie 2003, 264.

[34] Edwards 1981, 198–199; Romano 1994, 57–104; Gebhard/Dickie 2003, 268–269.

[35] Wiseman 1979, 494–496; Williams/Russell 1981, 27–29.

[36] Bookidis 2005, 149–150; Millis 2010b, 244–257. Engels (1990, 70) has a different opinion.

ceased to exist as a city and was relegated to the category of a village, but it did not completely disappear off the face of the earth.

The fame of this formerly important city, like the material remnants of Greek Corinth, could have aroused the colonists' interest in the history of the place where the colony was being built. The earliest traces of this interest, which are also examples of the colonists voluntarily referencing Corinth's past, can be found on coins. In Roman Corinth, as in many other cities of the empire, the decision to mint coins lay with the local authorities, i.e. the council of decurions. The production of coins was in turn supervised by the colony's highest officials, i.e. the *duoviri*. Now and then, an issue of coins was sponsored by wealthy benefactors, who provided the precious metal and sometimes paid the workers.[37] The obverse contained references to central authorities, i.e. emperors, while the colony authorities decided what images and symbols to place on the reverse. If the issue was financed by a benefactor, he could also influence the choice of motifs. The mint in Corinth, like other local mints, did not issue coins regularly, but only when needed or e.g. to commemorate an event. That said, in the period from 44/43 BC to 68/69 coins were issued regularly and in large quantities. Usually, the names of the *duoviri* currently in office were placed on the coins (duovirat coinage). Corinth briefly lost the right to issue coins following Vespasian's decision, but regained it under Domitian. In the second period, the names of the *duoviri* disappeared from coins and it became the norm to place the ruler's image on the obverse.[38]

Coins from the first year of the colony's existence already show scenes referring to local traditions and myths from the times of Greek Corinth. Reverses of coins from 44/43 show the image of Bellerophon sitting on a flying Pegasus.[39] According to the myth, Bellerophon had to leave Corinth after he had killed Bellerus and his own brother. After many adventures, he reached the court of the king of Lycia, who demanded that he kill Chimera. In order to accomplish this task, he first needed to capture Pegasus. Bellerophon managed to do so in Corinth, where Pegasus was drinking water from the spring Peirene, and then killed Chimera. Similar figures and symbols from the local tradition regularly appeared on coins issued in Roman Corinth. They included Poseidon, Chimera, a dolphin, Pegasus, and representations of Aphrodite. As we can see, the first officials of Roman Corinth deliberately and voluntarily referred to Greek Corinth, one of the most developed cities in Hellenic times in terms of culture and economy. Their decision provokes two questions. Firstly, where did they acquire their knowledge of Greek Corinth; secondly, why did they decide to refer to the past of the place where the colony was being built?

At least a few hypothetical sources of this knowledge can be named. Apart from the material remnants of the old city (mentioned above), we should again reiterate the fact that some of the colonists were of Greek origin. It is also known that some mythical stories connected to Corinth were familiar in Italy. To illustrate, we could quote the story of Melicertes-Palaemon known to Plautus, Virgil and Ovid.[40] We could also consider the possibility that stories connected to Corinth survived in other places in Corinthia, which

37 Mattingly 1962, 193–194.

38 Amandry 1998; Hoskins Walbank 2003a, 337–349.

39 *RPC* I 1124, 1116.

40 Plautus, *Rubens* 160–162; Verg. *Georg*. 436–437; Ovid. *Fast*. 6.583–582; *Met*. 4.416–542.

had not been destroyed by L. Mummius' army. Finally, it is a known fact that some inhabitants of Corinth managed to escape the slaughter in 146 BC and found shelter e.g. in Athens, in Egypt and on Rhodes, where they cultivated the traditions of their home city.[41] Thus, the Roman colonists' knowledge about the history of Greek Corinth had various sources. It is very unlikely, however, that the first officials deciding to place the images of Bellerophon and Pegasus on coins had conducted antiquarian studies.[42] It is simpler to assume that a group of the first colonists were well-versed in the history of the place they were sent to by Caesar's will.

It is more difficult to answer why the colony's authorities decided to make references to local mythical motifs from the very beginning. An interest in culture could have played a role, but this is unlikely given the low social status of the colonists, especially in the very earliest period of the colony's existence. Possibly, there was a desire to demonstrate to the Greeks from other cities that Roman colonists were favourably disposed towards and interested in Greek history and traditions.[43]

Regardless of the motives of the Corinthian elite soon after the foundation of the colony, the tendency to place symbols referring to the local past on Corinthian coins continued until the times of Caracalla and Geta, i.e. the last known issues from Corinth.[44] The greatest diversity of these symbols coincided with Hadrian's times. Under this emperor's rule, the most frequent motifs on Corinthian coins were scenes connected to the cult of Melicertes/Palaemon and mythical stories about Bellerophon's fight against Chimera. The next most used motifs on known coins were various representations of Poseidon and the temple or statue of Aphrodite in Acrocorinth.[45] The desire to highlight the classical background of Roman Corinth can also be seen in the case of a group of pseudo-autonomous coins from Hadrian's times, whose reverses depict Tyche, Bellerophon, Triptolemus on a chariot drawn by snakes, and the tomb of Lais, a famous courtesan from the 4th century BC. However, M. Hoskins Walbank warns against jumping to conclusions, stressing that even in the period of frequently referring to the Greek past, the Corinthians also took care to emphasise that they were Romans, for example placing the head of the goddess Roma on their coins. It is difficult not to agree with this historian, who stated, "The Corinthians were in the enviable position of having their cake and eating it, for they could enjoy the cultural cachet conferred by a Classical pedigree (…), and at the same time enjoy the privileges of Roman colony."[46]

The decision for the city to take over control of the famous Isthmian Games could also have been dictated by the desire to symbolically link the Roman colony with Greek Corinth. As we know, after Corinth was destroyed in 146 BC, the presidency over the games was taken over by the Sicyonians, who after a while moved them from the Isthmus

[41] Millis 2010b, 244–257.

[42] Therefore, they probably did not use various local historical accounts such as *Korinthiaka* by Eumelos of Corinth, or other such reports from the 2nd century known to Pausanias.

[43] Stansbury 1990, 154–155. Papageorgiadou-Bani (2004, 59) points out that the message of the images placed on coins was directed at receivers in the whole empire on the one hand, and at inhabitants of a given province on the other, so the iconography must have been comprehensible for the local population.

[44] Papageorgiadou-Bani 2004, 59–65.

[45] Hoskins Walbank 2003a, 345–347.

[46] Hoskins Walbank 2003a, 348.

to Sicyon.[47] Traditionally, it is thought that Corinth regained presidency over the games only in 2 BC. However, this date seems inconsistent with the fact that early Corinthian coins show many symbols directly referring to the games (e.g. wreaths to decorate the victors).[48] E.R. Gebhard's research shows that the Isthmian Games returned to Corinth soon after the colony was founded in 44 BC. However, they were not organised on the Isthmus, but in Corinth itself.[49] If we accept this date, Strabo's words become clear; he noted in 29 BC: "On the Isthmus is also the temple of the Isthmian Poseidon, in the shade of a grove of pine-trees, where the Corinthians used to celebrate the Isthmian Games."[50] The renowned geographer saw an element of the new reality, in which the games were not organised on the Isthmus, but this does not mean that they were not organised at all. If the task of organising and presiding over the games was taken away from the Sicyonians and handed over to the Roman colonists as soon as the time when the colony was founded, this would be a clear statement of intent not only on the part of the colonists, but also Caesar and his entourage.[51] They probably made deliberate efforts to show that the colony would not dissociate itself from the Greek past of the place where it was founded.[52] The Isthmian Games were part of the traditional *periodos*, and the way they were administered after 44 BC remained Greek through and through. In inscriptions, the person responsible for the programme is referred to by the Greek term *agonothetes*, the judges were called the *hellanodikai*, and Greek remained the language in which lists of victors were drawn up. The decrees honouring the *agonothetai* were written in Latin, however (Greek terms were transliterated), and publically displayed in Corinth.[53] Stansbury pointed out that the games must have played an important role in the "Hellenisation" of Roman Corinth, but he also emphasised that they had strong Roman overtones: their *agonothetes* was a Roman citizen, and they were the only Panhellenic games which included a special competition dedicated to the emperor, the *Caesarea*.[54] Therefore, the games did not so much contribute to the "Hellenisation" of Roman Corinth as be important for connecting the old local traditions with the new Roman reality.[55]

As has been mentioned before, the games were initially organised in Corinth itself. The sanctuary on the Isthmus, i.e. the traditional location of the games, was largely destroyed, and the first traces of repair works date back to the middle of the 1st century AD.[56] As M. Kajava showed, the Isthmian Games (but not the *Caesarea*, which continued in Corinth) returned to the Isthmus in 43 AD with the help of Cn. Cornelius Pulcher

47 Paus. 2.2.2.

48 Gebhard 2005, 182–183.

49 Gebhard 1993, 79–82.

50 Strabo 8.6.22.

51 Stansbury (1990, 228) rightly points out that the decision to take over control of the games must have either been made in Rome or approved by Roman authorities.

52 Consideration of economic benefits that the games and mainly the competitors and spectators coming to see them could have brought Corinth may also have been a factor. Amandry observed a tendency to increase the number of coins in the periods when the games were held: Amandry 1998; Stansbury 1990, 231; Spawforth 1989, 197.

53 *Corinth* VIII, 3.149–247; Geagan 1968, 69–80; Hupfloher 2008, 159–160.

54 Stansbury 1990, 231–232.

55 Walers 2005, 407.

56 Gebhard/Dickie 2003, 264–265.

from Epidauros.[57] He was one of the handfuls of Peloponnesian Greeks who decided to start a career in the Roman colony. We are familiar with his activity not only in Corinth, but also in Epidauros. The information provided by inscriptions pictures him as a man attached to Greek traditions on the one hand, and manifestly devoted to Rome on the other.[58] His father, Cn. Cornelius Sodamos, son of Nicatas, was a very influential figure in Epidauros. He was twice a priest of the imperial cult, as well as an *agonothetes* of the games called *Apolloneia kai Asklapeia*, to whose programme he added competitions dedicated to the emperor. During such combined games, his four-year-old son held the function of *gymnasiarchos* and *agoranomos*.[59] In the early 40s AD, the young Cornelius Pulcher moved to Corinth, where, as a member of a wealthy family, he was granted the colony's citizenship. In Corinth, he followed the local *cursus honorum* from *aedile* to *IIvir quinquennalis*. He was twice an *agonothetes*; during his second period in office he accomplished two things, important in the context of this discussion. He was the first to organise the *Isthmia* on the Isthmus, i.e. in their traditional location, which contributed to the restoration of the original character of the Isthmian Games. He also initiated a competition dedicated to deified Iulia, which he added to the programme of the games dedicated to the emperor.[60] He was, in a nutshell, a wealthy man originally from Epidauros, who pursued a public career in Corinth. In the Roman colony, Cornelius Pulcher appeared to be an active propagator of the imperial cult, but he also reformed the Isthmian Games so that they recaptured much of their original character. Other Greeks from outside Corinth, but pursuing a career in the colony, also became *agonothetai* of the Isthmian Games; however, none of them manifested their attachment to the Greek past in quite the same way as Cn. Cornelius Pulcher. It is likely that they became *agonothetai* because it was the most prestigious function in Corinth, not because they wanted to emphasise their Greek background.[61]

***

The Isthmian Games were inextricably linked to the cult of Melicertes/Palaemon. According to the myth, Melicertes was boy who, together with his mother, Ino, drowned in the sea. The boy's body was carried by a dolphin to the Isthmus, where the ruler of Corinth, Sisyphus, organised his burial and held the first Isthmian Games.[62] After her death, Ino was transformed into the goddess Leucothea, and Melicertes became the marine deity called Palaemon, connected to Poseidon. References to this myth appeared on Corinthian coins from Tiberius' times. The sanctuary of Palaemon on the Isthmus was built around the mid-1st century AD and was subsequently reconstructed multiple times. One of the reconstructions was sponsored by a generous euergetes, Publius Priscus Iuventianus, who repaired and decorated not only Palaemon's temple, but also a number of

[57] Kajava 2002, 171–176.

[58] Rizakis/Zoumbaki 2001, 302 (COR 226); 187–188 (ARG 116).

[59] Rizakis/Zoumbaki 2001, 186–187 (ARG 115).

[60] *Corinth* VIII, 3.153, I subscribe to the new reading of this inscription, proposed by N. Kajava (2002, 168–178).

[61] C. Iulius Laco: Rizakis/Zoumbaki 2001, 335–336 (COR 345); C. Iulius Spartiaticus: Rizakis/Zoumbaki 2001, 338 (COR 353); Cn. Cornelius Pulcher: Rizakis/Zoumbaki 2001, 302–305 (COR 228). See also below.

[62] Gantz 1993, 176–180, 456, 478, 733.

other cult buildings connected to Corinth's past, e.g. the temple of Demeter and Cora.[63] The circumstances of the "revival" of the cult of Palaemon in Corinth have become the subject of an interesting discussion, which illustrates well the problems encountered when studying the pantheon of Roman Corinth. According to M. Piérart, in the case of the cult of Palaemon on the Isthmus, we are not dealing with a simple continuation of cult practices from before 146 BC. In his opinion, the colonists had brought knowledge of the cult of Portunus-Palaemon from Italy and then, many decades after the colony was established, the cult was developed and new practices were added, which gave it a Mysteries-like character. This could have been the result of the antiquarian interests of parts of Corinthian elites, posing as direct heirs of the old Greek *polis*. An argument for Piérart's theory may seemingly be provided by Pausanias, who in passing mentions an altar of Melicertes in a place called Cromyon.[64] Pausanias was mainly interested in the past, and it is possible that he considered the cult of Melicartes/Palaemon to be too recent and did not include it in his depiction of Corinth and Corinthia.[65] It is worth remembering, however, that Pausanias' account is a specific one and should not be treated as a tourist guidebook of sorts.

Gebhard expressed a different opinion on the cult of Palaemon in Roman Corinth from Piérart's; according to her, the main elements of the cult of Palaemon had existed in Corinth before 146 BC and were continued by the colonists after the colony was established. By regaining control over the Isthmian Games and by reviving the cult of deities worshipped on the Isthmus, the colonists deliberately referred to one of the oldest traditions of the Greek city. However, the question arises about the manner in which the colonists had acquired their knowledge of the cult of Palaemon. Some of them may have derived their knowledge from Roman literature. The figure of Palaemon/Melicertes appears in the works of e.g. Plautus, Vergil, and Ovid.[66] Gebhard believes that the colonists could have gleaned further information from the Sicyonians, who administered the Isthmian Games from 146 to 44 BC. The memory of the cult of Palaemon may also have survived in those cities in Corinthia which, like Tenea, had not been destroyed by the Romans.[67]

Questions about continuity and change can be asked with reference to many other cults practised in Roman Corinth. It is obvious that the colonists brought with them many cults typical of Rome, such as Iuppiter Capitolinus, Iuppiter Optimus Maximus, Ianus, Saturnus, the Genius of the Colony and the Genius of Augustus.[68] Dividing the deities into Greek and Roman is risky, however, due to the progress that was made in the 1st century BC with regard to the process of identifying Greek gods with their Roman equivalents. In the case of cults such as Apollo Augustus, Neptunus Augustus or Mars

---

[63] Geagan 1989, 349–360; Rizakis/Zoumbaki 2001, 343–345 (COR 378).

[64] Paus. 2.1.3.

[65] Piérart 1998, 85–109; Lafond 2006, 290.

[66] Plautus, *Rudens* 160–162; Verg. *Georg*. 436–437; *Aen*. 5.823; Ovid. *Fast.* 6.538–552; *Met*. 4.416–542.

[67] Gebhard (2005, 165–203) summing up her analysis, concluded that: "There was thus both continuity and change in cult practice between the rites observed in Greek Corinth and in the Roman colony, but the debt to tradition seems to have been greater than previously supposed" (at p. 203); see also Wiseman (1979, 493–496) who suggests that it was the people living in Corinth before 44 BC that spread the knowledge of local cultures among the colonists.

[68] Bookidis 2005, 152–159; Hupfloher 2008, 154–155; Hoskins Walbank 2010, 362–364.

Augustus, we can never be sure whether we are dealing with a cult imported from Rome, or a Latin translation of the names of Greek gods, who became merged with Augustus.[69]

On the other hand, there is no doubt that the deities that used to be worshipped in the Greek city played an important role in the pantheon of Roman Corinth. Above all, we should name Aphrodite, Poseidon, Demeter and Cora, the cults of local heroes such as Sisyphus and Bellerophon, or the already mentioned Melicertes/Palaemon (Paus. 2.4.2; Strabo 8.6.21). Engels, who is a proponent of the theory that the colonists continued the cult practices of Greek Corinth rather than simply reviving them, pointed out several ways in which continuity was possible; e.g. he allowed the possibility that cult practices were carried on in Corinth in the transition period, something which is not documented by archaeological sources.[70] Another possibility is connected with those inhabitants of Corinth who were sold into slavery, but continued the religious traditions of their city, and subsequently their descendants settled in Corinth, bringing the traditions back. The continuity could have been a consequence of the antiquarian interests and searches of colonists themselves. It was also possible that the colonists wanted to secure the favour of Corinth's old gods of protection, especially Aphrodite and Poseidon. Engels himself concluded that the most likely possibility was the need to ensure the favour of the gods of protection and the colonists' interest in the history of the place.[71] He is probably right, although the list of factors he proposed is not exhaustive. However, before we suggest other ways, or rather reasons for the colonists worshipping local gods, it is worth noting that the factors he mentioned would play a role in the case not only of continuation, but also of revival of the old cults.

As has been mentioned above, there is much to indicate that the colonists sent to Corinth in 44 BC did not arrive at a sea of ruins. They saw many buildings in various states of repair and encountered some inhabitants. The fact that some of the old buildings, especially cult ones, survived, may have had some influence on adding the gods formerly worshipped in Corinth to the new pantheon.[72]

We do not know the technical details of the establishment of the colony in Corinth. To fill this gap in our knowledge, researchers very often refer to the *lex coloniae Genitivae* concerning the colony in Urso, Spain, established in 44 BC on Caesar's initiative. It follows from this law that decisions concerning cults practised in the colony, erecting temples, and performing public sacrifices, were made by the *duoviri* and decurions.[73] The situation was probably identical in Corinth (at least there are no reasons to think otherwise), where the first officials and members of the council also made the first decisions concerning the official pantheon. It was they who decided to place references to the local Corinthian hero Bellerophon on the reverses of coins. It was also they who decided to add Greek gods to the colony's religious calendar; archaeological findings show that it was these gods, i.e. Asclepius, Demeter and Cora, and Aphrodite, who were the earliest

[69] Engels 1990, 95; Hupfloher 2008, 154.

[70] Bookidis 2005, 149–150.

[71] Engels 1990, 94–95.

[72] Engels 1990, 94–95; Bookidis 2005, 151–164.

[73] *ILS* 6087; Bookidis 2005, 152; Hoskins Walbank 2010, 358.

to be worshipped.[74] Some of the sanctuaries devoted to the gods survived in good enough condition that the colonists did not necessarily have problems with their identification.[75] In the case of other cults, information could be retrieved from surviving inscriptions or oral accounts. However, it is not the sources of knowledge that are the most important, but the decision, made already at the time of the colony's establishment, to worship the gods that had formerly played such a big part in Greek Corinth. Naturally, one reason may have been and probably was the desire to ensure the protection of the old gods, but there was something else as well. By reviving the cults connected with old Corinth, the colonists wanted to show that the colony of *Laus Iulia Corinthiensis* was in no way trying to distance itself from Greek Corinth. Restoring old cult practices was a deliberate attempt to create a connection between Greek and Roman Corinth. All cities attached a great deal of significance to rites referring to the mythical past and their origins; the elites of Corinth wanted to act in the same manner, even at the price of creating the false impression that there was continuity between Greek Corinth and the Roman colony.

Decisions made at the point when the colony was established had an impact on the cultural character of the city in the future, in the sense that they set a model of behaviour and showed how the Greek past of the city could be referenced. Corinth was not lacking in wealthy people who sponsored the construction of new buildings, but also generously provided funds for the restoration or rebuilding of old Greek sanctuaries. There is a well-known example of Marcus Antonius Milesius, who, together with several others, rebuilt the temple of Asclepius and thus contributed to the revival of this god's cult.[76] References to Greekness sometimes took on a more surprising character. Greek terms transliterated into Latin appeared in Latin administrative titles. We know the term *theocolus Iovis Capitolini* from several epigraphic texts; the first example of its use is very early, and dates back to Augustus' rule.[77] The Greek term *theocolos* referred to the cult personnel at Olympia, and its addition to Roman terminology may have been dictated by snobbism and the desire to follow the Greek model. A. Hupfloher noted that all known examples of using the title *theocolus Iovis Capitolini* come from inscriptions placed on monument bases, which indicates that we are dealing with persons of high social standing.[78] Another interesting phenomenon was the divine worship of Octavia (sister of Octavian and wife of Mark Antony) in Corinth. She was never deified, but a temple was erected for her in Corinth and she was clearly included in the imperial cult. This practice can be interpreted as a local, Greek version of the imperial cult, which is explained by the role Octavia played in Roman politics. It cannot be ruled out that her cult was established in Corinth in the 30s BC by the supporters and clients of Antony. If this was the case, their act tells us much about their origin and religious customs.[79]

---

[74] Bookidis 2005, 159–160, who notes that the list of deities worshipped first should also include Zeus and Apollo. Cf. Hupfloher 2008, 153–154; Hoskins Walbank 2010, 365–368.

[75] Engels 1990, 94–95, for example the temple of Asclepius and Hygieia, or Demeter and Cora.

[76] *Corinth* VIII, 3. 311; Rizakis/Zoumbaki 2001, 263 (COR 65).

[77] *Corinth* VIII, 3. 152 (Sextus Olius Secundus – Augustus' reign), 194–196, 198.

[78] Hupfloher 2008, 156–159.

[79] Kantiréa 2007, 129–131; Hupfloher 2008, 154–155.

With time, as the influx of Greek population to the city increased, the presence of Greek elements became more and more visible. The pantheon of Roman Corinth became increasingly varied, with eastern cults, Judaism and Christianity entering the fold.[80]

***

The influx of Greek people must also have had an impact on the language prevalent in Corinth. It is commonly known that Latin was the language in which inscriptions were written throughout the 1st and in the early 2nd century. The situation changed in the 2nd century, with Hadrian's reign being the turning point. From the period of Augustus' rule to Trajan's times we only have six Greek inscriptions, while there are more than 100 Latin ones. From Hadrian's reign onwards, the trend changed; there are 39 Greek and 17 Latin texts in the period until Gallienus' rule.[81] Therefore, we can see that Latin, which was initially dominant, gradually gave way to Greek, although it did not disappear altogether. In the 2nd and 3rd centuries, honorific inscriptions for elite members continued to be written in Latin, which emphasised the privileged position of such persons in the local community.[82] The phenomenon of Latin being replaced by Greek as the language of inscriptions was typical not just of Corinth, since it also occurred in other colonies established on Greek lands.[83] Millis posed the question whether the fact that official inscriptions were written in Latin in the 1st century AD must mean that Latin was indeed a commonly used language in Corinth. In his opinion, public Latin inscriptions from the forum or theatre do not necessarily indicate this. In a Roman colony, Latin simply must have been used in the public sphere. However, Millis emphasised that Greek graffiti or writings on pottery are more numerous than Latin ones. Writing to the Christian community in Corinth, Paul the Apostle also used Greek, since he wanted to reach the greatest number of people. According to Millis, a "significant portion of the population" used Greek as the everyday language.[84] In light of what we have already said about the colonists, their habits, and their attitude to the Greek past of the city, Millis' conclusion seems correct.

***

Finally, it is time to consider what impact on the cultural transformation of Roman Corinth could have been made by members of influential Greek families from various Peloponnesian cities, who pursued a public career in the colony. Spawforth pointed out five such persons among the Corinthian elite during the period he analysed (i.e. until the end of Nero's reign).[85] They started to appear among Corinthian officials during Claudius'

[80] Hupfloher 2008: "…the Corinthian pantheon of imperial times was kind of an agglomerate containing different elements of different provenience: traditional Greek elements and newly imported elements from Rome and from the east and the south-east of the Roman Empire. The pantheon of Corinth was certainly not dominated by Roman gods." Cf. Bookidis 2005, 161; Hoskins Walbank 2010, 368–369, 371–372. Engels (1990, 102) however, saw a domination of Roman gods in Corinth.

[81] *Corinth* VIII, 3, 18–19 (Kent); Engels 1990, 71; Dixon 2000, 338; Lafond 2006, 303.

[82] Engels 1990, 73. The funerary dedication erected by L. Coranus Patrobius for himself and his family is dated to the early 3rd century: *Corinth* VIII, 3. 302.

[83] Rizakis 1995, 373–391; Baldwin Bowsky 2004, 50–95 (the example of Knossos).

[84] Millis 2010a, 23–29.

[85] It is known, however, that P. Caninius Agrippa had been connected with Corinth (his social background is uncertain; it is only known that he was Greek (see Rizakis/Zoumbaki 2001, 279–280: COR 135)) and so

reign, over 80 years after the colony was established. This is not a long period if we remember that the process of granting Roman citizenship to influential Greeks from the Peloponnese was a slow one. Holding Roman citizenship was necessary for the colony authorities to add someone from a different city to the list of citizens (*adlectio*). At least some parts of the elites of Greek cities viewed the possibility to sit on the colony's council of decurions, holding offices, and thus participating in governing the colony, as a special privilege crowning their efforts to join the political elite of the empire.[86] Among the Greeks pursuing a career in Corinth were C. Iulius Laco and C. Iulius Spartiaticus, the son and grandson, respectively, of the famous Spartan dynast Eurycles, who had already sided with Augustus at the Battle of Actium, for which he was rewarded with Roman citizenship, among other things. The group also included Cn. Cornelius Pulcher, who came from a family that had propagated the imperial cult in Epidauros since Augustus' times.[87] Each of these three men held the financially demanding function of *agonothetes* of the Isthmian Games, as well as other offices in Corinth. Possibly, the readiness to finance the games was a good enough reason for the Corinthian authorities to accept them as citizens. The men in question treated their careers in Corinth as a way to increase the prestige of their families, previously known and influential in local Greek communities and now announcing their presence on the provincial level. It seems doubtful that these few Greeks could have had an impact on the cultural identity of the city and its inhabitants. Only Cn. Cornelius Pulcher contributed, as mentioned earlier, to restoring the original character of the Isthmian Games. His achievement was a response to the growing interest of the colony's inhabitants in the city's Greek past. We have no knowledge of any similar achievements of the other men in question. Both Spawforth and Rizakis concluded that, through their activity in Corinth, the Greeks from good families from Sparta or Epidauros contributed to facilitating the integration of the colony with its Greek surroundings.[88] However, this seems rather doubtful. C. Iulius Laco, C. Iulius Spartiaticus and others pursued a career in Corinth above all because they wanted to be Romans and act like Romans.[89] It is difficult to see how they might have facilitated the integration with the Greek surroundings or other cities on the Peloponnese and in Achaea.

A large amount of data shows that Corinth's integration with its Greek surroundings was difficult. The Greeks' dislike of the colonists of low social status is recorded in the famous epigram of Crinagoras of Mytilene, writing in Augustus' times. He did not hide his contempt for the servile origin of the new inhabitants of Corinth.[90] Even if this was only his personal opinion, it can still be assumed that there were other Greeks who thought similarly. From the point of view of the Greek inhabitants of the Peloponnese, the very fact of sending the colonists to build a new city on the ruins of the old famous

had Eurycles of Sparta, who built a bathhouse in Corinth, but there is no indication that he held any offices in the colony.

[86] Raggi 2004, 55–68.

[87] We know nothing about the origin and ancestors of C. Iulius Polyaenus of Sicyon and P. Memmius Cleandr of Delphi.

[88] Spawforth 1996, 167; Rizakis 1996, 46.

[89] Walters 2005, 409.

[90] *Anth. Pal.* 9.284.

Greek centre might have caused distrust and dislike and encouraged them to keep their distance. The colonists were, after all, representatives of the new rulers of the world who had conquered the Greeks. In the turbulent period of the last decades of the Republic there were plenty of events that could only fuel the Greeks' negative feelings towards the Romans. Greece was the place where fights among the feuding Republic generals were taking place, and the warring sides did not hesitate to make use of the increasingly meagre resources of the Greek cities. The mentioned dislike may have focused on the colony's inhabitants, as they were the closest Romans. It should also be remembered that the very establishment of the colony may have been regarded by the local people as the most glaring manifestation of Roman domination.[91]

The dislike towards Corinth may have been intensified by the fact that its importance gradually increased, as it became the seat of the Roman governor. Traces of this dislike can be found as late as the second half of the 1st century. It was then that the city of Argos sought to regain the privilege that exempted it from paying for the organisation of the *venationes* in Corinth. The city had enjoyed this privilege since it bore the cost of organising the Panhellenic games called the *Nemeia*. However, it lost the privilege at some point as a result of a decision of the Roman authorities. In the letter concerning regaining the privilege, sent by Argos to the Roman governor, it was emphasised that the *venationes* were neither Greek nor ancient and that they were organised by others, i.e. the Corinthians. The authors of the letter also noted that Corinth was much wealthier than Argos.[92] The *venationes* referred to in the letter were one of the features of the celebrations connected with the imperial cult established in the Achaean *koinon* in 54 AD. The festivities took place in Corinth, which could also have been a source of frustration for the inhabitants of Argos. Previously, meetings of representatives of the cities participating in the *koinon* had been held in Argos. The letter shows that the causes of dislike towards the colony and its inhabitants may have been varied and may have existed at different times, not only at the moment of its establishment. It took time for such frictions to cease to have a negative impact on the mutual relations of the inhabitants of the colony and Greek cities.[93]

***

From a colony established by a few hundred people sent from Italy by Caesar, Corinth evolved into Greece's largest city within 150 years.[94] The increase in the population occurred as a result of migration from close and far corners of the Mediterranean world. Presumably, the majority of those who decided to settle in Corinth spoke Greek. The influx of immigrants had an impact on the ethnic identity of the city, although this does not mean that the Roman city became a Greek one. F. Millar's opinion, although formulated with regard to Greek cities in Roman times, seems to be correct; according to him, the

[91] Sartre 2001, 127; Rizakis 2004, 83–85.

[92] Spawforth 1994, 211–232.

[93] It is probably no coincidence that we know so little about these relations on the micro scale, i.e. on the level of normal families. One of the exceptions is a woman named Salvia from Thessaly, who married a wealthy Corinthian and went to live in her husband's home town (Rizakis/Zoumbaki 2001, 378–379: COR 545).

[94] Aristeides put forward such an opinion in the second half of the 2nd century.

cities remained under a strong influence of both Greek and Roman culture. Therefore, it is preferable to call them Greek-Roman cities rather than Greek cities.[95] Similarly, the Roman colony of Corinth remained under the influence of Greek culture. It is awkward, however, to talk about "Hellenisation" of Roman Corinth. The term "Hellenisation," similarly to "Romanisation," is used more and more cautiously by historians. Both these terms imply a one-sided process of absorbing Greek culture by the Romans (Hellenisation) or Roman culture by the Greeks (Romanisation). In fact, contacts between the two communities resulted in starting a dialogue in which both sides were active participants.[96]

The cultural identity of a city is decided by its inhabitants. As has been shown above, very early on, practically at the moment of the colony's establishment, the first colonists started to deliberately use various elements connecting it to the Greek *polis* destroyed in 146 BC. The reasons for this may have been varied, ranging from personal preferences, fascinations, or the wish to add prestige, to posing as heirs of the inhabitants of the old city. Let us remember that a considerable part of the elite of Roman Corinth were freedmen, with the desire to emulate their superiors, characteristic of this group.[97] In Corinth, thanks to Caesar, freedmen were granted the right to perform public functions (the privilege was later rescinded by Augustus), which satisfied their political ambitions. In order to increase their cultural prestige, they started to refer to the Greek history of the place where they happened to live.

The example came from the Roman authorities, and from Caesar to be specific. Cassius Dion noted that the dictator, establishing the colonies in Corinth and Carthage, wanted to restore the memory of the old inhabitants of these cities.[98] The first few decisions made by the colonists suggest that they had clear directions how to act, but also extensive authority (taking over the games). It is likely that Caesar's objective to create a city in which cultures could intermingle coincided with the objectives and ambitions of the colonists. In 16/15 BC, Augustus established another Roman colony, at Patras. The colony was built as a result of a procedure which slightly resembled synoecism. The new political structure was assigned the inhabitants of not only the territories closest to Patras, but also lands on the northern coast of the Gulf of Corinth. Augustus also ordered for the most important cult statues from Calydon (Artemis Laphria and Dionysus Calydonios) to be moved to Patras and placed in new temples.[99] In this way, he reorganised Patras' pantheon, founding it on old traditions. The cult of Artemis Laphria was quickly connected with the cult of the emperor, but this is beside the point.[100] What is crucial is that the reference to local traditions occurred on the initiative of the authorities, i.e. Augustus, who followed in Caesar's footsteps when it came to his policy on establishing colonies.

---

95 Millar 1993, 232–260.

96 Woolf 1994: 116–143; 1998, 22; Alcock 1997b, 109; Walters 2005, 397–417; Madsen 2006, 87–113 (the Greeks' attitude towards the Romans).

97 On the attitude of Roman freedmen, see Veyne 1990, 3–43.

98 Cass. Dio 43.50.4–5.

99 Paus. 7.18.8–9.

100 A. Rizakis (1996, 282–283; 2010, 129–154) analysing the cults and, mainly, the architectural development of the city, concluded that Patras was neither Greek nor Roman, but a typical Greek-Roman city. M. Kantiréa (2007, 98–101) analyses the case of Artemis Laphria in the context of the religious policy of Augustus, who sought to revive old cults not just in Rome, but also in the provinces.

Roman Corinth showed interest in its Greek predecessor from the very beginning of its existence. This followed both from Caesar's intentions and from the attitude and ambitions of the colonists themselves. With time, Greek elements in the Roman colony became more numerous and more visible. However, the inhabitants did not manage to convince everybody that they were heirs of the Greek inhabitants of the city. Pausanias, as a lover of Greek antiquities, was particularly sceptical; he was not fooled, and emphasised several times that in his time Corinth had not been inhabited by any of its old citizens.

Finally, one more thing must not be forgotten. Corinth was an important trade centre, visited by legions of merchants, sailors, games participants and spectators. It was these people that made it a buoyant and ethnically diverse city. Multi-ethnicity leads to cultural diversity, so caution should be called for whenever we try to classify Corinth using the terms "Roman" or "Greek."

BIBLIOGRAPHY

Alcock, S.E. (1997a): Greece: A Landscape of Resistance?, in: Mattingly 1997: 103–115.

Alcock, S.E. (ed.) (1997b): *The Early Roman Empire in the East*, Oxford.

Amandry, M. (1998): Le monnayage des duovirs corinthiens (*BCH* Suppl. 15), Athènes.

Baldwin Bowsky, M.W. (2004): Of Two Tongues: Acculturation of Roman Knossos, in: Salmeri/Raggi/Baroni 2004: 50–95.

Bookidis, N. (2005): Religion in Corinth: 146 B.C.E. to 100 C.E., in: Schowalter/Friesen 2005: 141–164.

Bowersock, G.W. (1965): *Augustus and the Greek World*, Oxford.

Broneer, O. (1941): Colonia Laus Iulia Corinthiensis, *Hesperia* 10: 388–390.

Bruneau, Ph. (1971): Lampes corinthiennes, *BCH* 95: 437–501.

Brunt, P.A. (1971): *Italian Manpower*, Oxford.

Di Napoli, V. (2010): Entertainment Building of the Roman Peloponnese: Theatres, *Odea*, and Amphiteatres and Their Topographical Distribution, in: Rizakis/Lepenioti 2010: 253–266.

Dixon, D. (2000): A New Latin and Greek Inscription from Corinth, *Hesperia* 69: 335–342.

Edwards, Ch.M. (1981): Corinth 1980: Molded Relief of Bowls, *Hesperia* 50: 189–210.

Engels, D. (1990): *Roman Corinth: An Alternative Model for the Classical City*, Chicago, Il.

Gantz, T. (1993): *Early Greek Myth: A Guide to Literary and Artistic Sources*, vols. 1–2, Baltimore–London.

Geagan, D.J. (1968): Notes on the Agonistic Festivals of Roman Corinth, *GRBS* 9: 69–80.

Geagan, D.J. (1989): The Isthmian Dossier of P. Priscus Juventianus, *Hesperia* 53: 349–360.

Gebhard, E.R. (1993): The Isthmian Games and the Sanctuary of Poseidon in the Early Empire, in: T.E. Gregory (ed.), *The Corinthia in the Roman Period. Including the Papers Given at a Symposium Held at The Ohio State University on 7–9 March, 1991* (*JRA Suppl.* 8), Portsmouth, Rhode Island: 78–82.

Gebhard, E.R. (2005): Rites for Melikertes-Palaimon in the Early Roman Corinthia, in: Schowalter/Friesen 2005: 165–203.

Gebhard, E.R., Dickie, M.W. (2003): The view from the Isthmus, ca. 200 to 44 B.C, in: Ch.K. Williams II, N. Bookidis (eds.), *Corinth the Centenary 1896–1996*, Athens: 261–278.

Hansen, F. (ed.) (1993): *The Ancient Greek City-State*, Copenhagen.

Hoskins Walbank, M.E. (1997): The Foundation and Planning of Early Roman Corinth, *JRA* 10: 95–130.

Hoskins Walbank, M.E. (2002): What's in a Name? Corinth under the Flavians, *ZPE* 139: 251–264.

Hoskins Walbank, M.E. (2003a): Aspects of Corinthian Coinage in the Late 1st and Early 2nd Centuries A.C., in: Williams/Bookidis 2003: 337–349.

Hoskins Walbank, M.E. (2003b): Unquiet Graves: Burial Practices of the Roman Corinthians, in: Schowalter/Friesen 2005: 249–280.

Hoskins Walbank, M.E. (2010): The Cults of Roman Corinth: Public Rituals and Personal Belief, in: Rizakis/Lepenioti 2010: 357–374.

Hupfloher, A. (2008): A Small Copy of Rome? Religious Organization in Roman Corinth, in: Rizakis/Camia 2008: 151–160.

Hutton, W. (2005): *Describing Greece. Landscape and Literature in the Periegesis of Pausanias*, Cambridge.

Kajava, M. (2002): When did the Isthmian Games Return to the Isthmus? (Rereading "Corinth" 8.3.153), *CP* 97: 168–178.

Kantiréa, M. (2007): *Les Dieux et les Dieux Auguste. Le culte imperial en Greèce sous les Julio-claudiens et les Flaviens. Etudes épigraphiques et archéologiques*, Athenes.

Lafond, Y. (2006): *La mémoire des cités dans le Péloponnèse d'époque romaine (IIe siècle avant J.-C. – IIIe siècle après J.-C.)*, Rennes.

Madsen, J.M. (2006): The Romanization of the Greek elite in Achaia, Asia and Bithynia: Greek Resistance or Regional Discrepancies?, *Orbis Terrarum* 8: 87–113.

Mattingly, D.J. (ed.) (1997): *Dialogues in Roman Imperialism. Power, discourse, and discrepant experience in the Roman Empire*, (*JRA Suppl.* 23), Portsmouth, Rhode Island.

Mattingly, H. (1962): *Roman Coins from the Earliest Times to the Fall of the Western Empire*, London.

Mattusch, C.C. (2003): Corinthian Bronze. Famous, but Elusive, in: Williams/Bookidis 2003: 219–232.

Millar, F. (1993): The Greek City in Roman Period, in: Hansen 1993: 232–260.

Millis, B.W. (2010a): The Social and Ethnic Origins of the Colonists in Early Roman Corinth, in: S.J. Friesen, D.N. Schowalter, J.C. Walters (eds.), *Corinth in Context. Comparative Studies on Religion and Society*, Leiden–Boston: 13–35.

Millis, B.W. (2010b): Corinthians in Exile 146–44 BC, in: R.W.V. Catling, F. Marchand with the assistance of M. Sasanow (eds.), *Onomatologos. Studies in Greek Personal Names presented to Elaine Matthews*, Exeter: 244–257.

Morris, I. (1992): *Death-Ritual and Social Structure in Classical Antiquity*, Cambridge.

Oliver, J.H. (1978): Panachaens and Panhellenes, *Hepseria* 47: 185–191.

Papageorgiadou-Bani, H. (2004): *The Numismatic Iconography of the Roman Colonies in Greece. Local Spirit and the Expression of Imperial Policy*, Athens.

Piérart, M. (1998): Panthéon et hellénisation dans la colonie romaine de Corinth: la "rédecouverte" du culte de Palaimon à l'Isthm, *Kernos* 11: 85–109.

Raggi, A. (2004): Cittadinanza colonaria e cittadinanza romana, in: Salmeri/Raggi/Baroni 2004: 55–68.

Rizakis, A.D. (1995): «Paysage linguistique» : Le grec face au latin. Le paysage linguistique dans la peninsule balkanique sous l'Empire, in: H. Solin, O. Salomies, U.-M. Liertz (eds.), *Acta colloqui epigraphici latini, Helsinki 3–6 sept. 1991*, Helsinki: 373–391.

Rizakis, A.D. (1996): Les colonies romaines des côtes occidentales grecques. Population et territoire, *DHA* 22: 255–324.

Rizakis, A.D. (1997): Roman Colonies in the Province of Achaia: Territories, Land and Population, in: Alcock 1997: 15–36.

Rizakis, A.D. (2004): La littérature gromatique et la colonisation romaine en Orient, in: Salmeri/Raggi/Baroni 2004: 69–94.

Rizakis, A. (2007): *Les Ti. Claudii* et la promotion des élites péloponnésiennes, in: Perrin Y. (ed.), *Neronia VII. Rome, l'Italie et la Grèce. Hellénisme et philhellénisme au premier siècle après J.-C. Actes du VIIe Colloque International de la SIEN*, Bruxelles: 183–195.
Rizakis, A.D. (2010): *Colonia Augusta Achaïca Patrensis*. Réaménagements urbains, constructions édilitaire et la nouvelle identité patréenne, in: Rizakis/Lepenioti 2010: 129–154.
Rizakis, A.D., Camia, F. (eds.) (2008): *Pathways to Power. Civic Elites in the Eastern Part of the Roman Empire. Proceedings of the International Workshop held at Athens Scuola Archeologica Italiana di Atene, 19 Dicembre 2005*, Atene.
Rizakis, A.D., Lepenioti, Cl.E. (eds.) (2010): *Roman Peloponnese III. Society, Economy and Culture under the Roman Empire: Continuity and Innovation*, Athens.
Rizakis, A.D., Zoumbaki, S. (2001): *Roman Peloponnese I. Roman Personal Names in Their Social Context (Achaia, Arcadia, Argolis, Corinthia and Eleia*), Athens.
Romano, I.B. (1994): A Hellenistic Deposit from Corinth: Evidence for Interim Period Activity (146–44 B.C.), *Hesperia* 63: 57–104.
Romano, D.G. (2003): City Planning, Centuriation, and Land Division in Roman Corinth: *Colonia Laus Iulia Corinthiensis* & *Colonia Iulia Flavia Augusta Corinthiensis*, in: Williams/Bookidis 2003: 279–301.
Romano, D.G. (2005): Urban and Rural Planning in Roman Corinth, in: Schowalter/Friesen 2005: 25–59.
Romano, D.G. (2010): Romanization of the Corinthia: Urban and Rural Developments, in: Rizakis/Lepenioti 2010: 155–172.
Salmeri, G., Raggi, A., Baroni, A. (eds.) (2004): *Colonie romane nel mondo greco*, Roma.
Sartre, M. (2001): Les colonies romaines dans le monde grec, *Electrum* 5: 111–152.
Schowalter, D.N., Friesen, S.J. (eds.) (2005): *Urban Religion in Roman Corinth. Interdisciplinary Approaches*, Harvard.
Spawforth, A.J.S., Walker, S. (1985): The World of Panhellenion I: Athens and Eleusis, *JRS* 75: 78–104.
Spawforth, A.J.S. (1989): Agonistic Festivals in Roman Greece, *Bulletin of the Institute of Classical Studies* 36: 193–197.
Spawforth, A.J.S. (1994): Corinth, Argos, and the Imperial Cult: Pseudo-Julian, *Letteres* 198 Bidez, *Hesperia* 63: 211–232.
Spawforth, A.J.S. (1996): Roman Corinth: The Formation of a Colonial Elite, in: A.D. Rizakis (ed.), *Roman Onomastic in the Greek East: Social and Political Aspects. Proceedings of the Inernational Colloquium on Roman Onomastics, Athens, 7–9 September 1993*, Athens: 167–182.
Stansbury, H.A. (1990): *Corinthian Honor, Corinthian Conflict: A Social History of Early Roman Corinth and Its Pauline Community*, University of California, Irvine.
Thomas, C.M. (2005): Placing the Dead: Funerary Practice and Social Stratification in the Early Roman Period at Corinth and Ephesos, in: Schowalter/Friesen 2005: 281–304.
Veyne, P. (1990): *La società romana*, Bari.
Walters, J.C. (2005): Civic Identity in Roman Corinth and Its Impact on Early Christians, in: Schowalter/Friesen 2005: 397–417.
Williams, C.K. II, Bookidis, N. (eds.) (2003): *Corinth the Centenary 1896–1996*, Athens.
Williams, C.K. II, Russell, P. (1981): Corinth: Excavations of 1980, *Hesperia* 50: 1–44.
Wiseman, J. (1979): Corinth and Rome I: 228 B.C. – A.D. 267, *ANRW* II 7.1: 438–548.
Woolf, G. (1994): Becoming Roman, Staying Greek: Cultural Identity and the Civilizing Process in the Roman East, *PCPhS* 40: 116–143.
Woolf, G. (1998): *Becoming Roman. The Origins of the Provincial Civilization in Gaul*, Cambridge.

ELECTRUM * Vol. 20 (2013): 163–176
doi: 10.4467/20800909EL.13.008.1437

Herulian Settlements in Byzantium under Emperors Anastasius and Justinian*

Stanisław Turlej
Uniwersytet Jagielloński, Kraków

Abstract: The aim of this article is to draw attention to the need to intensify historical research on Herulian settlements in Byzantium under Emperors Anastasius and Justinian based on the analysis of written sources. The starting point for studying the history of the Heruli in Late Antiquity should be a historical analysis of the excursus devoted to them by Procopius of Caesarea in the book VI *Wars*. As a result of a historical analysis based on literal interpretation and critical examination, taking into account legal circumstances and the historical context, it can greatly contribute to our knowledge of Herulian history.

To sum up the results of the conducted research, it is possible to give quite a precise description of the relations between the empire and the Heruli based on an analysis of the accounts of Procopius of Caesarea and Marcellinus Comes. In 512, Emperor Anastasius settled the tribe on the empire's lands. Taking advantage of their difficult situation, he probably forced them into full subordination. It seems that the Heruli, deprived of their tribal organisation and striving to keep their independence, rebelled and attacked the Romans at the first opportunity, i.e. ca. 514. The imperial army managed to defeat them as early as 515 or 516, and Anastasius refused to give them the status of allies, i.e. improve their position. In this situation it seems most likely that the empire completely broke its ties with the Heruli and the tribe left the empire's lands.

At this stage of the analysis it is difficult to determine to what extent Procopius was aware of the nuances of Anastasius' policy, as his account of the Herulian migration in search of new lands is very brief and schematic. All the details he provides, apart from the information about the Heruli crossing the Danube River on their own initiative, are in complete agreement with the reconstruction of events based on Marcellinus Comes' mention. Only after completing the analysis of Procopius' whole account on the Heruli will it be possible to formulate conclusions about its reliability and the sources he used.

Key words: Late Antiquity, Byzantium, Anastasius, Justinian I, Heruli, Procopius of Caesarea.

* The size of the material requires that the activities of Anastasius and Justinian be discussed separately.

There are two basic reasons for which the history of the Heruli in Late Antiquity arouses little interest from the perspective of historical studies: the tribe's modest significance and the scant number of sources.[1] Even reading renowned works, it is quite difficult to locate sufficiently complete information about the existence of their kingdom, let alone its role in the political life at the time.[2] Perhaps this situation will change with the publication of new materials about the tribe and with the current widespread popularity of the subject of ancient and medieval times.[3] Whether this will lead to actual progress in historical research is a different matter altogether. The history of the Heruli is still being painted in very broad strokes, and publications about the tribe are frequently based on compilations of out-of-context information from various sources. The only way to limit randomness and arbitrariness in selecting and assessing what information should be used and how is to broaden the analysis of current sources. Otherwise, general reconstructions or attempts to broaden our interpretation by referring to the general historical context may backfire and not only fail to lead to more detailed, established facts about the Heruli, but also blur the picture of the situation in which the Balkan provinces of Byzantium found themselves under Anastasius and Justinian.[4]

In the case of the Heruli, a serious obstacle encountered by researchers is undoubtedly not only the small number of available written sources but also the fact that they only refer to a handful of incidents, which, to make matters more complicated, show the tribe in a different light depending on the origin of a given tradition. Despite such unfavourable circumstances, we can at least try to systematise what we know about the Heruli in Late Antiquity thanks to the fact that in the early 6th century they bound their fate to the empire, and information about them was recorded in sources of Byzantine provenience. Particularly important is Procopius of Caesarea's account included in Book VI of the *Wars* which, although very well known, remains practically unused from the perspective of reconstructing the history of the tribe in Late Antiquity in relation to Byzantium.[5] In the later parts of his work, Procopius provides further valuable details about the Heruli when he discusses Justinian's policy towards the barbarians in the west and the Gepids' conflict with the Lombards.[6]

---

1 Studies on the Heruli: Rappaport 1912; Schmidt 1941, 548–564; Lakatos 1978, 89–90; Taylor 1999, 468–474; Goffart 2006, 205–210; Steinacher 2010, 319–360; Sarantis 2010, 361–362. For a survey of archaeological and linguistic research Brandt 2012, 7–8 (pdf version with introduction from 24 June 2012).

2 References to the Heruli appear in the context of analysing Byzantium's western policy under Anastasius and Justinian, especially when the military activities of the latter are discussed, e.g. Capizzi 1969, 171; Demandt 1989, 193; Whitby 2000, 714–715; Haarer 2006, 99; Mitchell 2007, 383; Meier 2009, 224, 235.

3 On the relatively negligible interest in the Heruli in comparison to studies on other tribes in Late Antiquity, see Sarantis 2010, 361–362; Steinacher 2010, 319.

4 For example, for a broad picture against the backdrop of Justinian's policy in the region, see Sarantis 2010, 374–375.

5 The works of Procopius of Caesarea are some of the most important sources for the history of Byzantium in the first half of the 6th century. For a discussion, see Rubin 1954: 80–81; 1960, 173–174; Cameron 1985, 3–4; Cataudella 2003, 393–394.

6 Chapters 33 and 34 of Book VII of the *Wars* are of particular importance for a comprehensive reconstruction of the situation in the territories at the Danube River. The topic of the Gepids' conflict with the Lombards has been a subject of discussion for a long time: Wozniak 1979, 148–149; Pohl 1996, 27–28; Sarantis 2009, 27–28.

It seems that the starting point for studying the history of the Heruli in Late Antiquity should, first of all, be a historical analysis of the excursus devoted to them by Procopius of Caesarea, based on a literal interpretation and critical analysis with references to the historical context.[7] It should be particularly emphasised that the digression is the only comprehensive account on the history of this tribe, and as such gives us an opportunity to systematise the discussion on controversial topics raised by fragmentary and often seemingly contradictory information from the other surviving sources, which is conducive to proposing hypotheses about, for example, divisions of the tribe.[8] We should also remember the significance of an analysis of this narrative for studies on the technique and reliability of the historian in the context of a comprehensive interpretation of his works.[9]

The description of the Heruli in Book VI of the *Wars* (VI 14,1–15,36) is a clearly separate excursus in an account of war activities in Italy in 538.[10] Having written about the arrival of Narses' army at Picenum (VI 13, 16–18), which included a substantial, 2,000-man contingent of Heruls, Procopius announces that he will characterise the tribe and present the circumstances in which it entered into an alliance with the empire.[11] After the perfunctory mention of the fact that they had lived beyond the Danube River for a long time, the account focuses on a description of their beliefs and customs (VI 14, 1–7). This is followed by a brief depiction of their victories over numerous unnamed tribes. They had subjugated the neighbouring barbarians and imposed their supremacy over the Lombards. After Emperor Anastasius came to power, the Heruli observed peace for three years (VI 14, 8–10). Later, they forced their king Rodolphus into an unjust war against the Lombards, which Procopius scrupulously relates (VI 14, 11–22). Defeated, the Heruli left their settlements and kept moving forward until they reached the territory previously inhabited by the Rugii. These were unpopulated lands, where they suffered hunger and could not support themselves. Forced by famine, they moved to the lands close to the Gepids, who allowed them to settle there. The good relations between the two tribes did not last long, since for no good reason the Gepids started to abuse the Heruli. The latter therefore crossed to the south bank of the river, into the Byzantine territory. Emperor Anastasius welcomed them, but his friendliness did not last when the Heruli in turn started to mistreat the Romans. The barbarians' conduct led to an intervention of

[7] The following analysis is preliminary and focuses on the source, and as such avoids sweeping commentaries, references to literature etc. The next stage of studies on the broad themes of the history of the Heruli in Late Antiquity should focus on interpreting Cassiodorus' information. It should be taken into account that he may have introduced changes due to the political situation not only after 519, which seems likely in the case of the *Chronica* (Prostko-Prostyński 1994, 224–225), but also after 535 in the case of his other works. Dating individual descriptions from *Varia* may prove to be of key importance, see Steinacher 2010, 347. Jordanes' account is also worth including. The Lombardic tradition certainly requires a separate analysis.

[8] For a discussion of research problems concerning the history of the Heruli in general, see Brandt 2012: 46–47. In Late Antiquity in relations with Byzantium: Sarantis 2009, 397–398.

[9] It is necessary to carry out a comprehensive analysis of Procopius' writings. The objective is to establish their message and dating, which will allow us to profile his whole work. In the light of recent research almost nothing is certain, see Greatrex 2003, 67.

[10] The numbers in brackets refer to fragments of the text of Procopius' *Wars*, and the cited passages from the work are from the Haury – Wirth edition. For a comprehensive commentary, see Rubin 1954, 177–185; Cameron 1985: 218–219; Rabanoglou 2005, 234–235.

[11] For the situation in Italy, see Rubin 1954, 177; 1995, 122; Cameron 1985, 188–189.

the imperial army. Defeated in battle, the Heruli could have been completely destroyed. Anastasius spared them, but did not accept them as allies (VI 14, 23–32). Emperor Justinian gave the Heruli fertile lands and persuaded them to convert to Christianity. From that time on, they helped Rome as allies and their manner of life became more civilised, but they still remained the worst rascals (VI 14, 33–36). The Heruli killed King Ochos, which led to yet another conflict with the empire. Although the barbarians did not respect the king and did not want to accept his authority, after the murder they came to the conclusion that they should have a king after all. They believed the best candidate would be a member of the royal family from the island of Thule (VI 14, 37–42).

In the next chapter of Book VI of the *Wars*, Procopius writes about a division among the Heruli. Some of them moved into Illyricum, and the rest, led by members of the royal family, went north to the island of Thule, where, following a long journey, they settled for good (VI 15, 1–4).[12] After a long description of the customs of the local barbarians (VI 15, 4–26), the historian relates the story about the arrival at Thule of envoys from their relatives remaining at the Danube River, who were looking for a suitable candidate for a king. They did find the right man, but he fell ill and died on the return journey. This forced the envoys to return to Thule, where they chose a man named Datius to be their king (VI 15, 27–29). This meant that the arrival of the new ruler was delayed; meanwhile, the Heruli from around Singidunum, concerned about Justinian's response, turned to the emperor, asking him to appoint their new ruler. The emperor chose one of their tribe living in Constantinople, Suartuas, who went to the Heruli at the Danube River and received their support. However, when he wanted to take military action against the approaching Datius, he was abandoned and ran for his life. This, reportedly, was the reason for the Heruli's revolt (VI 15, 30–36).

Earlier, when describing hostilities against the Persians and the Vandals, or the Nika riots in Constantinople, Procopius mentioned the Heruli several times, describing officers and soldiers fighting in the Roman army, and his characterisation was rather ambiguous. There were some good soldiers and notable, meritorious commanders, such as Pharas, but in general the historian associated the Heruli with drunkenness and faithlessness (IV 4, 28–31). They were Arians, which led to problems with maintaining their loyalty in Africa (IV 14, 11–13).[13] In the excursus, Procopius did not go back to what he had written earlier, but, true to his initial announcement, he aimed to describe the Heruli and the circumstances in which they entered into an alliance with Rome:

Ουτνες δS Βνθρώπων εσρν #Ĺρουλοι καρ Ǵθεν <Ńωμαίοις Τς ξυμμαχίαν Vρ™ν Vρχομαι.[14]

The account on the Heruli takes up two chapters of Book VI of the *Wars* and, in terms of the topics discussed, it falls into six basic parts:

1) 14, 1–6: a description of Herulian customs.

[12] Rabanoglou 2005, 237–238; Goffart 1988, 90; 2006, 416–417; Steinacher 2010, 353–354; Sarantis 2010, 369 n. 24; Brandt 2012, 22–23, 62–63. There is a lot of interest in the information about the presence of the Slavs on the route of the Herulian migration (VI 15, 2): Kobyliński 2005, 531 in the context of reconstructing their early history. The ongoing discussion is still lively, see Prostko-Prostyński 2011, 155–156.

[13] All mentions of the Heruli: Haury/Wirth 1964, 234; Lakatos 1978, 7–34; Goffart 2006, 208, 337 n. 108; Steinacher 2010, 349, 352.

[14] Haury/Wirth 1963, 208, 22–23.

2) 14, 8–10: the Heruli build a powerful kingdom, subjugating the neighbouring barbarians.

3) 14, 11–22: King Rodolphus is forced by his tribesmen into a war against the Lombards, which ends in utter defeat.

4) 14, 23–42: the Heruli's escape and their relations with Emperors Anastasius and Justinian.

5) 15, 1–26: a description of Thule.

6) 15, 27–36: Ochos is murdered and a new king is chosen. Internal strife follows and the tribe revolts against Justinian.

We can distinguish two threads, almost equal in volume, in the account: an ethnographical one, understood in broad terms, and a political one, with the latter also including paragraphs containing remarks about the Heruli, showing them in a very negative light as a people (14, 8; 14, 11; 14, 35–36; 14, 41). The ethnographic thread provides details about the tribe of Heruli, while the political one shows their history from a general historical perspective, unfortunately not only in connection with the tribe establishing direct political relations with the empire. Procopius interweaves the ethnographic and political threads and tells several stories about various aspects of the Herulian life, which may have been dictated by his concern about the best possible reception of his work in terms of its cognitive values. The origin and course of the conflict with the Lombards, as well as a considerable portion of the description of Thule, has nothing to do with the characterisation of the Heruli or with their relations with Byzantium. They may, however, be considered attractive from the point of view of the reader's interest. For Procopius' contemporaries, who had no close relations with Illyricum, let alone the barbarian world north of the Danube River, the excursus on the Heruli may have been worthwhile in terms of both its contents and its form. However, the frankly amazing generality and consequent incompleteness of his descriptions of purely political topics make literal interpretation and reconstruction of events difficult. The problem is not the fact that a story about wild barbarians and exotic lands is intermingled with descriptions of political events, because the author made sure that his account was clear and cohesive by skilfully combining the two threads so that the reader would not lose sight of the point. The problem is the obviously abridged and superficial account of strictly political topics. The events which were the turning points in the history of the tribe definitely stand out in the narrative, but the connections between them, as well as their consequences, are less clear. In the context of the author's announcement that he is going to present the circumstances in which the Heruli established their alliance with Rome, there is some inconsistency, since important events are summarised while secondary ones are given too much attention, e.g. the origin and course of the Heruli's conflict with the Lombards.

On the basis of a literal interpretation of this account, it is possible to reconstruct the most important moments in the history of the Heruli under Anastasius and Justinian, from the time when they were forced to migrate after the defeat inflicted by the Lombards:

1) Escape and settling near the Gepids.

2) Crossing the Danube River and settling on the empire's lands, the tribe's division.

3) Mistreatment of the Romans.

4) Victory of the imperial forces and Anastasius' handling of the defeated Heruli.

5) Justinian bestowing new lands on the Heruli and persuading them to convert to Christianity.

6) the death of King Ochos, the election of two kings, and the Heruli joining the Gepids.

The account on the political events directly concerning the Heruli's relations with Byzantium seems very general, full of ambiguities and abridgements, such as Procopius not finishing a story he started (for example the conditions on which Emperor Anastasius accepted the Heruli, or what happened to the Heruli after the revolt), or starting a new topic without any introductory information (e.g. about the sudden appearance of a Herulian king under Justinian). Next to the detailed facts and explanations of connections between the described events, there is almost no chronological data. The reason for all this information lacking was unlikely to have been the author's reluctance to make the text excessively long, since, as we have mentioned, he included some information exceeding what he had declared he would write about. In this context, it may be surprising that specific dates only appear when he describes the birth of the Herulian power at the beginning of Anastasius' reign.

The idea to present a comprehensive description of the tribe of Heruli probably occurred to Procopius when he was working on the account of the wars of Emperor Justinian, trying to grasp the complex political and military situation in the barbarian world and to include it in the description of the war in Italy. The historian explains who the Heruli were and how they found themselves in Byzantium's sphere of influence from the perspective of the mid-6th century. Therefore it is sufficient e.g. to mention briefly that they were a tribe that had long lived beyond the Danube River, and to give some basic facts from their history from the moment which was connected with the contemporary events. The excursus on the Heruli was probably meant to expand the political and military background of the commentary on the war in Italy, and to show not only the connection but also the influence of events in the barbarian world on the situation in the empire. It seems that Procopius was not particularly interested in the history of the tribe as such; he had probably not planned or prepared for tackling the subject, and had not looked for or gathered materials towards this aim, such as works of other authors or imperial documents. However, we have to reflect on the abridgements in the descriptions of recent or even contemporary events, since the author could acquire knowledge about them relatively easily. He participated in military campaigns in which Herulian troops took part and, serving at Belisarius' side, had direct contact with high-ranking military men from Illyricum. The latter could have known him personally, e.g. from the conflicts with the Heruli under Anastasius.[15] It seems that the information used by Procopius to describe Byzantium's relations with the Heruli could just as well have been provided by themselves, other barbarians (e.g. Lombards), or the Byzantines. The historian's dislike of Narses (who was very closely connected with the Heruli) may have considerably influenced his account,[16] e.g. the order of presentation of data (the description of Herulian cruelty opens the excursus), but we should not overestimate it in the context of possibly falsifying facts. Procopius paints the Heruli in a very negative light and there are clear

[15] Procopius was in contact with the Heruli and could obtain information from them, see Schmidt 1941, 552; Prostko-Prostyński 2011, 159; Brandt 2012, 20.

[16] Procopius disliked Narses: Goffart 2006, 207 n. 97; Steinacher 2010, 349.

tendencies to exaggerate their vices, also when describing their conflicts with the empire, but this alone does not constitute grounds for accusing him *a priori* of providing false information about political events regarding Byzantium, and known to many of his contemporaries.

The point of our historical analysis is to read Procopius' account in the correct way, which is very difficult given that he wrote a historical work devoted to events contemporary to himself, which in the reality of his time also meant that he took great care to ensure its literary value.[17] Concern about the best and widest reception of the work may have led to oversimplifying or abridging passages devoted to, for instance, politics or religion. Procopius reconstructed the political history of the Heruli in accordance with his own convention of presenting material, i.e. basing the narrative on just a handful of unrelated descriptions, skilfully put together. This makes the account difficult to understand fully, especially in the case of passages dealing with the emperors' critical decisions concerning the fate of the Heruli, all the more so since they had a legal aspect, and Procopius was not always very precise, even if he applied technical terms used in the imperial chancellery to describe the status of barbarians within the Byzantine legal system.[18] Due to the specificity of the account in this excursus, therefore, a historical analysis must take into account not only the literal meaning of the text, but also the broader context of the account, i.e. what he was writing about in a given passage, how he constructed his descriptions, e.g. the motif of the Herulian migration, etc.

Summing up, it must be emphasised that Procopius' excursus about the Heruli is of unique importance for the reconstruction of the history of the tribe. It is, at least in several places, possible to directly compare its information with accounts from a few independent sources from the era, which gives a more solid basis for reconstructing the Heruli's relations with Byzantium from 512 to the mid-6th century. The first step in such a reconstruction should be to establish the course of events, starting at the beginning of Justinian's reign. The last paragraph of the excursus devoted to the Herulian revolt after the murder of King Ochos refers to a later period and requires a separate analysis, taking into account the whole situation across the region in connection with the Gepids' war against the Lombards.

1) The description of the Herulian migration to the empire's lands is significant for learning about the situation and the distribution of forces in the region, as well as the method Procopius used to construct a description. The chronology of events remains debatable, because the Lombards' victory over the Heruli is dated to ca. 508 on the basis of an analysis of the historical context.[19] According to Procopius (VI 14, 10), this happened much earlier, ca. 494.[20] The origin of the conflict also remains unclear, since two different traditions have survived, while – regardless of provenience – the sources agree

---

[17] Kaldellis 2004, 15, 40.

[18] This is why it is so difficult to establish the exact relations between the Heruli and Byzantium. Using very general terms such as allies or *foederati* requires that the situation in the reality of the 6th century be taken into account: Schwarcz 1995, 290–291; Goffart 1988, 74 n. 263; Pohl 1997, 81–82; Scharf 2001, 71 n. 196; Sarantis 2010, 392.

[19] The most commonly used dating is ca. 508: Lakatos 1978, 89; Pohl 2001, 62; Goffart 2006, 208; Meier 2009, 224; Sarantis 2009, 20. Ca. 505: Schmidt 1941, 552. Ca. 510: Collins 2000, 128.

[20] In discussions on the dating, Procopius is also cited directly: Schmidt 1941: 552 n. 4; Krag 2003, 9 n. 4;

that the Heruli suffered a defeat and heavy losses.[21] The defeated set off in search of new lands, but Procopius does not mention any sort of division of the tribe.[22] According to him, following an unsuccessful stay on the lands formerly belonging to the Rugii, the Heruli settled near the Gepids, with their consent:[23]

> Dγχιστά που τ\ς Γηπαίδων χώρας Bφίκοντο. καρ α˘το†ς Γήπαδες τ@ μSν πρ™τα sκέτας γεJομένους Tνοικίζεσθαί τε καρ προσοίκους σφίσι ξυνεχώρουν εrναι.[24]

It is unknown how quickly the two tribes fell out. It follows from the description that it could have occurred when the newcomers had settled in. The Gepids first inflicted all manners of abuse on the Heruli, and then started to attack them outright, which made the Heruli leave the territory they were occupying.

2) According to Procopius, the Heruli crossed the Danube River directly after they had left the Gepids, in order to settle among the Romans. Emperor Anastasius reportedly showed them friendliness and assented to their settlement. On the basis of a literal interpretation of this account, it could be assumed that two separate events occurred. First, the Heruli crossed the Danube River on their own initiative, without asking the emperor's permission, in order to settle close to the Romans. The second incident took place after the Heruli crossed the river and found themselves in the empire's territory, because this is when they aroused the interest of Emperor Anastasius: he welcomed them and allowed them to settle there.

> Eπερ #Άρουλοι φέρειν τ{ λοιπ{ν ο˘χ οyοß τε Ђντες #Έστρον τε ποταμ{ν διαβαίνουσι καρ τοqς Tκείνf >Ñωμαίοις προσοικεqν Vγνωσαν, ¢νατασίου τ[ν α˘τοκράτορος Bρχ[ν Vχοντος Ϋσπερ α˘το†ς πολλi φιλοφροσύνf δεξάμενος sδρύεσθαι α˘το‡ ευασε.[25]

The barbarians' appearance on the empire's lands is dated precisely to 512, thanks to information related by Marcellinus Comes, contemporary to these events and seemingly well acquainted with the situation in the whole region.[26] His mention in the *Chronicle* is very laconic:

> *Gens Herulorum in terras atque civitates Romanorum iussu Anastasii Caesaris introducta*[27]

and, just as importantly, it is the only mention in this source concerning the tumultuous relations between the empire and the Heruli. Perhaps he disapproved of the policy of Emperors Anastasius and Justinian towards the Heruli,[28] and therefore focused on the fact of the barbarians' settlement, completely avoiding not only a broader description of how it came about, but also the subsequent failure of this policy caused by the Herulian revolt. It follows from the literal interpretation of this mention that the barbarians' settle-

[21] The origin and course of the conflict are described on the basis of the accounts of Procopius and Paul the Deacon: Goffart 2006, 336 n. 103; Steinacher 2010, 348–349; Sarantis 2010, 366–367.

[22] Rappaport 1912, 1160; Schmidt 1941, 552; Wolfram 1988, 318–319. Referencing Cassiodorus, *Variae* IV 45, it is posited that the Heruli arrived in Italy, and even that the tribe was divided: Sarantis 2009, 20.

[23] The Herulian migration to lands neighbouring with the Gepids is undisputed: Rappaport 1912, 1161; Schmidt 1941, 553.

[24] Haury/Wirth 1963, 212,15–18.

[25] Haury/Wirth 1963, 212,22–213,2.

[26] Prostko-Prostyński 1994, 234; Croke 2001, 48–49, 73–74.

[27] Marcellinus Comes ad. 512,11.

[28] Croke 1995, 117; 2001, 131; Goffart 2006, 336 n. 105.

ment was a one-off event which happened in 512 and consisted not in settling them in an empty territory, but among the Romans. The whole operation was very well prepared logistically and, as indicated by the terms used, based on a special imperial constitution.[29]

Determining the exact course of events in 512 is of fundamental importance, because it was then that the direct cooperation between the empire and the Heruli started. In the light of the literal interpretation of Marcellinus Comes' mention, it is clearly necessary to abandon the literal interpretation of Procopius' account regarding the barbarians' crossing the Danube on their own initiative in order to settle near the Romans.[30] Procopius' whole account of the Herulian migration in search of new lands is very schematic. According to him, the defeated barbarians wandered around looking for empty land, i.e. free of other tribes' settlements. *Rugiland*[31] was uninhabited but devastated, which is why the Heruli had to leave it. They moved close to the Gepids, and later – according to the logic of the account – crossed the Danube River in search of empty land on the empire's territory. However, the situation was probably different at the last stage of their migration, which follows not only from Marcellinus Comes' account, but also from Procopius' next passage. Starting from the Heruli's journey to Thule, Procopius states that those who did not want to cross the Danube set off there. Therefore, considering the whole narration about the Heruli's escape after their defeat against the Lombards, it can be determined unequivocally that the tribe divided when they left the Gepids' territory. It was then that some of the Heruli crossed the Danube and entered the Roman side, and the rest, led by members of the royal family, set off to Thule.[32]

After analysing the accounts of Procopius and Marcellinus Comes, the most probable hypothesis is that prior to their crossing, the Heruli had found out the conditions on which they would be allowed to enter the empire's territory. For one part of the tribe, including members of the royal family, they were unacceptable, and so they decided to set off to Thule. The rest of the Heruli agreed to the emperor's offer, crossed the Danube River and did not occupy an empty territory but, as follows from Marcellinus Comes' description, were "introduced" onto already populated lands under the effective control of the imperial administration. The Heruli were settled among the Romans, which seems to be confirmed by Procopius in the following passage, where he mentions their revolt. Marcellinus Comes' very precise mention allows us to verify the abridged, ambiguous and schematic description of the Heruli in Procopius' work. The historian, in turn, provides information which allows us to generally describe the conditions on which Anastasius agreed to accept them as difficult. In the light of our sources, the emperor most

[29] Sources and bibliography: Regesten 341. According to Croke (1995, 117; 2001, 74) the Heruli settled on depopulated lands.

[30] There are no grounds to base the reconstruction on a literal interpretation of Procopius, or to assume that Marcellinus Comes described only the second incident from his account, i.e. the Heruli's proper settlement on the empire's lands. Sarantis (2010, 372) posits that Anastasius approved the arrival of the Heruli and in subsequent years tried to impose his sovereignty.

[31] Pohl 2003, 458–459.

[32] Rappaport (1912, 1161) identified the reason for the division, which is interpreted ambiguously from the point of view of chronology: Sarantis 2010: 20; Brandt 2012, 22 n. 38, 46.

likely treated the Heruli as *dedici*.[33] There is no indication that they were given the status of *foederati* at the time.[34]

The lack of information regarding where specifically the Heruli were settled in 512 opened the door for various hypotheses. By far the most prevalent belief seems to be that they were assigned the area near the city of Singidunum, since this was where Procopius of Caesarea placed their settlements (VI 15: 30, and VII 33: 13).[35] It is worth noting, however, that the historian mentions such a location of the Heruli later in his narrative, discussing the situation in the times of Justinian, and it was probably true for the 540s, rather than the events described by Marcellinus Comes in 512.[36] Other proposed places are more general and limited to province names: Dacia Ripensis or Moesia I.[37]

Although there is no direct information as to where Anastasius settled the Heruli in 512, the area can be indirectly identified if we take Marcellinus Comes' description as a starting point. These must have been lands under the effective control of the imperial administration, urbanised and populated, which allows us to rule out the northern borders of the Western Balkans, which were hardly inhabited or empty.[38] In his description of the Heruli who set off to Thule (i.e. in a different passage than the account of the events connected to their settlement under Anastasius and Justinian), Procopius mentions that they settled down in Illyricum (VI 15, 1);[39] although the term is general, it allows us to glean further details. The lands where the Heruli ended up in 512 were probably under the effective control of the imperial administration and were situated in such a way that they were not limited to one province, but at least two, which is why a general term such as Illyricum was used.

3) Procopius provided unique information about the Herulian revolt under Anastasius, when the barbarians started to abuse the local Romans:

> χρόν¥ δS οˆ πολλ© ‹στερον προσκεκρούκασιν αˆτ© οs βάρβαροι οŹτοι, Βνϋσια Vργα Τργασάμενοι το†ς ταύτf>Ñωμαίους. (VI 14, 29)[40]

This is a wrongly underestimated and disregarded episode in the history of relations between Byzantium and the Heruli. Unfortunately, the historian did not say when exactly the Heruli became engaged in a conflict with Rome; he only wrote casually that it hap-

[33] Such a form of settlement meant that they were completely subordinate to Roman authorities: Tasler 1984, 286–287. Scharf (2001, 71) posits that the *symmachia* gave them the right of abode and the status of allies.

[34] They were not *foederati*, which is how their status is usually described: Wozniak 1981, 374; Rubin 1995, 142; Taylor 1999, 471.

[35] Stein 1949, 305; Wozniak 1981, 374; Goffart 2006, 208. Another place also identified as their settlement is Bassianae in Pannonia II, since the empire reportedly recaptured this area ca. 510: Regesten 326; Dušanić 1967, 74–75; Sarantis 2010, 369. They were connected with Pannonia in a later period: Menander Protector, frg. 5,4.

[36] Interpretations of Procopius' information on Singidunum: Prostko-Prostyński 1994, 242–243.

[37] Dacia: Schmidt 1941, 553; Rubin 1995, 142. Southern Pannonia: Vetters 1950, 49. The territories of Moesia I and Dacia: Lakatos 1978, 89.

[38] The destruction of the northern Balkans: Whitby 2000, 712–713; Sarantis 2010, 370.

[39] Without elaborating, this is how Rappaport describes the area of Herulian settlement: Rappaport 1912, 1161; Taylor 1999, 471.

[40] Haury/Wirth 1963, 213, 2–4.

pened "soon after", which probably does not refer to the general dating to 512–518.[41] An analysis of the situation at the time allows us to determine the supposed time of this event with relative precision. Defeated by the Lombards and severely weakened in numbers, the Heruli were unable to put up armed resistance against the Gepids, and only some of them crossed the Danube River into the empire's territory, since others migrated to Thule. Their military potential was, therefore, relatively small, and after the dramatic experience of neighbouring with the Gepids, it was highly reckless to provoke the emperor, with whom they had just come to an understanding. However, it is unlikely that their revolt was random; although one of its reasons could have been the tendency to disobey, and the wild, uncivilised disposition attributed to the Heruli, the decisive factor was probably their discontent with their living conditions. As Procopius' later description indicates, following their defeat the barbarians did not want to sever their ties with Byzantium, but to improve their situation. The most favourable conditions for taking a stand against the Romans occurred during Vitalian's revolt, which shook up Anastasius' reign.[42] It is likely that the barbarians could afford to risk a rebellion only when the emperor had lost control over Thracia and was forced to concentrate on keeping Constantinople. This would allow us to narrow the date down to 514, which would concur with Procopius' statement that it followed soon after they settled on the empire's territory.[43]

4) According to Procopius, the Herulian revolt was suppressed without problems, but it is not altogether clear what their subsequent relations with the empire were, since the relevant description is clearly shortened:

> δι{ δ[στράτευμα Τπ'α^το†ς Vπεμψε. νικήσαντες δS τi μάχf >Ρωμαqοι πλείστους μSv Vκτειναν, Τν ΤξουσίJ δS πολλi ξύμπαντας διαφθεqραι γεγόνασιν. Βλλ' ειςς sκετείαν τ™ν στρατηγ™ν οs κατάλοιποι α^τ™ν γεγονότες Τδέοντο διασώσασθαί τε α^το†ς καρ ξυμμάχους τε καρ βασιλέως ‰πηρέτας τ{ λοιπ{ν Vχειν. τα‡τÜ τε μαθόντα τ{ν ΆναστÜσιον _ρεσκε, καρ Βπ' α^το‡ λειφθ\ναι μέν τισιν <Åρούλων ξυνέβη, ο^ μέντοι οŠτε ξύμμαχοι >Ńωμαίοις γεγένηται οŠτε τι εργάσαντο α^το†ς Βγαθόν.[44]

The events related to the rebellion are discussed in general and, most importantly, contrary to the sources, the consequences it could have had for the Heruli are usually underestimated, as despite their defeat they seemingly maintained their lands and status.[45] In fact, the conflict was a serious one and the emperor's response was decisive: he sent an army, which defeated the barbarians on the battlefield and was capable of destroying them all.[46] The account indicates that Anastasius only agreed to spare the lives of the surviving Heruli, but rejected their request to become allies and serve the emperor.

[41] A mention of the revolt: Rappaport 1912, 1161; Schmidt 1941; Scharf 2001, 71; Sarantis 2010, 371; Steinacher 2010, 351.

[42] An in-depth discussion of sources: Martindale 1980, 1171–1176 (Fl. Vitalianus). The dating of breaking the bond: Capizzi 1969, 123–124; Meier 2009, 295–296; Külzer 2008, 87–88.

[43] Wozniak 1981: 374 posits the date to be 514, without giving any reasoning.

[44] Haury/Wirth 1963, 213,4–14.

[45] Rappaport 1912, 1161. They lost their subsidies but remained allies and kept their land in Moesia I: Wozniak 1981, 379–380. Their situation became generally worse because they were no longer allies: Scharf 2001, 71.

[46] Steinacher (2010, 351) suggests that they were decimated.

Procopius describes these events from a later perspective and very laconically. However, since after mentioning the Heruli's request he clearly states that they did not become allies and they did the Romans no good, it is most likely that the ties with them were broken at the time. Anastasius' conduct may seemingly appear absurd and harmful, since he had an opportunity to choose an evident solution which was beneficial for the state. Yet the emperors' decision not to destroy the defeated Heruli, and to reject their request to serve the empire, can easily be explained when we look at the situation in the region at the time. The military success against Vitalian in Thracia and against the Heruli in Illyricum did not give the emperor complete freedom of action. Vitalian was not crushed and the loyalty of the army in Illyricum was doubtful, as it sided with the opponents of Anastasius' religious policy.[47] Both destroying the Heruli and leaving them be meant that the army needed to stay on in the region, which could have been risky for the emperor's religious policy. Considering the revolt (i.e. the Heruli breaking their legal bond with Rome and the emperor rejecting their offers after the defeat), as well as the events in Justinian's times, it is most likely that there was a complete break in relations between the empire and the Heruli, who were allowed to leave the empire's territory.[48] According to Procopius' description of the situation, they had been in conflict with the Gepids,[49] so the only remaining neighbour who could give them shelter was Theodoric the Great.[50]

BIBLIOGRAPHY

a) Sources

Procopii Caesariensis, *Opera Omnia*, vol. I–IV, rec. J. Haury, add. et corr. G. Wirth, Lipsiae 1962–1964. *De bellis libri VIII*, vol. I–II. *De Aedificiis*, vol. III. *Arcana Historia*, vol. IV.

Cassiodori senatoris variae, ed. Th. Mommsen, MGH, AA XII, Berolini 1894: 1–385.

Marcellini Comiti Chronicon, ed. Th. Mommsen, MGH, AA IX, Berolini 1894.

The History of Menander the Guardsman, ed. R.C. Blockley, Liverpool 1985.

Pauli Historia Langobardorum, ed. G. Waitz, MGH, SRG, t. XLVIII, Hannoverae 1878.

Regesten der Kaiserurkunden des Oströmischen Reiches von 476 bis 565, bearbeitet von T.C. Lounghis, B. Blysidu, St. Lampakes, Nicosia 2005.

b) Secondary literature

Brandt, T. (2012): *The Herules* (pdf version with introduction from 24 June 2012).

[47] Marcellinus Comes ad 516.3. Anastasius' relations with the pope and the religious situation in Illyricum: Schwarcz 1992, 3–4; Meier 2009, 311–312; Turlej 2011, 175–176.

[48] Procopius' account about Justinian's activities regarding the Heruli at the beginning of his reign is quite brief and therefore unclear, but other sources allow us to posit that most likely the emperor renewed cooperation with the tribe on completely new principles. This is discussed in a separate article.

[49] There are no grounds to assume that the Heruli cooperated with the Gepids and jointly attacked Sirmium ca. 527: Wozniak 1981, 377; Sarantis 2010, 378.

[50] It is generally assumed that they could rely on Theodoric the Great for help after the defeat against the Lombards: Ensslin 1959, 148. Theodoric supported Vitalian: Demandt 1989, 193 and the Herulian rebellion against Anastasius was also beneficial for the Ostrogoths because it weakened the empire.

Cameron, A. (1985): *Procopius and the sixth century*, London.
Capizzi, C. (1969): *L'Imperatore Anastasio I (491–518)*, Roma.
Cataudella, M.R. (2003): Historigraphy in the East, in: G. Marasco (ed.), *Greek & Roman Historiography. Fourth to Sixth Century A.D.*, Leiden–Boston: 391–447.
Collins, R. (2000): The Western Kingdoms, in: A. Cameron, B. Ward-Perkins, M. Whitby (eds.), *CAH*², vol. XIV: 112–134.
Croke, B. (1995): *The Chronicle of Marcellinus. A Translation and Commentary*, Sydney.
Croke, B. (2001): *Count Marcellinus and His Chronicle*, Oxford.
Demandt, A. (1989): *Die Spätantike*, München.
Dušanić, S. (1967): Bassianae and its Territory, *Archeologia Iugoslavica* 8: 67–81.
Ensslin, W. (1959): *Theoderich der Große*, München.
Gillett, A. (2003): *Envoys and Political Communication in the Late Antique West, 411–533*, Cambridge.
Goffart, W. (1988): *Narrators of Barbarian History (A.D. 550–800): Jordanes, Gregory of Tours, Bede, and Paul the Deacon*, Princeton.
Goffart, W. (2006): *Barbarian Tides*, Philadelphia.
Greatrex, G. (2003): Recent Work on Procopius and the Composition of Wars VIII, *Byzantine and Modern Greek Studies* 27: 45–67.
Haarer, F. (2006): *Anastasius I. Politics and Empire in the Later Roman World*, Cambridge.
Haury, J., Wirth, G. (1963): Procopii Caesariensis, *Opera Omnia*, vol. II: *De bellis libri V–VIII*, edidit J. Haury et G. Wirth, Lipsiae.
Haury, J., Wirth, G. (1964): Procopii Caesariensis, *Opera Omnia*, vol. IV: *De Aedificiis*, edidit J. Haury et G. Wirth, Lipsiae.
Kaldellis, A. (2004): *Procopius of Caesarea: Tyrany, History and Philosophy and the End of Antiquity*, Philadelphia.
Kobyliński, Z. (2005): The Slavs, in: P. Fouracre (ed.), *Cambridge Medieval History*, vol. I, Cambridge: 524–544.
Krag, C. (2003): Rodulf, *RGA* 25: 58–59.
Külzer, A. (2008): Ostthrakien, *TIB* 12, Wien.
Lakatos, P. (1978): *Quellenbuch zur Geschichte der Herulen*, Szeged.
Martindale, R. (1980): *The Prosopography of the Later Roman Empire*, vol. II, Cambridge.
Meier, M. (2009): *Anastasios I*, Stuttgart.
Mitchell, S. (2007): *A History of the Later Roman Empire*, London.
Pohl, W. (1996): Die Langobarden in Pannonien und Justinians Gotenkrieg, in: H.D. Bialeková, J. Zábojnik (eds.), *Ethnische und kulturelle Verhältnisse an der mittleren Donau vom 6. bis zur 11. Jahrhundert*, Bratislava: 27–35.
Pohl, W. (1997): The Empire and the Lombards, in: W. Pohl (ed.), *Kingdoms of the Empire: The Integration of Barbarians in Late Antiquity*, Leiden–New York–Köln: 75–133.
Pohl, W. (2001): Langobarden, II. Historisches, *RGA* 18: 60–69.
Pohl, W. (2003): Rugiland, *RGA* 25: 458–459.
Prostko-Prostyński, J. (1994): *Utraeque Res Publicae. The Emperor Anastasius I's Gothic Policy (491–518)*, Poznań.
Prostko-Prostyński, J. (2011): Herulowie między Wisłą a Bugiem w VI w.?, *Slavia Antiqua* 52: 155–161.
Rappaport, B. (1912): Heruli, *RE* VIII, 2: 1150–1167.
Rebanoglou, A.M. (2005): Γεωγραφίκα και εθνογραφίκα στοιχεία στο έργο του Προκοπίου Καισαρείας, Thessalonike.
Rubin, B. (1954): *Prokopios von Kaisareia*, Stuttgart.
Rubin, B. (1960): *Das Zeitalter Justinians*, Bd. 1, Berlin.
Rubin, B. (1995): *Das Zeitalter Justinians*, C. Capizzi (Hg.), Bd. 2, Berlin–New York.
Sarantis, A. (2009): War and Diplomacy in Pannonia and the Northwest Balkans during the Reign of Justinian. The Gepid Threat and Imperial Responses, *DOP* 63 (2009): 15–40.

Sarantis, A. (2010): The Justinianic Herules: From Allied Barbarians to Roman Provincials, in: F. Curta (ed.), *Neglected Barbarians*, Turnhout: 361–402.
Scharf, R. (2001): *Foederati. Von der völkerrechtliche Kategorie zur byzantinischen Truppengattung*, Wien.
Schmidt, L. (1941): *Die Ostgermanen*, München.
Schwarcz, A. (1992): Die Erhebung des Vitalianus, die Protobulgaren und das Konzil von Heraclea 515, *Bulgarian Historical Review* 20: 3–10.
Schwarcz, A. (1995): foederati, *RGA* 9: 290–299.
See von, K. (2006): Ultima Thule/Thule, *RGA* 31: 416–420.
Stein, E. (1949): *Histoire du Bas-Empire*, vol. 2, Paris–Bruxelles–Amsterdam.
Steinacher, R. (2010): The Heruls. Fragments of a History, in: F. Curta (ed.), *Neglected Barbarians*, Turnhout: 321–360.
Tasler, P. (1984): Dediticii. I. Historisches, *RGA* 5: 286–299.
Taylor, M. (1999): Herules, *RGA* 14: 468–474.
Turlej, S. (2011): *Justyniana Prima. Niedoceniony aspekt polityki kościelnej Justyniana*, Kraków.
Vetters, H. (1950): *Dacia Ripensis*, Wien.
Whitby, M. (2000): The Balkan and Greece, in: *CAH*², vol. XIV: 701–730.
Wolfram, H. (1988): *History of the Goths*, Berkeley.
Wozniak, F. (1978): Byzantine Diplomacy and the Lombard – Gepidic Wars, *Balkan Studies* 20: 139–158.
Wozniak, F. (1981): East Rome, Ravenna and Western Illyricum: 454–536 A.D., *Historia* 30: 351–382.

„ELECTRUM" – VOLUMES PUBLISHED:

1. *Donum Amicitiae. Studies In Ancient History Publisher on Occasion of the 75th Anniversary of Foundation of the Department of Ancient History of the Jagiellonian University*, ed. by E. Dąbrowa, Kraków 1997, pp. 249; ISBN 83-233-1054-8.
2. *Ancient Iran and the Mediterranean World. Proceedings of an International Conference in Honour of Professor Józef Wolski held at the Jagiellonian University, Cracow, in September 1996*, ed. by E. Dąbrowa, Kraków 1998, pp. 236; ISBN 83-233-1140-4.
3. S. Sprawski, *Jason of Pherae. A Study on History of Thessaly In Years 431-370 BC*, Kraków 1999, pp. 193; ISBN 83-233-1242-7.
4. *Grupy społeczne, ich organizacja i funkcja w świecie starożytnym. Materiały konferencji naukowej PTH, Kraków, 4-6 września 1997 [The Social Groups In the Ancient World, their Organisation and Functions* (In Polish with the English and French summaries)], pod red. E. Dąbrowy, Kraków 2000, pp. 117; ISBN 83-233-1321-0.
5. *Roman Military Studies*, ed. by E. Dąbrowa, Kraków 2001, pp. 191; ISBN 83-233-1422-3.
6. *Tradition and Innovation in the Ancient World*, ed. by E. Dąbrowa, Kraków 2002, pp. 117; ISBN 83-233-1578-7.
7. *The Roman Near East and Armenia*, ed. by E. Dąbrowa, Kraków 2003, pp. 143; ISBN 83-233-1792-5.
8. *Titulus. Studies in Memory Dr. Stanisław Kalita*, ed. by E. Dąbrowa, Kraków 2004, pp. 151; ISBN 83-233-1849-2.
9. *Freedom and its Limits in the Ancient World. Proceedings of a Colloquium held at the Jagiellonian University, Kraków, September 2003*, ed. by D. Brodka, J. Janik & S. Sprawski, Kraków 2003, pp. 262; ISBN 83-233-1819-0.
10. *Ancient Iran and its Neighbours. Studies in Honour of Prof. Józef Wolski on Occasion of His 95th Birthday*, ed. by E. Dąbrowa, Kraków 2005, pp.126; ISBN 83-233-1946-4.
11. *Greek and Hellenistic Studies*, ed. by E. Dąbrowa, Kraków 2006, pp.201; ISBN 83-233-2109-4.
12. *Studies on the Late Roman History*, ed. by E. Dąbrowa, Kraków 2007, pp. 113; ISBN 978-83-233-2286-3; ISSN 1897-3426.
13. *Continuity and Change. Studies in Late Antique Historiography*, ed. by D. Brodka & M. Stachura, Kraków 2007, pp. 211; ISBN 978-83-233-2374-7; ISSN 1897-3426.
14. *Studies on the Greek and Roman Military History*, ed. by E. Dąbrowa, Kraków 2008, pp. 155; ISBN 978-83-233-2578-9; ISSN 1897-3426.
15. *Orbis Parthicus. Studies in Memory Professor Józef Wolski*, ed. by E. Dąbrowa, Kraków 2009, pp. 272; ISBN 978-83-233-2821-1; ISSN 1897-3426.
16. E. Dąbrowa, *The Hasmoneans and their State. A Study in History, Ideology, and the Institutions*, Kraków 2010, pp. 228; ISBN 978-83-233-2821-1; ISSN 1897-3426
17. D. Brodka, *Ammianus Marcellinus. Studien zum Geschichtsdenken im vierten Jahrhundert n. Chr.*, Kraków 2009, pp. 164; ISBN 978-83-233-2845-2; ISSN 1897-3426
18. *New Studies on the Seleucids*, pp. 196, Kraków 2011; ISBN 978-83-233-3053-0; ISSN 1897-3426
19. *The Greek World in the 4th and 3rd Centuries BC*, pp. 178, Kraków 2012; ISBN 978-83-233-3483-5; ISSN 1897-3426